Economic Growth and the Origins of Modern Political Economy

Economic Growth and the Origins of Modern Political Economy addresses the intellectual foundations of modern economic growth and European industrialization. Through an examination of both the roots of European industrialization and the history of economic ideas, this book presents a uniquely broad examination of the origins of modern political economy.

This volume asks what we can learn from 'old' theories in terms of our understanding of history, our economic fate today and the prospects for the modern world's poorest countries. Spanning across the past five hundred years, this book brings together leading international contributors offering comparative perspectives with countries outside of Europe in order to place the evolution of modern economic knowledge into a broader reference framework. It integrates economic discourse and the intellectual history of political economy with more empirical studies in economic history and the history of science. In doing so, this innovative volume presents a coherent and innovative new strategy towards a reconfiguration of the history of modern political economy.

This book is suitable for those who study history of economic thought, economic history or European history.

Philipp R. Rössner is Lecturer in Early Modern History at the School of Arts, Languages and Cultures, University of Manchester, UK.

Economic Growth and the Origins of Modern Political Economy

Economic reasons of state, 1500–2000

Edited by Philipp R. Rössner

Routledge
Taylor & Francis Group

LONDON AND NEW YORK

First published 2016
by Routledge

2 Park Square, Milton Park, Abingdon, Oxfordshire OX14 4RN
52 Vanderbilt Avenue, New York, NY 10017

Routledge is an imprint of the Taylor & Francis Group, an informa business

First issued in paperback 2020

British Library Cataloguing in Publication Data
A catalogue record for this book is available from the British Library

Library of Congress Cataloging in Publication Data
Names: Rössner, Philipp Robinson, editor.
Title: Economic growth and the origins of modern political economy : economic reasons of state, 1500 - 2000 / edited by Philipp R. Rössner.
Description: New York : Routledge, 2016.
Subjects: LCSH: Economics--History. | Economic development--History. | State, The--History.
Classification: LCC HB75 .E324 2016 | DDC 330.1--dc23
LC record available at https://lccn.loc.gov/2015045830

ISBN: 978-1-138-93040-7 (hbk)
ISBN: 978-0-367-66837-2 (pbk)

Typeset in Times New Roman
by Saxon Graphics Ltd, Derby

Contents

PART VI
**Economic reason of state and its survival in modern economic
discourse**

Illustrations

Figures

Tables

Contributors

William J. Ashworth is Senior Lecturer, Department of History at the University of Liverpool, UK.

Jürgen Backhaus is Professor emeritus in Public Finance and Fiscal Sociology at the University of Erfurt, Germany.

Francesco Boldizzoni is Research Professor in Economic History at the University of Turin, Italy.

Kenneth E. Carpenter is former Assistant Director for Research Resources at Harvard University, USA.

Ann Coenen is Lecturer in History at the University of Utrecht, The Netherlands.

Moritz Isenmann is Lecturer in History at the University of Cologne, Germany.

Lars Magnusson is Professor of Economic History at the University of Uppsala, Sweden.

Prasannan Parthasarathi is Professor of History in the Department of History, Boston College, USA.

Erik S. Reinert is Professor of Technology Governance and Development Strategies at Tallinn University of Technology, Estonia and chairs The Other Canon Foundation in Norway.

Sophus A. Reinert is Assistant Professor at Harvard Business School, Harvard University, USA.

Philipp R. Rössner is Lecturer in Early Modern History at the University of Manchester, UK.

Marcus Sandl is Assistant Professor in History, Department of History at the University of Zurich, Switzerland.

Bertram Schefold is Senior Professor in the Department of Economics, Goethe-Universität Frankfurt am Main, Germany.

Peer Vries is Professor in Global Economic History at the University of Vienna, Austria.

Carl Wennerlind is Associate Professor, Department of History at Barnard College, USA.

Part I

Manufacturing matters

The history of an old idea

1 New inroads into well-known territory?

On the virtues of re-discovering pre-classical political economy

Philipp R. Rössner

Mercantilism, Cameralism, economic reason of state: an alternative geneology of the free market

Recent years have seen a notable increase in historians' curiosity about the state and its involvement in the economic process, prior to as well as during the great transition known as industrialization.[1] This went together with a reconceptualization of the role of markets in the economic process and the debunking of the myth of 'free markets'. Since the path-breaking studies by Epstein (*Freedom and Growth*) or Harcourt's *Illusion of Free Markets,* it is difficult to take issue with the notion that markets – the cornerstone of any well-functioning economy – performed best when regulated, in varying intensity, and guarded by a strong and proactive state. The latter provided an effective regulative framework that made sure that markets performed well: at least this is what people held as a commonplace in European economic discourse since the Renaissance. Moreover, many European states can be proven to have acted – at least by intention – quite interventionist since the dawn of the early modern age, actively facilitating economic growth by promoting select branches of domestic industry by various means such as bounties, premiums and protective custom duties. By no means did this process commence during the industrial age; we find ample traces of it in the recorded economic history of medieval and early modern history, in the shape of royal acts, *Fürstenspiegeln* (Princes' Mirrors), learned treatises, customs and excise legislation and so on. More and more evidence has been accumulating over the recent years confirming that without such states that were interventionist at least in principle (and usually tried to implement as many of the principal stances in practice also) things such as the 'European miracle', the first industrialization and the 'great divergence' are unlikely to have happened. It had been the state – in varying shapes and degrees – that effected, facilitated and guarded European economic development since the middle ages, more often than not with positive success.

This somewhat flies in the face of what many modern textbooks still tell the aspiring students. Just consider Mankiw's very learned and eminently influential *Principles of Economics*. In his classical statement of the 'ten golden rules of economics', Rule Six says that:

Markets Are Usually a Good Way to Organize Economic Activity. Households and firms that interact in market economies act as if they are guided by an 'invisible hand' that leads the market to allocate resources efficiently [...].[2]

The empirical record of Europe's economic history of the past six hundred years or so tells a different story. States have been necessary actors in the market process, curbing and ruling out negative behavioural aspects such as usury, arbitrage, speculative gains and other forms of rent-seeking behaviour that lead to Pareto-suboptimal allocation effects, i.e. the detriment of the common weal. Most states also actively interfered with the economy or at least made attempts consciously directed at this task, since the middle ages, in order to facilitate and stimulate economic growth and development.[3] Until now the historical record has failed to produce unambiguous evidence of anything that would even closely resemble 'free' markets. In fact, European states became increasingly dirigiste and interventionist over the past five centuries, notwithstanding Adam Smith's famously evocative claim that the opposite should become the rule for future bliss. Neither the waiver of the British Corn Laws, sometimes seen as the onset of the great deregulation of the nineteenth century, or some attempts at financial market liberalization in the wake of the 'neoliberal' turns in western politics post-1979 have managed to revert a growing tendency exhibited by European states to interfere with and regulate their economies, both internal as well as external. Since the past two hundred years the modern capitalist northern economies became more densely-regulated than ever before in the recorded history, and societies have progressively moved away from free markets. This process ran somewhat counter to mainstream economic dogma increasingly emphasising the inherent goodness of free and unregulated markets for good economic performance and growth. Reasons and motivations for these processes are manifold – some of them will be discussed in the following chapters.

It seems just as though the recent economic and financial crises in the world economy have also led to a renewed interest in a strange beast we call 'mercantilism'. Obviously both aspects are related: markets and growth on the one, mercantilism on the other hand, although scholars by no means always or readily appreciate this. Here we find the main angle-point of the present book. There still are many myths and unclear areas regarding the evolution of modern economic discourse, as well as the interaction between economic discourse, political economy and real economic development over the past five centuries that are in desperate needs to be cleared up. European economic history and political economy do not start with either the Enlightenment or the industrial revolution (as many historical and economic studies and textbooks still claim, if implicitly). Therefore, any discussion of the state in the economic process should start with what we have come to know as 'mercantilism', prior to moving on to more contested research fields and terminologies and even stranger creatures such as 'Cameralism' or, ultimately, alternative concepts such as 'economic reason of state'. This exercise should provide ways and means towards an attempt at an integrated study of economic thought and practice better explaining Europe's transition to industrialization, c. 1500–1900 AD, or in a different framework of analysis from the one usually chosen.

Scholars have, in the more recent past, rather been wary to define what mercantilism was: an economic theory, policy, political economy, economic discourse[4] or historical moment? Heckscher, in his magnificent two-volume work *Merkantilismen* (1931), expressed a rather sceptical view of it but never doubted its existence as such: For Heckscher, mercantilism was a very concrete and well-identifiable beast to attack.[5] For Werner Sombart, alongside Max Weber one of the towering figures in German historical and economic sociology in the years preceding the First World War, the situation was similar. In Sombart's model, mercantilism was begotten of the *Stadtökonomie* – an untranslatable term (its literal translation, 'city economy' does not even come close). Sombart was on the same page with Heckscher (or, rather, Heckscher echoed Sombart, really, as the first version of *Der Moderne Kapitalismus* predated Heckscher's *Merkantilismen* by almost exactly three decades, with only the second and considerably-altered version of it, published between 1915 and 1927, somewhat nearer to Heckscher's opus magnum). According to Sombart, Europe's medieval city economies had been focused on provisioning and securing foodstuffs and regular supplies by encouraging grain imports into the cities and discouraging exports, trying to regulate urban markets in favour of the urban *bonum commune*. The later 'states' of pre-industrial Europe would do just what the city economies of the middle ages had done, transforming the notion of the urban-civic common good onto a larger scale of 'national economy' (*Nationalökonomie, Volkswirtschaft*). Mercantilism thus provided the foundations of modern capitalism, according to Sombart,[6] in the same way as it paved the way for the rise of modern states after the 1500s. Markets and states were linked by symbiotic coevolution. The two depended upon one another and were connected within a functional nexus, in a similar way as it was not the market that had 'created' money as a means facilitating exchange deep down in history, but the state, in its desire to raise taxes. Sombart's idea that mercantilism was a strategy aimed at 'unification' of the territorial and later national economies that emerged out of the medieval city economies even goes back to German historical economist Gustav Schmoller, writing in the 1880s, although many would probably also associate it with Heckscher.[7]

Sombart would argue that the mercantilistic programme, especially the building-up of export industries, was from the beginning subjected to the overarching goal of strengthening the state and its finances. Obviously, within the idiosyncratic situation of the Germanic lands between the Middle Ages and modernity these measures would all have amounted to the same: small, open and vulnerable economically as well as politically, the mere survival of the German micro-'state' in the post-Westphalian system depended upon a sound economy in the same way as a sound economy depended upon the existence of a sound state and its functional apparatus, such as soldiers for defence and civil servants for administration of the common weal. Economics and politics were too closely entangled to be analysed separately. Economic policy and analysis of their time were contingent upon the political conditions of the day, in the same way as mercantilism and Cameralism as theories and practical programmes of development were closely intertwined with all matters of domestic economic performance.[8] In this way Jan de Vries' summing up of the current state of the art in research on mercantilism in the 1960s and 1970s that 'the state, the military, and the private economy could each stimulate the growth of the others' still holds true. But we need to make some important qualifications. First, this all to common stance was derived from Werner Sombart's *Der Moderne Kapitalismus* without scholars usually acknowledging this (partly but not exclusively because *Der Moderne Kapitalismus* was, until 2016, never translated into the English language). Secondly, such stimulations could, as de Vries himself would admit, work only 'where institutions and social structure were effective in transmitting their varied impulses to each other'.[9] The papers assembled in the present volume will shed more light on this important aspect. This is also one of the reasons why the alternative term 'economic reason(s) of state' is chosen as the more appropriate descriptive label here, as a variation upon a political-historical argument on states and international competition in the seventeenth and eighteenth century developed by the late I. Hont.[10] But any attempt to study (economic) reason of state or mercantilist theory on political theory grounds exclusively will impose the same intellectual limitations upon the analysis as would the study of mercantilism from the vantage point of its purely economic content (and worse, its 'modern' economic content, as though economic thought could have evolved in a quasi-linear fashion over time from bad to moderately good and finally 'good' economics). So the term 'economic reason(s) of state' is chosen here as a compromise term and, hopefully, a better analytical framework.

Some scholars have spotted the ascendance of economic liberalism and the people's liberation from misgiven ideas of the past during the process commonly known as the (economic) 'enlightenment'.[11] This notion, albeit tempting, is once again considerably at variance with the historical evidence. Mercantilist policies and ideas continued to live on beyond 1750, and on many accounts even grew stronger during the nineteenth and twentieth centuries.[12] In the 'mercantilist' age (roughly between 1500 and 1900[13]) politics and economics were intertwined but without a clearly-discernible precedent of one over the other; traditionalist interpretations of mercantilism or Cameralism as strategies chiefly aimed at boosting tax income or the power of the state should likewise be rejected. But as late as 2014 a very learned textbook could still happily formulate insights so fundamentally at variance with the textual (discursive) as well as factual record that we may wonder to what extent some modern mainstream economists are still stuck within the Foucauldian age, i.e. an age where 'myth' has either equal weight or even a slight precedence over 'facts' in guiding, forming and shaping not only humans' cosmological belief system but also their practical actions and processes of decision forming. To the economic disciples in our modern age of disenchantment, statements such as 'to the Mercantilists, however, prosperity in the sense of increased per-capita income was secondary to the concentration of economic power in the hands of the state'; or that 'money, not real goods, was commonly equated to real wealth', or that '[m]any mercantilists feared the consequences of too much freedom, so they relied on the state to plan and control economic life'[14] sound all-too familiar, representing a famous and somewhat comfortable tune, almost akin to a lullaby. Yet what if they simply do not match historical 'reality'? Compared to modern states mercantilist 'states' in early modern Europe were decidedly under-regulated – where no modern strong Weberian bureaucracy and state existed, it could hardly have had any more than a superficial impact upon economic behaviour. Furthermore, the notion of the 'Midas fallacy' or the imputed mercantilists' confusion of money with wealth can also be easily dismantled as mythical (see below). And it is hard to retain the notion, based upon the studies assembled in the present volume, that economic growth was in any way or usually a sub-ordinate goal in mercantilist and Cameralist thought. In fact, economic reason of state theory rested fundamentally upon the desire to promote growth and development as a valuable goal in itself.

Historical economists such as Wilhelm Roscher and Gustav Schmoller had, during the 1870s and 1880s, stated that mercantilism as a strategy was chiefly addressed at national economic integration and economic development (but they also reiterated Adam Smith on the 'bullion fetishism' line of argumentation).[15] Their interpretation can perhaps best be understood given the double context of German political-imperial unification (1871) as well as the on-going economic crisis of the early 1870s (*Gründerzeit* crisis). The next fundamental economic crisis was, of course, the Great Depression which brought us not only Heckscher's rather critical interpretation of mercantilism,[16] but also Keynes' famously positive assessment of it. Heckscher corresponded intensely with Keynes upon the launch of an English translation of his *Merkantilismen* (1931) in 1935.[17] Keynes maintained that the Mercantilists, in their emphasis on low interest rates as a means to keep the marginal productivity of capital high, the need to stimulate domestic investment and employment and economic activity and the maintenance of a positive balance of trade, prefigured certain pillars of what he laid out as his *General Theory* in 1936. Such a positive assessment became a rather partisan interpretation in the subsequent decades when neoclassicism took over in the economics faculties all across the Western world. It was mainly German economists and economic historians who would retain a more positive assessment even after the great cultural and political watershed of 1945[18], certainly but not exclusively in connection with the German economic programme of state-led growth and arms race after 1936 and the unholy consequences of this, but partly also due to post-war macro-economic strategies aptly named by one scholar 'coordinated capitalism'.[19] Towards the later twentieth century when the neoliberal turn was in full swing in the wake of the turbulent 1970s which were, in many a European and North Atlantic country, a decade of economic crisis, 'stagflation', rising unemployment, soaring interest rates and a failing pubic sector, British and American writers then stressed the rent seeking aspect of mercantilist political economy.[20] This assessment appears, upon hindsight and when interpreted as a historical moment in its own right, as much an expression of personal desire, the discursive culture and the public intellectual climate of the age as an accurate description of some aspects of mercantilist reality: a fashion – in the same way as

Keynes' or Heckscher's rival interpretations had been. In the wake of Ekelund/ Tollison's powerful *Mercantilism as Rent Seeking Society* many would argue that the mercantilist creed reflected the rent seeking interests of particular groups at the expense of the larger rest of society.[21] This interpretation chimed well with the general cultural flow of the age: 'free' markets were best (with a reliable definition lacking just what such free markets should look like), and that on top of this, nearly all aspects of human action and interaction could be explained using an economistic approach.[22] This discourse, fuelled by Friedman's influential essay on *Freedom and Capitalism*, was mirrored in politics, in the landslide regime changes from socialist to liberal-conservative in the most powerful economies of their age (1979: Thatcher; 1980: Reagan, and 1982: Kohl, in the Federal Republic of Germany).

The fashionable 'new' interpretation of mercantilism as an applied political economy in Europe's early modern worlds stressed its costs to society, including the 'costs of empire' in the British case. However, such reasoning begged one crucial question. Would the observable dynamics of the mercantilist age, for instance in the colonial trades after the 1660s, which continued until the American War (1776–83), especially the permeation of goods such as sugar, tobacco and coffee into the landscape of consumption and the transformation of Europe's landscape of production for the market and consumption *via* the market since c. 1660, sometimes labelled a 'consumer revolution'[23] or 'industrious revolution'[24] … would these dynamics have unfolded in a similar way, if the regulatory framework of the Atlantic economy and the Navigation Acts had *not* existed in the first place? As Pomeranz suggested in his influential *Great Divergence*, it was the 'ghost acreages' provided by the Atlantic economy and its institutional framework (customs, tariffs and regulative frameworks) that would have made a crucial contribution toward England's successful economic development.[25] And whilst Pomeranz did not pay much attention to the state as an economic *actor* in setting up the 'ghost acreages' system – nor did Bin Wong's *China Transformed* (1997) – recent research has stressed the importance of pro-active European states as economic actors in terms of explaining global economic divergence over the last five centuries or so.[26] As early as 1993 some researchers would start challenging the 'rent seeking' model of mercantilism.[27] Others on the other hand would never give in, even in the face of accumulating contrary evidence. A recent account on British economic development that appeared well within the on-going third global economic crisis since the 1870s is still outspokenly sceptical about Mercantilist political economy, heralding the Smithian-Ricardian model as the 'better' long-term solution.[28] It is somewhat in fundamental conflict with recent empirical evidence that demonstrates the contrary.[29] Mercantilism is still as much a question of metaphysical belief, obviously,[30] in the same way as it still serves as a useful guideline for historical enquiry as well as current problems of development.

Comparatively little attention has been paid to developments in political economy outside England; even though we find, on the continent, a discourse on political economy called 'Cameralism' that was as rich and powerful in terms of discursive variation and theoretical insights as mercantilist discourse in England or Scotland ever were.[31] The Cameralists may have had a stronger focus on the fiscal aspects of the economy, as well as the allocative role of the state, impersonated by a 'strong' (what former research would have called absolutist) ruler and the state regulating the market, coordinating economic decision-making processes and in this way initiating economic development. Some have argued that Cameralist writers had a better understanding of economic development. Compared to England and the Netherlands most continental European economies were 'backwards' in the early modern period.[32] But we find essentially the same core set of recipes here as in the English economic discourse, i.e. within the nation that would become the first industrializing country. It was indispensable for any country – poor and rich alike – to build up a native domestic export industry, no matter at what costs or how uncompetitive some of these industries might be in the first place: this – and not free trade and specialization according to initial absolute or comparative advantage – is what made poor countries rich and rich countries even richer.[33] Sometimes the search for a better policy of development begins in later fifteenth-century England (Tudor economic policy directed at import substitution and developing a native woollen export industry by prohibiting the export of raw wool in 1485), in the 'turning point years' of nascent liberalism expressed in English political economy writing nipped in the bud by a return to outright protectionism 1696–1713[34], or in eighteenth-century England under the stout First Minister Sir Robert Walpole, when a delicate mix of customs barriers, bounties and encouragements on domestic industrial production helped England (and Scotland) build up a competitive manufacturing economy that would in the nineteenth century come to dominate world markets. Only in the wake of the Corn Law waivers (1846) would England adopt a less regulated framework for international trade.[35] But by no means does the story begin or end with England, being one of the richest nations of her time. It seems as though the 'rich' countries of early modern Europe (especially Holland and England) had used essentially the same strategies and economic recipes that the 'poorer' or catch-up countries (France, Austria-Habsburg, Prussia and the other German states) would use in their idiosyncratic processes of industrialization. Friedrich List, in his historical sketch of European development (*Das Nationale System der Politischen Ökonomie*, 1841, chs. 1–4) was obviously right.

But the idea that protectionism can be a useful tool for development goes back much further than List.[36] It has a much longer pedigree and much wider geographical spread: it was a pan-European discourse. It may have been that (English) mercantilism was more trade-orientated (*handelsorientiert*), whilst Cameralism was production-orientated (*produktionsorientiert*).[37] But surely such aspects were differences in terms of nuance rather than essence. In fact, the 'mercantilist' or Cameralist programme of development, combined with the emphasis on the role of the state and the fisc (Cameralism) was so common in pre-modern Europe that we may call the 'English way' (where the emphasis on the needs and goals of the state as the origin of all political economy was perhaps less pronounced than in continental economic thought) the *Sonderweg*, and Cameralism, which was neither peculiarly 'German' nor in any way exceptional,[38] the general or 'mainstream' economic paradigm in early modern Europe. Here, the North Sea and Atlantic also provided a huge cultural barrier: for landlocked economies such as the German states Anglo-maritime doctrines such as mercantilism often made little sense, as several of the following chapters will state. With Britain being an island and turning – by destiny or chance – into the first industrial economy in history it is clear that economic recipes and strategies were considerably different than elsewhere, in economies in many ways less exposed to the sea and sea-borne economics than England and Scotland. But since 'Cameralism' has been somewhat reserved by later scholars for describing the German experience, the present volume will use the more neutral and generic term 'economic reason(s) of state'[39] as a less value-laden item and reserve, for the time being but strictly speaking incorrectly, 'Cameralism' to German economic thought.

Mercantilism and the origins of modern capitalism

So what new can we add to the debate? Ironically, we must turn our view back in order to do answer this question. Perhaps the clearest notion ever offered was in chapter 54 of the first volume of Werner Sombart's magnificent *Der moderne Kapitalismus*:

> In fact, the entire mercantile policy was born from the fundamental endeavour which may be summarized thus: many wars require many men and much money; increasing 'manufactories' creates a demand for many men; much money will be brought into the country through foreign trade, if it is 'active'. Manufactories and foreign trade will be supported by the aspiring economic elements: the results will be a community of interest between capitalism and the principalities; therefore, capitalistic interests must be promoted. But to promote capitalistic interests means to give capitalistic enterprise the right of way. That is, the well-understood state interests became 'friendly to enterprise', and labour policies were pursued from the viewpoint of employing measures to secure for the employer an abundant, industrious, efficient and a cheap labouring class. Where the interest of the employer and that of the labourer were in conflict, the employer's interests were unconditionally guaranteed. The mercantile labour policy was, therefore, almost wholly a protection to employer, but not to labour.—Because the welfare of the state demanded it and for no other reason—certainly not because popular sympathies would have been with the employers as such rather than with the labouring class.[40]

Sombart's insight was appropriated by a number of scholars stressing the collaborative nature or coevolution of merchant capitalism and, more modern, merchant networks on the one hand that fuelled European economic life and integration of larger regions into international capitalist 'world systems'. On the other hand the states and their fiscal and military might would not only facilitate this process but in fact provide the necessary preconditions for its set-up and beneficial coalition between private and government interests.[41] It is difficult to overlook, if Sombart's assessment were true, the parallels in the mercantilist creed with certain strands of modern 'supply-side' ideologies and policies. In Sombart's sketch of capitalism's ascendance, mercantilism reflected the interest of domestic entrepreneurs in general, not monopolistic rent-seekers. Or, turned on its head, is not every entrepreneur automatically prone to rent seeking?[42] The package came in combination with a cost and blessing at the same time: the emerging modern fiscal-military states. Their existence and permanency was based, given the times and circumstances of early modern Europe, upon practically constant warfare. War was the father of the modern state. By the same token it was the origin of modern capitalism (and Sombart would characterize certain military occupations as archetypical in terms of closely matching capitalistic behavioural traits).[43] We may today, of course, doubt the validity of the concept of 'modern' or 'modern capitalism', from a cultural vantage point that has provided us with such valuable concepts as post-colonialism, deconstructivism, or the cultural turn. But Sombart's general message is powerful still. His conception of entanglement between states, wars and political economy is timeless. States could, during the early modern economy, not survive without sound and strong (emerging national) economies; nor could the emerging national economies and markets survive without states.[44] This has been true until today, as recent 'histories' of 'failing' states have suggested in an unintended (and usually unacknowledged) resurrection of the younger German Historical School and early twentieth century institutionalism hundred years ahead of the current *Zeitgeist*.[45] Historians and economists have paid only very rarely attention to this.

We can safely skip the debate about whether or not the term 'mercantilism' is a particularly lucky choice (we know that it is isn't). Contrary to its name mercantilism was primarily concerned with the promoting of manufacturing, industry and domestic competitiveness in *production*, not trade (trade simply was a subordinate variable contingent upon the former: whether a nation was competitive or not naturally showed in her *balance of trade*, i.e. the connectivity with the outer world: did she manage to export her manufactures – then this should be a good sign. If not, something was wrong and had to be corrected within, that means on the *production* side *again*). We also know that no epistemologically coherent or 'closed' theory stood behind mercantilism.[46] Quite the same is true with the modern economic sciences where there is a lot of epistemological drift and discursive competition, manifested for instance in the debate about whether or not modern economics can be called paradigmatic, non-paradigmatic or pre-paradigmatic (the mere fact that there is such a debate suggests the third answer is probably correct). Even though neither 'mercantilism' nor 'Cameralism' were strictly speaking contemporaneous terminologies (no English mercantilist would have called himself by that name, but at least the German authors sometimes called themselves *Kameralisten*) we can clearly say that as a historical moment and theory, both mattered a lot for European history. They usually included a core set of shared beliefs. These beliefs centred on the idea that states should actively interfere in the economic process. Economic development was – inter alia (but neither primarily nor exclusively) – seen as a means to raise taxes and thus state income. But the reverse was equally true. Without states and rulers, the existence of modern free markets, modern entrepreneurship and economic growth would have been unthinkable. As noted above we may therefore as well call this theory 'economic reason of state' – for those of us uncomfortable using '-isms' in the discourse.

Clearly too little expense has been paid, in terms of research efforts and intellectual stealth, on what went on beyond Britain and the first British Empire during the 'mercantilist age'. Cameralism has often (but wrongly)[47] been named as 'German mercantilism',[48] and it was certainly much more than 'a form of academic pedagogy aimed at the future administrators of the eighteenth-century German territorial states'.[49] It has been given only orphan-like attention in the English-speaking literature, in parts without doubt because '[i]ts very nature and purpose as a pedagogic discourse rendered it unsuitable for contemporary translation into English, French, or Italian; consequently it had no manifest resonances among those writers who provided the foundations of political economy'.[50] This statement of course begs the question to what extent political economy necessarily 'originated' in England at all? How original was English political economy, really; and how much did the other cultures of Europe contribute to the rise of European economic thought, 1500–2000 AD?[51] Without doubt Cameralism also contained the key ingredients of a general economic theory of development that made Europe rich in the crucial centuries between the dawn of the early modern age and the age of industrialization and globalization. If anything, Cameralism was the origin of modern political economy.[52] Cameralism was also not simply a variant of mercantilist theory; it seems as though it was the other way round. English and French mercantilism may have been a side strand of a much larger continental theory which we may for want of a better term label 'Cameralism' or 'economic reason of state'. Nor did Cameralism ever represent either a peculiarly *German* thing or a *Sonderweg* in general; in fact we find Cameralism all over the place; from Sweden to Italy. Perhaps the worst accusation has it that Cameralism was not a theory in its own right (read: not a 'modern' theory i.e. fulfilling the benchmark criteria of modern mainstream economics) but a random set of principles extending across the entire spectrum of economic activity, from raising pigs, horticulture, to building up a manufacturing industry and financing a standing army, subject to the overall strategic goal of filling the state's coffers.

As on-going research has confirmed, the Cameralists actually *had* a theory. They *had* a clear set of axiomatic principles on how good markets should work; how exchange should be governed and put on fair grounds, and how an economy could be developed towards a more effective production frontier. Many of their ideas about 'free' markets (in a sense of 'just' or 'fair' exchange) have found their way into modern neoclassical and liberal theory.[53] There is much more continuity than break in tradition between the modern economic sciences, the modern economy and early modern European economic reason of state theory.

Economic reason of state and the origins of modern economic growth

It seems quite ironic that modern economic theory lost its emphasis on *production*, becoming focused on *circulation* instead (with the emergence of Physiocracy and later on classical economic thought) right at the time when the processes known as industrialization and the fundamental transformation of European manufacturing began to gather full momentum towards the end of the eighteenth and the early nineteenth century: i.e. processes of transformation and productivity growth within the *producing* rather than *distributing* spheres of the economy. This discursive drift arguably led to considerable cognitive distortion, not only in historical portrayals of the economy but also within economic beliefs in general.[54] Two basic ideas were once held important in Europe's transition to capitalism, but got forgotten over time as 'modern' economic discourse and economic theory evolved. These ancient insights were that first, that manufacturing mattered, and second: that a strong and pro-active state was important to safeguard and nurture the precarious plant that became later on known as 'economic growth and development'. They represent the cornerstones of 'economic reason(s) of state', reflecting mutual interest and feedback processes between state, finance and economy that influenced the writing of these theories. They were widely shared across Europe. Their pedigree is ancient. And they continue to matter today – particularly in the light of the current crises in the world economy.

If we look at pre-industrial Europe we find that many of the key ingredients and ideas usually identified as crucial to modern economic growth were already in it – for a long time. A strong manufacturing base? Known to sixteenth-century Italian economic writers. The role of knowledge management, technology and science? Known to early seventeenth-century Swedish thinkers. The notion that infinite growth is principally possible? Again, Sweden, around 1600 AD. A strong state that safeguards its subjects' economic interests and property rights, up to the point of actively promoting growth and development? We find this idea in seventeenth-century and eighteenth century German economic discourse, but, of course, much earlier in the texts produced in Renaissance Italy. We also find states that repeatedly tried to apply these ideas in practice. The best example perhaps is post-1688 England. Since the fourteenth century a developmental-protectionist state had laid the foundations for the subsequent transition into England's becoming the 'first industrial nation'. Less-well understood, however, is how deeply permeated continental Europe's intellectual landscape was by these ideas. We also lack a deeper understanding of the interaction between these ideas and economic practice and policy. We find the idea of a state that actively promoted development – with a focus on *manufacturing* – very early on, i.e. around 1500 AD at latest. Thus – in Chapter 2 of this volume – Erik S. Reinert and Ken Carpenter propose to utilize a newly-tapped source, Harvard Business School's Kress Library, and a unique collection of economics bestsellers that circulated across continental Europe in near complete series of editions since the late sixteenth century. By tracing the pattern of editions and translations into other languages of 65 economic bestsellers between the late sixteenth and nineteenth century – from

Giovanni Botero's *Ragion di Stato* to Johann Heinrich Justi's *Policeywissenschaft* – the development of a very peculiar canon of economic works is reconstructed. The authors suggest that the modern epistemological paradigm in the economic sciences is biased towards writers that were, during their lifetime, neither particularly widely read nor, if ever, republished. Contrary to much received wisdom, it was 'mercantilist' and 'Cameralist' textbooks that were widely read, republished and used in academic teaching and research in economics well into the nineteenth century. And these laid a focus on promoting manufactures as the main source of domestic economic growth. Lars Magnusson takes up the story in Chapter 3. In standard textbooks concerning the history of economic thought it is often taken for granted that Cameralism was a kind of German *Sonderweg* or native version of mercantilism, rooted in its peculiar history, as well as geographical position. Magnusson's paper examines to what extent this standard interpretation makes sense at all, or whether it would be more fruitful to take a different departure point. The paper argues that our understanding of the relation between mercantilism and Cameralism hinges to a large extent on modern definitions. There were not one but many German responses to 'jealousy of trade' and 'reason of state' as main action points in early modern political economy. Moreover, it is important to abandon the kind of 'blue print' history so often connected to a Whig interpretation of history. Instead, Magnusson urges us that we should not limit our view to the search for 'better' or 'superior' strategies in history, but acknowledge that different responses existed – more or less rational – to different, and sometimes changing, circumstances of time and space.

That ideas and theories varied over time, attaining different configurations over different spaces seems only natural; but just how they unfolded differently in different contexts (idiosyncrasy) has seldom been studied. Therefore, exemplary-specific case studies on 'German' Cameralism, provided in Part II, will shed more light on this. Jürgen Backhaus follows this task up in Chapter 4. The basic goal of the Cameralist and the mercantilist state was, Backhaus suggests, essentially the same, i.e. to have 'as many healthy inhabitants as possible'. The Cameralists, however, emphasized the point that it was important not to have just many, but rather many *healthy* subjects. For this reason, Cameralist writers usually suggested a number of very specific policies, which cannot be readily found in the Mercantilist writers' texts. The paper discusses six policy areas in order to contour the difference between mercantilist and Cameralist policies. Whilst the basic goals of the states and the basic policy doctrine were similar, due to their specific geo-political position the Cameralists made radically different proposals at times. The policy areas surveyed comprise customs duties and fiscal policy in general, monetary policy and monetary stability; demographic and health policies; and finally – interestingly, as it underscores Cameralism's main purpose (policies to have many happy healthy people), the avoidance of winter wars, as these tended to have many and futile casualties. In Chapter 5, Bertram Schefold shows us a nuance in this grand German poet unbeknownst to most of us. Goethe the poet is well known; Goethe the economist isn't. His insights into money creation and paper money's effects, as well as the forces of modern capitalism, are apparent in his *Faust*, where paper money is represented as a realization of the project of alchemy. Goethe's vision of the active liberal man, who is, through entrepreneurial activity, capable of altruism and trustworthiness, is clearly visible in *Wilhelm Meister*. His experiences as a businessman and princely administrator are likewise important. The background to Goethe's multifaceted economic activities is his remarkably comprehensive knowledge of economic schools of his day. He was educated as a Cameralist but enthusiastic of the Physiocrats when young. For some time, he would adopt a German form of Smithian liberalism, but also had a critical interest in French socialism when old. He eventually read and approved of authors who anticipated the German Historical School. He never was an analytical economist, however. Instead, Goethe approached economics like other aspects of reality: as the observer with the inimitable ability to transform his vision into *Anschauung*, i.e. into 'visual' or 'intuitive' theory.

That ideas may also change according to political climate and social context – i.e. may represent vested interests of the actors formulating the theories – is shown by two essays on France under Colbert and Britain towards the end of the American War. They especially apply to the configuration of the free trade and comparative advantage ideology, two of the most prominent discursive figures and concepts in modern economic theory. This is the guiding topic for Part III. Moritz Isenmann, in Chapter 6, argues that the idea that countries should specialize in what they could do best as a principle in international economics (later on refined in the shape of the comparative advantage argument) originated in its proto-form in early eighteenth-century vested mercantile interests representing the outcome of a distinctly French institutional, political and economic setting. Upon the introduction of a new tariff on manufacturing imports after the ascendancy of Colbert in 1661, the representatives of France's agricultural provinces, such as the Guyenne or the Bretagne which depended on the export of wine and other agricultural goods constantly argued *against* the extension of the protective tariff list to their provinces. They did so by pointing to their local privileges, at first without reference to the Common Good. When asked for their expert advice in the newly established Council of Commerce (1701), however, their privileges and interests metamorphosed into 'economic laws'. These 'laws' would suggest that every country had to follow its advantage by specializing on those goods which could be produced more cheaply at home – and for France this meant: wine and other agricultural goods. The story is taken up by William J. Ashworth, in Chapter 7, in which he says that by 1780 the British State was on the verge of consuming the people more than the people were consuming. The Seven Years War had greatly increased the National Debt. The situation became dire in 1776 after the breakout of war with the mainland American colonies, followed quickly by a maritime clash with France and Spain. To add to the woes, it now seemed a real possibility that the West Indies and Ireland would soon follow colonial North America. State finances seemed to be in a extremely precarious situation. This situation entailed a major dismantling, restructuring and withdrawal of the state from regulatory functions, particularly at first, within the domestic economy. It also meant a sustained emphasis upon the new lightly or untaxed industries of cotton, potteries and iron. To eventually achieve these goals this would require a supporting creed accompanied by an epistemology that would come to be filled by a new political economy. Increasing emphasis would be put on the opposite of past experience: stressing an idealized market free of 'unnatural' regulations.

Useful knowledge, i.e. science and knowledge management were as important in pre-Enlightenment economic thought as they were later on in the 'classical' context – contrary to a widely-held notion that claims this exclusively for the classical economic tradition that emerged in the wake of the Scottish Enlightenment and philosophers such as David Hume or Adam Smith.[55] This comes across from the case studies assembled in Part IV. Marcus Sandl emphasizes that in contrast to earlier studies which have stressed Cameralism's axiomatic and deductive character, the Cameralists were committed to the principle of *change*. The following aspects were relevant:

1   Economic backwardness: being underdeveloped meant that every political measure had to be a turning point. Cameralists therefore defined the initial situation of policy as *crisis*, requiring flexible and effective decision-making processes.
2   Decision-making situations arose from specific visions of reality. Cameralists were especially concerned about the question of how information could be connected, and which medial forms were important in that process (influential German sociologist Luhmann's 'doubling of reality' comes to mind).
3   The Cameralists usually emphasized upheaval and repeatedly drew attention to figures of dis-quietness. The most important one was the *Projektemacher* (project-maker). He generated opportunities out of crises and changed the world – not always for the better – so as to be able to 'regenerate' himself.

Therefore, risk and chance stood at the heart of Cameralist epistemology. Carl Wennerlind, in Chapter 9, takes up the story, moving from the German states to early modern Sweden. A new spirit of improvement was actively promoted in Sweden by powerful state officials, great merchants, and university professors during the nation's *Age of Greatness*. The aim was to discover a method to generate enough wealth to support Sweden's pursuit of prosperity and prominence. Embracing the Hartlibian reform program sweeping across northern Europe, Sweden's improvement discourse came to focus on how to discover and catalogue the nation's natural resources and how to enhance humanity's capacity to transform nature. A number of writers also offered suggestions on how to best organize the economy to secure a continuous material expansion and advancement of society's general well-being – infinite growth. This paper explores the ideas of Johan Classon Risingh (1617–1672), famous as Sweden's first writer on political economy, first secretary of Sweden's Board of Trade, and last governor of New Sweden. Risingh offered a detailed account of national prosperity and carefully elaborated on the ideal interplay between agriculture, manufacturing, and commerce. Drawing heavily on the new ideas promoted by the Hartlib Circle, often quite directly, Risingh consistently highlighted the advancement of science and the flourishing of commerce as the key ingredients in the recipe for progress and refinement, but also the active role of the state in the market process.

The idea that the state should interfere with the economy is not only ancient, but also one that can be found in many other places outside Europe. But it may have worked exceptionally well in Europe since the Middle Ages. This is drawn out by adopting a global perspective, with essays on India, China, the Austrian Netherlands and Italy in the early modern period (Part V). This does not mean, however, that extra-European states did not – or not at all efficiently – interfere with the domestic economy. In Chapter 10, Prasannan Parthasarathi convincingly demonstrates that states made a visible contribution to economic growth and development in South Asia from the heyday of the Mughal Empire in the seventeenth century to the post-Mughal regional polities of the eighteenth century. It begins with a discussion of agriculture, which was a major arena of state activity. It then moves on to trade and manufacturing, for which we possess less information but which was of the utmost concern to rulers. Armaments production, in particular, was essential to the maintenance and exercise of state power. The paper concludes with an examination of knowledge producing activities. While the links to economic growth are not always immediately evident, the accumulation and dissemination of technical knowledge was perceived to be of great political and economic importance and loomed large in the minds of states and their officials in the seventeenth and eighteenth century. In Chapter 11, Peer Vries says that, notwithstanding the fact that several highly influential social scientists continue to claim that Great Britain after the Glorious Revolution was turned into a state that 'facilitated' the market but did not itself actively intervene in the economy, most historians actually studying its history now agree that Great Britain when it took off was a fiscal-military and in many respects interventionist, mercantilist state. Notwithstanding the fact that several highly influential social scientists continue to claim that in Qing China the state disturbed the market mechanism and subordinated economic efficiency and development to its political goals, most historians actually studying its history now agree that it in several respects was closer to a laissez-faire, minimal state than that of Great Britain. In his article the author discusses in what ways studying the state in Great Britain and China in the long eighteenth century might change our thinking about the role of the state in economic development. In Chapter 12, Ann Coenen explores whether during the eighteenth century the Austrian Netherlands's administrators succeeded in developing an economic policy that favoured new industries, in other words: a proto-ISI-approach. It shows that over the course of the eighteenth century, a strongly interventionist central government emerged in the Austrian Netherlands. Research into its economic policy shows that the latter was a dynamic tool to support the industry. The administration operated on the basis of a number of overarching economic goals, specifically tailored to the local economy. While its results were probably not uniformly beneficial in every regard, the active role that the new economic administration played had a major impact on the sectors involved. Sophus A. Reinert's Chapter 13 urges us to adopt a broader concept of what the early modern state was and what it could do as an actor in the economy, using eighteenth-century Italy as a case study. Though often marginalized or approached from a 'social' and frequently utopian perspective, bandits have historically occupied the very core of political philosophy and political economy. And they naturally occupy an important role in Max Weber's classic definition of 'the state'. Not only do bandits by their very presence disrupt successful governmental monopolies on violence, they destabilize territories and challenge the very legitimacy of states. It goes without saying that this is as much a problem of state formation as of market formation. And with this new viewpoint on early modern state territoriality Reinert also offers a fundamentally different approach to the genealogy of markets and modern market-based exchange in Europe (which has often, for instance through the econometric interpretation of market integration, been seen as the key feature of 'good' development and global economic divergence before and in the wake of the industrial revolution[56]). Few regions offer a richer history of banditry, market formation and state building than the Italian peninsula.

These contributions, reflecting on-going cutting-edge research chiefly on the intellectual genealogy of the modern economic mind, suggest that it is time to reconfigure the origins of modern political economy and give those ideas more place and weight that were lost, forgotten and sometimes deliberately displaced in the modern economic discourse – by denial of parentage and genealogy – from the academic canon of the modern economic sciences. We have only lost a true sense of credentials for those ideas, not the ideas as such: they have stayed with us ever since the Renaissance and in all likelihood are responsible for making us rich. They provided the intellectual blueprint both of Europe's long road towards industrialization as well as the Great Divergence. This is what the concluding Chapter 14 by Francesco Boldizzoni suggests. This final chapter takes this story into the nineteenth and twentieth centuries and shows how the 'economic reason of state' theory evolved into modern political discourse. Cameralism, unlike mercantilism, was a response to the specific needs of landlocked economies and, as such, it survived industrialization. When Victorian Britain embraced free trade as a means to increase the dependence of the rest of the world on its fully mature economy, the industrializing nations of continental Europe reacted fiercely. The war was fought on the battleground of ideas as much as on the actual battleground of two world wars. In the nineteenth century the laissez-faire doctrines of Smith, Ricardo and the likes were challenged by the 'national system of political economy' of List and the German Historical Schools. In the twentieth century the two great wars that nearly destroyed Europe originated from economic interests but, more importantly, from what German jurist and political philosopher Carl Schmitt called the fundamental opposition between civilizations of 'land' and 'sea'. Indeed, the wheel has turned, but we find the same opposition at the root of much of today's conflict between the advocates of globalization and its discontents.

Off the beaten track: *Sonderwege*, why it pays to walk on them and the origins of the modern economy

By adopting a non-Anglo-centric and non-teleological view on Europe's transformations towards industrialization as well as the evolution of modern economics, pinned against the canvas of ideas and discourses that supported such reconfigurations of the productive landscape, we can observe that the former *Sonderwege* may actually have been the 'norm'. There was, perhaps, less variation or deviation in continental European economic thought from the English way than we used to think. And Cameralism certainly was neither really German nor in any way a special case. Rather, there were many idiosyncratic ways – both to the modern economy, as well as modern economics as a science addressed at understanding economic behaviour, economic change and growth. What we have called 'economic reason(s) of state' was the mainstream economic thought, widely shared across contemporary Europe in the early modern period; clearly with much idiosyncratic regional drift and temporal variance. The science of economics and political economy is not hewn into stone – it never was.

We must one last time contrast these findings with earlier vantage points and thus stake the way for possible future research exercises. We have reasserted ourselves once again of the older insights by Sombart, Heckscher and Keynes that mercantilism mattered – for European history, even for her transition towards capitalism.[57] There may not even be much of a divergence in later, i.e. post-1800, economic thought from the earlier mercantilist or Cameralist paradigm in the way it has been portrayed by many modern scholars of political economy, trying to earmark zones of rupture and breaking points in the genealogy of the modern economic sciences where no such junctures strictly speaking ever existed. The mercantilists and economic reason of state theorists used theoretical abstraction where appropriate and empirical evidence where necessary.[58] They cherished the principle of self-interest as much as later classical writers and utilitarian authors would. But they also accepted that self-interest and markets must have rules to perform well. Most modern economists would probably concur.[59] Economic reason of state (mercantilism, Cameralism, Colbertism…) has in fact always been with us, ever since the days it emerged in its raw shape between the thirteenth and sixteenth centuries with its ancestor called 'bullionism'.[60] Surely it changed its shape over the centuries; but was it therefore a chameleon? Rather it adapted to the idiosyncratic conditions, possibilities and limitations of its respective countries and fields of application. But this seems quite natural. Any economic theory or strategy, if it should be realistic and helpful, should be expected to do just that. What is good for the British economy will be very different from what is good for Iceland or the US. And what was good for the nineteenth century British economy may have been bad for the fifteenth, sixteenth, seventeenth and eighteenth-century English or British common weal.

Economic reason of state theory had much commend to it when applied wisely and within favourable institutional environments. This was as true in fifteenth-century Flanders as in twentieth-century Europe or twenty-first century China.

Many a mercantilist and Cameralist text was concerned with the abolition of monopolies and configuring the free market. Surely such strategies did not always work to the desired extent, especially not in those cases where policies were rather soft and weak – and certainly not the kind of entity we would recognize nowadays as a 'state' – and where society was still fragmented in terms of claims to economic resources and political power. In many regions in pre-industrial Europe rulers competed with the local nobility for different types of privileges (freedoms and liberties, *Freiheiten*) and different layers of political as well as economic 'governance' and claims to political and economic resources. Today we may call to mind A. Sen's 'capability' approach as a way to look at problems of resource distribution – political, social, legal-institutional, economic and cultural resources – that is in a way similar to Europe's Ancien Règime economies, i.e. societies in which particular interests directed at rent seeking and monopoly counteracted attempts by the government to create a more equitable environment for market exchange. It was, in fact, not necessarily mercantilist economic thought and practice that was about rent seeking – as many historians still argue[61]: it was the institutional or cultural environment that did not always do the trick. Mercantilist and Cameralist principles were quite apt to promote domestic growth and industrial development. As theories and political economy discourse they were expressively and principally directed *against* rent seeking and aimed at achieving Pareto-optimal results in resource allocation. And they can indeed be shown to have worked exceedingly well in post-1688 England.[62]

But perhaps the most interesting task for further intellectual efforts is to tease out more closely how some modern economists came to believe in the 'truth' of principles that are, in many instances, empirically 'wrong', meaning profoundly at variance with what happens in practice ('reality'). Harcourt's study does a good job in terms of kicking off the debate,[63] but the following chapters suggest that there is a lot more out there. Especially the case studies presented in this volume on Colbert's France (by M. Isenmann) and Britain under W. Pitt (W. Ashworth) suggest that there may be something fundamentally wrong not only with the rent-seeking approach to the history of political economy (see above), but also with our much-cherished free market and free trade paradigm. The free trade argument seems an issue of persuasion, as German economist Friedrich List knew: sometimes free trade is good, sometimes bad. Often actors are two-faced when proposing its general applicability as a 'best practice' model when drinking wine whilst preaching water. As the history of Martin Luther and the German monopoly debate of the 1520s shows[64] in the same way as the discourse on 'free trade' in the French wine exporting provinces under Colbert, or British economic discourse in the wake of the American War of Independence in the 1780s – the free trade idea, whenever we find it emerging in the past five hundred years in European history, usually reflected the economic interests of some sort of pressure group. Was this not a peculiarly deceitful version of rent-seeking economics? Free trade – and unregulated domestic exchange in the fashion of the modern textbook paradigm – may have mattered much less in the Great Divergence and Europe's long road towards industrialization than some super-enthusiasts used to suggest.[65] In this way the following essays contribute not only towards a re-balancing of the history of economics and political economy and the economic history of Europe in general, but also – it is hoped – to a better economics for future generations.

Notes

1 This chapter partly draws on Philipp Robinson Rössner, "Heckscher Reloaded? Mercantilism, the State and Europe's Transition to Industrialization (1600–1900)," *The Historical Journal,* 58,2 (2015), 663–683 and id., "Manufacturing Matters: From Giovanni Botero (c.1544–1617) to Friedrich List (1789–1846), or: The History of an Old Idea," in *Through Wealth to Freedom,* ed. Harald Hagemann, Stephan Seiter and E. Wendler (Milton Park / New York: Routledge, 2016) (in preparation). For the pre-industrial period see, e.g., William J. Ashworth, *Customs and Excise: Trade, Production, and Consumption in England, 1640–1845* (Oxford and New York: Oxford University Press, 2003); David Ormrod, *The Rise of Commercial Empires: England and the Netherlands in the Age of Mercantilism, 1650–1770* (Cambridge and New York: Cambridge University Press, 2003); Prasannan Parthasarathi, *Why Europe Grew Rich and Asia Did Not: Global Economic Divergence, 1600–1850* (Cambridge and New York: Cambridge University Press, 2011), as well as other contributions too numerous to name here. For an earlier period, see also S. R. Epstein, *Freedom and Growth: The Rise of States and Markets in Europe, 1300–1750* (London: Routledge, 2000).
2 E.g. N. Gregory Mankiw, *Principles of Economics* 5th ed. (Mason, Ohio: South-Western; London: Cengage Learning distributor, 2008).
3 Bernard Harcourt, *The Illusion of Free Markets: Punishment and the Myth of Natural Order* (Cambridge, MA: Harvard University Press, 2011); Epstein, *Freedom and Growth*; Alessandro Stanziani, *Rules of Exchange. French Capitalism in Comparative Perspective, Eighteenth to Early Twentieth Centuries* (Cambridge: Cambridge University Press, 2012).
4 The older literature on mercantilism is nearly endless. For more recent surveys, see Lars Magnusson, *Mercantilism: The Shaping of an Economic Language* (London and New York: Routledge, 1994). See also id., *The Political Economy of Mercantilism* (Milton Keynes and New York: Routledge, 2015), as well as the essays collected in Moritz Isenmann, ed., *Merkantilismus: Wiederaufnahme einer Debatte* (Stuttgart: Franz Steiner, 2014), or in Fritz Neumark, ed., *Studien zur Entwicklung der ökonomischen Theorie* II (Berlin: Duncker & Humblot, 1982), as well as the excellent book edited by Philip J. Stern and Carl Wennerlind, eds, *Mercantilism Reimagined: Political Economy in Early Modern Britain and its Empire (*Oxford: Oxford University Press, 2013).
5 Eli F. Heckscher, *Mercantilism,* 2nd ed. (London: Allen & Unwin, 1955). I have used the German edition transl. G. Mackenroth (Jena, G. Fischer, 1932) of which Heckscher approved more than the English translation by M. Shapiro. See Lars Magnusson's introductory chapter to the new English edition of Heckscher's *Mercantilism* (Pickering & Chatto).
6 Werner Sombart, *Der moderne Kapitalismus; historisch-systematische Darstellung des gesamteuropäischen Wirtschaftslebens von seinen Anfängen bis zur Gegenwart,* 2 Vols. 4th ed. (Munich and Leipzig: Duncker & Humblot, 1921/1928). An English translation will be published soon (ed. Erik S. Reinert, Philipp R. Rössner and Jürgen Backhaus: London and New York: Anthem, 2016). In the original this reads 'daß diese Politik (trotz beträchtlicher nationaler Verschiedenheiten) in ihren Grundzügen doch in allen europäischen Ländern sich gleich gestaltet hat.' (Vol. I/1, 374).
7 Heckscher, *Merkantilismus.*
8 Sombart, *Der moderne Kapitalismus,* Vol. I/1, 370.
9 Jan de Vries, *The European Economy in an Age of Crisis 1600–1750* (Cambridge: Cambridge University Press, 1976), 243.

10 Istvan Hont, *Jealousy of Trade. International Competition and the Nation-Trade in Historical Perspective* (Cambridge/MA and London: The Belknap Press of Harvard University Press, 2005), introduction (1–158), esp. 6–17.

11 E.g. Robert B. Ekelund, Jr. and Robert F. Hébert, *A History of Economic Theory and Method*. Sixth Edition (Longgrove/Ill. Wave Land Press, 2014), 50 and 72ff.

12 On neo-mercantilism and mercantilism's place in modern economic theory, see essays in Lars Magnusson, ed., *Mercantilist Economics* (Boston: Kluwer, 1993).

13 For the long continuity of mercantilist ideas in European policy, see Ha-Joon Chang, *Kicking Away the Ladder: Development Strategy in Historical Perspective* (London: Anthem, 2003), chs. 1, 2; Erik S. Reinert, "The Role of the State in Economic Growth," *Journal of Economic Perspectives*, 26, 4/5 (1999), 268–326, id., *How Rich Countries Got Rich...And Why Poor Countries Stay Poor* (New York: Carroll & Graf, 2007), ch. 3, or Sophus A. Reinert, *Translating Empire. Emulation and the Origins of Political Economy* (Cambridge, MA: Harvard University Press, 2011), ch. 1.

14 Ekelund and Hébert, *A History of Economic Theory and Method*, 49, 48; Joel Mokyr, *The Enlightened Economy: Britain and the Industrial Revolution, 1700–1850* (New Haven: Yale University Press 2009), ch. 4.

15 See Magnusson's contribution to the present volume, as well as his *Political Economy of Mercantilism*.

16 Magnusson, Introduction to new ed. of Heckscher, *Mercantilism*.

17 *General Theory of Employment, Interest and Money* (London: Macmillan, 1935).

18 E.g. Cilly Böhle, *Die Idee der Wirtschaftsverfassung im deutschen Merkantilismus* (Jena: Gustav Fischer, 1940).

19 See Hans Joachim Röpke, Die Wachstumstheorie der deutschen Merkantilisten (Ph.D. diss. Marburg 1971); Ingomar Bog, *Der Reichsmerkantilismus. Studien zur Wirtschaftspolitik des Heiligen Römischen Reiches im 17. und 18. Jahrhundert* (Stuttgart: Gustav Fischer, 1959); id., "Ist die Kameralistik eine untergegangene Wissenschaft?," *Berichte zur Wissenschaftsgeschichte* 4 (1981), 61–72. The term 'coordinated capitalism' comes from Barry Eichengreen.

20 R. B. Ekelund and R. D. Tollison, *Mercantilism as a Rent-Seeking Society. Economic Regulation in Historical Perspective* (Texas: A&M University Press, 1981).

21 A good example is Stanley L. Engerman, "Mercantilism and Overseas Trade, 1700–1860," in *The Economic History of Britain since 1700, Vol. I: 1700–1860* ed. Roderick Floud and D. McCloskey (Cambridge, 2nd ed. 1994), 182–204.

22 Milton Friedman, *Capitalism and Freedom* (Chicago: University of Chicago Press, 1962); Gary S. Becker, *The Economic Approach to Human Behavior* (Chicago: University of Chicago Press, 1976). Paul Seabright, *The Company of Strangers: A Natural History of Economic Life* (Princeton: Princeton University Press, 2004). More recently and from a journalistic perspective T. L. Friedman, *The World is Flat. A Brief History of the Twenty-first Century* (New York: Farrar, Straus and Giroux, 2005).

23 E.g. John Brewer, ed., *Consumption and the World of Goods* (London et al.: Routledge, 1994); Maxine Berg, ed., *Consumers and Luxury: Consumer Culture in Europe 1650–1850* (Manchester: Manchester University Press, 1999).

24 Jan de Vries, "The Industrial Revolution and the Industrious Revolution," *Journal of Economic History*, LIV, 2 (1994), 249–270; id., *The Industrious Revolution: Consumer Behavior and the Household Economy, 1650 to the Present* (Cambridge: Cambridge University Press, 2008).

25 Kenneth Pomeranz, *The Great Divergence: China, Europe, and the Making of the Modern World Economy* (Princeton: Princeton University Press, 2000).

26 Parthasarathi, *Why Europe Grew Rich*; Peer Vries, *State, Economy and the Great Divergence: Great Britain and China, 1680s–1850s* (London: Bloomsbury, 2015). See the chapter by Peer Vries in the present volume.

27 See especially the essays collected in Magnusson, ed., *Mercantilist Economics*.

28 Mokyr, *Enlightened Economy*, ch. 4.

29 Lars Magnusson, *Nation, State and the Industrial Revolution: The Visible Hand* (London and New York: Routledge, 2009).
30 E.g. Mokyr, *Enlightened Economy*, or Deirdre N. McCloskey, "It was Ideas and Ideologies, not Interests or Institutions, which changed in Northwestern Europe, 1600–1848," *Journal of Evolutionary Economics* 25/1 (2015), 57–68.
31 Magnusson, *Mercantilism*. On Scotland see, e.g., G. Seki, "Policy Debate on Economic Development in Scotland: the 1720s to the 1730s," in *The Rise of Political Economy in the Scottish Enlightenment*, ed. T. Sakamoto and H. Tanaka (London and New York: Routledge, 2003), 22–38.
32 Reinert, *How Rich Countries Got Rich*, ch. 3.
33 Chang, *Kicking Away the Ladder*; Parthasarathi, *Why Europe Grew Rich*; E. Reinert, *How Rich Countries Got Rich*; S. Reinert, *Translating Empire*, ch. 1.
34 Different models of explanantion have been put forth inter alia by Joyce Oldham Appleby, *Economic Thought and Ideology in Seventeenth Century England* (Princeton, NJ: Princeton University Press, 1978), and more recently Steven Pincus, *1688: The First Modern Revolution* (New Haven, CT: Yale University Press, 2009). See the still eminently useful debate in D. C. Coleman, "Mercantilism Revisited," *The Historical Journal* 23, 4 (Dec., 1980), 773–791. For the earlier period, see Reinert, "The Role of the State in Economic Growth," and for the Walpolean moment in the 1720s, Chang, *Kicking Away the Ladder*.
35 Parthasarathi, *Why Europe Grew Rich*; Chang, *Kicking Away the Ladder*. Frank Trentmann, *Free Trade Nation: Commerce, Consumption, and Civil Society in Modern Britain* (Oxford: Oxford University Press, 2008).
36 David Levi-Faur, "Friedrich List and the Political Economy of the Nation-State," *Review of International Political Economy* 4, 1 (Spring, 1997), 154–178.
37 Thomas Simon, "Merkantilismus und Kameralismus. Zur Tragfähigkeit des Merkantilismusbegriffs und seiner Abgrenzung zum deutschen 'Kameralismus,'" in *Merkantilismus. Wiederaufnahme einer Debatte*, 65–82.
38 Ernest Lluch, "Cameralism Beyond the Germanic World: A Note on Tribe," *History of Economic Ideas*, 5/2 (1997), 85–99.
39 Adopted and modified from Arthur Weststeijn and Jan Hartman, "An Empire of Trade: Commercial Reason of State in Seventeenth-Century Holland," in *The Political Economy of Empire in the Early Modern World*, ed. Sophus Reinert and Pernille Røge (Basingstoke: Macmillan, 2013), 11–31.
40 Transl. K. F. Geiser, ed. Reinert, Rössner and Backhaus, forthcoming 2016. See note 6 above.
41 E.g. Immanuel Wallerstein, *The Modern World System I. Capitalist Agriculture and the Origins of the European World-Economy in the Sixteenth Century* (New York: Academic Press, 1974); id., *The Modern World System II. Mercantilism and the Consolidation of the European World-Economy, 1600–1750* (New York: Academic Press, 1980), or Erik H. Mielants, *The Origins of Capitalism and the 'Rise of the West'* (Philadelphia: Temple University Press, 2007). I have taken the treatise of Jonathan Daly, *Historians Debate the Rise of the West* (London and New York: Routledge, 2015) as a departure point.
42 Sombart, *Der moderne Kapitalismus*, German ed., Vol. I/2, p. 811.
43 For a full exposition of this see Sombart, *Der moderne Kapitalismus*, German ed. See, most recently, the quantitative discussion in Steven Pinker, *The Better Angels of our Nature: Why Violence has Declined* (New York: Viking, 2011) and general elaborations of the political and fiscal origins, consequences and ramifications of European wars by Jan Glete, *War and the State in Early Modern Europe: Spain, the Dutch Republic, and Sweden as Fiscal-Military States, 1500–1660* (London and New York: Routledge, 2002); Bartolomé Yun Casalilla and Patrick O'Brien, eds, *The Rise of Fiscal States: A Global History, 1500–1914* (Cambridge and New York: Cambridge University Press, 2012), Martin L. van Crefeld, *The Rise and Decline of the State* (Cambridge: Cambridge

University Press, 2000), and Geoffrey Parker, *The Military Revolution: Military Innovation and the Rise of the West, 1500–1800* (Cambridge and New York: Cambridge University Press, 1988). Most recently Philip T. Hoffman, *Why did Europe Conquer the World?* (Princeton: Princeton University Press, 2015).

44 See, e.g., Harcourt, *Illusion of Free Markets*; Stanziani, *Rules of Exchange*.

45 Daron Acemoglu and James A. Robinson, *Why Nations Fail: The Origins of Power, Prosperity, and Poverty* (New York, Crown: 2012). The concept of 'failure' is interesting in its own right – see an unpublished paper by Francesco Boldizzoni.

46 We should note, however, that to think of mercantilism as either a coherent theory or policy programme would make it quite unique in world history, as it would be hard to pinpoint any other period or world region in history where there has ever been either a dominant and 'unified' paradigm, or a unified policy agenda when applied in practice.

47 See the discussion by T. Simon, which is not free of misconceptions but ultimately very useful: mercantilism was trade orientated, whereas German or Cameralist political economy can be called production-orientated.

48 Most recently in the consensual definition by eminent historian of economic thought, Horst Claus Recktenwald, in the Palgrave Dictionary of Economics: 'Cameralism is the specific version of mercantilism taught and practised in the German principalities (Kleinstaaten) in the 17th and 18th centuries'. See H. C. Recktenwald, "Cameralism," in *The New Palgrave Dictionary of Economics*, Second Edition, ed. Steven N. Durlauf and Lawrence E. Blume (online version, 2008), last accessed 9 September 2015.

49 Keith Tribe, "Cameralism and the Sciences of the State," in: *The Cambridge History of Eighteenth-Century Political Thought*, ed. Mark Goldie and Robert Wokler (Cambridge: Cambridge University Press, 2006), 525–546, at 525.

50 Ibid.

51 A fascinating analysis of the skewed nature of modern economic tradition in political economy is provided in Sophus A. Reinert, "The Empire of Emulation: A Quantitative Analysis of Economic Translations in the European World, 1500–1849," in *The Political Economy of Empire in the Early Modern World*, 105–128.

52 See the essays in Jürgen G. Backhaus, ed., *The Beginnings of Political Economy: Johann Heinrich Gottlob von Justi* (Boston, MA: Springer, 2009). See also the works referred to above. A good discussion may also be found in Johannes Burkhardt and Birger P. Priddat, *Geschichte der Ökonomie* (Frankfurt am Main: Deutscher Klassiker Verlag, 2009); Birger P. Priddat, "Kameralismus als paradoxe Konzeption der gleichzeitigen Stärkung von Markt und Staat. Komplexe Theorielagen im deutschen 18. Jahrhundert," *Berichte zur Wissenschaftsgeschichte* 31 (2008), 249–263; Keith Tribe, *Strategies of Economic Order. German Economic Discourse, 1750–1950* (Cambridge: Cambridge University Press, 1995), ch. 1; Bertram Schefold, "Glückseligkeit und Wirtschaftspolitik: Zu Justis 'Grundsätze der Policey-Wissenschaft,'" in *Vademecum zu einem Klassiker des Kameralismus: Johann Heinrich Gottlob von Justi, Grundsätze der Policey-Wissenschaft*, ed. Bertram Schefold (Düsseldorf: Verlag Wirtschaft und Finanzen, 1993), as well as the volumes specifically devoted to pre-classical continental economics in the *Studien zur Entwicklung der ökonomischen Theorie/Schriften des Vereins für Socialpolitik*, V, X, XI, XVI, XXI and XXIV (Berlin, 1986–2010).

53 William D. Grampp, "An Appreciation of Mercantilism," in *Mercantilist Economics*, 59–85.

54 Francesco Boldizzoni, 'The Domestication of the Economic Mind: A Response to the Critics,' *Investigaciones de Historia Económica - Economic History Research* 9 (2013), 71–74, abstract.

55 Mokyr, *Enlightened Economy*.

56 See, e.g., Karl Gunnar Persson, *Grain Markets in Europe, 1500–1900: Integration and Deregulation* (Cambridge and New York: Cambridge University Press, 1999), or the recent attempt and synopsis of the economistic literature on early modern European market integration and global divergence by Roman Studer, *The Great Divergence*

Reconsidered: Europe, India, and the Rise to Global Economic Power (New York: Cambridge University Press, 2015).

57 Grampp, "An Appreciation."

58 Ibid.

59 Harcourt, *Illusion of Free Markets.*

60 John H. A. Munro, *Wool, Cloth, and Gold. The Struggle for Bullion in Anglo-Burgundian Trade, 1340–1478* (Brussels: Editions de l'Université de Bruxelles/Toronto: University of Toronto Press, 1972); Peter Spufford, *Monetary Problems and Policies in the Burgundian Netherlands 1433–1496* (Leiden: Brill, 1970).

61 Including Mokyr, *Enlightened Economy.*

62 See, e.g., Parthasarathi, *Why Europe Grew Rich*; Ashworth, *Customs and Excise*; Julian Hoppit, "Bounties, the Economy and the State in Britain, 1689–1800," in *Regulating the British Economy, 1660–1850* ed. Perry Gauci (Farnham, Surrey; Burlington, VT: Ashgate, 2011); Julian Hoppit, "The Nation, the State, and the First Industrial Revolution," *The Journal of British Studies*, 50/2 (2011), 307–331; Raymond L. Sickinger, "Regulation or Ruination: Parliament's Consistent Pattern of Mercantilist Regulation of the English Textile Trade, 1660–1800," *Parliamentary History*, 19/2 (2000), 211–32; Anna Gambles, "Free Trade and State Formation: The Political Economy of Fisheries Policy in Britain and the United Kingdom, circa 1780–1850," *Journal of British Studies* 39/3 (2000), 288–316, and C. Dudley, "Party Politics, Political Economy, and Economic Development in Early Eighteenth-Century Britain," *Economic History Review*, Second Series, 66:4 (2013), 1084–1100.

63 Harcourt, *Illusion of Free Markets.*

64 Martin Luther, *On Commerce and Usury*, ed. P. R. Rössner (London and New York: Anthem, 2015), introduction, esp. 142–146.

65 David S. Landes, *The Wealth and Poverty of Nations. Why Some Are So Rich and Others So Poor* (New York: W.W. Norton, 1998), or Eric L. Jones, *The European Miracle: Environments, Economies and Geopolitics in the History of Europe and Asia*, 3rd ed. (Cambridge: Cambridge University Press, 2003).

2 German language economic bestsellers before 1850

Also introducing Giovanni Botero as a common reference point of Cameralism and mercantilism[1]

Erik S. Reinert with Kenneth E. Carpenter

The major legacy of Cambridge economist Herbert Somerton Foxwell (1849–1936) was to form the nucleus of two of the greatest collections of economics books. Indirectly it is essentially thanks to Herbert Foxwell, and later to the curator of one of these collections, that we are able to produce a fairly accurate list of the economic bestsellers in the German language before 1850.

Foxwell's first collection, of about 30,000 books, was sold to the Worshipful Company of Goldsmiths in London for 10,000 Pounds in 1901. This collection forms the core of what is now Goldsmiths' Library of Economic Literature at the University of London. With his duplicates Foxwell then started a second collection, which became Kress Library of Business and Economics at Harvard Business School. Based on Foxwell's book collection at Harvard – and the work of Ken Carpenter who became its curator in 1968[2] – we are now able to measure, to a reasonable degree, which economics books, in any Western language, have been the most influential, measured using the number of editions as a proxy.

Foxwell collected books published before he was born, i.e. stopping with 1849, a year after the Revolutions in Europe and the publications – all in that same year – of John Stuart Mill's *Political Economy,* of Marx' and Engels' *Communist Manifesto*, and of Bruno Hildebrand's *Die Nationalökonomie der Gegenwart und Zukunft.* Foxwell's choice of date limits the scope of Ken Carpenter's work and this paper. With Foxwell's collection as a basis Carpenter investigated and made a list of the 40 bestselling economics books in terms of editions published before 1850.[3] Based on Carpenter's continuous work on economics translations from 1968 to date, Carpenter and Reinert are now putting together a new publication on the economic bestsellers before 1850, with a biography and bibliography of the authors. The updated number of bestselling books – achieving more than ten editions before 1850 – is likely to be 65. Carpenter's list is astonishing reading because so many presently unknown economists figure so prominently there, while authors that present students of the history of economic thought would be convinced they would find there are conspicuously absent.

The first list had five authors who were either Germans or wrote the first edition of the work in question in German. On the forthcoming list two will be added (Seckendorff and Hirzel), and one (Schröder 1686) will have to be deleted because we seem unable to find more than nine editions, and the cut-off point has been established at ten. Still, this paper lists Wilhelm von Schröder's 1698 *Fürstliche Schatz- und Rent-Kammer* because it was a very important book, and also the works of Johann Heinrich Gottlob von Justi, whose textbook would definitively have made it to ten editions if it had not been published in so many different versions.

Of the 65 bestsellers that are likely to make it into the new bestseller volume, one was published in the 1500s, ten during the 1600s, thirty-nine in the 1700s, and 15 from 1800 to 1850. It is slightly surprising to find that the German authors – including Schröder here – are so early in the chronology: three in the 1600s, three in the 1700s and Marx' and Engels' *Manifesto* as the only one in the 1800s. As opposed to the other works, the *Manifesto* is so well known that it will not be discussed here.

Herbert Foxwell, Kress Library, and the economic bestsellers

In Cambridge Herbert Somerton Foxwell (1849–1936) was a contemporary of John Maynard Keynes' father John Neville Keynes (1852–1949), of Alfred Marshall (1842–1924), the founder of neo-classical economics, and of economic historian William Cunningham (1849–1919). In 1890 John Neville Keynes published *The Scope and Method of Political Economy*. In the same year the first edition of Marshall's *Principles of Economics* appeared. Both volumes were published by Macmillan, and the authors thank each other in the introduction for having read and commented on their respective manuscripts. It may be argued that Keynes Senior's book – e.g. with its insistence on history and on the inseparability of economics and ethics – lies surprisingly close to the German Historical School approach. The same thing applies to Foxwell, whose own writings are marked by an ardent anti-Ricardianism.

John Maynard Keynes (1883–1946) has given us a loving obituary of Foxwell,[4] and one can almost imagine that his father's sympathies shine through in his comments. Like his German counterparts at the time, Foxwell argued strongly against the abstract economic methods of David Ricardo, and like the members of the German Historical School, he equally disliked liberalism and communism. Foxwell wrote several pieces on the history of English socialist economics and ninetenth-century economics in general. Together with Edwin Seligman of Columbia University (another serious collector of economics books), Foxwell is a main source of information on minor English economists, both socialists and anti-Ricardians, of the nineteenth century. Foxwell's 110 page introduction to Anton Menger's *The Right to the Whole Produce of Labour*[5] brings a scathing criticism of Ricardo's negative influence on economics on two accounts: Ricardo both gave the whole course of mainstream economics a 'wrong twist', making it unhistorical and unrealistic, and his 'crude generalization' gave 'modern socialism its fancied scientific basis'.

Foxwell thus very early saw the point that lately has been made by Joseph Stiglitz[6] and Geoffrey Hodgson[7] that both communism and liberalism have the same intellectual roots in David Ricardo. So strong was Foxwell's dislike of Ricardo, that he failed to deliver his Presidential Address on Ricardo to the Royal

Economic Society 'on the ground that his onslaught of the man, who had convinced the world of the dreadful heresy of a necessary conflict between the interests of capital and labour, would have been too provocative'.[8] Foxwell also wrote on finance and banking, emphasizing the advantages of the continental banking practices over English.

It was Foxwell who spelt out the danger of what Schumpeter later labelled 'The Ricardian Vice' in economics:

> Ricardo, and still more those who popularised him, may stand as an example for all time of the extreme danger which may arise from the unscientific use of hypothesis in social speculations, from the failure to appreciate the limited applications to actual affairs of a highly artificial and arbitrary analysis. His ingenious, though perhaps over-elaborated reasonings became positively mischievous and misleading when they were unhesitatingly applied to determine grave practical issues without the smallest sense of the thoroughly abstract and unreal character of the assumptions on which they were founded.[9]

Foxwell's collection of economics books – still today the core of the Kress Collection – reflects the collector's understanding that economics must be studied in its economic and social context, and Foxwell's 'special sympathy for all heretics against the bondage of economic orthodoxy'.[10] Schumpeter's defiance of economic orthodoxy – of the normally uncontested superiority of the canonical writings from the Physiocrats to 'A. Smith' – is very much in the spirit of Foxwell and of his book collection, where Schumpeter was physically based when he wrote the *History of Economic Analysis.* Schumpeter's well known scepticism towards 'A. Smith' is paralleled in Foxwell's critical attitude towards the English tradition. Schumpeter is indeed open to see positive aspects of most economic ideas, perhaps with the exception of the German Romanticists.

Being an English economist, Foxwell was unique in his intuitive closeness to the German philosophical and economic approach from which Schumpeter came. Against the backdrop of Foxwell's own economics and his book collection, Schumpeter stands out as a kindred spirit. He refers to Foxwell five times in the History of Economic Analysis, but – somewhat surprisingly – always only as a collector or editor, never as an economist and historian of economic thought in his own right.

In his 110-page introduction Foxwell discusses the role of the English socialists and gives the reader a tour de force of the history of economics in the nineteenth century as it relates to socialist ideas. Here are some quotes from Foxwell's introduction to Menger:

> just as we may avoid widespread physical desolation by rightly turning a stream near its source, so a timely dialectic in the fundamental ideas of social philosophy may spare us untold social wreckage and suffering. (xxi)

> the merely mechanical philosophy of Malthus (xl)

as Jevons has observed, Ricardo gave the whole course of English economics a wrong twist. (xli)

The fact seems to be that, after the appearance of Ricardo's Principles, the economists were largely given over to sterile logomachy (*i.e. disputes about words, controversy turning on merely verbal points, ER*) and academic hair-splitting. (lxxii)

The work on Schumpeter's 'filiations' of economic thought was continued in Kress Library through publications on bibliographical matters and on unknown economists. In the 1970s Kenneth Carpenter, the Kress Librarian, did very important work on Schumpeterian filiation of ideas in economics. Carpenter worked both on establishing the impact and influence of economics books published before 1850 (as already mentioned, this year is the cut-off point for Foxwell's collection, the year after his birth) and on tracing the spread and influence of economic ideas through translations from and into German.[11] His *The Economic Bestsellers before 1850* (see above) is a standard reference work for economic books. Carpenter's massive work on *Translations of Economic Literature before 1850* still remains unpublished.

Giovanni Botero and the origins of mercantilism and Cameralism

It is probably fair to say that Cameralist and mercantilist tradition grew out of two much older and overlapping traditions:

1 The *Fürstenspiegel* tradition with roots back to Roman times, bringing advice to the rulers on how to govern. Even in peripheral Norway, this tradition goes back to a text from around 1250: *Konungs skuggsjá* (Old Norse for 'King's mirror').
2 The tradition of accurate country surveys and descriptions dating back to *De magnalibus urbis mediolani* of Bonvesin de la Riva (1288) and later works also on the Florentine state. Such descriptive surveys were the purpose of costly and extensive *visitas* in the Spanish provinces of the New World, the result of which were published.

We have now come to think that the apparently different traditions – Cameralism and mercantilism – did not grow independently out of the two traditions mentioned above, that many authors both Cameralist and mercantilist used the extremely widely diffused works of Giovanni Botero (1544–1617) as a common platform and point of reference. Botero's work *Ragion di Stato* (1589) satisfied the *Fürstenspiegel* tradition, while his *Relazioni Universali* (1591) satisfies the need for surveys and the fact-finding missions' quest for geographical, cultural, and anthropological knowledge. All in all, at the time when the knowledge of the whole world and its cultures became codifiable, Giovanno Botero provided an unusually complete range of social sciences. It is worth noting that in contrast to the many utopias of the period, Botero's reasoning was based on the observation of history and of facts.[12] In his work he clearly distances himself from *bullionism* – from the idea that a nation's wealth consists in the amount of precious metals owned – of which mercantilism is sometimes accused.

Botero was born in the small town of Bene Vagienna in the province of Cuneo in the Italian Piedmont region. As a Jesuit, he was keenly interested in non-European cultures.[13] From the point of view of now long-standing Western eurocentrism, the ability of the Jesuits also to engage in two-way cultural communication reminds us that Eurocentrism is not necessarily a 'natural' state of affairs. Jesuit Matteo Ricci (1552–1610) – a contemporary of Botero – ventured with a small group to China, where he not only translated Christian and Western scientific texts into Chinese, but also Chinese texts into Latin.[14] The Jesuits in China 'went native' to the extent that they sometimes dressed like Chinese literati. By entering inside foreign cultures – from Chinese to the Guaraní in South America – Jesuit travellers also played the role of anthropologists. As one observer says, Botero 'brought together an immense mass of geographical and anthropological information, which he tried to organize according to broad methodological categories (like "resources", "government", and "religion")'.[15]

Apparently few things unite Sir Walter Raleigh (1554–1618), Tommaso Campanella (1568–1639), English economist Edward Misselden (1608–1654), and Swedish technologist and economist Christopher Polhem (1661–1751). But one thing does: they all convey key insights found originally in Giovanni Botero and they do not quote him or anyone else as to the origins of these insights. Clearly also the work of the first German bestseller, Veit von Seckendorff (1626–1692)[16] is Botero. There are still 30 editions of Botero's works (mainly uncatalogued) in the Gotha Library that Seckendorff formed for Ernest the Pious (Ernst der Fromme) of Sachsen-Gotha-Altenburg, and Botero was on the reading list Seckendorff made for the education of princes.[17] The start of this chapter attempts to scratch the surface of the links between Giovanni Botero and early economics, particularly German economics. The large number of translations of Botero's works – especially the *Relazioni Universali* – that appeared in Germany, both in Latin and German translations, testifies to his strong influence on the German seventeenth century *Zeitgeist* (see Tables 2.1 and 2.2 below for a list of editions).

Many years ago, rambling through the uncatalogued parts of the Gotha Library – in search of material relating to its first librarian, Veit von Seckendorff – Reinert was struck by the large number of editions of Giovanni Botero's works. Curiosity grew even more when he found that his 1622 Venice edition of Botero's *Relazioni Universali* – combining geography, anthropology and *Staatswissenschaften* (and to some people a very early book on oceanography) – according to his bibliographer is the sixty-first edition of this book, the first being in 1591.

During the authors' quest to produce a new, more complete and more broadly conceived edition of the economic bestsellers before 1850, it became clear that Botero's small book (3 + 79 pp) *The Cause of the Greatnesse of Cities / Sulla Grandezza delle Città* (first edition 1588) is the first economic bestseller, reaching a record 40 editions before 1850, 38 of them between 1588 and 1671. Only one year later, this volume was included in the much larger work *Ragion di Stato* (8 + 368 pp) which in English came to be called *Reason of State* and in German *Staatsräson*. In his 1925 work on *Staatsräson* Meinecke mentions Botero's many followers and the 'true catacombs of forgotten literature', which follow in Botero's paths.[18]

For details of the publication record, see Table 2.1 below. It is not yet completely clear which editions of *Ragion di Stato* contained *Greatnesse of Cities* and which did not. There is a new (2012) translation of Botero's *The Cause of the Greatnesse of Cities*[19] with an excellent introduction by Geoffrey Symox.

As was the habit with translations at the time,[20] sources frequently were not acknowledged. In early economic thought, it has seemed to us, sometimes very assertive statements are made, as if everyone should know where they came from. In various forms, the statement that manufactures were the real gold mines, much more valuable than the gold mines themselves, is found all over Europe from the late 1500s through the 1700s. It now appears that this statement and this understanding originate with Giovanni Botero's 1588 work. We find them from Tommaso Campanella (1602) and Antonio Genovesi (in the 1770s), both in Italy, to Sir Walter Raleigh in England, Gerónimo Uztáriz in Spain, and Anders Berch, the first economics professor outside Germany, in Uppsala in Sweden in the 1740s.

These people shared a basic understanding that only in barren areas lacking natural resources and with few possibilities for food production – such as in Venice and in the Dutch Republic – economic development would tend to come 'naturally'. In other areas the transition from diminishing returns activities (agriculture) to increasing returns activities (manufacturing) – as they were identified by Serra (1613) – from 'natural activities' to 'artificial activities' – using the terminology of Thomas Mun (1621) which may have originated with Botero – required heavy-handed government policies. What Venice and the Dutch Republic had achieved – rather than the policies of Venice and the Dutch Republic – was the object of attention of foreign economists and foreign rulers alike.

The theoretical conflict between the forefathers of today's mainstream canon and what we could call the Renaissance canon has existed at least since the 1622–23 'English' debate between Gerard de Malynes[21] and Edward Misselden,[22] in which Malynes represented a static theory rooted in *barter* and Misselden represented a theory centred around *learning* and *production*. In the history of economic thought, their debate is interpreted as being about exchange controls and the balance of trade.[23] The controversy between the two was an 'acrimonious, even abusive' one, in which 'ink was shed like water'.[24]

However, by going back to the sources, one finds that the main line of attack by Misselden against Malynes is his 'mechanical' view of Man – Malynes has left out Man's 'art' and 'soul'. Misselden quotes at length a paragraph from Malynes, where Malynes reduces trade to three elements, 'namely, Commodities, Money, and Exchange'.[25] Objecting to this definition, Misselden says: 'It is against Art to dispute with a man that denyeth the *Principles* of Art'. Misselden scorns Malynes for not seeing the difference between a heap of stones and logs and a house – because Man's productive powers and his soul, which produce the house, have been left out. Typically, the wealth of a nation was seen as lying in its capacity to produce, its 'productive powers' as Friedrich List put it.

The importance of the difference between 'heaps of stones and logs and a house' rings a bell when reading Botero, the first English translation of which was in 1605:

> some will ask me; whether Fertilitie of Land, or Industrie of Man, importeth more to make a place Great, or populous? Industrie, assuredly. First because Manufactures framed by the skilfull hand of Man, are more in number[26], and price[27], than things produced by Nature: For Nature giveth matter, and subject: but the Curiositie and Art of Man addeth unspeakable varietie of formes. Wool, from Nature, is a rude and simple Commoditie: What fair things, how various, and infinite, doth Art make out of it?[28]
>
> Compare the Marbles, with the Statues, Colossuses, Columns, Borders, and infinite other Labours, taken. Compare the Timber, with the Galleys, Galleons, Vessels of many sorts, both of Warre, Burthen, and Pleasure: Compare also the Timber, with the Statues, the Furnitures for Building, and other things innumerable, which are built with the Plane, Chesill, and Turners-Wheele. Compare the Colours with the Pictures… (etc.)[29]

Botero's distinction between raw materials and the finished goods which are created by the arts certainly recalls Thorstein Veblen's insistence on the instinct of workmanship – rather than Adam Smith's barter instinct – as the origin of wealth. Misselden represents the acute Renaissance awareness of the vast territory to be covered between Mankind's present poverty and ignorance, and the enormous potentials of human learning. This released enthusiasm and energy. The situation recalls Keynes' frustration with the suboptimal situation of the world under the Great Depression. Both the Renaissance philosophers/economists and Keynes were searching for the formula needed to liberate society from its obviously inferior position at the time. It recalls what Keynes called 'Salvation through Knowledge'. This attitude is very different from Man as the passive victim of 'two sovereign masters, pain and pleasure',[30] which is the philosophical foundation of English classical and modern neo-classical economics.

In England, Sir Walter Raleigh was also studying Botero's treatise; his 'Observations Concerning the Causes of the Magnificency and Opulence of Cities' is a precis of Botero's text.[31] For example: Raleigh's final section, 'The Causes That Concern the Magnificency of a City' closely follows Botero's translation of the conclusion to Book III of 'On the Causes'. Raleigh's interest in 'On the Causes' seems to be linked to his colonial projects. Echoing Botero's conception of a civilizing process in which cities were instrumental (Book I, ch. 2), Raleigh's opening statement alludes to the need to 'civilize and reform the savage and barbarous lives and corrupt manners of such People', presumably the American Indians.[32] Recognizing the 'uncivilized' nature of most non-European cultures could lead to a desire to protect them, as were the policy of Botero and also the official policy of the Spanish monarchy towards the Indians. It could also lead to a desire to colonize and exploit them as cheap labour.

It is also likely that William Petty (1623–1687), who entered a Jesuit college in Caen in France at the age of 14, would have been exposed to the ideas of Botero whose ideas were very much in fashion at the time.

The Spanish mercantilist Geronimo de Uztáriz (1670–1732), whose main work was translated into both French and English, commented from a particularly good vantage point, being a Spaniard and having lived in Holland and Italy for 23 years. Uztáriz' conclusion reflects Botero's line on the role of manufactures and the sterility of gold *per se*: '[Manufactures] is a mine more fruitful of gain, riches, and plenty, than those of Potosí'.[33]

The text below, from an economics student in Uppsala in 1747, sums up the mercantilist argument with emphasis on population density. We find the same much earlier argument in William Petty, who developed it into a policy recommendation: move the population from sparsely populated areas in the periphery of the realm to London where they are more useful. This also reflects the policies of the Jesuits in Latin America, where the native populations were brought into city-like *reducciones*. The author, Gustav Westerbeck, was a student of Anders Berch who held the Chair of Economics in Uppsala:

> How things really are in national economics, is nowhere clearer than in the case of the United Netherlands. They have virtually no domestic (resources), but still, through the industry of its large population, exceed in strength the immense but sparsely populated and idle Spain. (The Netherlands) knows well how to use the folly of others to its own benefit. We see how poor Spain is with all its gold and silver mines, the best ports and the best soil in the world, because of its lack of inhabitants. On the other hand how its large number of inhabitants make the United Provinces mighty, with their miserable ports and the worst climate on earth.[34]

The explosive spread of Botero's *Grandezza delle Città* is shown in Table 2.1. Counting Strasbourg – where Seckendoff had studied – as Germany, there were four editions of the work published in Germany before the start of the 30 Years' War. The others were one in Ursellis/Oberursel (near Frankfurt am Main) and two in Cologne. All were in Latin. The first German translation appeared in Frankfurt in 1657. It is interesting to note how the editions grew fewer during the war, all over Europe, and how the frequency picked up again afterwards.

Table 2.1 includes all editions found so far of *Cause della Grandezza delle Città* (first edition Rome 1588), all editions of *Della Ragion di Stato* (first edition Venice 1589), and all editions of *Relazioni Universali* (first edition Rome 1591) when they are bound with *Ragion di Stato*.

Table 2.2 lists 83 independent editions of the *Relazioni Universali* between 1591 and 1796 (there were no editions between 1796 and 1850). *Relazioni Universali* was published in Italian (from 1591), German (first two editions Cologne 1596), Latin (first two editions in Frankfurt am Main and Cologne 1598), English (first in London 1601), Spanish (first in Valladolid 1599), and Polish (first in Krakow 1613). Botero's bibliographer Assandra[35] informs us that the *Relazioni* was a prohibited book in France.

Table 2.1 Giovanni Botero, *Cause della Grandezza delle Cittá / Della Ragion di Stato.*
Editions before 1850.

1	Rome	1588 (only *Grandezza*)
2	Rome	1588 (only *Grandezza* + historical piece on Rome)
3	Venice	1589 (1st edition of *Ragion di Stato*, also including *Grandezza*)
4	Ferrara	1589 (from here on, clean entries indicate both works in one)
5	Ferrara	1590 (only *Grandezza*)
6	Ferrara	1590
7	Rome	1590
8	Madrid	1593 (Spanish)
9	Milan	1596 (only *Grandezza*, publisher Pacifico Ponzio)
10	Milan	1596 (only *Grandezza*, publisher S. Barberino)
11	Turin	1596
12	Milan	1596
13	Milan	1597-98 (*Ragione* 1597, *Cause* 1598)
14	Venice	1598
15	Pavia	1598 (without *Cause*)
16	Venice	1598 (without *Cause*)
17	Paris	1599 (French, without *Cause*)
18	Barcelona	1599 (Spanish, without *Cause*)
19	Venice	1601
20	Ursellis /Oberursel	1602 (Latin)
21	Strasbourg	1602 (Latin)
22	Burgos	1602 (Spanish, without *Cause*)
23	Burgos	1603 (Spanish, without *Cause*)
24	Barcelona	1605 (Italian + *Relazioni*)
25	London	1606 (English, only *Grandezza*)
26	Burgos	1606 (Spanish, without *Cause*)
27	Turin	1606
28	Paris	1606 (French, *Maximes d'estat militaires et politiques…*)
29	Venice	1606
30	Venice	1608 (+ *Relazioni*)
31	Milan	1609
32	Bologna	1609
33	Turin	1610
34	Cologne	1613 (Latin)
35	Cologne	1615 (Latin)
36	Venice	1619
37	Venice	1619
38	London	1635 (English, only *Grandezza*)
39	Venice	1640 (+ *Relazioni*)
40	Frankfurt	1657 (German)
41	Venice	1659 (+ *Relazioni*)
42	Venice	1659
43	Frankfurt	1661 (1664?) (German)
44	Helmstedt, Germany	1666 (Latin)
45	Venice	1671 (+ *Relazioni*)
46	Milan	1830
47	Milan	1839

Table 2.2 Giovanni Botero, *Relazioni Universali*. Editions before 1850.

1	Rome	1591
2	Rome	1592–93
3	Ferrara	1592
4	Bergamo	1594–96
5	Rome	1595
6	Rome	1595
7	Venice	1595
8	Vicenza	1595 publisher G. Greco
9	Vicenza	1595 publisher Eredi di Perin libraio
10	Brescia	1595–96
11	Rome	1596
12	Bergamo	1596
13	Venice	1596 publisher G. Vincenti
14	Venice	1596 publisher G. B. Vssio
15	Venice	1596 publisher G. Angelieri
16	Bergamo	1596
17	Venice	1596
18	Cologne	1596 German, publisher J. Gymnici Erben
19	Cologne	1596 Latin, publisher C. Andree
20	Manuscript in British Museum, London	1596 German
21	Venice	1597
22	Vicenza	1597
23	Rome	1597
24	Venice	1597
25	Frankfurt	1598 Latin
26	Brescia	1598
27	Venice	1598
28	Cologne	1598 Latin
29	Brescia	1599
30	Venice	1599
31	Venice	1599
32	Cologne	1599 German
33	Valladolid	1599 Spanish
34	Venice	1600
35	Lübeck	1600 Latin
36	Turin	1601
37	London	1601 English
38	Venice	1602
39	Ursellis/Oberursel	1602 German
40	Ursellis/Oberursel	1603 Latin
41	Barcelona	1603 Spanish
42	Venice	1605
43	Barcelona	1605 Spanish
44	Turin	1607
45	Venice	1608 publisher A. Angelieri
46	Venice	1608 publisher G. Bertano
47	Barcelona	1608 Spanish
48	Valladolid	1609 Spanish
49	London	1611 English
50	Venice	1611
51	Munich	1611 German
52	Munich	1611 German

Table 2.2 Giovanni Botero, Relazioni Universali. Editions before 1850 *continued*

53	Venice	1612
54	Cologne	1613 Latin
55	Krakow	1613 Polish
56	Frankfurt	1614 Latin
57	Venice	1618
58	Marburg	1620 Latin
59	Helmstedt	1620 Latin
60	Gerona	1622 Spanish
61	Venice	1622
62	Leyden	1625 Latin
63	Leyden	1626 Latin
64	Leyden	1627 Latin
65	Leyden	1629 Latin
66	London	1630 English
67	Leyden	1633 Latin
68	Venice	1640
69	Venice	1640
70	Leyden	1642 Latin
71	Leyden	1642 Latin
72	Leyden	1647 Latin
73	Jena	1648 Latin, translated from German
74	Venice	1650
75	Venice	1659
76	Venice	1662
77	Helmstedt	1664 Latin
78	Leipzig	1667 Latin
79	Bologna	1668
80	Helmstedt	1670 Latin
81	Venice	1671
82	Gerona	1748 Spanish
83	Venice	1795
84	Venice	1796

Note: Not all editions are complete. Except for corrections in chronology, we have followed the entries by Assandra. In contrast to Botero's *Grandezze*, this book was prohibited in France, which explains the lack of French translations. Publishers are indicated only when the editions of the same year in the same city were by different publishers. For more details, see Assandra (op.cit.).

Boterians in Sweden: a parenthesis

Sweden is an interesting country to study because – in spite of being in the geographical periphery of Europe – starting in the early 1500s with the Reign of Gustav Vasa, Sweden played an important role in European politics.[36] In the habit of the period, Sweden also attracted important foreign academics to work for them, like Hugo Grotius, René Descartes, and Samuel Pufendorf.

Just like in other countries, sometimes early economists assertively make comments which leave the reader in doubt about their origin. Here we shall briefly discuss the case of three early Swedish economists, Christopher Polhem (1661–1751), Anders Bachmansson (1697–1772), and Anders Berch (1711–1774). Berch was the first professor of economics outside Germany, in Uppsala in 1741.

Figure 2.1 Christopher Polhem (1661–1751), Swedish inventor and economist. In this 1745 speech and pamphlet, Polhem uses the argument first used by Antonio Serra (1613): diminishing returns in the mining sector are a reason why Sweden must cultivate manufacturing. Raw materials (*Rudimaterier*) must be worked into manufactured goods (*Manufacturer*).

With kind permission from Erik Reinert.

The second was probably at the opposite geographical point in Europe: Antonio Genovesi in Naples in 1754. Berch's chair was in *jurisprudentiæ oeconomiæ et commerciorum* and Genovesi's in *commercio e meccanica.*

It is not so surprising to find Tommaso Campanella (1568–1639), Neapolitan author of the utopian *Città del Sole* (1602), echoing Botero on the need to encourage national industries on the basis that they were 'more prolific than mines'.[37] It is more surprising to find the same insight that manufactures have the quality of 'inexhaustible gold mines' almost 150 years later, in 1747, in the work of Anders Berch. [38]

Christopher Polhem, inventor and economist, is still portrayed on Swedens's 500 kronor banknote. The other side of the banknote pictures the contemporary King Carl XI, and the building that housed what was probably the world's first central bank (Riksbanken, 1666). Polhem not only testifies to the need for manufacturing in order to produce national wealth, he also restates the theoretical point which Antonio Serra[39] (fl. 1613) added to Botero's understanding: that diminishing returns (in Sweden's case in mining) make it impossible to grow richer by continuing to produce what Polhem calls *Rudimaterier* (raw materials), therefore they must be worked into *Manufacturer* (manufactured goods). This was also the basic message of the Marshall Plan following World War II and classical development economics until the late 1970s.

The sixteenth century was surprisingly cosmopolitan. We find Botero's early works in first editions in Krakow and Nürnberg, as well as in Milan. We should keep in mind that not only the higher echelons of the clergy, but also artisans – through guild membership – could move around and work in different European countries. Obviously also the nobility was mobile, and so were students.

The diary of an important Swedish nobleman, Per Brahe d.y. (1602–1680) – whose library was to hold a copy of Botero's *Ragion di Stato* – testifies to the two last points. His diary gives us information on how it was to grow up and live during the Thirty Years' War, and how the founder of the first university in Finland was matriculated at two of the oldest universities in Europe: Bologna and Padova.[40] Brahe's travels and the naturalness with which he moves around and stays with the nobility is amazing, but perhaps with a hint of bragging ('in Greenwich I was with "Konung Jacob"' (King James)). Impressive is the trip he makes starting in January 1623 traveling through a Germany at war – mentioning many cities he travels through – how he learns to fence in Strasbourg, crosses the St. Bernardo on foot, goes to Milan and on to Bologna, where he is matriculated at the university, South to Naples (where he had a *démelé* with a nobleman), then on to Rome, Florence, and Padova ('where I was also matriculated'). In Hamburg-Harburg he is almost killed by a *Hollsteiner,* and breaks his leg, but is back again in Sweden just after Christmas 1626.

In 1640 Per Brahe is the most important founder of Åbo Akademi,[41] a university in Turku/Åbo, in Finland. Sweden had an interesting colonial practice in that they established universities in conquered territory, in Dorpat/Tartu in Estonia in 1632, and in Lund, in Southern Sweden, in 1688, in a territory just conquered from the Danes. From 1648 to 1814 the University of Greifswald (founded 1456) was also a Swedish administered university. Swedish policies in the occupied territories were of a very different kind than later types of colonialism. One sign of this is that the Estonian equivalent of 'in the good old days' is still today 'in the good old Swedish days'.

Like Polhem, Bachmansson combined the interest in economics with that of mechanical work. His large 1730 volume *Arcana Oeconomiae et Commercii* always appeared to be slightly out of context, an early bird in the explosion of economics writings. However, going through the volume, the first thing that strikes the reader is that the page layout – what the Germans call the *Satzspiegel* – of Bachmansson's volume when he talks about the different nations and cultures of the planet is identical to that of Botero's *Relazioni Universali*. And this layout is not very common. Indeed, Bachmannson's work appears to blend the subjects of Botero's two main works, *Ragion di Stato* and *Relazioni Universali*.

Looking for original works of Botero in Swedish libraries – which may have inspired our three authors – we found them only in a single library which Google maps places in the middle of a forest not far from Uppsala, where Sweden's first university is located: Skokloster. The Skokloster librarian informs that Botero's *Grandezza delle Città* was found in four of the private historical collections that make up the present library, Carl Gustaf Wrangel (1613–1676), who built the library, Per Brahe d.y (1602–1680), Nils Brahe (1633–1699), and Carl Gustaf Bielke (1683–1754).[42] Enlightenment Sweden apparently held impressive private libraries. It should also be mentioned that a peculiar manifestation of the Swedish love of books was that in times of war they specialized in taking libraries for a ransom.[43]

German language economists on the economics bestseller lists

Apart from the works on Seckendorff and Justi this list reflects the work of Harvard Librarian Ken Carpenter, former curator of the Kress Library, since he started working in Kress in 1968. The entries on the different bestsellers are given in the state they are at the time of writing, reflecting various degrees of completeness. These entries are all the more impressive since most of the work was done before access to online library catalogues was possible.

Listed are all bestsellers originally written in German. It was thought for a long time that the work of the Swiss author Hans Caspar Hirzel – *Le Socrate Rustique* – had first been published in French. This publication was rendered as *The Rural Socrates* in English. However, the authors have recently found that the work was originally published in German.

Veit Ludwig von Seckendorff (1626–1692). Teutscher Fürsten-Staat (1656)

Teutscher Fürsten-Stat/ Oder: Gründliche und kurtze Beschreibung/ Welcher Gestalt Fürstenthümer/ Graff- und Herrschafften im H. Römischen Reich Teutscher Nation, welche Landes, Fürstliche und Hohe Obrigkeitliche Regalia haben/ von Rechts- und löblicher Gewonheit wegen beschaffen zu seyn/ Regieret/ mit Ordnungen und

Satzungen/ Geheimen und Justitz Cantzeleyen/ Consistoriis und andern hohen und niedern Gerichts-Instantien, Aemptern und Diensten/ verfasset und versehen/ auch wie deroselben Cammer- und Hoffsachen bestellt zu werden pflegen.[44]

1   Frankfurt, Götze, 1656.
2   Frankfurt, Götze, 1660.
3   Frankfurt, Götz, 1665 (at this point the publisher's name is not conjugated anymore).
4   Frankfurt, Götz, 1670.
5   Frankfurt, Götz, 1678.
6   Frankfurt & Leipzig, Meyer, 1687.
7   Frankfurt & Leipzig, Meyer, 1695.
8   Frankfurt, Meyer, 1700.
9   Frankfurt, Meyer, 1703.
10   Frankfurt & Leipzig, Meyer, 1711.
11   Jena, no publisher, 1720.
12   Jena, Meyer, 1737.
13   Jena, Güth, 1754.

Figure 2.2 Frontispiece and title page of the 1737 edition of Veit von Seckendorff's *Teutscher Fürstenstaat* ('The German Principality').

With kind permission from Erik Reinert.

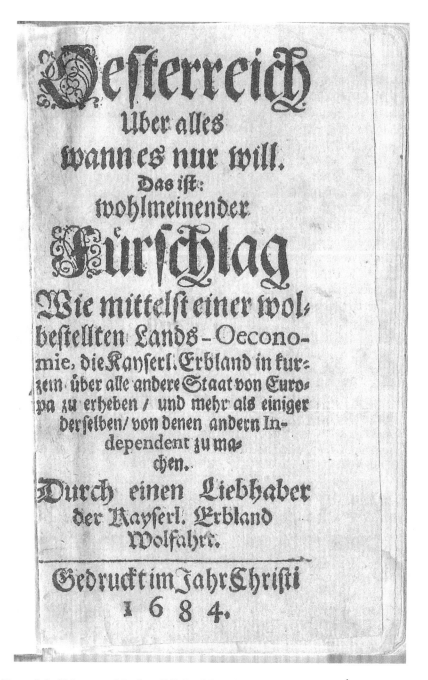

Figure 2.3 Title page of the first (1684) edition of Philip von Hörnigk's *Ôesterreich über
alles wann es nur will* ('Austria Supreme, if she so wishes').

Philip Wilhelm von Hörnigk (1638–1712). Österreich über alles wann es nur will *(1684)*

Oesterreich über alles wann es nur will. Das ist: wohlmeinender Fürschlag wie mittelst einer wolbestellten Lands-Oeconomie, die Kayserl. Erbland in kurzem über alle andere Staat von Europa zu erheben / und mehr als einiger derselben / von denen andern Independent zu machen. Durch einen Liebhaber der Kayserl. Erbland Wolfahrt.

[No place, but Nürnberg] Gedruckt im Jahr Christi 1684.

1   [Nürnberg] 1684. According to the preface to the 1708 edition, the printer was Johann Hoffmann, who brought it out in 1684.
2   [n.d., 1684?] Otruba notes an edition without place of publication [1684?] with the title page statement: 'zum anderen Mal auffgelegt'.
3   [Nürnberg, no publisher] 1685.
4   [Passau, no publisher] 1685.
5   [No place, no publisher] 1705.
6   Leipzig, Fritschen, 1707.
7   Regensburg, Seidel, 1708.
8   Regensburg, Seidel, 1712.
9   Regensburg, no publisher, 1717.
10   [No place, no publisher] 1719.
11   Regensburg, Peetz, 1723.
12   Regensburg, Peetz, 1727.
13   Frankfurt, no publisher, 1729.
14   Frankfurt & Leipzig, no publisher, 1750.
15   Frankfurt & Leipzig, no publisher, 1753.
16   Frankfurt & Leipzig, no publisher, 1764.
17   Berlin & Stettin, Friedrich Nikolai, 1784.
18   [Vienna, Wucherer] 1784. Pirated edition.
19   [No place, but probably Vienna, no publisher] 1784. Pirated edition.

Wilhelm von Schröder (1640–1688). Fürstliche Schatz- und Rent-Kammer *(1686)*

This book seems unfortunately not to make ten editions, and will therefore not be part of the Carpenter/Reinert updated version of the *Economic Bestsellers* before 1850. However, the book is so interesting that it is included here, and since it will not be included in the new bestseller list we give some more information regarding the book. [45]

German-Austrian scholar Heinrich Ritter von Srbik lists the following editions: 1686 (Leipzig), 1704 (Leipzig), 1708 (mentioned in *Zincke, Cameralisten-Bibliothek*, Leipzig 1751/52), 1713 (Leipzig: Thomas Fritsch), 1718 (Leipzig, including Zugabe by Karl Ferdinand Pescherin), 1737, 1744 and 1752 (all three Leipzig und Königsberg).

Srbik has used many of these editions himself, and says: 'Nur die Existenz einer Auflage von 1718 ist mir nicht völlig sicher'. But this edition is in the Reinert collection 1718 (1718, Leipzig: Boetio), also 1686, 1713, and 1744. Worldcat has 1686, 1704, 1713, 1721, 1744, 1752 (January 2014). Hitotshubashi and Syracuse universities have the 1737 edition (see Carpenter 1975).

The frontispiece of the 1718 edition (illustrated below) seems to have created a political scandal by confronting the 'good ruler' who shears the wool of his sheep with the 'bad ruler' who fleeces them.

1   Leipzig, Gerdesius, 1686.
2   Leipzig, no publisher, 1704.
3   Leipzig, Fritschen, 1713.
4   Leipzig, Boetio, 1718.
5   Leipzig, no publisher, 1721.
6   Leipzig & Königsberg, 1737.
7   Königsberg, no publisher, 1752.
8   Leipzig & Königsberg, no publisher, 1774.

Figure 2.4   Title page and frontispiece of the first (1686) edition of Wilhelm Schröder's *Fürstliche Schatz- und Rentenkammer* ('The Treasury of the Principality').

With kind permission from Erik Reinert.

Figure 2.5   Title page and frontispiece of the 1718 edition, published 30 years after Schröder's death. The frontispiece is added by Karl Ferdinand Pescherin who wrote a new introduction. Contrasting the 'good ruler', who is happy with the wool of his serfs, with the 'bad ruler', who fleeces them, recalls an old German saying. According to Schröder's biographer Srbik (1910) this frontispiece discredited Schröder's economic ideas (Srbik, p. 89).

With kind permission from Erik Reinert.

Johann Heinrich Gottlob von Justi (1717–1771). Cameralist writings.

Of all the Enlightenment 'Vielschreiber' (polygraphs) in economics, Johann Heinrich Gottlob von Justi[46] appears to have been the most prolific anywhere. A recent bibliography[47] lists 67 books and 7 periodicals written and edited by Justi. In addition, there are 13 translations into five languages: French, Spanish, Dutch, Russian and English. This paper shows that while key German mercantilists before Justi – Seckendorff, Hörnigk and Schröder – were not translated at all, there are 13 translations made from eight different books by Justi. So Justi in a sense breaks the 'autarkic' mold in which German economics had worked until then: with him German (including Austrian) economic ideas for the first time become export items.

Justi's career was marked by frequent moves and also by the Seven Years War, so he would tend to issue new and slightly changed editions of his main textbooks when he took up teaching positions at new universities. Chronologically and professionally Justi – with his contemporary Johann Friedrich von Pfeiffer (1718–1787) – represents the intermediary step between Hörnigk and Sonnenfels – and is also therefore included here. Clearly, if fewer different book titles had been given to present his work, Justi would have made it into the bestseller list.

Below we have listed those of Justi's publications which are closest connected to the core subject of cameral sciences. His other works are excluded. The numbers refer to the numbers in the H. & E. Reinert bibliography.

1 Deutsche Memoires, oder Sammlung verschiedener Anmerkungen, Die Staatsklugheit, das Kriegswesen, die Justiz, Morale, Oeconomie, Commercium, Cammer- und Polizey- auch andere merkwürdige Sachen betreffend, welche im menschlichen Leben vorkommen, Von einigen Civil- und Militairbedienten, auch von andern gelehrten und erfahrnen Personen aufgezeichnet und hinterlassen worden. Leipzig 1741. [2nd edition with additional volume Vienna (1750?)], 3rd edition: Deutsche Memoires; oder Sammlung vermischter Anmerkungen, die Staatsklugheit, Oekonomie, Polizey- und Finanzwesen betreffend, 3 volumes, Vienna 1760.

13 Auf höchsten Befehl an Sr. Röm. Kaiserl. und zu Ungarn und Böhmen Königl. Majestät erstattetes allerunterthänigstes Gutachten von dem vernünftigen Zusammenhange und practischen Vortrag aller öconomischen und Cameralwissenschaften; wobey zugleich zur Probe die Grundsätze der Policeywissenschaft mit denen dazu gehörigen practischen Arbeiten vorgetragen werden; benebst einer Antrittsrede von dem Zusammenhange eines blühenden Zustandes der Wissenschaften mit denjenigen Mitteln, welche einen Staat mächtig und glücklich machen. Leipzig 1754.

14 Progr. Abhandlung von den Mitteln, die Erkenntnis in den öconomischen und Cameral-Wissenschaften dem gemeinen Wesen recht nützlich zu machen. Göttingen 1755, 2nd edition (?), Göttingen 1775.

15 Staats- Wirtschaft, oder Systematische Abhandlung aller Oeconomischen und Cameralwissenschaften, die zur Regierung eines Landes erfordert werden. 2 volumes. Leipzig 1755, 2nd edition Leipzig, Breitkopf (1758?), reprint: Aalen, Scientia, 1963.

16 Entdeckte Ursachen des verderbten Münzwesens in Teutschland, nach ihren ersten und wahren Quellen; wobey zugleich neue und wirksame Mittel dagegen vorgeschlagen werden, die ein jeder Reichsstand vor sich, ohne Mitwirkung des Reichs und ohne Recesse mit seinen Mitständen, in Ausübung bringen kann. Leipzig, Breitkopf, 1755. [Authorship not entirely certain].

19 Der Handelnde Adel dem der Kriegerische Adel entgegen gesetzet wird. Zwey Abhandlungen über die Frage: Ob es der Wohlfarth des Staats gemäss sey, dass der Adel Kaufmannschaft treibe? Aus dem Französischen übersetzt und mit einer Abhandlung über eben diesen Gegenstand versehen. Göttingen, Wittwe Vandenhöck, 1756. [Abhandlung von dem Wesen des Adels und

dessen Verhältniss gegen die Commercien, pp. 241–288]. Original in French by Abbé Gabriel François Coyer (1707–1782). Coyer's work is one of the Economic Bestsellers before 1850.

19   Russian. Torguëiiushchee dvorëiianstvo, 1766. Library of Congress gives other authors as Justi and Fonvizin, Denis Ivanovich (1745–1792).

20   Grundsätze der Policey-Wissenschaft in einem vernünftigen, auf den Endzweck der Policey gegründeten Zusammenhange und zum Gebrauch Academischer Vorlesungen abgefasset. Göttingen 1756, 2nd edition, Wittve Vandenhöck, 1759, 3rd edition 1782. Reprints: Frankfurt, Sauer & Auvermann, 1969, and Düsseldorf, Wirtschaft und Finanzen, 1993.

20   French. Élémens géneraux de police, démontrés par des raissonnemens fondés sur l'objet & la fin qu'elle se propose. Par M. Jean-Henri Gottlobs de Justi, conseiller du Roi d'Angleterre, commissaire général de police des duchés de Brunswick & de Lunebourg, Paris, Rozet, 1769, [reprinted 1969?]. Translated by Marc Antoine Eidous.

20   Spanish. Elementos de policía general de un estado, in: 'Memorias instructivas y curiosas sobre agricultura, industria, economía, chymica, botánica, historia natural....', Vol. XII, Madrid 1791, pp. 377–496. Translated via the French edition.

24   Die Chimäre des Gleichgewichts von Europa; eine Abhandlung, worinnen die Nichtigkeit u. Ungerechtigkeit dieses zeitherigen Lehrgebäudes der Staatskunst vor Augen gelegt, und dabey allenthalben neue und rührende Betrachtungen über die Ursachen der Kriege und den wesentlichen Grunde, worauf die Macht eines Staats Ankommt, beygebracht werden. Altona 1758. Alternative entry: Die Chimäre des Gleichgewichts von Europa, aus den wichtigsten Gründen der Staatskunst erwiesen und aus den neuesten Weltbegebenheiten erläutert. 2 parts (2 Teile). Altona 1758.

24   Dutch. De chimere of hersenschim van het evenwigt in Europa. Of Verhandeling, waarin de nietigheid [...] dit systéma der staat-kunde duidelyk ontvouwd wordt. The Hague, P. van Cleef, 1767.

25   Vollständige Abhandlung von denen Manufacturen und Fabriken, 2 volumes, Copenhagen, Rothenschen Buchhandlung, 1758–61. [2nd edition of 2nd vol. 1780], 2nd edition of both volumes 1789.

25   Dutch. Volledige verhandeling der manufaktuuren en fabrieken. Utrecht, wed. J. v.Schoonhoven, 1782.

28   Die Chimäre des Gleichgewichts der Handlung und Schiffahrt, oder: Ungrund und Richtigkeit einiger neuerlich geäusserter Meinungen von denen Maassregeln der freyen Mächte gegen die zu befürchtende Herrschaft und Obermacht zur See, wobey zugleich Neue und wichtige Betrachtungen über die Handlung und Schiffahrt der Völker, und über den höchsten Punkt der daraus entstehenden Macht und Glückseligkeit beygebracht werden. Altona, David Iversen, 1759.

28   French: La Chimère de l'equilibre du commerce et de la navigation. Copenhagen & Leipzig, Veuve de Rothe, 1763.

29 Der Grundriss einer Guten Regierung in fünf Büchern verfasset. Frankfurt & Leipzig, J.G. Garbe, 1759.

31 Systematischer Grundriss allen Oeconomischen und Cameral-Wissenschaften. Frankfurt & Leipzig 1759.

32 Die Wirkungen und Folgen, sowohl der wahren, als der falschen Staatskunst in der Geschichte des Psammitichus, Königes von Egypten und der damaligen Zeiten. 2 vols. Frankfurt & Leipzig, Johann Gottlieb Garbe(n), 1759–1760.

35 Politischen und Finanzschriften über wichtige Materien der Regierungsangelegenheiten, des Kriegeswesen und der Cameralgeschäfte. 2 volumes. Copenhagen 1760.

37 Die Natur und das Wesen der Staaten, als die Grundwissenschaft der Staatskunst, der Policey, und aller Regierungswissenschaften, desgleichen als die Quelle aller Gesetze, abgehandelt. Berlin, Stettin, Leipzig, Johann Heinrich Rüdigers, 1760. [New annotated edition, Mietau, Steidel, 1771, reprint: Aalen, Scientia, 1969].

37 Dutch: De aart der wetten afgeleid uit de natuur en het weezen der staaten, 1773.

37 Russian translation 1: Suscestvennoe izibrazenie estestva narodnych obscestv i vsjakago roda zakonov / Soc. gospod. Justi. S nemeck. na ross. jazyk perev. [A]vr[aa]m V[o]lk[o]v. [Moskva, Univ, 1770].

37 Russian translation 2: Suscestvennoe izobrazenie estestva narodnych obscestv i razlicnych zakonov / Socinenie Justi. [St. Petersburg 1802].

39 Abhandlung von der Macht und Glückseeligkeit und Credit eines Staats. Ulm, Frankfurt, Leipzig, Gaum, 1760.

43 Oeconomische Schriften über die wichtigsten Gegenstände der Stadt- und Landwirthschaft. 2 volumes. Berlin & Leipzig, Buchladens der Real-Schule, 1760 (1761?), [new edition 1766–67].

45 Die Grundfeste zu der Macht und Glückseligkeit der Staaten; oder ausführliche Vorstellung der gesamten Policey-Wissenschaft. 2 volumes. Königsberg & Leipzig, Gerhard Luddewig Woltersdorfs Wittwe, 1760–61, second edition 1774, reprint Aalen, Scientia, 1965.

47 Onomatologia oeconomico-practica, oder ökonomisches Wörterbuch... 3 volumes. Ulm 1760–63.

49 Abhandlung von der Vollkommenheit der Landwirtschaft und der höchsten Kultur der Länder. Ulm 1761.

50 Gesammelte Politische und Finanzschriften über wichtige Gegenstände der Staatskunst, der Kriegswissenschaften und des Cameral- und Finanzwesens. 3 volumes. Copenhagen & Leipzig, Rothenschen Buchhandlung, 1761–64, [reprinted Aalen 1970].

51 Abhandlung von denen Manufactur- und Fabriken-Reglements zur Ergänzung seines Werkes von denen Manufakturen und Fabriken, Berlin & Leipzig, Verlag des Buchladens der Real-Schule, 1762.

53 Ausführliche Abhandlung von denen Steuern und Abgaben nach ächten, aus dem Endzweck der bürgerlichen Gesellschaften abfliessenden Grundsätzen, und zur Wohlfahrt der Völker dienlichen Maassregeln abgefasset. Königsberg

Vollständige
Abhandlung
von denen
Manufacturen
und
Fabriken.

Erster Theil
welcher die allgemeinen Grundsätze und
Betrachtungen in sich enthält.

Von
Johann Heinrich Gottlob von Justi,

Königl. Großbrittanischen Bergrathe und Ober=Policey=Commissario, wie auch Mitglied
der Königl. Großbrittanischen Gesellschaft der Wissenschaften
daselbst.

Koppenhagen,
Auf Kosten der Rothenschen Buchhandlung. 1758.

Figure 2.6 Title page of volume one of Johann Heinrich Gottlob von Justi's *Vollständige
    Abhandlungen von denen Manufakturen und Fabriken* ('A Complete Treatise
    of Manufactories and Factories'). In Justi's terminology, all textile industry
    falls under the heading of '*Manufacturen*'. All other industries are '*Fabriken*'.

& Leipzig, G. Ludwig Wolterdorffs Wittwe, 1762, reprint Wiesbaden, Gabler, 1977.

54 Vergleichungen der Europäischen mit den Asiatischen und andern vermeintlich Barbarischen Regierungen, in drey Büchern verfasset. Berlin, Johann Heinrich Rüdigers, 1762, reprint: Königstein, Auvermann, 1978.

60 System des Finanzwesens, nach vernünftigen aus dem Endzweck der Bürgerlichen Gesellschaften und aus der Natur aller Quellen der Einkünfte des Staats hergeleiteten Grundsätzen und Regeln ausführlich abgehandelt. Halle, Renger, 1766, reprints: Aalen, Scientia, 1969 and Dillenburg, Gruber, 1998.

62 Betrachtungen über den Ackerbau, in Abhandlungen der churfürstlichen baierischen Akademie der Wissenschaften, 1767.

Journals

J 3 'Physikalisch-oeconomische Real-Zeitung, aus denen von der Natur- und Haushaltungs-Wissenschaft, Feld-Bau, Heilungs-Kunst, Cameralwesen, Policey, Künsten, Manufacturen und Handlung handelnden Schriften zusammen gelesen und mit neuen Stücken, Versuchen und Anmerckungen versehen nebst einer allgemeinen Anzeige alles dessen, was bisher in diesen Sachen geschrieben worden', Stuttgart 1754. – Continued under the title 'Physikalisch-ökonomische Wochenschrift', 2 vols, Stuttgart: 1755–1758. – Continued under the title: 'Etwas für alle, oder neue Stuttgardter Realzeitung' in the years 1765–1766 – then under the title: 'Allgemeines Stuttgardter Magazin ökonomischen und physikalischen inhalts, aus den grössten und kostbarsten Werken gesammelt auf das Jahr 1767, 1768 etc'.

J 4 'Schlesische Oekonomische Sammlungen', Band 1–3 (= Stück 1–24), Breslau 1754–1762 (Korn).

J 6 'Göttingische Policeyamts-Nachrichten, oder vermischte Abhandlungen zum Vortheil des Nahrungsstandes aus allen Theilen der oeconomischen Wissenschaften, benebst verschiedenen in das Göttingische Policeywesen einschlagenden Verordnungen und Nachrichten', 1755, 1756 & 1757 (until July). Continued 1768 under the title 'Wochentliche Anzeigen von gemeinnützigen Sachen'.

J 7 'Politische und Finanzschriften über wichtige Materien der Regierungsangelegenheiten, des Kriegeswesen und der Cameralgeschäfte', Copenhagen 1760.

Hans Caspar Hirzel (1725–1803). **Die Wirthschaft eines philosophischen Bauers *(Zürich, 1761)***

This work was known primarily through its French translation, which first appeared in 1762, under the title of Le Socrate rustique.

1   In vol. 1 (1761): pp. 371–496, of Abhandlungen der naturforschenden Gesellschaft in Zürich, German.

2   Zürich, Heidegguer & Co., 1761, German. Either an offprint or a reprint of the text, as it appeared in the periodical.

3   Zürich, chez Heidegguer & Compagnie, 1762, French.

4   Zürich & Limoges, Martial Barbou, 1763, French.

5   Zürich, Heidegguer, 1764, French.

6   Zürich, Fuesslin, 1768, French.

7   Wien, Joseph Kurtzböck, 1768, German.

8   London, Becket, 1770, English, as 'The Rural Socrates' in Arthur Young's Rural oeconomy.

9   Dublin, Exshaw *et al.*, 1770, English, as 'The Rural Socrates' in Arthur Young's Rural oeconomy.

10   London, Becket, 1773, English, as 'The Rural Socrates' in Arthur Young's Rural oeconomy. Reissued in 1779, with a new title page and with the sheets of the 1773 printing rearranged so as to place Hirzel first and Young's Rural oeconomy second.

11   Zürich, Orell. Gessner, Füeslin u. Comp., 1774, German.

12   Philadelphia, Pa., James Humphreys, 1776, English, as 'Le Socrate rustique: or, the Rural Socrates', in Arthur Young's Rural oeconomy.

13   Lausanne, Grasset, 1777, French.

14   Florence, Vanni [1782?] Italian, as 'L'economia d'un contadino filosofo descritta dal sig. dottore Hirzel'.

15   Burlington, N.J., Isaac Neale, 1792, English, as 'The Rural Socrates' in Arthur Young's Rural economy.

16   Vicenza, Rossi, 1793, Italian, 'Il Socrate rustico, o descrizione della condotta economica, e morale d'un contadino filosofo'.

17   Hallowell, Maine, Edes, English.

18   Paris, Dusacq, 1847, French.

Josef von Sonnenfels (1732–1817). Grundsätze der Polizey, Handlung und Finanz (1765–76, 3 vols.)

Sonnenfels' three-volume work well represented the liberal humanitarianism of Maria Theresia and Joseph II. It was the most important textbook in the Catholic German-speaking areas. In addition to at least eight editions of all three volumes, there was even a one-volume, truncated edition for students, of which there were three editions. L. B. M. Schmid's *Ausführliche Tabellen über die Policey-Handlungs- und Finanzwissenschaft* (1785) is an outline of Sonnenfels' *Grundsätze* for students. There were also three Italian translations, the latest in 1832, and a Latin edition. Sonnenfels' text continued to be used into the 1840s. Professors were required to do so by law. However, Joseph Kudler, whose *Grundlehren der Volkswirthschaft* (1846), replaced Sonnenfels, explains that the law was violated in spirit through using Sonnenfels' text as the basis for attack on cameralistic economics. As with all multivolume works, library catalogues do not provide details about each volume, and instead give inclusive dates, despite sets being made up of volumes from different printings. In its bibliographical detail, the list below is far from definitive, but it does show the widespread influence exerted by Sonnenfels.

1 Vienna, no publisher, 1769–76, German.
2 Vienna, Trattner, 1770, German.
3 Vienna, no publisher, 1776, German.
4 Vienna, Edlen von Trattnern, 1777, German.
5 Gesammelte Schriften, 1783–87, German.
6 Milano, Galeazzi, 1784, Italian, 'Scienza del buon governo'.
7 Venice, Vitto, 1785, Italian, partial translation, 'La scienza del buon goerno del signor di Sonnenfels…'.
8 Vienna, no publisher, 1786–87, German.
9 Munich, no publisher, 1787, German.
10 Moscow, Novikov, 1787, Russian, partial translation, Иосифа Зонненфелса Начальныя основания полиции или благочиния.
11 Vienna, no publisher, 1798, German.
12 Munich, no publisher, 1801, German.
13 Vienna, Camesina, 1804–05, German.
14 Vienna, no publisher [1819?], German.
15 Venice, Santini, 1806, Italian, partial translation.
16 Posonii [Bratislava/Pressburg], no publisher, 1807, Latin, 'Principia politiae, comercii, et rei aerariae. E germanicus lucubrationibus… latine reddita a Wolfgango Beke'.
17 Budapest, Typis regiae universitatis hungaricae, 1808. Latin, partial translation 'Summaria institutionum politicarum adumbration. Excerpta principiis politiae, commerciorum et rei aeriae. Pars prima'.
18 Vienna, no publisher, 1818–22, German.
19 Tübingen, no publisher, 1820, German.
20 Posonii [Bratislava/Pressburg], Typis haeredum Belnayanorum, 1823, Latin.
21 Milano, Silvestri, 1832, Italian, partial translation.

Notes

1 All images depicted in the text are taken from the private *Reinert Collection*, built up by the author, and are free of copyright.
2 Carpenter later worked in other positions in the Harvard Library system, and retired in 2001. But since 1968 his passion has been to record translations of economics books. On Carpenter at Harvard, see http://hul.harvard.edu/publications/hul_notes_1299/carpenter.html.
3 Kenneth E. Carpenter, *The Economic Bestsellers before 1850* (Boston: Baker Library, Graduate School of Business Administration, Harvard University, 1975). Downloadable at http://www.othercanon.org.
4 "Herbert Somerton Foxwell," originally published in *Economic Journal*, December 1916, and as chapter 17 in *The Collected Writings of John Maynard Keynes. Vol. X. Essays in Biography* (Cambridge: Cambridge University Press, 1972), 266–296.

5 London: Macmillan, 1899. Downloadable on http://www.othercanon.org/papers/.

6 Joseph Stiglitz, *Whither Socialism* (Cambridge, MA: MIT Press, 1994).

7 Geoffrey M. Hodgson, *Economics and Utopia* (London: Routledge, 1999).

8 Keynes 1972, op.cit, 270.

9 Foxwell 1899, xli.

10 Keynes 1972, op.cit, 281.

11 Kenneth E. Carpenter, *Dialogue in Political Economy: Translations from and into German in the 18th Century; Issued on the Occasion of an Exhibition in the Kress Library* (Boston, MA: Baker Library, Graduate School of Business Administration, Harvard University, 1977).

12 Of course Botero made mistakes, as when his sources were not correct. The remarkable thing, however, is the acuteness of his policy prescriptions that came to typify the centuries of economics that go under the name of Cameralism and mercantilism.

13 'Indeed the very purpose of the group Loyola gathered during his studies in Paris was the apostolate with the Muslims in the Holy Land.' Robert Alexander Maryks, *Saint Cicero and the Jesuits, The Influence of the Liberal Arts on the Adoption of Moral Probabilism* (Aldershot: Ashgate, 2008).

14 See Jonathan D. Spence, *The Memory Palace of Matteo Ricci* (London: Penguin, 1983).

15 Joan-Pau Rubies, *Travel and Ethnology in the Renaissance* (Cambridge: Cambridge University Press, 2000), 294.

16 For an overview, see Reinert, Erik S., "A Brief Introduction to Veit Ludwig von Seckendorff (1626–1692)," *European Journal of Law and Economics* 19 (2005), 221–230.

17 See Reinert, Sophus A., "Cameralism and Commercial Rivalry: Nationbuilding through Economic Autarky in Seckendorff's 1665 Additiones," *European Journal of Law and Economics* 19 (2005), 271–286.

18 'Wahre Katakomben von vergessener Literatur.' Friedrich Meinecke, *Die Idee der Staatsräson in der neueren Geschichte,* second edition (Munich: Oldenbourg, 1925), 83n.

19 Toronto: University of Toronto Press, 2012.

20 On translations, see Sophus A. Reinert, *Translating Empire* (Cambridge, MA: Harvard University Press, 2011).

21 Gerard Malynes, *The Maintenance of Free Trade, According to the three essentiall (sic) Parts...Commodities, Moneys and Exchange of Moneys* (London: William Sheffard, 1622), and *The Center of the Circle of Commerce, or, A Refutation of a Treatise,.....,lately published by E.M.* (London: Nicholas Bourne, 1623).

22 Edward Misselden, *Free Trade and the Meanes (sic) to Make Trade Flourish* (London: Simon Waterson, 1622), and *The Circle of Commerce or the Ballance (sic) of Trade* (London: Nicholas Bourne, 1623).

23 Schumpeter discusses the controversy between the two men in his *History of Economic Analysis* (New York, NY: Oxford University Press, 1954), 344–345. See also their respective entries in 'The New Palgrave'. In all cases these references are purely to the mechanics of money and exchange.

24 Buck, Philip, *The Politics of Mercantilism* (New York, NY: Henry Holt, 1942), 23.

25 Misselden, *op. cit.*, (1623), 8.

26 I.e. greater diversity of products.

27 This could be interpreted as meaning more imperfect competition due to higher barriers to entry.

28 The second English translation is clearer on this and is used here: *The Cause of the Greatnesse of Cities. Three Bookes, With Certaine Observations concerning the Sea. Written in Italian by John Botero...* (London: Printed by E.P. for Henry Seile, 1635), 85–86.

29 Ibid, 88–89.

30 Jeremy Bentham, *An Introduction to the Principles of Morals and Legislation* (1780) (London: University Paperback), Ch. I, 11.

31 Sir Walter Raleigh (ed. Thomas Birch), *The Works of Sir Walter Raleigh, Kt. Political, Commercial, and Philosophical; Together With His Letters and Poems...* (London: Printed for R. Dosley, 1751), vol. 2, 321–329.

32 The discussion of Botero an Raleigh is based on Geoffrey Symcox, "Introduction" to Giovanni Botero *On the Causes of the Greatness and Magnificence of Cities* (Toronto: University of Toronto Press, 2012), xiv.

33 Potosí, at about 4,000 metres above sea-level in present-day Bolivia, was the richest of all mines in the world. At the time, it was the probably the largest city in the Americas (with a population of around 150,000 in the mid-1600s, it was about double the size of Lima).

34 Gustaf Westbeck, *Tankeförsök om Särskilda Näringars Idkande*, Thesis (Uppsala, 1747), 4–5.

35 Guiseppe Assandra (1926 & 1928), "Giovanni Botero. Note biografiche e bibliografiche di Giuseppe Assandra suo concittadino" (ed. Gino Borghezio), in *Bollettino storico-bibliografico subalpino*, XXVIII, (Turin: Bene Vagienna, 1926), 407–442, and ibid. (1928), 29–63, 307–351.

36 See also the chapter by Carl Wennerlind in the present volume.

37 Tommaso Campanella and Edmund Chilmead, *A Discourse Touching the Spanish Monarchy: Wherein Vve Have a Political Classe, Representing Each Particular Country, Province, Kingdome, and Empire of the World, with Wayes of Government by Which They May Be Kept in Obedience. As Also, the Causes of the Rise and Fall of Each Kingdom and Empire. Written by Tho. Campanella. Newly Translated into English, According to the Third Edition of this Book in Latine* (London: printed for Philemon Stephens and are to be sold at his shop at the Gilded Lion in Paul's Church-Yard, 1653); discussed in Tommaso Fornari, *Delle Teorie Economiche nelle Provincie Napolitane dal Secolo XIII al MDCCXXXIV* (Milan: Hoepli, 1882), 165–191.

38 Anders Berch, *Inledning til Almänna Hushålningen, innefattande Grunden til Politie, Oeconomie och Cameralwetenskaperna* (Stockholm: Lars Salvius, 1747). The term used is 'outlöselige Guldgrufwor' (216). For an account of Berch and the teaching of economics in eighteenth-century Sweden, see Sven-Eric Liedman, *Den Synliga Handen* (the visible hand) (Stockholm: Arbetarkultur, 1986).

39 Antonio Serra, *A 'Short Treatise' on the Wealth and Poverty of Nations (1613)*, ed. with an introduction by Sophus A. Reinert (London: Anthem, 2011).

40 *Svea Rikes Drotset Grefve Per Brahes Tänkebok* (Stockholm: Delén, 1806).

41 Carl Magnus Schymanson, *Per Brahe och Åbo Akademi* (Helsinki: Helsingfors Tidnings- & Tr.-Aktiebolagets Tryckeri, 1915). Series publisher: Svenska litteratur-sällskapet i Finland.

42 Mail from the librarian at Skokloster Library, 21 May 2014.

43 Otto Walde, *Storhetstidens Litterära Krigsbyten. En Kulturhistorisk Bibliografisk Studie*, 2 Vols. (Uppsala: Almquist & Wicksell, 1916/1920).

44 See also E. Reinert, "A Brief Introduction to Veit Ludwig von Seckendorff."

45 On Schröder, see Heinrich Ritter von Srbik, *Wilhelm von Schröder. Ein Betrag zur Geschichte der Staatswissenschaften* (Vienna: Kommission bei Hölder, 1910).

46 See Erik S. Reinert, "Johann Heinrich Gottlob von Justi (1717–1771): The Life and Times of an Economist Adventurer," in *The Beginnings of Political Economy: Johann Heinrich Gottlob von Justi*, ed. Jürgen Backhaus (New York, NY: Springer, 2009), 33–74. A version of this chapter can be downloaded from http://www.othercanon.org/papers/.

47 Hugo Reinert and Erik S. Reinert, "A Bibliography of J.H.G. von Justi," in *The Beginnings of Political Economy*, 19–31.

Part II

Economic ideas and idiosyncrasy

The example of Cameralism

3   Was Cameralism really the German version of mercantilism?

Lars Magnusson

Introduction

In standard textbooks concerning the history of economic thought it is often taken for granted that Cameralism was a kind of German *Sonderweg* or native version of mercantilism – or the mercantile system – rooted in its peculiar history, as well as territorial position in Europe. For example in the *Palgrave Dictionary of Economics* it is stated right on that Cameralism was 'a version of mercantilism, taught and practised in the German principalities (*Kleinstaaten)* in the 17th and 18th centuries'.[1] Moreover it is often taken for granted that German *Nationalökonomie* which emerged in the beginning of the nineteenth century was a direct offshoot of earlier versions of Cameralism, in the same vein that British Classical political economy stemmed from the 'boom of the 1690's' with the development of a 'science of trade' especially with the so called 'Tory free-traders' including Child, Law, Davenant, Barbon and others.[2] Hence it was possible to speak of two different traditions of economic thinking and practice in Europe. Joseph Schumpeter talked in this context of '[n]eglecting smaller countries we find the main difference was between England and the Continent' (here, besides Germany, Schumpeter also included France and Italy).[3]

The idea of a German *Sonderweg* goes back at least to Wilhelm Roscher's grand opus dating from 1874, *Geschichte der National-Oekonomik in Deutschland.* Moreover, Roscher was most probably the first to characterize German economic thinking and practice before the nineteenth century as 'Cameralism'. *Cameral-wissenschaft* both in single and plural form was of course used from the beginning of the eighteenth century onwards, but he was the first to allude to it in order to characterize a whole period after 1648, up to the middle of the eighteenth century as the 'polizeilich-cameralistische Zeitalter der deutschen Nationalökonomik' (the latter concept was of course not used at that time).[4]

In his series of chapters starting with 1648 Roscher begins with lamenting the situation in the German territories after the Thirty Years War: its cities and countryside diminished in population with people roaming around trying to carve out a meagre existence.[5] Hence out of this turmoil the first task was to establish territorial states built on law, order and stable taxation. Out of this grew some different 'schools' of economic thought and (particularly) policy and practice.

With a start in the seventeenth century Roscher mentioned particularly three of them: a *conservative* '*Nationalökonomik*' (especially represented by Veit Ludwig von Seckendorff with his *Teutsche Fürstenstaat*, 1655), a '*rein wissenschaftliche*' (purely scientific-theoretical) school in North Germany including polymaths such as Samuel von Pufendorff and Hermann Conring, and lastly '*a praktisch-progressive*' (practical-progressive) school especially emerging in Austria (with Johann Joachim Becher, Wilhelm von Schröder, or Philipp Wilhelm von Hörnigk etc.).[6] Especially the Austrians were influenced by what Roscher calls the *Mercantil-system*. Broadly he defined it as a system of thinking and practice which emphasised the importance for a state of having a great population, much money in the country and a foreign trade to receive it if the state had no mines of its own. To this he added the importance of working up production at home, avoiding importation of value added manufacture goods from abroad. Lastly what held the *Mercantil* system together was *Staatshätigkeit*, a sense of belonging to a certain state, which built on the notion that 'Jedes Staatsgebiet wurde im schroffsten Gegensatze zur ganzen übrigen Welt gefasst' (every state territory was defined in sharp contrast and opposition to the rest of the world).[7]

Such an interpretation was even more clearly emphasized by another historical economist (of the 'younger historical school'), Gustav (von) Schmoller. In his *Studien über die wirtschaftliche Politik Friedrich des Grossen*, published from 1884 to 1887, he proposed that the German *Sonderweg* of mercantilism was caused by the underdevelopment of Germany, its lateness to inaugurate territorial states and its commercial dependence upon England (and France). Hence its distinctive variety of mercantilism – also here regarded as a system of selfish economic policies in a word of combating national powers – originated not from 'whether a mercantilist policy was necessary and desirable; about that there was agreement and properly so'. What differed instead was Germany's landlocked position, its political anarchy and still underdeveloped economy. In a German context the theories of mercantilism, Schmoller propounded 'meant, practically, nothing but the energetic struggle for the creation of a sound state and a sound national economy, and for the overthrow of local and provincial economic institutions'.[8] Hence '[t]he victories of the Prussian army served the same end as the financial and commercial policy of the state; between them they raised Prussia to a place among the Great Powers of Europe'.[9]

In turn, both Roscher and Schmoller had of course learnt their lesson from Friedrich List. Hence to their interpretation of Germany as a late-comer to the industrialisation spurt (using the vocabulary of Alexander Gerschenkron)[10] can be connected List's emphasis on Britain being the great hypocrite – a perfidious Albion – which first developed a draconic system of protection during the seventeenth century with its famous Navigation Acts as only the tip of a much bigger iceberg and then, in the early nineteenth century, complaining when other countries used basically the same methods in order to develop their economies. We can cite Schmoller again: 'does it not sound to us to-day like the irony of fate that the same England, which in 1750–1800 reached the summit of its commercial supremacy by means of its tariffs and naval wars, frequently with extraordinary violence and always with the most tenacious national selfishness, that this England at the very same time announced to the world that only the egoism of the individual would be justified – but never the egoism of the states and nations; the doctrine which dreamt of stateless competition of all the individuals of every land, and of the harmony of the economic interests of all nations?'[11]

Hence the idea of a German *Sonderweg* originating from the disaster of the Thirty Years War creating a tradition of economic thinking and practice that was very different from what occurred in the British Isles played an important role in the formation of both the older and younger Historical school in Germany in the late nineteenth century. Pointing out the overall defensive character of nascent state formation in the German *Länder* since the seventeenth century the historicists provided a historical construction, a kind of backward narrative of 'invention of tradition', which we are so familiar with in the history of economic thinking.[12] The closure of this tradition is also part of this narrative. Hence 1945 has often been used to signal the demise of the Cameralist influence in German economic discourse. Germany lost the war and the old tradition of *Nationalökonomie* was replaced by Anglo-Saxon economics.

Cameralism and mercantilism: two different 'schools of thought'?

In this chapter, I will discuss to what extent this standard interpretation of Cameralism as a German *Sonderweg* makes sense or whether it is more fruitful to take another point of departure in order to understand the development of different economic discourses in Europe before the nineteenth century. A number of questions may be put. First, to what extent is it really fruitful to speak in terms of specific 'schools' of mercantilism and Cameralism during the seventeenth and eighteenth centuries? Secondly, if we still choose to do so, can we more specifically discern the differences between the two '-isms'? Lastly, does it make any sense to speak about a specific German *Sonderweg*? Is perhaps the German case only a variant of a broader European discussion on economic growth and modernisation while perhaps England with its emphasis on international trade was the special case (something which Schumpeter hinted at, as we saw when he drew the contrast between England and the Continent)?[13]

First to the issue of mercantilism and Cameralism as specific 'schools'. As we know a heated debate has raged over a long time whether mercantilism ever was a 'school' or even a system-like phenomenon. The concept *systeme mercantile* first appeared in print in Marquis de Mirabeau's *Philosophie Rurale* in 1763. In France during this period the concept was utilized in order to describe an economic policy regime characterized by direct state intervention in order to protect domestic merchants and manufacturers in accordance with seventeenth-century Colbertism. However, the main creator of 'the mercantile system' was Adam Smith. According to Smith the core of the mercantile system – 'the commercial system' – consisted of the popular folly of confusing wealth with money. The practical orientation of the mercantilist writers were founded upon one general principle: that a country must export more than it imported leading to a net-inflow of bullion, the so-called 'positive balance of trade theory'.[14]

Adam Smith's viewpoint was contested by the German historical school a century later. Instead it identified mercantilism as a rational expression of nation building during the early modern period. According to Gustav Schmoller, *Merkantilismus* was the policy of unity and centralization pursued especially by the rulers of Brandenburg-Prussia during the seventeenth and eighteenth centuries. Hence also mercantilism expressed the economic interest of the state and viewed economic wealth as a rational means to achieve political power. The much debated balance of trade theory was perhaps misguided as a general analytical tool. However, David Hume's specie-flow theory relied upon the assumption that market forces were really at work and that the quantity theory of money was applicable to more distant times. Given the war-like situation of the early modern period in Europe this could not be taken for granted, Schmoller argued. In this particular situation of imperfect markets the adoption of protectionism, infant industry tariffs and even restrictions regarding the export of money could have been the perfect rational choice at the time.

A next step in the discussion came after Eli Heckscher had published his 'Mercantilism' in two volumes in the beginning of the 1930s.[15] First out was A. V. Judges in 1939 who rejected the notion of 'a mercantile state'. Was mercantilism even a coherent 'system', he asked? His objection was that mercantilism 'never had a creed; nor was there a priesthood dedicated to its service'. Moreover, it did not, he argued, offer a coherent doctrine or 'at least a handful of settled principles'. Thus, mercantilism was a straw man constructed 'in the eighteenth century by men who found security for their own faith in a system of natural law'.[16] This view was further reiterated two decades later by the British economic historian D. C. Coleman, stating that retaining mercantilism as a label for economic policy would be 'not simply misleading but actively confusing, a red-herring of historiography'. Moreover it served to 'give a false unity to disparate events, to conceal the close-up reality of particular times and particular circumstances, to blot out the vital intermixture of ideas and preconceptions, of interests and influences, political and economic, and of the personalities of men which is the historian's job to examine'.[17]

From this the discussion has gone on. Even though Judges and Coleman a long time ago denounced the usefulness of the concept mercantilism it is still with us today. Not only for nostalgic reasons or convenience though: it still seems to make sense to have a name for some general shared views – very much prevalent during the seventeenth and eighteenth centuries – on how wealth and power as a combined goal of early modern states in their vigorous political and economic competition with each other could be achieved through economic means. Most of them shared the opinion that such goals could be achieved by regulating and protecting foreign trade and installing native value-adding manufactures. This does not mean, of course, that mercantilism was a coherent economic theory (emerging from any mistaken identification between bullion and wealth), *nor* an always very systematic set of practical policies. Instead it was not unusual that the goals of such policies were in opposition to each other and often served different (special) interest groups.[18]

Shifting interpretations of Cameralism

As mercantilism, Cameralism is a very much contested concept. Also in this case it has been argued that it had very little in common and that it is impossible to talk of a 'school' in this context. By explicitly referring to different 'traditions' in German economic thinking from the early seventeenth century onwards Roscher was the first to admit this variety even though he chose the concept 'polizeilich-cameralistische Zeitalter' (see above) for the whole period from 1648 up to the end of the eighteenth century. In the *conservative Nationalökonomik* he finds traces back to the *Hausväter* literature, but explicitly refers to Seckendorff's *Teutscher Fürstenstaat* (1655) as something of a starting point. Then this 'conservative' tradition leads further via von Rohrs *Einleitung zur Staatsklugheit* (1718) to become part of the university subject of Economics, Polity and Cameralism after the 1720s.[19] As a *Hofjunker* to the Duke Ernst von Gotha and later on serving as chancellor (*Kanzler*) *und Consistorial-Präsident in Sachsen* Seckendorff was well versed in the administrative chores of small-state Germany.[20] Hence to Albion Small he was 'the Adam Smith of Cameralism'.[21] In the *Teutscher Fürstenstaat* he argued that a good prince must know his domains well through inspection and good maps. He must organise the well-being of its inhabitants both in a moral and material sense. The third and longest part of his book was devoted to 'Cameralism'. Here Seckendorff listed the revenues open to the ruler and how his income might be improved. But most of all, his book was an instruction for a good ruler. He especially emphasised the moral obligations of the prince who must respect hereditary dispositions and accept the customs of his people.[22] Without doubt from this there is a rather long leap to – as Roscher notes – to the great *polyhistors* and moral philosophers, from Pufendorff to Wolff and Thomasius, who were involved in the great tradition to develop a discourse of natural rights, which influenced discussions on economy and polity far beyond Germany in the eighteenth century.[23] In Habsburg Austria yet another discourse appeared (which we will return to).

Moreover, also in a new contribution to the discussion the German legal historian Thomas Simon emphasises the difference between different varieties of political economy in Germany during the seventeenth and eighteenth century. For him the Austrians are very close to being mercantilists with their emphasis on commerce and foreign trade while the 'real' Cameralists are more *produtionsorientiert* (literally 'production-orientated') and take their point of departure from the Aristotelian concept of *oeconomy* as house-holding (*oikonomia*). Cameralism in its eighteenth century as a university subject – in its threesome Policy, Economy, and Cameralism – was thus at the base a version of Neo-Aristotelianism.[24]

Against this backdrop it is not peculiar that there exists strong disagreement about what kind of creature Cameralism was at its core. Schumpeter never spoke about Cameralism as such but rather chose to speak about 'consultant administrators' and Cameralism as administrative science.[25] Even though he never cites him Schumpeter could have found much food for such thought in Albion

Small's thick book on Cameralism published in 1909. Here Small defined Cameralism as 'primarily a theory and a technique of government'. Hence the Cameralists 'were servants of the state'. Or according to the longer version: 'the cameralists were a series of German writers, from the middle of the sixteenth century to the end of the eighteenth century, who approached civic problems from a common viewpoint, who proposed the same central question, and who developed a coherent civic theory, corresponding with the German system of administration at the same time in evolution'. Moreover to the Cameralists 'the central problem of science was the problem of the state', and their theories 'radiated from the central task of furnishing the state with ready means'.[26]

While government and the interest of state still seems to be central in Keith Tribe's more restricted definition of Cameralism there are gross dissimilarities between him and Small. Tribe agrees that Cameralism can be regarded as a type of 'administrative economics'. However, he restricts it to have emerged – as a specific language or discourse – in the Prussian universities after 1720. Hence his emphasis on Cameralism as 'a university science', which by 1770 had 'an established place within the teaching programmes of many of the thirty-one German universities that functioned at the time'.[27] The first chairs in the sciences of *Kameral-wissenschaft, Polizei* and *Ökonomie* had been inaugurated in places such as Halle, Frankfurt-an-der-Oder and Rinteln in the 1720s. During the coming decades a stream of textbooks appeared that were written by teachers and professors. Their aim was undoubtedly to educate civil servants who would be able to administer matters of the state but also to teach good practices in order to develop the national economy. They should be able to understand the principles of taxation but also those of good 'policey' in order to create a larger population, establish manufactures and a prosperous agriculture.

In a more recent contribution to the discussion Andre Wakefield seeks to expand the definition yet again. Like Tribe, he regards Cameralism as some kind of common discourse mainly developed during the eighteenth century (he even connects it to the emergence of the industrial revolution in continental Europe) but he extends it far from being merely a 'university science'. Moreover it was not 'economics' and 'administrative economics' in any narrow sense: 'German Cameralists existed at the nexus between science and economic development (and were) […] proponents of the notion that one could promote development through the systematic application of the natural and human sciences'.[28] Hence Wakefield's Cameralists, besides being university professors in state administration, also included natural scientists, brave inventors and cranks experimenting in chemistry and mineralogy at the time, explorers in the natural sciences, as well adventure seekers and perhaps even simple rogues (Wakefield's favourite Cameralist Johann Heinrich Gottlob Justi could perhaps be attributed to most of these roles).

Juxtaposing Cameralism and mercantilism

Hence it is at least debatable whether it is very fruitful to regard Cameralism as one particular school of thought and practice. Rather we should perhaps talk about a variety of traditions and discourses, which to some extent were intertwined but also differed from each other. As Ingomar Bog stated more than fifty years ago – in a polemic against Judge's and Coleman's insistence upon mercantilism as a non-concept – that does not in principle rule out that we cannot find *some* common themes in these different discourses and policy schemes.[29] But whether this very general common ground was a specifically German *Sonderweg* is a totally different matter – as I will return to in the end.

This connects also to our second question how to juxtapose Cameralism and mercantilism. This is not an easy matter. Here perhaps the case of the Austrian 'Cameralists' – Roscher's third 'school' as we saw – can bring some light. There has always been bewilderment concerning whether such Austrian 'Cameralists' as Johann Joachim Becher, his brother-in-law Philipp Wilhelm von Hörnigk, or Wilhelm Schröder were not in fact 'mercantilists' rather than Cameralists.

Becher (1635–1682) was born in Speyer in the Palatinate (Rheinland-Pfalz) and during a hectic lifetime attained fame as a physician, alchemist, precursor of chemistry and perhaps most of all for his development of the phlogiston theory. In 1657, he was appointed professor of medicine at the University of Mainz and physician to the archbishop there. After publishing a number of works on metallurgy and chemistry he was in 1666 made councillor of commerce at Vienna, where he had gained the powerful support of the prime minister of Emperor Leopold. Sent by the emperor on a mission to the Netherlands he afterwards, among other things, wrote his *Politischer Discurs von den eigentlichen Ursachen des Auf- und Abnehmens der Städte, Länder und Republiken* (1668). It was because of this book that he has been recognized as a Cameralist as well as, alternatively, a mercantilist. But most of all Becher was a man who sought opportunity where he could find it. He started manufactures and opened workhouses in wool, linen and silk. He involved himself in a colonisation project of Guyana under the auspices of the *Kurfürst* (imperial elector) of Bavaria. Furthermore, for the count of Hanau he made up a detailed plan to colonise the area between Orinoco and the Amazonas. Besides, he outlined plans for new industrial and manufacturing projects, for example with the *Kurfürst* of Mainz. In Vienna, where he stayed during most of the 1670s, he became the head of the *Manufakturhaus* manufactory supported by the Emperor. At the same time he projected the building of Rhine-Danube-Canal – another wild scheme that failed. Perhaps understandably the Emperor got tired of his many (and costly) schemes. He emigrated to London, where he died in 1682.[30]

As a person Becher might fit well with Wakefield's definition of a true Cameralist: *metallurg* (alchemist!) and maverick adventurer. He fits less well with the loyal state administrator which Schumpeter (and Small) talked about, or with a typical (Prussian) university professor after 1720. He was not even particularly interested in state administration. For the bulk of *Politische Discurs* mainly deals with matters of commerce and trade. Thus he spent most of the discussion on how badly commerce and trade were organised in Germany and how they could be improved. In general, he proposed the principle of free trade.[31] At the same time he proposed a significant restriction to this principle of freedom. Thus free trade may rule only if it did not interfere with the goals of population increase, subsistence and good community (*Volksreichheit, Nahrung und Gemeinschaft*), he pointed out.[32] It was in this context that he brought in his famous distinction between *Monopolium, Polypolium* and *Propolium*. All these forms implied great threats to a well-organized trade. Thus monopolies kept the population down, polipoly (a form of ruinous competition) endangers subsistence, and the propolium or forestalling disturbs society ('Monopolium verhindert die populosität, das Polypolium die Nahrung, das Propolium die Gemeinschaft').[33] With *polypolium* Becher referred to a situation where there are too many competitors, which destroys business, and the term *Propolium* alluded to forestalling and cornering of necessities.

It is obvious that Becher's ideal was the free institutions and flourishing trade and industry he found prevailing in the Dutch republic. He speaks of how the Dutch miraculously enough had been able to rise from rags to riches, becoming the most prosperous nation in the world: 'wordurch Hollandt ein schlechte Grafschafft zu solchem Standt kommen seye, das es allein nun mehr am Mitteln als das gantze Römische Reich vermag'. The only reason for this Becher says is its commerce and liberties: 'Commercien, ihr libertät und resolution'. More specifically it was the 'verarbeiten' (processing) of raw material (silk) in its own 'Industrien' that has been the most important reason behind Holland's rise. His aim in the *Politische Discurs* is mainly to demonstrate 'welcher gestalt die Commercien einem Land Schaden und Nutzen bringen könnte' (literally: to what extent commerce may benefit or ruin a country).[34] To fill the state's coffers with specie is not the most important aim. Rather – and here he uses the C-word – 'das Cameral-Wesen bestehet nich allein in Einnahm und Aussgab, und dieser richtiger Verrechnung, sondern es beruhet auch dass man dess gantzen Lands interesse befördere, und dem gemeinen Mann zu Mitteln verhelffe' ('Cameralism means not only the balancing of means and income, but also to promote the entire country's wealth and to raise the common man's subsistence').[35] The main litmus test for a prosperous civil society (*Civil Societät*) was that it was 'volkreiche narhafte Gemein' (i.e. populous *as well as* prosperous). It was the same with a state as with a town: 'je volkreicher also ein Stadt ist, je mächtiger ist sie auch' (literally: the more populous a city is the more prosperous it is).[36] For Becher, wealth lay in production. Furthermore, a well-ordered agriculture, many handicrafts and manufactures would act as a stimulus to increased consumption. This meant that there should be a certain proportion between these three main sectors of the economy. Consumption in its turn was the centre and source of a country's well-being.

On the other hand, Becher believed that 'money was the soul and nerve of the land' (*das Geld gleichsamb die Nerve und Seel eines Landes ist*). Consequently, it should be kept in the country.[37] Roscher interprets Becher on this point not to house any bullionist illusions but to consider money as a form of *Verlag* or putting-out (circulating as opposed to fixed) capital. Hence, with a great *Verlag* it was possible to employ many workers and increase the riches of the country.[38]

In order to decide whether Becher was a 'mercantilist' or a Cameralist it must be added that he by no means was a lone figure. Possibly born in Frankfurt am

Main, his brother-in-law Philipp Wilhelm von Hörnigk graduated in law at Ingolstadt (but was, contrary to the older literature, never promoted to a doctoral degree) in 1661.[39] Hörnigk's most famous work *Öesterreich über alles wann es nur will* (1684)[40] must be regarded in the context of war and the national humiliation inflicted upon Germany during at this time. France had seized Trier and Strasbourg in 1684, and the same year the Turks had stood before the gates of Vienna. Hence, Hörnigk's tone was aggressive and nationalistic. However, Austria's weakness was her own fault, he argued. She had given away her wealth to foreigners, for example her vast linen trade.[41] But Austria was able to change this 'whenever she wanted'. In this context Hörnigk presented a program for national recovery, which resembled Antoine Montchrétien's receipt for the recovery of France, put forward in his tract from 1615, *Traicté de l économie politique* (he was by the way the first to use the concept 'political economy'). His main solution was to establish economic and administrative means by which Austria could provide enough national independence and subsistence at home (*Subsistenz in ihrem eigenen Haus*).[42] In order to establish such self-sufficiency Hörnigk presented a long list of principles which included the necessity to work up raw materials in *Fabriquen* (manufactories or manufacturing enterprise); to find the right means to increase the amount of people that would contribute to the *Verarbeitung* (processing) of raw materials; see to that gold and silver, as far as possible, is not transported out of the country; and to watch that the *landsinwohner* (inhabitants of the country) mainly use wares of their own produce (*dass sie sich an ihren einheimischen gutern begnugen*). In this context the *Missbrauch* (misuse) of foreign wares must be averted and, to the extent that importation is necessary, it must be exchanged for other wares and not money. In fact no wares should ever be imported that could be produced within the country.[43]

Roscher found Hörnigk's program to be mercantilistic.[44] This is basically also Thomas Simon's position who points out the great difference between for example Seckendorff's *Hausväter*-inspired language and the Austrians' emphasis on trade and commerce.[45] However, to be honest in form and content, Hörnigk was much closer to the program of self-sufficiency connected with Montchrétien in France than to what the English mercantilist writers of the seventeenth century had proposed. Perhaps then Colbertism is a better word to use than mercantilism. But then how shall we see the connection between Colbertism and mercantilism? Perhaps we should not, as Simon suggests, overestimate their differences.[46] But Colbertism in France was much more inclined to emphasize infant industry protection than the English. We seem to be running in circles. How shall we be able to come out of what increasingly looks like a terminological *cul-de-sac?*

Similarities and variants in early modern European economic thought

After this exercise, despite the strong image that Roscher provided of the situation in Germany after 1648, we perhaps still will have to reject the notion of *one* German *Sonderweg*; one unbroken 'tradition' originating from Germany's special backward situation after 1648. As Tribe and others have suggested it is surely relevant to speak of specific Cameralist university teaching discourse roughly from the establishment of the first chairs in Polity (*Policey*), Economy, and Cameralism in Prussia during the 1720s, with a probable highpoint fifty years later. But with this exception Germany is perhaps not such a special case at all. We have seen the resemblance between Colbertism and the Austrians. We have referred to the development of a natural right discourse, which surely involved many countries. It is also important to note that a genre of Aristotelian-inspired *Hausväter* discourse was not an exclusive German phenomenon. Treatises of everything from good husbandry, instructions for morally correct commerce to Princes' Mirrors (*Fürstenspiegel*) with roots back to he the Greeks and the Romans (Xenophon in particular) were widespread in Europe from Medieval times.[47] Especially the latter can be found from Hungary in the East to Norway in the North to Spain in the West, but also outside Europe in the Byzantine as well as in Islamic world.

We can also trace other similarities between discourse and practice in Europe. Hence in many parts of Europe during the whole epoch from the seventeenth and up until the late eighteenth century we find different responses to what David Hume called 'Jealousy of Trade': how to achieve *power* in a situation of fierce international competition and nascent state making with economic means, something which at this time often was called *plenty*.[48] As many have noted it makes no sense to decipher whether *plenty* or *power* was the most important aim of economic writers or politicians during this era. Instead, both endeavours were regarded as potent and largely identical.[49] It is also true that such responses in many cases – but not always – grew out of an envy of the Dutch miracle. We have already seen Becher's admiration of Holland, which without doubt also included a large sense of envy. Hence what the Dutch case seemed to illustrate more than anything else was that increased international trade was the foundation upon which military strength and national power could be built. At the same time national power was regarded as a pre-condition for the accumulation and preservation of wealth.

Contemporary seventeenth-century observers in England and elsewhere contemplated different answers to the Dutch miracle. One way to react was to say that the Dutch had snatched the trade of other countries through ruthless competition, but also admittedly through hard work, parsimony and a public (and patriotic) spirit. In England the merchant and political writer Thomas Mun in the 1620s emphasised how the Dutch had been able to out-compete the English herring fishermen in the North Sea. It was on this basis according to him that the Dutch monopoly of the trade between the Baltic and the North Sea had been developed during the early seventeenth century.[50] Another explanation was proposed by writers such as William Temple – for a while British ambassador in Holland. Temple especially emphasised the wealth-creating effects of specialisation and division of labour. For him trade was not a zero-sum game but created instead spirals of increased demand, which in turn further stimulated the growth of trade. A country of tradesmen is much richer than a country of farmers, he noted. Moreover, a trading country can host many more citizens than an agricultural one. A dense population is thus both a sign of riches, but will at the same also stimulate increased demand and more riches.[51]

However, *Jealousy of Trade* was not directed exclusively against the Dutch. In France the seventeenth century saw the emergence of economic nationalism. Around 1600 the *valet du chambre* to the King Henry IV, Berthélemy Laffemas, had published a number of treatises in which he argued for the establishment of manufactures in France in order to avoid 'unnecessary' imports. According to Laffemas the problem was that France sold out its raw materials too cheaply in order to buy foreign goods.[52] In a more aggressive tone some decades later his message was reinforced by Montchretien, as we saw above. For him the very concept 'political economy' presupposed strong protectionist measures taken by a *dirigiste* state. He was strongly propounding the thesis that political and military power went along with economic development and modernisation at home. Later on during the seventeenth century this would form the backbone of the so-called *Colbert System*. For Colbert the truth behind the principle of developing an own manufacture industry based upon their own natural resources showed itself in the quite successful wars that France fought with England and the Dutch republic.[53]

We find the same theme exposed also in the Kingdom of Naples, where Antonio Serra would ponder over how a small nation without own resources in silver and gold could be able to survive and thrive. In his influential tract *Breve Trattato*, published in 1613, he emphasised that a small state like Naples would have to export both to cover the importation of necessities and luxuries as well as for the import of money (silver). In turn this meant that Naples had to develop a 'favourable balance of trade' in goods; it must export more goods than it imported. Without doubt Serra's insistence upon the necessity of a favourable balance of trade became a much-discussed topic later on. For example England, where this debate was especially intense, was a country without own resources in silver and gold.[54]

Finally, also in Spain the ways and means to become prosperous and powerful were widely-discussed as early as the sixteenth century. Here of course the lack of native silver and gold resources was not the main problem, as specie was amply provided for from the Americas. Instead it was recognized that an import of bullion rather than riches could create dire problems.[55] Already in 1556 Martin de Azpílcueta formulated the famous so-called quantity theory of money. What would happen when there was such a great inflow of silver and gold that money would fall and goods rise in value, he argued. Hence the so-called Price revolution was a well-known phenomenon amongst contemporary Europeans. When the price level increased in Spain this meant that domestic wares became dearer and imports cheaper. As a consequence, domestic industries as well as agriculture suffered from cheap foreign competition. In Spain controller of the public finance Luis Ortiz in the 1580s struggled hard to find remedies for this problem. He came up with the proposition – familiar to us by now – that the Spaniards should stop buying foreign (manufactured) goods but rather work up their own native raw materials. In the seventeenth century Gerónimo de Ustáriz and others would develop this into a full-fledged system of protection and import-substitution.[56]

Cameralism: a *Sonderweg*?

So where does this lead us? Should we abandon the notion of Cameralism as the German version of a more general mercantilist discourse? Instead of providing a definitive answer I would like to fuel the discussion by providing some brief comments and ideas.

First, it is a question of terminology whether we want to put the name 'Cameralism' on the German response(s) to *Jealousy of Trade* or state interest by economic means in early modern Europe. In a sense it was – as Tribe or Wakefield emphasize – a more strictly-defined discourse and practice carried out by people in or outside academia in Prussia and other German lands with a common aim to improve and innovate. But then we would have to find a new name for the wider phenomenon of responses to the *Jealousy of Trade* paradigm. Should we perhaps call this 'mercantilism', or should we abandon this term also?

Secondly, *Cameralism* is clearly a misnomer if we believe that it was *the* German response to *Jealousy of Trade* and reason of state using economic means. Realizing that mercantilism was a much more varied phenomenon than for example Adam Smith admitted we must also acknowledge that there existed a variety of such responses in the German speaking countries. Still it is clear that many of them – in different ways – tried to understand and find means to improve the position of the particular state in a struggle for European recognition and power. That states like Prussia and Austria found other strategies to follow than France and England is perhaps not so difficult to understand. For England it seemed only natural to claim that its riches lay in its foreign trade. For a Prussian ruler around the turn of the century 1700 this would have made no sense.

Thirdly, it is important to abandon the kind of 'blue print' history that so often is connected to a Whig interpretation of history. Instead we must acknowledge that there is no 'better' or 'superior', but only different responses – more or less rational – to the circumstances of a certain place and time. This is not a paper on methodology. If it had been, it would have been necessary here to discuss how ideas and practices were 'translated' and through this transformed in content, shape and design, and how the process of emulation can be characterized. In this sense there were many *Sonderwege* (or none at all).

Not only those who have regarded themselves, in a sense, as the 'blue-print' can be blamed for this sin, however. In his great work Wilhelm Roscher compares the *goldene Zeit britischer Nationalökonomik* (golden age of British economics) from Hume to Ricardo with the kind of 'Vorrang, wie ihn die Italiener im 15. und 16. Jahrhundert auf dem Gebiete der Malerei besessen haben' (literally: the superiority of Italian painting in European art during the fifteenth and sixteenth centuries).[57] Attractive as it might be such an approach most often makes bad and prejudiced history. It neglects the historical context and our ability to understand historical actors.

Notes

1 Horst Claus Recktenwald, 'Cameralism', in *The New Palgrave Dictionary of Economics*, Second Edition ed. Steven N. Durlauf and Lawrence E. Blume (2008), online version on http://www.dictionaryofeconomics.com/article?id=pde2008_C000011&edition=current&q=cameralism&topicid=&result_number=1 [last accessed Wed 2 September 2015, 1:57 p.m.].

2 The boom is referred to in Terence Hutchison, *Before Adam Smith. The Emergence of Political Economy 1662–1776* (Oxford: Blackwell, 1988), while Lars Magnusson, *The Political Economy of Mercantilism* (London: Routledge, 2015) speaks about a science of trade emanating from this period.

3 Joseph A. Schumpeter, *A History of Economic Analysis* (New York: Oxford University Press, 1954), 147.

4 Wilhelm Roscher, *Geschichte der National-Oekonomik in Deutschland* (Munich: R. Oldenbourg, 1874), 219.

5 Roscher, *Geschichte*, 219f.

6 Ibid., 228

7 Ibid., 231.

8 Here in the English translation; Gustav Schmoller, *The Mercantile System and Its Historical Significance* (New York: MacMillan, 1897), 76.

9 Ibid.

10 Alexander Gerschenkron, *Economic Backwardness in Historical Perspective* (Cambridge Mass.: The Belknap Press of Harvard University Press, 1966), 1.

11 Schmoller, *Mercantile System*, 80.

12 For a discussion particularly on Adam Smith but also in general terms, see Lars Magnusson, *A Tradition of Free Trade* (London: Routledge, 2004).

13 Also suggested by Donald Winch and Patrick O'Brien, eds, *The Political Economy of British Historical Experience, 1688–1914* (Oxford: the British Academy by Oxford University Press, 2002), introduction.

14 Magnusson, *A Tradition of Free Trade*, ch 1. Also Magnusson, *The Political Economy of Mercantilism*.

15 The first Swedish edition came out as *Merkantilismen*, vol 1–2. (Stockholm: Norstedts, 1931), the German in 1932 (*Der Merkantilismus*, Jena: Gustav Fischer 1932) and the English one in 1935 entitled *Mercantilism* (London: George Allen & Unwin, 1935).

16 A. V. Judges, "The Idea of a Mercantile State," in *Revisions in Mercantilism*, ed. D. C. Coleman (London: Methuen, 1969), 35–60, at 35f.

17 D. C. Coleman, "Eli Heckscher and the Idea of Mercantilism," in id., ed., *Revisions in Mercantilism*, p. 117.

18 Magnusson, *Political Economy of Mercantilism*, ch 2. The emphasis on rent-seeking as an important aspect of Mercantilism is (perhaps too much) highlighted in Robert B. Ekelund and Robert D. Tollison, *Politicized Economies. Monarchy, Monopoly and Mercantilism* (College Station: Texas A&M University Press, 1997).

19 Roscher, *Geschichte*, 238.

20 On Seckendorff, see ibid., 238ff.; Albion Small, *The Cameralists* (Chicago: Chicago University Press, 1909), 60ff.

21 Small, *Cameralists*, 69.

22 For a longer description of this book, see ibid., 63ff.

23 On the influence of natural rights discourse for example on the Scottish enlightenment it is still worth the while to consult *Wealth and Virtue. The Shaping of Political Economy in the Scottish Enlightenment*, eds. István Hont and Michael Ignatieff (Cambridge: Cambridge University Press, 1983).

24 Thomas Simon, "Merkantilismus und Kameralismus. Zur Tragfähigkeit des Merkantilismusbegriffs und seiner Abgrenzung zum deutschen 'Kameralismus,'" in:

Merkantilismus. Wideraufnahme einer Debatte, ed. Moritz Isenmann (Stuttgart: Franz Steiner, 2014), 65–82.

25 Schumpeter, *History*, 159.

26 Small, *Cameralists*, viii, 3,4,

27 Keith Tribe, *Governing Economy. The Reformation of German Economic Discourse 1750–1840* (Cambridge: Cambridge University Press, 1998), 11.

28 Andre Wakefield, *The Disordered Police State: German Cameralism as Science and Practice* (Chicago: University of Chicago Press, 2009), 20f, 25.

29 Ingomar Bog, "Mercantilism in Germany," in *Revisions in Mercantilism*, 162–189, at 171, 181. The same argument in A. W. (Bob) Coats, "Mercantilism Yet Again," in *Gli economisti e la politica economica*, ed. N. Piero Roggi (Naples: Edizione Scientifiche Italiane, 1985), 66–88.

30 On Becher, see Louise Sommer, *Die österreichischen Kameralisten in dogmengeschichtlicher Darstellung, II* (Vienna: Konegen, 1925), 1–78; Herbert Hassinger, *Johann Joachim Becher, 1635–1682. Beitrag zur Geschichte des Merkantilismus* (Vienna: A. Holzhausens Nfg., 1951); Roscher, Geschichte, 270ff; Small, *Cameralists*, 107ff; and Erhard Dittrich, *Die deutschen und österreichischen Kameralisten* (Darmstadt: Wissenschaftliche Buchgesellschaft, 1974), 58f.

31 'Freiheit in Zu und Ausfuhr der Waaren, wenig oder keine Imposten darauf, dass sich ein Jeder man ehrlich nähren, wie er kann und weiss, und sich in Wohnung, Kleider und Trank möge seinen Willen nach betragen'. Quote from Becher's *Psychosophia oder Seelenweisheit* (1707), after Roscher, *Geschichte*, 278.

32 Ibid.

33 Johann Joachim Becher, *Politischer Discurs von den eigentlichen Ursachen dess Auf- und Abnehmes der Städt, Länder und Republicken….*(Frankfurt: Johann David Zunners, 1668), 25.

34 Ibid., 19.

35 Ibid., 23.

36 Ibid., 28.

37 Ibid., 2.

38 Roscher, *Geschichte*, 276.

39 On Hörnigk, see the introduction in the forthcoming Philip Wilhelm von Hörnigk, *Austria Supreme (if only it wills so). A Strategy for European Economic Supremacy* ed. P. R. Rössner, transl. K. Tribe (London and New York: Anthem, 2016). Sommer, *Die österreichischen Kameralisten*, II, 124ff.; Roscher, *Geschichte*, 287ff; Kurt Zielenziger, "P. W. von Hörnigk," *Encyclopedia of the Social Sciences* (New York: MacMillan, 1951); Dittrich, *Kameralisten*, 66ff, and most recently Erik S. Reinert, *How Rich Countries Got Rich…and Why Poor Countries Stay Poor* (London: Constable, 2007), 95f. and 313f.

40 See the forthcoming English translation in Rössner, ed., *Austria Supreme*.

41 Philipp Wilhelm von Hörnigk, *Oesterreich über alles wann es nur will* (1684) (Frankfurt am Main: Klostermann, 1948), 32.

42 Ibid., 70, 222.

43 Ibid., 33ff.

44 Roscher, *Geschichte*, p.292.

45 Simon, "Merkantilismus und Kameralismus."

46 Ibid., 69.

47 For example, see Keith Tribe, *Land, Labour and Economic Discourse* (London: Routledge & Kegan Paul, 1978), ch. 4.

48 On such themes, see István Hont, *Jealousy of Trade. International Competition and the Nation-State in Historical Perspective* (Cambridge Mass: The Belknap Press of Harvard University Press, 2005).

49 For this rather diffuse discussion see Magnusson, *Political Economy of Mercantilism*, ch.2.

50 Thomas Mun, *England's Treaure by Forraign Trade* (1664) (New York: Augustus M Kelley, 1986). This treatise was probably written in the early 1620s but only published forty years later by his son John Mun.

51 William Temple, *Observations upon the United Provinces of the Netherlands (1673)* (Cambridge: Cambridge University Press, 1932).

52 On Laffemas, see for example Charles W. Cole, *Colbert and a Century of French Mercantilism* (New York: Columbia University Press, 1939), part 1.

53 For an overview see Magnusson, *Political Economy of Mercantilism*, ch 3.

54 On Serra see Sophus Reinert, "Introduction," in Antonio Serra, *A Short Treatise on the Wealth and Poverty of Nations (1613)* ed. Sophus Reinert (London and New York: Anthem 2011).

55 See Cosimo Perrotta, "Early Spanish Mercantilism: the First Analysis of Underdevelopment," in *Mercantilist Economics* ed. Lars Magnusson (Boston: Kluwer 1993), 17–58.

56 Ibid., 22f.

57 Roscher, *Geschichte*, 236.

4 Mercantilism and Cameralism

Two very different variations on the same theme

Jürgen Backhaus[1]

Cameralism: logics, purposes, goals

Take a look at any historical map of the Palatinate after the Thirty-Years-War (see Figure 4.1). Contrast this with one of the contiguous states of the time, such as France. You will notice immediately that the geo-political conditions differed and suggested drastically different policy options. The purpose of this contribution is to draw on some of my earlier work as well as by others and explain some of these differences in more detail.

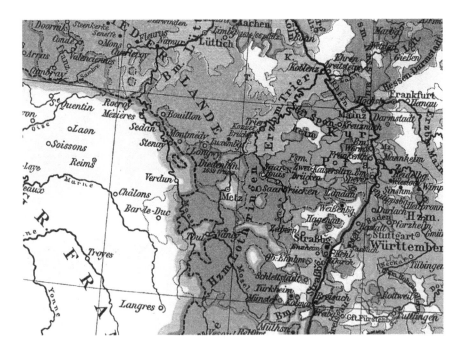

Figure 4.1 South-west Germany in 1688.

Source: Putzger's *Historischer Weltatlas*, 1905.

In the German language area, the ultimate Cameralist was, of course, Johann Heinrich Gottlob von Justi (1717–1771). Starting from about twelve pages of Christian Freiherr von Wolff's (1679–1754) path-breaking contribution,[2] Justi produced a monumental theory of Cameralism, which at the time was designed to be the material from which future civil servants could be taught. It therefore also included management and technology, notably forestry.[3] The basic goal of the Cameralist and the mercantilist state was essentially the same, to have as many healthy inhabitants of the country as possible. Actually, the Cameralist writers emphasized the point that the main aim was not simply to have many but 'many healthy inhabitants'. For this reason, the Cameralist writers suggested a number of very specific policies addressed at a healthy state of the population, which cannot be readily found in the mercantilist writers' publications, as the latter tend to emphasize the population's size, next to studies on mortality and morbidity.

The geo-political situation in Germany as exemplified by the Palatinate after the Thirty-Years-War, a country which stretched from the Upper Danube to the Lower Rhine, in many discontiguous patches and pieces, forced the rulers to look for ways to increase the competitive position of their states, when they could never be certain of the dominance of their position.[4] I use six policy areas to demonstrate the difference between mercantilist and Cameralist policies. It should be understood that the basic state goals and policy doctrines were the same; but due to the geo-political position the Cameralist advisers made radically different proposals from their mercantilist counterparts.

A structural comparison of Cameralism and mercantilism

The first aspect relates to *customs duties* and *protective tariffs*. Take the problem of customs duties first. Obviously, one aim would be to raise maximum revenue. If you have a discontiguous state, however, you have to be careful not to deter the trade from coming in but instead circumventing your country. If the customs duties are so high as to divert the trade elsewhere, the towns with staple rights will suffer from the loss of trade and staple duties; local industry will not benefit from imports and also miss out on the export opportunities. Hence, in order to maximize revenues from customs duties, these have to be set as low so as to divert the trade from competing areas and markets into one's owns. This requires a policy of low customs duties.

In the mercantilist states, in contrast, the rulers controlled substantial empires so that resource mobility was relatively low. In mercantilist empires, the rent-seeking explanation offered by Robert Ekelund and Robert Tollison follows as a natural extension of public choice reasoning. There was a considerable degree of resource immobility along with sizeable differences in organizational costs among interest groups. As a result, investment in rent-seeking activity became more profitable relative to investment in productive activity, in comparison to what would have existed if resources were highly mobile and if differences in organizational costs were small.

In the Cameralist regimes, however, resources were highly mobile, and organizational costs differed only slightly among interest groups. The Cameralist states existed in a thoroughly competitive environment, in which the scope for taxation was tightly circumscribed, both by the persistence of feudal institutions and by the high mobility of resources due to the fragmented nature of the German territories. With over 300 states in the German-speaking territories, soldiers, craftsmen, merchants and peasants could easily walk from one state to another in search of better circumstances. These territories provided a nice historical application of what since 1956 has come to be called the 'Tibout Model'.

Although most peasants were nominally indentured, such indenture had no force in the aftermath of the Thirty Years War. People were highly valued assets, and a ruler of, say, Hildesheim, would have no interest in returning peasants or craftsmen who might have come from neighbouring Halberstadt. While rulers would welcome migrants from other states, they could not force people to remain within the boundaries of their states. With the technologies of transportation and communication that existed at the time, an effort to prevent emigration would have been exceedingly costly. It would have conflicted severely with economic development, thereby reducing the state's prospects of survival. In terms of practice, peasants were free to choose where to live; rulers could not compel people to live in their jurisdictions, but rather had to attract them.[5]

Interestingly enough, Friedrich List[6] stood firmly in the Cameralist tradition. Even when he advocated protective tariffs, he had this objective in mind.[7] This is why his protective tariffs actually represented wise tariff policy and not, as we find it described in most textbooks on international trade, barriers to competition. The argument in most textbooks on international trade is that protective tariffs would last forever and hinder economic development. Friedrich List proposed a radically different policy. In fact, protective tariffs that are merely set up for political reasons disappear when they are not effective. The rationale behind that is simple. When a particular import is protected by a high tariff, this will either allow a local industry to form behind the barrier of protection, or the policy will not succeed at all. If the policy is successful, ultimately the tariff will disappear because it will not yield any revenue and, for that reason, it will be abolished as a consequence of practical fiscal policy, since ineffective tariffs are routinely abolished as a matter of practical policy. If, on the other hand, the policy of protective tariffs is not effective and no local industry develops, pressure will mount on the government to correct the tariff policy. This political pressure comes from two sides. On the one hand, local industry will insist on receiving the cheaper imports, since local products are not available and the tariff makes the imports unnecessarily expensive. The high tariff, however, also results in a competitive disadvantage of the local importers, who may want to leave the country altogether. This is contrary to economic policy, and hence internal government pressure from the ministry of commerce will mount to reduce the protective tariff to its normal measure.

The second policy area is concerned with tax rates and the tax base. A state eager to raise its revenues from taxation, notably revenues from the excise tax, at the time must be concerned with the tax base. As Arthur Laffer explained on a napkin to President Reagan at the time, there is a long-run relationship between the tax base, the tax rate and the tax revenue. This insight was not new with Arthur

Laffer.[8] It was standard fare in Cameralist economic thought. With a given tax base, the tax revenue is always the same at two tax rates, with the exception of the maximum revenue. If the tax rate is one hundred per cent, the tax revenue is zero and so is the tax revenue at a rate of zero per cent. Somewhere between one hundred and zero per cent is the maximum yielding tax rate. Another matter is, however, the care for the tax base. The tax base can be shrunk or expanded. If the tax rate is excessive, the tax base will dwindle. Hence, the policy maker should always aim for a tax rate as low so as not to shrink the tax base. The tax rate should therefore always be on the left part of the Laffer curve, not on the upper part where the tax base is going to dwindle all the time.[9] Taxation is a matter of building the tax base and raising tax revenues, when a long-term maximum of tax revenue can only be gained from a stable tax base. For this reason, Cameralists held that the excise taxes should be levied moderately. Necessities such as beer can yield more than goods that cannot be readily substituted.

A third aspect concerns monetary stability and the role of gold. Currency debasement represented, in many countries, a standard tool of economic policy, but it is a very poor instrument of Cameralist economic policy. In fact, the Rhenish florin was stable for almost a thousand years, as Werner Sombart (1863–1941)[10] pointed out in his monumental 'Modern Capitalism' (1916).[11] This was sensible economic policy, because the Cameralist state was looking for the revenue from seigniorage, which is highest when the currency is stable and an export item. In this case, minted gold earns the seigniorage through export, when unminted gold needs to be imported. It is unminted gold that needs to be attracted through Cameralist economic policies. Gold was not a fetish of economic policies in mercantilist and Cameralist times. It was rather a typical element of security policy.

Both Cameralist and mercantilist states needed mercenary armies, and those armies ran away and over to the enemy if they were not paid regularly. Armies also disliked being paid in debased currencies, which is why they needed to be paid in stable money. For this reason, it is important to have a war treasure of unminted gold at hand so as to be able to mint fresh currency when armies need to be either hired or held within the country.

A fourth policy area identified as important by Cameralist economics was demographic policies. Demographic economic policy or 'population management' was extensive and rather imaginative. Keep in mind that the goal was to have a large, prosperous and healthy population.[12] In order to foster this goal, Cameralist advice was to set up savings banks where future brides could save for their dowry. Since a maid might take ten to fifteen years to save for a dowry, it would be necessary to have a savings bank at her disposal so at the time of marriage the dowry would indeed be there. At the same time, setting up savings banks would change the behaviour of the population with a view to fostering parsimonious behaviour, and it would make the future brides all the more attractive due to the dowry.[13]

A fifth issue was Cameralist health policy. Today health policy is mostly carried out by the state in order to engage in the redistribution of life's chances. This policy pioneered by the York school of health economics (Anthony Culyer) sees state health policy primarily as a means of redistribution. The nationalization of health in Britain and Canada had primarily this goal, as did the policies in Germany in the 1990s (Norbert Blüm). In France, these policies through holding back the prices for pharmaceuticals led to a shortfall of medication and an uncounted number of deaths since vital drugs were not available. This is the opposite to Cameralist health policy, which generally aims at promoting the health of as many people as possible, not redistributing life chances. In such, the policy adviser would point out the cost in terms of the inhabitants' health losses due to redistributive health policies.

A sixth policy field was represented by the strive to avoid winter wars. An interesting example of this policy can be found in Johann Heinrich Gottlob von Justi's insistence on avoiding war campaigns in winter. In winter, the losses from military campaigns were heavier than in summer, as measured in terms of casualties and the wounded.[14] For this reason, Justi wished for agreements among warring parties to avoid winter campaigns. Rather, campaigns should take place in late summer when the fields had already been harvested. This illustrates the practicality of Cameralism as an economic and policy doctrine. It underscores again the main purpose of Cameralism, policies to have as many happy healthy people as possible: winter wars tend to have many and futile casualties.

Conclusion

In six policy areas some fundamental differences between mercantilist and Cameralist policies could be shown. It should be understood that the basic goal of the states and the basic policy doctrine were the same. But due to the geo-political position the Cameralist advisers made radically different proposals from their mercantilist counterparts.

Notes

1   Shortly after an international workshop on mercantilism and Cameralism held in July 2014 at the University of Leipzig (from which the present paper emerged), organized and hosted by the editor of the present volume, Jürgen Backhaus fell seriously ill due to a stroke and therefore was unable to complete his contribution to the present volume. The present chapter therefore retains the original characteristics of a manuscript prepared for oral delivery. Only the most necessary revisions have been made by the editor, who is particularly grateful to Dr Ursula Backhaus, for taking much care and effort in working-up the paper.

2   Christian Wolff, *Grundsätze des Natur- und Völkerrechts* (*Principles of Natural Law and the Law of Nations*) (Halle 1754), reprint. Collected Works, 1. Division, German Writings, Vol. 19, ed. Marcel Thomann (Hildesheim and New York: Olms, 1980). In his *Principles of Natural Law*, Christian von Wolff introduced the concept of the State as follows: 'Es ist also nötig, dasjenige durch gemeinschaftliche Kräfte zu erhalten, was eintzelne Häuser vor sich nicht erhalten können. Und zu dem Ende müssen Gesellschaften errichtet werden (§ 836). Eine Gesellschaft, die zu dem Ende gemacht wird, heisset ein Staat (civitas)'. Tranlates as: 'Thus it is necessary to retain by common force what single households or individuals cannot maintain by themselves. To this end society is created. We call such a community or society, if it is formed to these ends, a state (civitas)'. Wolff, Vol. 19, *Principles of Natural Law, op. cit.*, § 972. Although it was not

acknowledged by Justi, Wolff's concept was basic to what later became known as Cameralism.

3 Compare Johann Heinrich Gottlob von Justi, *Grundsätze der Policeywissenschaft* [Reprint of the third improved edition with comments, Johann Beckmann (ed.) 1782, (3) Göttingen: Vandenhoek 1756 (1), 1759 (2)] (Frankfurt am Main: Sauer & Auvermann KG, 1969), and Johann Heinrich Gottlob von Justi, *Staatswirthschaft oder Systematische Abhandlung aller ökonomischen und Cameralwissenschaften* (Leipzig: Breitkopf, 1758).

4 Cf. Jürgen G. Backhaus and Richard E. Wagner, "The Cameralists: A Public Choice Perspective," *Public Choice* 53 (1987), 3–20. The Peace of Westphalia in 1648 recognized more than 300 independent states within the Cameralist lands in the German Empire, and not only shaped the constraints for Cameralist states, but also for mercantilist countries such as the Netherlands. Compare the essay by Gerrit Meijer, "The Peace of Münster at the Background of the History of Thought," in *Taking up the Challenge! Festschrift for Jürgen Backhaus* ed. Helge Peukert (Marburg: Metropolis, 2015), 495–505.

5 Cf. Backhaus and Wagner, "The Cameralists: A Public Choice Perspective," 5f.

6 Cf. Jürgen Backhaus, "Die politische Ökonomie der Schutzzolltheorie," in *Studien zur Entwicklung der ökonomischen Theorie*, X, ed. Bertram Schefold (Berlin: Duncker & Humblot, 1992), 103–114.

7 List argued that the development of a nation's productive powers leads to a higher welfare of the state and is to the benefit of the inhabitants. Compare Erik S. Reinert, "Daniel Raymond 1820: A US economist who inspired Friedrich List, with notes on other forerunners of List from the English-speaking periphery," in *Taking up the Challenge!*, 517–536, at 530.

8 See, e.g., Victor A. Canto et al., *Foundations of Supply-Side Economics, Theory and Evidence* (New York: Academic Press, 1983).

9 The Laffer curve is typically depicted as a diagram with tax revenue on the vertical axis and tax rate on the horizontal axis. It takes the form of a reversed U-shape.

10 Cf. Jürgen Backhaus, ed., *Werner Sombart (1863–1941) – Social Scientist, 3 vols.* (Marburg: Metropolis Verlag, 1996).

11 Werner Sombart, *Der moderne Kapitalismus. Historisch-systematische Darstellung des gesamteuropäischen Wirtschaftslebens von seinen Anfängen bis zur Gegenwart*, 2nd ed. (Munich and Leipzig: Duncker & Humblot, 1916), ch. 23, first half volume, section 2.

12 The reduction in population during the Thirty Years' War (1618–1648) was immense. 'The overall population in the German-speaking territories fell by roughly one-third, from about 21 million to around 13 million. This carnage was far from evenly distributed. The population of Württemberg fell from 400,000 to 50,000. The Palatinate lost more than 90 per cent of its population. Three million people in Bohemia were reduced to 800,000. Cities too withered before the onslaught of rampaging armies. Berlin and Colmar lost half their populations. Augsburg was reduced from 50,000 people to 20,000. Chemnitz lost 80 per cent of its population. And the toll in Magdeburg reached 90 per cent'. Backhaus and Wagner, "The Cameralists: A Public Choice Perspective," 4.

13 The original German quote reads as follows: 'Der Endzweck der meisten und fast aller Mannspersonen ist, ihre eigene Haushaltung und Gewerbe zu führen. Hierzu läßt sich ohne alles Vermögen nicht gelangen. Der Vortheil also, daß man mit einem Mägdchen die gewünschte Absicht erreichet, schließt die Augen bey vielerlei anderen Betrachtungen zu […] Wann ein jedes Mägdchen nur 50 Rthrt. (Rix Dollars) Ausstattung hätte; so würden alle Handwerker und Arbeiter alle nach ihren Neigungen heyrathen, die Ehen würden viel glücklicher seyn, jederman würde sich selbst setzen können, und der Staat würde viel bevölkerter seyn'. Johann Heinrich Gottlob von Justi, *Politische und Finanzschriften über wichtige Gegenstände der Staatskunst, der Kriegswissenschaften und des Cameral- und Finanzwesens* (Copenhagen and Leipzig: Rothen, 1761), vol. 3, Part IV. Entitled 'Abhandlung von denen Brautcassen', 272.

14 The discussion by von Justi reads as follows: 'Daß man die Soldaten zu keinen Unternehmungen wider die Jahreszeit und Beschaffenheit der Natur gebrauchen solle. Es ist noch sehr zweifelhaftig, ob die Winterfeldzüge, welche seit 1740 angefangen haben, in dem mitternächtlichen Theil von Europa gewöhnlich zu werden, zu billigen, oder zu verwerfen sind. Man kann allerdings einige Gründe ausfündig machen, welche dergleichen Feldzügen das Wort zu reden scheinen. Es läßt sich öfters der Feind, der in keiner Gegenverfassung stehet, durch einen solchen Winterfeldzug mit einem Male über den Haufen werfen; und so viel Elend, Unglück und Blutvergießen, welches allemal einen langwierigen Krieg zu begleiten pfleget, kann dadurch vermieden werden. Gleichwie auch die große Hitze des Sommers denen Soldaten vielerley Ungemach verursachet, worauf öfters häufiges Kranken und Sterben zu entstehen pfleget; so scheinet auch dieses durch die Winterfeldzüge gehoben zu werden, wie denn in der That dieser Ursachen wegen in Portugal und Spanien, auch öfters in Italien, die Kriegsverrichtungen im Winter vorgenommen werden, und dargegen in der Hitze des Sommers die Erfrischungsquartiere bezogen werden. Allein diesen Gründen stehet entgegen, daß ein Winterfeldzug nur alsdenn über den Feind Vortheil zuwege bringet, wenn er ganz unerwartet ist. Dahingegen wenn es einmal zur Gewohnheit geworden ist, der Feind sich gleichfalls in Gegenverfassung setzet, und mithin dadurch die Langwierigkeit des Krieges nicht vermieden wird. Es ist auch gewiß, daß die Winterfeldzüge viel mehr Ungemach bey sich führen, als die ordentlichen Feldzüge im Sommer; es ist ungewiß, ob nicht daraus noch mehr Krankheiten entstehen müssen. Wenigstens sind die Sachsen, Franzosen und Bayern nach den ersten Winterfeldzügen in Böhmen häufig dahin gestorben. Dahingegen sind so viele Gründe wider dergleichen Winterfeldzüge vorhanden, daß man fast keinen Anstand nehmen kann, sie gänzlich zu verwerfen. Da man dennoch auch nicht aufhöret, die Kriegsverrichtungen im Sommer vorzunehmen; so wird dadurch das Elend des Krieges, welches dem menschlichen Geschlecht bereits ohnedem schädlich genug ist, verdoppelt. Ja! die Natur selbst widerstreitet dergleichen Kriegsverrichtungen im Winter'. Johann Heinrich Gottlob von Justi, *Politische und Finanzschriften über wichtige Gegenstände der Staatskunst, der Kriegswissenschaften und des Cameral- und Finanzwesens* (Copenhagen and Leipzig: Rothen, 1761). Cf. Part XX, pp. 282/3. A translation of the quote is to be found in Ursula Backhaus, *A History of German and Austrian Economic Thought on Health Issues* (Frankfurt am Main: Haag+Herchen, 2007), 92f.

5   Goethe's economics

Between Cameralism and liberalism

Bertram Schefold (translated by Jim A. Underwood)

Goethe: an economist?

Goethe as business expert—an anachronism, surely? And who am I to dare offer him a collegial pat on the back? Yet it must be legitimate for an academic to ask: where did Goethe stand on the economic problems of his time; how did he manage his budget; what did he seek to learn about business science; why, wherefore, and how successfully did he promote business; what, in his official capacity, did he actually do for the economic good of Saxe-Weimar? In particular, it is the connection between Goethe's economic virtues as a representative of his day and the economic visions that we find in his poetry and prose that I want to look at here.

'The veil of poetry furnished by truth'[1] transforms its object in such a way that a new reality, a new truth comes into being that enriches or questions—at any rate, changes—our previous understanding of the world. That Goethe cast the 'veil of poetry' over the business world too in order to give it a new appearance is not something many people realised in the nineteenth century. He was not so much an economist abreast of his day as a poet ahead of it, and he attained economic visions that escaped even the late nineteenth and early twentieth centuries. Among the economic authorities of the time, only Wilhelm Roscher, in his 1874 history of German political economy, *Geschichte der National-Oekonomik in Deutschland*, came close to accepting Goethe as an economist. Referring to studies by A. Schöll, he said it was now firmly established that Goethe's 'practical economic activity' had been 'as assiduous as it was skilful' as well as 'chiming perfectly with his development as a writer'.[2] Roscher cites key economic insights addressed in Goethe's prose work such as the duties accompanying rights of ownership and how 'the wealthy are valued according to how others benefit from their wealth'.[3] However, Roscher takes the view that the treatment of the miracle of paper money in *Faust II* does not 'go to the heart of the matter' and that all the 'damming of oceans, digging of canals, etc.', even coupled with the image of an 'active, flourishing people as life's highest aim', amounts to no more than 'images from a *laterna magica*'[4]—his comments on what Goethe has to say about individual sectors of the economy are positively disparaging.

Why do we today see the dull colours of the magic lantern as vivid flashes casting a terrifying light on the landscape of modern economic crises? Hans

Christoph Binswanger shows how in *Faust II* Goethe, highlighting the compulsive growth of the modern money economy, its susceptibility to crises brought about by speculation and inflation, its ownership structure, and its destructive dynamic as regards cultural tradition and the environment, dramatizes these things as apocalyptic menace. No one seems to have noticed in this connection that Goethe, in presenting his vision to us, is taking his images from an ancient 'adventure capitalism', as Max Weber would have called it in contrast to 'modern capitalism', because that kind of piracy and dam-building, that kind of land-reclamation and destruction of the Philemon and Baucis idyll, is the stuff of the pre-industrial capitalism of the Netherlands in the era of mercantilism—whence Roscher's mention of the *laterna magica*—whereas the effect on ourselves clearly stems from the fact that this version of how things would develop in post-industrial service capitalism appears prophetic. Perhaps the kind of capitalism we are used to does not, in our eyes, despite—or indeed because of—its overgrown financial sector, seem quite as 'modern' and 'rational' as Max Weber thought.

Why, then, this change in the historical effect of Goethe's economic diagnoses, which are presented not analytically but intuitively, as it were, and which were not taken seriously in his own century, whereas his overall rank in the world of literature remained undisputed? At the same time the question arises: how does the critique of capitalism to be found in Goethe's work relate to his liberal attitude, his affirmation of the bourgeois world, and his fond harking-back to aspects of the lifestyle of the *ancien régime*? We cannot expect to be able to reduce Goethe's economic thinking rapidly to a simple formula. I suggest below that Goethe should be categorised slightly differently than has been done hitherto; I try to place him as a connecting link between an earlier Cameralist tradition and the historicism that came after it. To get closer to him, let me begin with his practical work.

Goethe's practical economic attainments and achievements

Goethe's income was high—combining his family inheritance, the salary the Duke paid him, and his literary earnings—but so was his expenditure: for his household, his hospitality, his travels, his collections. He could conduct himself like an entrepreneur who has the ability to create the means of meeting his substantial ends. There are some famous examples of his shrewd business sense.

For modern economists, perhaps the most astonishing of these is the way he anticipated what has become known as the 'Vickrey auction', the modern reinvention of which—in a more generalised form—was awarded a Nobel Prize. Goethe wished to find out what his works were worth to a respected publisher. So he offered his latest epic, *Hermann and Dorothea*, to the publisher Vieweg, accompanying his offer, which was delivered by an agent, with a sealed letter. Vieweg was to disclose his bid, likewise to an agent, before opening the letter. The agent was then to compare Vieweg's bid with the offer contained in Goethe's letter, which was now opened. If Vieweg's bid was higher than Goethe's offer, Vieweg was to receive the right to publish the work—but at the price named by Goethe; if Vieweg's bid was lower, no deal ensued.

To Vieweg, Goethe's proposal must have felt like an affront; he had not seen the manuscript but was obliged to make an estimate of its value nonetheless. However, the way Goethe went about things meant that Vieweg had to disclose his estimate, because had he bid less than the manuscript was worth to him he ran the risk, not knowing how much Goethe had offered, of not securing the coveted right to publish; had he bid more in order to tempt Goethe he risked having to go through with the deal at a higher price than he had actually wished to pay. What Vickrey proved in a generalised way is that, if at auctions the second-highest bid is established as the purchase price, the participants in the auction will base their bidding on true estimates of value and not be diverted therefrom for strategic reasons. It was only after Vickrey's Nobel Prize that people understood the importance of the discovery Goethe had anticipated here.[5]

This is just one example of Goethe's feeling for business, such as I[6]—and others before me—have examined in greater detail elsewhere. However, Goethe was not in this instance behaving as an economist who seeks to disseminate a theoretical discovery. He did not describe and discuss the principle of the second-price auction in the abstract; he simply came across it and exploited it for his own purposes. As another example shows, he did not necessarily act like a businessman maximising profit, because although he obtained the monopoly for the distribution of the so-called '*Ausgabe letzter Hand*' [the German term for the last edition personally supervised by the author]—the title page of each volume proudly announces as much[7]—he did not sell the privilege at the highest price, as his son August urged, but instead chose a publisher, Cotta, whom he could expect to manage his business reliably and in a way that would ensure that the interests of his heirs, too, were looked after.[8] Goethe bore less resemblance to a capitalist striving for the highest possible return than to one of those householders in the classical world for whom wealth was a means to the good life. He was not so much like the householder in Cicero's *De officiis*,[9] seeking to use his fortune to gain honour for his family through public attainments. He was even less like the householder portrayed by Philodemus the Epicurean, taking his pleasure in silent enjoyment. No, Goethe most resembled Aristotle's *eleutherios* or 'civilised person', who does not find it easy to stay rich because he knows how to give properly.

The young Goethe had come to Weimar not for the purpose of writing but in order to join the government. Consequently, in the years before his Italian journey he attended more than five hundred meetings of the Privy Council. After the Italian journey Goethe was also involved in government work in an advisory capacity. The most interesting case from the standpoint of economic policy—it was spoken of as an 'exceptionally intricate Gordian knot'[10]—concerned the coinage and currency system. Liberally supplied with documents, Goethe was asked to investigate how the official exchange rate, as used to determine tax payable, differed from that customary in the marketplace and whether the public should be permitted to settle tax debts using the cheapest means of payment available. The official basis of calculation was the French *écu, called* 'leaf thaler' [*Laubtaler*], but minting of this ceased in 1792, when the French government introduced the *assignats*, a form of paper currency.[11] Goethe acknowledged in his report that the leaf thaler as still in circulation continued to form the basis of the exchange and payment system but said it was not really suitable for two reasons: leaf thaler coins varied in value, because before and during the years of the Revolution the quality of their minting had not remained entirely constant, the earlier vintages being better; secondly, even the inferior leaf thaler coins were disappearing. They became scarce and were increasingly driven from circulation by an excessive issue of the *Scheidemünze*.[12] Goethe's objection: 'Every currency standard, no matter what, needs to be solid'.[13]

In the examples relating to his own household, we see Goethe as a shrewd connoisseur of economic affairs, deploying his funds like a good manager, not going for maximum yield but instead making use of his resources to foster and maintain the desired lifestyle. His report on the coinage system is written more from an economic standpoint and in it he stresses that age-old principle of financial policy: maintaining a fixed monetary standard. However, he does not develop the elements of abstract economic theory in order to analyse an inconsistent tendency not encountered under modern conditions (deflation in connection with silver money, inflation in connection with *Scheidemünzen*). Clearly he was aware that the policy laid down in the '*Rescript*', requiring taxes to be paid in good coin, was one that the public would find oppressive. The Duke's approach was that of a modern government that—as Great Britain once did for the sake of the gold standard—clings to a high exchange rate; in this analogy the Weimar taxpayers, who were accustomed to deal in small change, resembled importers needing to go to great expense in order to be able to pay in foreign currency (the costly leaf thaler).

Influences of economic thought

Goethe's behaviour was probably, his writing certainly and verifiably, influenced by advances in the economic sciences. His lifetime overlapped with no fewer than five different 'schools' of political economy. In other words, he lived through all the discipline's basic developmental phases. Before his day there had really only been the economics of the Ancient World and the Middle Ages, of which as a historically and philosophically educated person he will inevitably have had some notion. That Goethe made a study of the five contemporary schools is vouched for in detail by Mahl[14] in his thorough examination of the writer's knowledge of economics. I intend to state here my own view of those schools, and in one respect my findings differ from those of Mahl. As we shall see, Goethe moved away from the ideas of the Cameralist authors, who all championed their respective princes and were primarily concerned with filling the royal coffers. On the whole, Mahl rightly stressed this, although Goethe, particularly in the coinage report, did eventually come down in favour of the fiscal interest. However, what strikes me as even more important is that Goethe clung to concepts and approaches that were Cameralist in a further sense—despite his liberal championing of tolerance and market freedom. This needs explaining in greater detail.

In the early modern period, long before industrialisation and the emergence of modern capitalism, the expanding web of commerce, guild-controlled craft-trade production, then the outwork system and manufacturing, began first to complement and later to supplant feudal forms of production until eventually, in parts of Europe—Britain, especially—even agriculture became capitalistic in that the land, while remaining the property of the aristocracy, was let out to tenant farmers in return for rent. National economic units came into being, held together politically by Absolutism, a system of rule that promoted trade within the territory, curbed the local power of the aristocracy, and encouraged merchants to settle colonies by granting them certain privileges. In this so-called 'mercantile' period money and credit, notably exchange business, were supported by the minting and circulation of gold or silver coins, the purchasing power of which was essentially governed by precious-metal costs. Without such coinage the payment system could not function. Countries that had no precious-metal resources of their own were therefore obliged to acquire this indispensable means of money-circulation by exporting goods to such silver-producing countries as Saxony, Tyrol, or—following the discovery of America—Spain. The mercantilists, however, took things a step farther: they went from promoting trade, exports, and colonisation for the purpose of acquiring precious metals to investigating the prerequisites for developing an export-oriented system of production as well, eventually, as one that suited the domestic market; they discussed mobilising the workforce and investing in infrastructure such as dikes, canals, roads, and harbours.

In the smaller sovereign territories of the Reich and in the imperial cities, discussion of development policy was from the outset directed more strongly towards the circumstances of domestic development and the resources of the state with regard to supporting these—that is to say, towards taxation. Sovereigns whose luxurious lifestyles and military requirements had previously been funded by their domains, gained additional income from customs duties, indirect taxation, and capital levies but still not—not for many years to come—by taxing individual incomes, since these stemmed from too wide a variety of sources and could not be assessed with sufficient reliability. Just as the achievements of mercantilism were subsequently belittled by being pilloried as a mere striving to increase a country's fortune in gold and silver, the Cameralist variant was caricatured as a theory of the fleecing of subjects through ever more taxes to satisfy the ruling class's taste for luxury. Such truncated forms of Cameralism and mercantilism existed, but there were also some excellent writings that went far beyond this viewpoint and took in the whole landscape of economic affairs. Genuinely understanding mercantilists were aware that entrepreneurs could drive economic growth forward only where markets were sufficiently free. Far-sighted Cameralists saw the good of the state as lying in applying its resources to the development of agriculture and manufacturing, which is why they promoted agricultural reforms and vocational training.

In Goethe's youth, Cameralism dominated the German-speaking world. Although the more systematic main works of the earlier[15] or more recent[16] versions of Cameralism were missing from Goethe's father's library, the shelves did contain travel books, portrayals of countries and cities, and works of cameral and commercial law[17] describing the Cameralistic practices of sovereign governments, and with these Goethe became well acquainted—not least in connection with his own legal studies and with his work as an attorney. Before leaving Frankfurt he tried to shrug off their intellectual influence,[18] but he ordered the work of James Steuart, the most important of the late mercantilists,[19] for himself, and throughout the Weimar years he was working within the Cameralistic tradition trying to simplify the tax system, to move on from the demesne economy to taxing aristocratic estates as well, and to organise and place limits on government spending: in every sphere, as we saw in the case of the coinage system, the forces of conservatism proved hard to overcome.

Goethe's youthful idealism became attached not to the France of the Revolution but to a tendency that, in overcoming the mismanagement of Versailles intellectually, helped pave the way for change. Physiocracy, which in the last twenty years or so preceding the Revolution had gained the intellectual upper hand in Paris, turned against mercantilist interventionism and claimed that social generation was productive solely through agriculture; the physiocrats wanted to replace the complex Cameralistic tax system with a single tax on the true source of wealth—namely agriculture, which at that time still employed over three-quarters of the population.[20] Goethe's ten-year older friend and brother-in-law, Johann Georg Schlosser, was involved in certain physiocratic experiments that the Margrave of Baden, a patron of the French physiocrats, was carrying out in his own territory, but increasingly Schlosser moved away from the pure version of the theory.[21]

Certainly, Goethe resisted a dirigist form of Cameralism, even though as a minister he did occasionally act in this way, and he was attracted by physiocracy's ideas of order, by its aversion to state intervention, and by its exalted view of nature and agriculture, particularly during the period when, like Schlosser, he was reviewing for the periodical *Frankfurter Gelehrte Anzeigen*. According to Ruppert,[22] Goethe had bought a number of books by Johann Georg Büsch in which to study the problems of trade and monetary policy. But the system of political economy he studied in the greatest detail was that of Adam Smith, championed in Germany by a series of not internationally read but nationally significant scholars who included a personal friend of Goethe, Smith's German translator Georg Friedrich Sartorius. On several occasions, too, Goethe met Georg von Buquoy, who made several original contributions to so-called 'classical' political economy. Buquoy also occupied himself with maths and physics and is today best known as an early mathematical economist, although his approach was more widely based and took in more than pure theory.[23] According to information supplied by S. Richter, Buquoy dedicated a copy of his principal work to Goethe with the observation that he, who interested himself in everything 'that the human mind [had] devised', ought also to take an interest in the 'distribution of earthly goods among the nations'. Two groups of pages have been cut: those bearing the 1815 introduction, in which Buquoy sets out his particular systematics of political economy, and, from a supplement added in 1817, those devoted to Buquoy's highly original *Tabellerische Übersicht des Zusammenhangs der Gewerbe unter einander* ('Table Representing the Way the Trades Interconnect')—a kind of input-output table, as we should say nowadays, but captured verbally, showing what the different sectors of the economy from agriculture to transport produce in terms of primary and secondary products, i. e. what which sector supplies to and receives from which other. It looks from this as if Goethe was interested in the material substratum of the classical theory of value but not in taking the subsequent step towards abstraction: which commodity, as a result of production outlay, was worth how much?

Goethe took a more critical stance in relation to another German Smithian, Ludwig Heinrich Jakob.[24] Adam Smith, the true founder of classical political economy, whose work Goethe possessed in his Weimar library, as well as related works in translations by Sartorius,[25] borrowed the idea of laissez-faire from the physiocrats but considered not only agriculture but also commodity-producing labour to be productive. Division of labour could also increase productivity in the industrial sphere. It made production cheaper and therefore contributed to an expansion of sales; however, the larger the markets, the more it was worthwhile taking division of labour further and ultimately using machinery as well. Nowhere does Goethe appear to have taken up the questions relating to theory of value dealt with by Sartorius in his *Abhandlungen* ('Treatises').[26] On the other hand, I do see a similarity when Sartorius contrasts Smith's 'natural' freedom with a 'beneficial' kind[27] and therefore, for all his polemicizing against mercantilism and the natural services of feudalism, extols charitable work by the state like a good Cameralist. What suits Britain does not suit everyone; things do not always work without the state taking the initiative.[28] In a typically German way he takes particular exception to Smith's idea that education may in essence be imparted on a private basis,[29] and he places himself in a German tradition reaching all the way back to Reformation times when he says that the state must curb the dominance of big capital over small.[30] Numerous reviews of books on political economy dealing with this area appeared in periodicals co-published by Goethe, beginning in his Frankfurt period, and there is documentary evidence of the great care and attention he devoted to questions of detail touching on publication of a review of Thornton's book about the circulation of paper money in Great Britain.[31] Thornton's *Enquiry into the Nature and Effects of the Paper Credit of Great Britain* is a work of monetary theory belonging in the classical tradition of political economy, the importance of which for the history of economics was stressed by no less an authority than Hayek. The book includes an analysis of the conditions under which paper money, when issued on the basis of a precious-metal currency, remains stable in value.

Yet the author who was probably a particular favourite of Goethe's from 1773 onwards was someone who is usually mentioned among historians of economic dogma only for having had Goethe as a reader. This was the 'magnificent' Justus Möser, as Goethe called him. 'This incomparable writer's short essays on civic themes had been appearing in the *Osnabrücker Intelligenzblätter* for several years and were brought to my attention by Herder.' Thus begins the passage in *Dichtung und Wahrheit* ('Poetry and Truth') that over three pages,[32] up until 'Such a man impressed us enormously', eulogises a work based not on theory but purely on visual perception,[33] a 'true whole'—although in the form of a collection of essays—in which Goethe extolled the 'most intimate knowledge of bourgeois life', the tension between 'tradition' and 'change', the unprejudiced portrayal of the 'conditions of the classes', towns and villages, the civic and family spheres, ownership and public contributions, the outstripping of craft-trade production by factories, and the place of overseas trade: A 'consummate businessman addresses the nation [...] in many different forms that might be termed poetic and must certainly, in the highest sense of the word, be deemed rhetorical'.[34] Clearly, in Goethe's opinion, Möser was the very embodiment of liberality and humanity, civic understanding and political form—a writer to whom he was deeply attracted because his intuitive approach combined the theoretically systematic and the legally binding so gracefully that no harshness appeared anywhere yet a sensible way forward was indicated none the less. That kind of direct view of development— in this case a metamorphosis not of plants but of society—runs through Goethe's entire work. It is what connects Cameralism—still present today to an extent of which we are barely aware—with the historicism that succeeded it; possessing an importance that modern economists seriously underestimate, it constitutes the living element of their subject.

In Germany, certainly in a more pronounced sense than in other countries, the classical phase of political economy gave way to one marked by historicism. People ceased to believe that economic behaviour was guided purely by self-interest and stressed how it was also affected by cultural factors characterising particular periods and particular nations. The morality that freedom of trade amongst people presupposes is not spontaneously generated thereby but must have its roots in tradition and be watered by education and the law. This is confirmed by the events that followed the break-up of the Soviet Union in Russia, when the world saw that, unless institutions based on the rule of law are created first, the market cannot become established in other than an anarchistic form. The historicist school also saw a role for the state in creating infrastructure, raising the general level of education and training, and protecting younger, newly emergent industries unable to hold their own against foreign competitors such as have already reached a higher stage of development. The true representatives of historicism, Roscher first among them, did not come into their own until after Goethe's death, but they were preceded by economists who used a historicist approach. Marx[35] recalled Gustav von Gülich, whom Goethe read in 1830, praised, and used for the conclusion of his *Faust*.[36] Gülich, who visited a whole series of countries, Britain foremost among them, to make a comparative study of industrialisation, addressed the 'men of state', thinking that:

[they] would be happier to see a single text that takes a historical look at the way the contemporary conditions of industry have emerged, thus throwing more light on the present situation of the same, than many volumes of political economy that, while discussing trade, agriculture, and manufacturing, describe these less in terms of how they have become what they are as of how they should be if they were to fit what the respective authors' theories require.[37]

This kind of historically based, economically coloured empiricism was very much in line with the programme of the historicist school. Certainly, a link to the historicist school can be found in Goethe so far—as is the case, basically, with Cameralism—as the moral foundations of economic conduct and state responsibility for infrastructure and education are concerned. For the rest, Goethe's economic views bore the stamp of a personal liberalism, the nature of which we need to explore more closely.

Goethe was also acquainted with Adam Müller, chief representative of what is known as the romantic school of political economy, and Müller's 'organicism' will have been much to his taste. However, the surviving letters and records of conversations indicate not economic but literary and religious discussions between the two.[38] In Goethe's final years, early socialist writings were beginning to spread throughout Europe, championing cooperatives, trade-union amalgamations, socio-political reforms, and communist Utopias. He read about, had people tell him of, took an interest—sometimes favourable, sometimes sceptical, even disapproving—in the social experiments carried out by American colonists. He was particularly critical of the Frenchman Saint-Simon and his followers. On 28 June 1831 he wrote to Zelter that he:

> had occasion to think about the *Réligion Simonienne*. The sect is headed by some very clever people who are well aware of the shortcomings of our time and good at talking about what is desirable; but when they think they can abolish all wrong and foster and promote what is desirable, their thinking is full of holes.[39]

Goethe's response to the different economic schools and theories

The five approaches of Cameralism/mercantilism, physiocracy, and the liberal/classical, early socialist, and historicist/romanticist schools all left traces in Goethe's work—sometimes in the modest form of brief allusions revealing that Goethe has taken cognisance of a newly fashionable doctrine (physiocracy, for instance), sometimes in the form of a major programmatic discussion, such as when his economic striving has Faust discover the dangers of unregulated capitalism, sometimes (as has perhaps been least commented on before) when Goethe informally grasps older economic forms as being the living expression of local conditions, temporal limits, or national characteristics.

Physiocracy he tackled in a farce-like play, *Der Bürgergeneral* ('Citizen General'), in the context of wider allusions to the economic and political causes of the French Revolution. The play opens with a happily married young peasant couple who, like the farmers so extolled by the physiocrats, contentedly till their little acre. The woman opines, 'And if father simply can't fathom how he is going to save the French nation from its debts, I say: George [her husband; B. S.], we'll just have to make sure we never get into debt'.[40] A fellow villager who acts like a Jacobin turns out to be a complete fool. The nobleman, unlike the judge who behaves like an over-zealous policeman, is shrewd enough not make a big fuss about a French uniform hidden by the phoney revolutionary and says soothingly:

> Calm down! Untimely dictates and untimely forfeits lead only to trouble. In a country whose prince cuts himself off from no one, where all classes think fairly of one another, where no man is prevented from going about his business, where useful views and insights are held in common, there no parties will form.[41]

In other words it is the mismanagement of the French ruling class and the monarchy that paved the way to disaster. So far as the people are concerned, it was a case of: 'Let each man get on with his own life; he'll not lack things to do. Let him make use of the peaceful time vouchsafed to us; let him and his family cultivate their own rightful advantage: that way he'll bring advantage to all'.[42] Developments in France must have struck Goethe as all the more unfortunate for the fact that he had himself, back in the Frankfurt period, looked for salvation through the reforming endeavours of the then Minister of Finance, Turgot. In *Dichtung und Wahrheit* he recalls:

> [...] one wished the Americans every good fortune [...], and now that a new and benevolent King of France was even demonstrating the best of intentions as regarded personally abolishing so many abuses and confining himself, out of the noblest of motives, to introducing a properly adequate system of political economy, forgoing all arbitrary authority [...], there spread throughout the world a mood of the most cheerful hope, with trusting youth believing that they and their contemporaries might look forward to a fine, not to say splendid future.[43]

The unsophisticated return to natural economic forms and benevolent patriarchal government that we find outlined in *Der Bürgergeneral* and this harking-back to the efforts of the physiocrats did not constitute the entirety of Goethe's response to the challenges of the Enlightenment. Keeping to the economic sphere, consider this famous passage from '*Wilhelm Meisters Wanderjahre*' ('Wilhelm Meister's Journeyman Years'). Here Goethe is talking about the risk of technical progress undermining outwork employment in mountain districts, where virtually every house contained a loom that offered the possibility of supplementing the family's meagre income from farming.

> The increasing dominance of machine production torments and frightens me; it is rolling on like a storm, slowly, slowly; but it is headed this way, and it will arrive and strike. [...] The pretty, happy life you witnessed there must still be vividly before you, and the dressed-up crowd gathering from all sides yesterday was wonderful testimony. Think how all this will gradually collapse, wither, and the wilderness, enlivened and populated over centuries, will once more revert to its primeval solitude.[44]

Goethe knows there is a way out, of course:

> Here are but two choices, one as sorry as the other: either to seize on the new development and thus hasten our ruin, or to set out, taking the best and worthiest people with us, and seek a kinder fate across the seas. […] I know perfectly well that people nearby are considering setting up machines and snatching the people's livelihood for themselves.[45]

The writer's prevailing sentiment is one of sadness at the loss of a moribund world; knowing that a new one may emerge—through emigration, for instance—gives consolation but does not take away the sadness. Where Schumpeter saw the development of capitalism as a process of creative destruction, the writer is first overwhelmed by the destructive effect before acknowledging any new creation—if that is the word for it. The economic alternatives of embracing mechanisation or fleeing abroad led to conflicting discussions among classical economists influenced by physiocracy and the followers of Adam Smith. Smith's chief successor, David Ricardo, recognised that lowering the cost of production by introducing machines releases purchasing power, and that this may lead to fresh employment, although not inevitably. In the ancient world and in the Middle Ages, inventions were sometimes suppressed in order to protect existing jobs, but no one wished to abandon the plough and go back to the spade. Goethe took no part in the arguments that raged at the time about the effects of progress on employment. His basic attitude was that the fit must help themselves. We learn as much in another passage of the same book:

> As little as the steam engines can be throttled can anything similar be done in the moral realm. The liveliness of commerce, the continual rustle of paper money, the increase in debts to pay off other debts–all these are frightful elements that the young man of the present confronts. He is fortunate if he is endowed with a moderate, peaceable disposition that neither makes excessive demands on the world nor allows itself to be determined.[46]

Even more clearly does Goethe address the active individual elsewhere in the book when he compares and contrasts physiocratic contentment in landownership with the products of the home, by which he means the results of handicraft and—going beyond Smith—intellectual work, and ultimately with making a fresh start in a foreign land:

> Yes, Nature has ordained it so! A man, born on the land, comes through habit to belong to it; the two grow together, forming the most beautiful ties. […] And yet one may say: even though a man's property is of great worth, even greater worth must be ascribed to his deeds and achievements. Hence, in the large perspective, we may consider landholding as a smaller part of the blessings granted to us. Most of these, and the best of them, are actually to be sought in a life of movement and in that which is gained through such an active life.[47]

Goethe parades before the reader the entrepreneurs, the people who get things done: craftsmen, artists, dealers, people who create something new by relocating to other countries. For Goethe, successful entrepreneurs are responsible; they are prepared to share with their dependants. As we read in the earlier *Wilhelm Meisters Lehrjahre* (Wilhelm Meister's Apprenticeship Years):

> Do I not make much better use of my assets than my father did? Will I not drive my income even higher? And shall I be the only one to enjoy this burgeoning benefit? Shall I not treat the man who works with me and for me in the persons of his family, too, to benefits that expanded knowledge and advancing time offer us?[48]

Goethe's free and open attitude to the world and his faith in the creative power of the individual can be interpreted as liberalism, but despite his friendship with the Adam Smith translator Sartorius he did not unreservedly identify himself with classical liberalism and the free-trade system. Smith himself, thinking of Britain, had overlooked irrefutable items of government spending—in the field of education, for example—and in such backward countries as Germany the state, Sartorius felt, should assume additional economic responsibilities. And Sartorius was the intellectual leader of the German liberal economists. In *Wilhelm Meister*, those who create are not entrepreneurs in the Schumpeterian sense of a process of creative destruction; they do not realise new ideas with the kind of ruthlessness to which profit-maximisation so seductively beckons. Rather they are seen as exemplary figures, capable of looking beyond their own advantage to pursue the interests of a greater whole, and what happens is that cooperative economic ideals and communal forms of upbringing are tried out. Following what later became known as the tradition of 'German political economy', Goethe turned against the one-sided prevalence not only of self-interest but also of eudemonist principles; he also considered the Kantian view of morality as duty to be excessively narrow, writing as an example of what he called a 'meditation on experience':

> Some have taken self-interest to be the mainspring of all moral conduct; others have claimed to identify the desire for well-being, for happiness, as being alone effective; others again gave pride of place to the apodictic sense of duty, and since none of these prerequisites has proved generally acceptable one has ultimately had to derive both the moral and the beautiful from the whole complex of sound human nature.[49]

Here Goethe claims the right, in opposition to the philosophers and their derivation from principles, to describe the moral as well as the beautiful in terms of their appearance as phenomena. There are models of moral conduct in economic affairs in *Wilhelm Meister*, while *Faust* tells of the dangers and limits encountered by the person who, following his own development, infringes the bounds of morality. Here, though, rather than tracing Goethe's explicit portrayals of a good and moral or dubious and dangerous mode of economic conduct, I would prefer to show by means of an example how, as a condition of both, Goethe rendered the economic perceptible on an everyday (weekday and feast-day) basis, combining Intuitive Theory and a Cameralist view of economics.

Goethe's intuitive theory and the Cameralist vision of economics

'I too in Arcadia!' is the motto Goethe attached to his *Italienische Reise* ('Italian Journey'), the record of the beautiful time he spent in the pre-Revolutionary south, discovering the joyful Mediterranean lifestyle and the art of the Ancient World that underlay it. He described the journey in letters, and it is these, with the addition of a number of essays, that constitute the essence of the book. He gives proof of his almost unbelievable productivity not only in his reception and portrayal of all he saw but also in writing, continuing, and indeed even completing several major works on his travels and while living in Rome. He writes of tracks, roads, and carriages, of inns and amorous encounters, of fig trees and cornfields, of volcanism and primitive plants, of Raphael's paintings and of temples, of the chaotic Vatican state and of Magna Graecia, mostly in a cheerful manner and with the kind of sense awareness that, according to Friedrich Gundolf, marks Goethe's genius and the way he saw the world:

> Goethe *looked for intuition*, not feeling or even elevation. Visual perception: that, for him, was the union of 'I' and external world: it is in the eye that the seeing person […] places him/herself and the world on the same level […]. It was primarily as a seeing person, educating his eye, that Goethe undertook his Italian journey.[50]

Few authors have pointed out that the *Italian Journey* also contains sense awareness of economic circumstances, the reason being that we are used to talking about these in such non-sensory, abstract terms as 'gross domestic product', 'share price', or 'employment gap'. The other programme—so-called 'Intuitive Theory'—is one that Edgar Salin, following on from Gundolf and Edith Landmann, developed from the scientific approach of the group of economists around Stefan George,[51] using it to characterise the method of describing the economic sphere adopted by Werner Sombart and the most recent historical school. Let us start with Goethe's own words:

> Visual perception is akin to *imagination*; it is first *imitative*, simply rehearsing objects. Subsequently, it is *productive* in that it animates what it has captured, developing it, extending it, transforming it. […] Here we see the desirability of analogy, which moves the mind on many related points in order that its activity may re-unite everything relevant, everything that matches. This gives direct rise to *allegories* which are of greater value, the more closely they approximate to the thing they are called upon to elucidate. But the finest allegories are those that coincide with the thing completely and appear identical with it.[52]

Intuition does not simply see things in given forms; it also has at its disposal a 'living power of imagination' that 'pursues the thing perceived into the unseeable depths of nature lying beyond the senses'.[53] In this way, visual perception ultimately captures a whole from which the parts are understood. Goethe, for instance, experiences the city of Rome with its two-thousand-year history as a whole that through visual perception and imagination takes shape within him as he strolls its streets. That kind of seeing needs to be learnt:

> One realised, then, how necessary it is, in bringing up a child, not to eliminate imagination but to direct it, to impart to it, by presenting it early on with noble images, a yearning for beauty, a thirst for magnificence. In vain do we seek to suppress sensuality, to educate the intellect, to secure the dominance of reason; the imagination lies in wait like the most potent enemy. Nature has endowed it with an irresistible impulse towards the absurd that even in educated minds wields great power and in the most respectable company, countering every civilising influence, will resurrect the innate coarseness of the grimace-loving barbarians.[54]

Faced with the undirected imagination, the artist's whole duty is to learn to 'make it precise, to hold it fast, and finally to imbue it with presence'.[55]

Regarding the intuitive theory of economists, it is particularly the examinations of economic styles in the interwar years made by Bechtel, Spiethoff, and others that matter.[56] Spiethoff draws up a somewhat formal but nonetheless useful and much-quoted schema of the principal features of economic styles. According to him, these are characterised by the coherence of (1) an economic approach or mentality, (2) the natural and technological foundations of the economy, (3) the constitution of the economy, (4) the constitution of society, and (5) a specific dynamic. However, as I have tried to show elsewhere,[57] the endeavour is very much older, at least in Germany. The hierarchical theories of the historicist school are already, in the work of Bruno Hildebrand and Karl Bücher, aimed essentially at stylising previously existent economic forms in the sense of ideal types, not at nailing the chimera of faithful representation. In the historicist school, economics in the strict sense of material reproduction overflowed, as in Cameralism, into sociology, and politics. The historicist school is rooted in descriptions of the various different national economic forms of the mercantilist period; it delighted in portraying, comparing, and contrasting the ways in which economic forms varied geographically and in temporal succession in conjunction with political ideas and institutions, national character, resources currently available, and the economic operations and industries that had developed as a result. Conditions as they had existed in classical antiquity offered an ideal standard of measurement, as did still uncivilised peoples one of comparison, oriental empires a challenge, and the competitiveness of European nations the chief object of investigation— the findings of which were of course often given in purely anecdotal terms.

A famous summary of this literature nourished by travel accounts and voyages of discovery was made by Giovanni Botero.[58] Even more comprehensive and systematic is Kaspar Klock, writing two generations later, during the Thirty Years' War. As part of a massive study of national finances, Klock presented a survey of the countries of the world, their political systems, and their economic output, in conjunction with their respective 'national natures' and state funding potential. He specified five headings under which he intended to structure the study of each country. This was not in fact executed consistently, but there are astonishing parallels between his headings and those of later research into economic styles:

Klock (1651)

1 *Ratio Reipublicae*
2 *Populi natura*
3 *Regnorum jura*
4 *Populi condition*
5 *Reditus Regnorum*

Spiethoff (1932)

1 Economic spirit
2 Natural and technical foundations
3 Constitution of the economy
4 Constitution of society
5 Economic dynamic

Differences and similarities are easy to spot. Klock's *Ratio Reipublicae* is the same as *raison d'état* or the *raggione di stato* that goes back to Botero and Machiavelli, while 'economic spirit' refers not so much to the political as to the economic mode of thinking. *Populi natura* is the manner in which people conduct themselves; it relates to properties of physique and character. There follow, in Klock's list, the system of law and the conditions in which people live, seen both outwardly and socially—examples being their housing and the forms their families take. Finally comes the presumed key to understanding. With Klock, this lies in state financing and state revenues; with Spiethoff, a state's economic dynamic provides the foundation for its capacity to develop.

Goethe's autobiographical writings—notably the *Italian Journey*—reveal him as standing in this Cameralist tradition, not in the sense of the 'evil' Cameralism that squeezes the people in order that its rulers may live in greater luxury but in the sense of an interest that takes account of every detail of economic institutions with a view to understanding and promoting the whole as an organism. The 'Italian journey' made by Goethe's father already shows signs of such interests— for example, when its author compares the states of Genoa and Venice and their patrician yet republican constitutions. Johann Caspar affords Genoese families scope to pursue their mercantile interests in the belief that these serve the interests of the whole, while according to his son particular institutions in Venice are designed to curb differences in wealth among its leading families, the better to secure their political dominance.[59] Goethe's own son August continues his father's observations in describing the climate, institutions, agriculture, and manners of Lombardy.[60] All three of them, for instance—father, son, and grandson—take an interest in silkworm breeding. The Cameralistic tradition is also in evidence in connection with Goethe's reading habits. Granted, we have seen how he took issue with Smith and the advocates of free trade, and he was also a personal friend of Buquoy's, who pioneered the introduction of mathematical ideas into economics, but the books he bought and read for preference were Cameralist studies concerning problems of agriculture, how to combat pests, concrete monetary institutions. There are more of such studies on the shelves of his library before the turn of the century, but there are also some dating from the 1820s. When he reaches the south of Italy, as he reports on 12 April 1787, he is shown coins belonging to the countries of Magna Graecia. 'The brilliance of the Sicilian cities, now dimmed, gleams freshly again from these moulded metals. The splendour of Sicilian cities, now obscured, shines out of these shaped pieces of metal with its original freshness.'[61] He recalls how, in the Ancient World, Sicily was the granary of Italy, yet he finds the potential for grain production in the hinterland of Palermo, his first stop, almost non-existent. To this 'whim' he sacrifices Syracuse, the chance of seeing archaeological remains, possibly a more comfortable journey by boat to the east coast, instead crossing the interior to Catania in the hope of understanding Sicily's wheat culture. He acquires a book on the subject and does not regret the digression despite the fact that spending days travelling through fields also bores him and he yearns occasionally for 'the winged chariot of Triptolemos [...] to escape from this monotony'.[62] The book[63] of course he never reads—it still lies in his library uncut—because he has now *seen* and can concentrate on art again.

Economic life from the Alps to Sicily

From the start of the trip Goethe seeks to take an 'interest in the world'. He is keen, he writes, to 'try out my spirit of observation, test [...] whether my eye is clear, pure, and bright, how much I can take in at speed [...]'.[64] A lot of what he saw can be arranged under Klock's headings (see above). Take *populi natura*, the 'character of the people'. Goethe has travelled no farther than Bolzano:

> Seeing so many merchant faces gathered in one spot pleased me. Their expression very clearly bespeaks a purposeful, comfortable existence. On the square were sitting female fruit vendors with flat, round baskets over four feet in diameter, in which peaches lay side by side, so as not to press each other. The pears likewise.[65]

When he reaches the plain of Verona, the people no longer seem to him so full of life but the townsfolk look better.[66] Venice: 'What again claims my attention above all else is the populace, a great mass, a necessary, instinctive existence'.[67]

He does not praise everything about the character of the people. He is thoroughly displeased—repeatedly so, throughout the journey—with the lack of cleanliness. On his first arrival he is horrified when he enquires of a manservant about performing a certain business and the man, gesturing towards the courtyard below, utters the words, 'qui abasso può servirsi!'[68] And in Venice this statesman, on leave from Weimar, writes, 'As I strolled along, I could not resist drafting a set of regulations for this purpose, preparing the way, in my thoughts, for a sanitary supervisor who would take his task seriously. Thus one is always ready and eager to sweep before someone else's door'.[69]

Then again there are times when he can identify very happily with the character of the people. When someone calls out 'Felicissima notte!' to him, he writes, 'Thus the idiomatic expressions of one language cannot be translated into another; for, from the basest to the most sublime, every word relates to the nation's peculiarities, whether of character, sentiments, or conditions'.[70] On the other hand: 'the papal state seems to survive only because the earth refuses to swallow it'.[71] Klock's verdict was similar: the Vatican State, he said, was like vinegar made from the finest wine.[72]

Wherever he goes Goethe comments on agriculture; he is critical of the fact that the Tuscan plough has no wheels and that the ploughshare is fixed; he examines fertilisation, mentions details regarding wheat, beans, flax, and olive trees, extols diligence, and rails against the inadequacy of his carriage: 'This Italy, which enjoys nature's richest favour, has lagged very badly behind other countries with respect to mechanics and technology, which after all are the basis of a more modern and comfortable way of life'.[73]

Following his first stay in Rome, which was almost wholly taken up with art-watching: 'We approached Naples in an atmosphere of the purest brightness'. Goethe's first impression is almost a cliché: 'Everybody is out on the street and sitting in the sun, as long as it goes on shining. The Neapolitan believes himself in the possession of Paradise, and has a very dismal conception of the countries in the north: '*Sempre neve, case di legno, gran ignoranza, ma denari assai*'.[74] 'Immediate gratification, temperate enjoyment, cheerful toleration of temporary afflictions!'[75] or: 'I find these people to be the most eagerly and ingeniously industrious, not in order to become rich, but to live in a carefree manner'.[76] But then, admiring the equilibrium with which agriculture is practised, after his Sicilian excursion, he takes a different view. When others maintain that Naples contains tens of thousands of idlers, he retorts:

> Of course, very soon after I had acquired some knowledge of conditions in the south, I surmised that this might well be the Northern way of thinking, according to which anyone who does not toil scrupulously the entire day is considered an idler. Therefore I paid particular attention to the common people, whether in action or at rest, and could, to be sure, see many poorly clothed persons, but no unoccupied ones.[77]

There follows detailed evidence of those various occupations: the bearer, the bargee, the fisherman, even children appeared to Goethe to be 'occupied in a number of ways'.[78] He describes how he sees a very serious-looking lad moving about carrying melons and selling them by the slice:

> It is true that one cannot go many steps without encountering some very poorly clothed or even ragged individual, but that does not mean he is an idler, a sluggard. Indeed, I am tempted to advance the paradox that in Naples, comparatively speaking, perhaps the greatest industriousness is to be found among the lowest classes.[79]

Goethe wonders how far the explanation should be sought in climatic conditions, but then, thinking of the Ancient World, recalls how Pliny praises Magna Graecia, criticises the common view as too general and gives it as his opinion of the 'humble folk' of Naples that 'Without exception this class of people has very lively temperament and a candid, straightforward gaze.[80]

One question that remains unasked is that of the incomes of the upper classes, the well-to-do bourgeoisie, the clergy, and the nobility, amongst whom Goethe moved easily during his journey, sometimes incognito, sometimes as a celebrated young author of European standing. This was not a case of repression; rather, any critical, analytical approach or taking of sides, whether revolutionary or reactionary in tendency, was supplanted, as the mirror image of a feeling of belonging to the upper class, by a sense of identification with the lower orders, a participation in the lives of innkeepers, carriage drivers, farmers, and fisherfolk.

Goethe scattered his observations of the Italian economy rather by the by; he would have devised his own system had he had occasion to bring those observations together. Summarising his findings ourselves, we can perhaps characterise his distinguishing features of an economic style as follows:

1   Nature of the people and their religion.
2   Agriculture.
3   Buildings.
4   Language and custom.
5   Order as kept by police.

Agriculture and buildings attract the highest number of detailed references, which of course cannot be listed here. Order—or the lack of it—is about more than mere cleanliness; it also concerns questions of labour organisation, leisure time and such ceremonies as church-going and theatre-going, for it still goes without saying—this too was for Cameralists a 'police matter'—that the state lays down a template for life's courses, which here distinguishes the countries of Italy in harmony with their differing political forms.

Adopting this standpoint gives one a fresh view of the Roman carnival portrayed at the end of the *Italian Journey*. Goethe researchers tend to read this with some unease: why such consideration of a custom that Goethe did not actually like? He himself writes, 'The Roman carnival is a festival that really is not given to the people, but one the people give themselves. The state makes few arrangements for it, and goes to little expense'.[81] Here too, intuition is primary and the imagination called upon, albeit not without method. Recalling the cruder aspects of the carnival, the risk involved in racing horses in such limited space, Goethe concludes:

> If we may continue to speak more seriously than the subject seems to warrant, then we shall make the observation that the most intense and extreme pleasure, like those horses flying past, appear to us only for a moment, stir us, and scarcely leave a mark on our mind; that freedom and equality can be enjoyed only in the frenzy of madness; and that, in order to spur us to the highest pitch of excitement, the greatest delights must come into very close proximity with danger and let us want only to savour, in their vicinity, feelings of pleasure mixed with fear.[82]

A few pages later Goethe apologises for having become reconciled to the mad tumult on the grounds that he saw it 'as one more significant natural product and national event'; he had, he says, to 'mingle with the masquerading crowd' although they 'often made a repulsive, weird impression'.[83] The carnival solves the riddle of the unmentioned inequality in yet another fashion—this time not through amiable participation in the life of the people but through level-headed—so far as possible—observation of the 'heat of madness', in which equality becomes reality for the blink of an eye but at the same time leads *ad absurdum*, prompting revulsion and dread. Goethe's *Das römische Carneval* ('The Roman Carnival') came out in 1789, the year of the French Revolution, and in the city of the Pope it touches on all the issues that were also of concern to the French kings in Paris: the opposite poles of law and its overthrow, government and anarchy, nobility and bourgeoisie, rich and poor, self-control and unbridled passion, grace and terror.

A rationally thought-through capitalism *à la* Max Weber is not something Goethe seems to see anywhere. The question of the justice of the entire order is left open; that order is experienced. Rational capitalism is not something we find in Goethe, either as vision of the future or as interpretation of the present, either as lure or as danger. In his positive vision of market economics or capitalism, the world of business and entrepreneurship is imbued with a morality that holds extreme forms of profiteering and exploitation in check. Goethe's bogeyman of a capitalism that looks modern to us—such as that evoked in '*Faust*'—bears essentially irrational features. His interpretation of a more moderate, earlier world such as we have just traced in connection with the *Italian Journey* is associated by religion, morality, and political forms with the circumstances of pre-Revolutionary Europe. Historically, politically, and economically his liberal ideal—liberal in the classical sense, as outlined above—of a society of educated, responsible, sensitive, and kind-hearted people stood at the centre of his world. We might say that this ideal becomes *Anschauung* for us, becomes visual perception, through the poems and through Goethe's life, but his liberalism—unlike Smith's, for whom it stood for a theory and a system—his liberalism was different: a liberality of outlook, as in the Ancient World, a stance, the way one lived one's life. For Faust it is action that takes precedence, not words; similarly, in *Maximen und Reflectionen* ('Maxims and Reflexions') Goethe writes:

> When I hear talk of liberal ideas, I am always amazed at how people offer one another empty verbal husks. An idea should not be liberal; let it be forceful, hearty, self-sufficient—that way it will obey the divine injunction to be productive [...].[84]

Notes

1 ['Der Dichtung Schleier aus der Hand der Wahrheit']. Johann Wolfgang Goethe, *Sämtliche Werke. Briefe, Tagebücher und Gespräche*, 40 vols. (Frankfurt am Main: Deutscher Klassiker Verlag, 1985–1999). Henceforth referred to as: FA, part, vol. Here: part I, vol. 1, p. 11.

2 Wilhelm Roscher, *Geschichte der National-Oekonomik in Deutschland* (Munich: Oldenbourg, 1874), 477.

3 Ibid., 478f.

4 Ibid., 479.

5 Benny Moldovanu and Manfred Tietzel, "Goethe's second-price auction," *Journal of Political Economy* 106/4 (1998), 854–859.

6 Cf. Bertram Schefold, "Goethe und das Wirtschaftsleben," in *Liber Amicorum. Katharina Mommsen zum 85. Geburtstag* ed. Andreas Remmel (Bonn: Bernstein, 2010), 483–516.

7 *Goethe's Werke. Vollständige Ausgabe letzter Hand* (Stuttgart: J. G. Cotta, 1827–1842).

8 Cf. Manfred Tietzel, *Literaturökonomik* (Tübingen: Mohr, 1995).

9 Bertram Schefold, *Beiträge zur ökonomischen Dogmengeschichte*, selected and ed. by Volker Caspari (Darmstadt: Verl. Wirtschaft und Finanzen, 2004).

10 *Goethes amtliche Schriften*, ed. Willy Flach, 4 vols. (Weimar: H. Böhlaus Nachfolger, 1950–87), vol. II.1, 353–355.

11 Cf. ibid., col. III, p. 145.

12 German technical term for small change or token coins with an upper limit on the purchaser's requirement to accept them in payment as legal tender.

13 *Goethes amtliche Schriften*, vol. II.1, 383.

14 Bernd Mahl, *Goethes ökonomisches Wissen* (Frankfurt am Main: P. Lang, 1982).

15 Kaspar Klock, *Tractatus juridico-politico-polemico-historicus De Aerario* [1651], ed. and introduced by Bertram Schefold (Hildesheim and New York: Olms, 2009).

16 J. H. G. von Justi, *Grundsätze der Policey-Wissenschaft* [1756]. Facsimile edition with a commentary volume, ed. by Bertram Schefold (Düsseldorf: Verl. Wirtschaft u. Finanzen, 1993).

17 Franz Götting, "Die Bibliothek von Goethes Vater," in: *Rechts- und Staatswissenschaften, Geographie. Nassauische Annalen* 64 (1953), 59–64.

18 Mahl, *Goethes ökonomisches Wissen*, ch. II.1.

19 FA, II/2, no. 112; cf. Bertram Schefold, "Die Verbindung von Theorie, Geschichte und Politik bei James Steuart," in *Vademecum zu einer klassischen Synthese von Theorie, Geschichte und Politik. Kommentarband zur Faksimile-Ausgabe der 1767 in zwei Bänden erschienenen Erstausgabe von James Steuart*, An Inquiry into the Principles of Political Oeconomy (Düsseldorf: Verlag Wirtschaft u. Finanzen, 1993), 5–16.

20 Rainer Gömmel and Rainer Klump, *Merkantilisten und Physiokraten in Frankreich* (Darmstadt: Wissenschaftliche Buchgesellschaft, 1994).

21 Johann Georg Schlosser, *Xenocrates oder Ueber die Abgaben, 1784*, ed. Rainer Klump (Marburg: Metropolis Verlag, 2000).

22 Hans Ruppert, *Goethes Bibliothek. Katalog* (Weimar: Arion Verlag, 1958).

23 Christos Baloglou and Bertram Schefold, "Einleitung," in: Georg von Buquoy, *Die Theorie der Nationalwirtschaft*, reprint of the 1918 edition (Hildesheim: Olms, 2005), V–XXXVII.

24 Bertram Schefold, introduction to Ludwig Heinrich Jakob, *Grundsätze der National-Oekonomie oder National-Wirtschaftslehre* (Hildesheim: Olms, 2004), pp. V–XLV.

25 Cf. Ruppert, *Bibliothek*, 434.

26 Georg Sartorius, *Abhandlungen, die Elemente des National-Reichthums und die Staatswirthschaft betreffend* (Göttingen: J. F. Röwer, 1806).

27 Ibid., 205.

28 Ibid., 494.

29 Ibid., 497.

30 Ibid., 477.

31 Henry Thornton, *An Enquiry into the Nature and Effects of the Paper Credit of Great Britain* (London: Printed for J. Hatchard et al., 1802).

32 FA, I/14, 648–650.

33 On the contrast between visual perception and theory, cf. Bertram Schefold, "Edgar Salin and his concept of Visual Theory During the Interwar Period," *Annals of the Society for the History of Economic Thought* 46 (2004), 1–16.

34 FA, I/14, 648–650.

35 Karl Marx, *Das Kapital. Kritik der politischen Ökonomie*, 3 vols. (Berlin: Dietz, 1962–1983), vol. 1 (Marx-Engels-Werke 23), 19.

36 As shown in Mahl, *Goethes ökonomisches Wissen*, 472–483.

37 Gustav von Gülich, *Geschichtliche Darstellung des Handels, der Gewerbe und des Ackerbaus*, 2 vols. (Jena: F. Frommann, 1830), VII.

38 FA, II/6, no. 174; cf. also *Briefe an Goethe*, collected with commentary and notes by Karl Robert Mandelkow, 2 vols. (Hamburg: C. Wegner, 1965–1969), vol. I, nos. 330 and 334; Johann Wolfgang Goethe, *Gedenkausgabe der Werke, Briefe und Gespräche*, 27 vols., 3rd ed. (Munich: Artemis, 1977), vol. XXII, pp. 468, 470, 858, vol. XXIII, 39.

39 FA, II/11, no. 828.

40 FA, I/6, p. 115.

41 FA, I/6, p. 149

42 FA, I/6, p. 148.

43 FA, I/14, p. 770.

44 Johann Wolfgang von Goethe, Wilhelm Meister's Journeyman Years, in: Goethe, *The Collected Works*, vol. 10, Conversations of German Refugees + Wilhelm Meister's Journeyman Years, ed. Jane K. Brown (Princeton, NJ: Princeton University Press, 1994), 93–435, at 396.

45 Goethe, Wilhelm Meister's Journeyman Years, see above, 396.

46 Ibid., 298.

47 Ibid., 364.

48 FA, I/9, 807.

49 Taken from a 'report' [*Zeugnis*] that Goethe wrote for his friend, interpreter, and translator Carlyle, in: *Goethes Briefwechsel mit Thomas Carlyle*, ed. by Georg Hecht (Dachau: Einhorn [1913]), 39.

50 Friedrich Gundolf, *Goethe*, 2nd ed. (Berlin: G. Bondi 1917), 364f.

51 Cf. Schefold, "Edgar Salin"; Bertram Schefold, "Die Welt des Dichters und der Beruf der Wissenschaft," in *Wissenschaftler im George-Kreis. Die Welt des Dichters und der Beruf der Wissenschaft*, ed. Bernhard Böschenstein, Jürgen Egyptien, B. S. and Count Wolfgang Vitzthum (Berlin: De Gruyter, 2005), 1–33; Bertram Schefold, "Politische Ökonomie als 'Geisteswissenschaft'. Edgar Salin und andere Ökonomen um Stefan George," in *Studien zur Entwicklung der ökonomischen Theorie* XXVI ed. Harald

Hagemann (Berlin: Duncker & Humblot, 2011), 149–210; Korinna Schönharl, *Wissen und Visionen. Theorie und Politik der Ökonomen im Stefan Georg-Kreis* (Berlin: Akademie Verlag, 2009).

52 From a letter Goethe wrote to Knebel on 21 February 1821, FA, II/9, no. 463.

53 FA, II/9, no. 457; cf. Shu Ching Ho, *Über die Einbildungskraft bei Goethe. System und Systemlosigkeit* (Freiburg: Rombach, 1998), 90.

54 *Annalen*, 1805, FA, I/17, p. 178.

55 Goethe, *Wilhelm Meister's Journeyman Years*, 271; FA, I/10, p. 521; cf. Ho, *Einbildungskraft*, 104.

56 Cf. Bertram Schefold, *Wirtschaftsstile*, 2 vols. (Frankfurt: Fischer Taschenbuch-Verlag, 1994–1995), vol. 1: *Studien zum Verhältnis von Ökonomie und Kultur*.

57 Introduction to Klock, *Tractatus*.

58 Giovanni Botero, *Le Relationi Universali di Giovanni Botero* (1596).

59 Johann Caspar Goethe, *Reise durch Italien im Jahre 1740* (*Viaggio per l'Italia*), ed. by the German-Italian League [*Deutsch-Italienische Vereinigung*], Frankfurt, transl. from the Italian and annotated by Albert Meier in conjunction with Heide Hollmer, 4th ed. (Munich: C. H. Beck, 1999), 60f., and 436.

60 August von Goethe, *Auf einer Reise nach Süden. Tagebuch 1830*, ed. by Andreas Beyer and Gabriele Radecke, (Munich: Hanser, 2003), 93–97.

61 Goethe, *The Collected Works*, vol. 6, *Italian Journey*, ed. by Thomas P. Saine and Jeffrey L. Sammons (Princeton, NJ: Princeton University Press), 201.

62 Ibid., 225.

63 Anon., *Riflessioni su l'economia e l'estrazione de' frumenti della Sicilia fatte in occasione della carestia* (Palermo, 1785).

64 Goethe, *Italian Journey*, see above (fn. 61), p. 2.

65 Ibid., 25.

66 Ibid., 35f.

67 Ibid., 58.

68 Ibid., 29.

69 Ibid., 61.

70 Ibid., 69.

71 Ibid., 94.

72 Klock, *Tractatus*, vol. I, 27.

73 Goethe, *Italian Journey*.

74 Ibid., 151f.

75 Ibid., 163.

76 Ibid., 164.

77 Ibid., 263.

78 Ibid., 263.

79 Ibid., 265.

80 Ibid., 266f.

81 Ibid., 390.

82 Ibid., 414.

83 Ibid., 419.

84 FA, I/13, 117.

Part III

Vested interests, contingency and the shaping of the free trade doctrine

6 From privilege to economic law

Vested interests and the origins of free trade theory in France (1687–1701)

Moritz Isenmann

Adam Smith and the international division of labour: an 'intellectual' success story?

In the 'Conclusions on the Mercantile System' in the fourth book of his *Wealth of Nations*, Adam Smith identified as the 'two great engines' by which this alleged system 'proposes to enrich every country', the encouragement of exportation and the discouragement of importation, especially with regard to manufactured goods.[1] While certain other parts of the 'mercantile system' such as the imputed confusion of wealth with money were arguably an Aunt Sally set up by the moral philosopher for the sole purpose of being knocked down,[2] Smith was certainly right as far as the 'two great engines' were concerned. A great deal of government attention during the seventeenth and eighteenth centuries – be it in England, France or the Netherlands – centred indeed (although to varying degree) on the protection of home industries by such 'mercantilistic' means.[3] According to Smith, however, this policy was severely flawed. It not only had turned commerce, which should be a 'bond of union and friendship' among individuals as well as among nations into the 'most fertile source of discord and animosity'.[4] From a more strictly economic point of view, by restricting imports through high import duties or outright prohibitions of similar foreign commodities, governments had created monopolies for producers on the home market, prescribing merchants somehow where to invest and thereby diverting their capital into less profitable employments for the national economy. Furthermore, it had inverted the relationship between production and consumption, enriching a small group of merchants and manufacturers at the expense of the wider population:

> Consumption is the sole end and purpose of all production; and the interest of the producer ought to be attended to, only so far as it may be necessary for promoting that of the consumer. The maxim is so perfectly self-evident, that it would be absurd to attempt to prove it. But in the mercantile system, the interest of the consumer is almost constantly sacrificed to that of the producer; and it seems to consider production, and not consumption, as the ultimate end and object of all industry and commerce.

In the restraints upon the importation of all foreign commodities which can come into competition with those of our own growth, or manufacture, the interest of the home-consumer is evidently sacrificed to that of the producer. It is altogether for the benefit of the latter, that the former is obliged to pay that enhancement of price which this monopoly almost always occasions.[5]

Smith himself proposed a very different system based on free international trade, in which merchants – not protected any more against foreign competition by the government but instead guided by the 'invisible hand' of the market – automatically invested their capital in those branches of the national economy which were most profitable for the country, while the 'public' would profit by being offered the products it needed always at the lowest possible price. Thereby, Smith put forward what has later been named the theory of 'absolute advantage' in international trade:

> If a foreign country can supply us with a commodity cheaper than we ourselves can make it, better buy it of them with some part of the produce of our own industry, employed in a way in which we have some advantage. [...] Whether the advantages which one country has over another, be natural or acquired, is in this respect of no consequence. As long as the one country has those advantages, and the other wants them, it will always be more advantageous for the latter, rather to buy of the former than to make.[6]

Smith's idea of an international division of labour based on the element of production costs proved tremendously influential. From his theory of 'absolute' advantage, there would be a relatively small step to the concept of 'comparative' advantage developed by David Ricardo some years later in his *Principles of Political Economy and Taxation* (1817),[7] which since then and for a very long time has been one of the undisputed cornerstones of the theory of international trade.[8]

Recent trends in economics and in the history of economic thought suggest, however, that 'mercantilist' policy was most probably not as flawed as Smith would have thought. Far from being based solely on the balance of trade theory, which Smith qualified as completely 'absurd',[9] the rationale behind the protection of home industries was that there existed a fundamental difference between the agrarian and the industrial sector and that the latter – creating more added value, more possibilities of employment and not being constantly threatened by climatic vagaries that remained beyond human control – was so essential for the well-being of a country as to definitely deserve protection.[10] In order to be able to put the element of production costs at the centre of thinking about international trade, Smith and Ricardo had to go by this basic difference between the agrarian and the industrial sector and the (fairly obvious) fact that profits made in the latter are in general by far greater than profits made in the former.[11] As early as 1979, Fernand Braudel, in the third volume of his *Civilisation matérielle, économie et capitalisme*, therefore mocked the theory of cost advantage as an 'allegedly "irrefutable" pseudo-theorem'.[12] Over the past years, some economists have further underscored the problems posed by this bedrock of classical trade theory.[13] On top of the aforementioned aspects, these economists point out that the production of manufactured goods shows increasing returns to scale (meaning that output increases over-proportionally compared to the input of the productive factors, for instance due to learning and specialization/division of labour effects), while production in the agricultural sector usually leads to diminishing returns to scale upon the extension of production. Therefore, as Erik Reinert has put it, a country that specializes in the production of agricultural goods specializes in 'being poor'.[14]

In what way does the fact that Smith's idea of the international division of labour has lost a great deal of its persuasive force affect our understanding of the idea of free international trade from a historical point of view? The answer to this question depends considerably on the way in which we conceive its origins. Because of their supposed irrefutability and 'self-evidence', the idea of free trade and of cost advantage have generally been considered as the result of intellectual advancement during the eighteenth century.[15] If we stick to this 'intellectual' version of its origins, we might have to see it as just another confirmation of Arthur Cecil Pigou's famous sentence that the history of economic ideas is about 'wrong ideas of dead men'. I think, however, that we can obtain far more interesting insights if we question this 'intellectual' explanation of its origins and investigate other factors, which might have substantially contributed to its development such as the fundamental element Smith went by in his theory, i.e. the difference between the agrarian and the manufacturing sector.

As Erik Reinert explains, one of the keys to a country's successful economic development is an equilibrated relationship between agricultural activities and manufacturing (or 'Schumpeterian' activities). Even more interesting for the present analysis, however, is Reinert's fundamental insight that there are different groups or classes supporting these different activities and that they may have vested interests in the development of their respective sectors. Reinert identifies several occasions in history where such differing vested interests entered into conflict. One example was sixteenth-century Castile, where the victory of landowners over artisans and manufacturers led to a deindustrialization of the country, which proved extremely unfavourable for its economic development.[16] Similarly, the American Civil War to Reinert 'was essentially [a war] between Southern landowners with vested interests in agriculture [...] and the North with vested interests in industrialization'.[17] From the vantage point of this hypothesis I would like to suggest in this essay that the theory of an international division of labour based on the criterion of absolute production costs, as it emerged during the eighteenth century in European economic discourse, was essentially the outcome of a conflict between such vested – agricultural and manufacturing – interests. We find the origins of this conflict and accordingly the formulation of the absolute cost advantage theorem in late seventeenth- and early eighteenth-century French debates about taxation and industry. These ideas were later on picked up by Scottish and other British philosophers and political economists turning them – wittingly or unwittingly – into 'eternal truths'. Whilst it would be interesting to trace the analytical background of this mutation in late eighteenth- and nineteenth-century political economy further, only the origins of this very powerful idea will be considered here.

Possible sources and 'forerunners': the trail leads to France...

What can be said about possible sources and 'forerunners' for Smith's theory of 'absolute advantage'? According to Jacob Viner, there was an 'eighteenth-century rule' held by many authors stating 'that it pays to import commodities from abroad whenever they can be obtained in exchange for exports at a smaller real cost than their production at home would entail'.[18] But unfortunately Viner does not cite many examples for such authors. English authors prior to Adam Smith normally hailed as predecessors of classical political economy or at least as 'moderate mercantilists' such as Nicholas Barbon, Dudley North or Charles Davenant do not mention it at all. In fact, Viner misinterprets the traditional vision of a providential distribution of goods amongst different countries as a forerunner of absolute and comparative cost theory. There was indeed a widespread opinion which had originated in late Antiquity and which was still present in the seventeenth and eighteenth centuries that God had distributed His goods amongst different countries in order to make human beings depend on each other and force them to enter into peaceful contact by means of international commerce.[19] As Edward Misselden noted:

> And to the end there should be a *Commerce* amongst men, it hath pleased *God* to inuite as it were, one Country to traffique with another, by the variety of things which the *One hath*, and the *other hath not*: so that which is wanting to the *One*, might be supplied by the *Other*, that all might have sufficient.[20]

Such statements sound already very much like Smith and Ricardo – but only if we see them through Viner's neoliberal looking glass.[21] For this theory of a 'universal economy' did not contain any reference to prices or production costs. Far from that, this definition of commerce meant an exchange of 'necessaries' against 'superfluities', i.e. of goods that were lacking in one country at least in the necessary quantity but were over-abundant in another – not of goods that could be respectively produced at lower cost. It did not resolve the problem of international competition, namely with respect to manufactures. The only example Viner provides in his *Studies in the Theory of International Trade*, which does contain an argumentation involving costs of production, is a tract with the title *Considerations on the East-India Trade* (1701), supposedly written by one Henry Martyn.[22] In this tract, Martyn argued that it would be more convenient for England to import certain products from India since they could be produced there at a lesser cost, instead of producing them at home.[23] But apart from the fact that this treatise seems to have been literally unknown prior to the nineteenth century and therefore does not qualify as a likely source of inspiration for Smith, it is concerned with colonial and re-export trade, not with direct trade between two countries, say England and France or England and Portugal.

If we look further at English debates about direct trade between two countries, we may find authors that were in favour of 'free trade' in the sense of a general possibility to exchange wares and goods, but none who did it on the basis of economic reasoning foreshadowing classical theory. Tories in favour of an Anglo-French commercial treaty in the wake of the Peace of Utrecht (1713) pleaded for freer trade with France on rather 'mercantilist' grounds. The case made by the supporters of that treaty, such as Daniel Defoe in the *Mercator* rested on the assumption that trade with France was favourable for England as it showed a positive balance of trade and that the lower tariffs promised by the treaty would allow crushing French woollen manufactures. David Hume, another alleged 'forerunner' of modern trade theory, in his pleas for freer trade did not advance anything close to absolute or comparative cost theory. In his Essays 'Of Commerce', 'Of the Balance of Trade' and 'Of Jealousy of Trade' he emphasized the beneficial consequences of competition only in the sense that they would lead to emulation.[24] In the latter Essay he actually argued – as every good 'mercantilist' would have done – that his free-trade-arguments did not apply when a higher productivity and possibilities of employment could be obtained by prohibiting a foreign commodity.[25]

Yet even more astonishingly, Adam Smith himself seems to have ignored the principle of cost advantage as a solution to international competition for a fairly long time of his life. Neither is there a hint made at it in the *Theory of Moral Sentiments* (1759), nor in his *Lectures on Jurisprudence* (1762–1764), and if we look at the sections concerning international trade in an *Early Draft of the Wealth of Nations* written most likely in the first half of the year 1763, there is equally no trace of it. The *Lectures on Jurisprudence* and the *Early Draft* are in fact extremely telling when compared to the fourth book of the *Wealth of Nations*. Already in the former Smith stated the principles that 'national or public opulence consists in the cheapness of commodities in proportion to the wages of labour' and that 'whatever tends to raise their price above what is precisely necessary to encourage the labourer tends to diminish national or public opulence', naming as causes excises and other taxes upon industry as well as monopolies.[26] But he did not yet apply the argument against monopolies to the case of import prohibitions and high duties on foreign commodities. Arguing for freer trade between England and other countries he compiled in the *First Draft* a list of six reasons supporting this claim, but the argument of monopoly and production costs is not to be found among them. Also his ferocious and somewhat obsessive attack on manufacturers, which would become a leading theme of the *Wealth of Nations*, is entirely missing.[27]

The question thus is: what happened between the revision of the *Lectures on Jurisprudence*, the *First Draft* and 1776, when the completed *Wealth of Nations* appeared, which could have turned Smith from moderate mercantilist into the 'free trader' cherished in the modern economic sciences? Shortly after the revision of the *First Draft*, from 1764 to 1766, Smith undertook a journey to France accompanying the future Duke of Buccleuch on a cavalier tour. As has been argued several times, this journey and especially the encounter made with the group of Physiocrats around Quesnay and Mirabeau in the French capital, proved decisive for Smith's future work on political economy.[28] And what regards absolute cost theory the trail indeed leads to France, although not to the Physiocrats, who did not think that there could arise anything good out of trade for they considered agriculture the only economic sector which could produce additional wealth. The first known statement – in print – was actually made by someone of rather 'mercantilist' belief, Jean-François Melon, who had been secretary to John Law during his disastrous experiment with paper money, which had led to the 'Mississippi bubble'. In a chapter on 'Exports and Imports' included in the second edition of his *Essai politique sur le commerce* (1736),[29] he developed the following hypothesis. As a general rule, Melon said, the entry of raw materials should be favoured while that of wrought goods should be prohibited. However, this rule should not be followed blindly:

> It is thereby dangerous to act invariably according to this rule, which suffers some exceptions. For if the commodity received costs little, & and the Nation which delivers it takes from us another overabundant merchandise, this maxim leads to error. I do not cite the commerce of wine and draperies between France & England as a sweeping example; but I present it as an article that deserves a discussion applicable to this maxim.[30]

With even more conviction the argument was restated thirteen years later by René Louis d'Argenson, a French nobleman and administrator, who had served as royal intendant in the Hainaut and as Secretary of State for Foreign affairs. In an open letter published in 1751 in the *Journal Œconomique* as a critique of an extract drawn from a 'mercantilist' tract written by an Italian nobleman, the Marquis of Belloni, which had been published in the *Journal Œconomique* the month before, d'Argenson attacked the notion that foreign manufactures had to be excluded and the exportation of domestic commodities had to be favoured by means of import and export duties. The nation that had followed this principle first, lamented d'Argenson, had set to the others the example to follow and turned commerce into a perpetual war. Such a policy had been inspired by 'the particular good' (*bien particulier*) winning over 'the common good' (*bien public*). Commerce could not be directed by the government, it was the 'science of the particular', and should therefore left be free:

> The whole of Europe should be one general and common trade fair [...]. The distance and the costs of transportation are sufficient to make the commodities of one's own country preferable to those of the others; wherever these obstacles cease, the foreigner is to be preferred to our fellow countryman, otherwise you will ruin your subjects instead of favouring them.[31]

That Smith had read Melon's *Essai* can be proven by several references to it in the section on public credit of the *Wealth of Nations*. It is also extremely likely that he knew d'Argenson's article in the *Journal Œconomique*. D'Argenson had died seven years before Smith's journey to France. But discussing economic issues in the salons of Paris, one of his interlocutors might well have shown or indicated d'Argenson's open letter to him, a translation in English of which had appeared together with other select articles from the *Journal* already in 1754.[32]

Yet, there is still another source, which bears even closer resemblance to the passages in the *Wealth of Nations* referred to in the first sections of the chapter and which might have served to inspire Melon, d'Argenson and Adam Smith: a series of *mémoires* delivered by members of the French Council of Commerce established in 1700, which did not circulate in print in the eighteenth century, but of which several manuscript copies existed. In order to understand why several of these deputies in their memoirs made statements so very much at odds with the principles of political economy followed in France until that moment, we must first go back to debates about taxation in the period of the great figure that gave French mercantilism its name and label: Jean Baptiste Colbert.

Provincial economic privileges and the 'common good'

It is probably no exaggeration to say that the French tariff list of 1667 is one of the most important and at the same time most thoroughly misinterpreted documents in early modern economic history. It was issued in April of that year by Jean-Baptiste Colbert, who sought to strengthen the manufacturing basis of the French economy. In order to achieve this goal, import duties on several goods including wrought textiles were increased. In the case of English and Dutch woollens (*draperies*) the duty was raised from 40 *livres* to 80 *livres*. This seems to be a lot, and therefore historians have labelled the tariff of 1667 as 'ultra-protectionist', as a 'fighting tariff' designed to 'injure drastically' the trade of neighbouring countries.[33] For Lionel Rothkrug in his study on the *Political and Social Origins of the French Enlightenment* (1965) it was the main reason for an alleged opposition to Colbert's policies by the French merchant community, who wanted to continue trade as before and held that this tariff was utterly damaging to the French themselves.[34]

The outbreak of a merchant opposition against Colbert is very much a product of Rothkrug's own imagination. There are only few traces of fundamental dissent against the Comptroller general's customs policies; moreover they were usually advanced by Colbert's political adversaries. And there are two principal reasons for the fact that there was no unified 'merchant opposition' against Colbert. As I have argued elsewhere, the tariff of 1667 was in fact far from being as 'prohibitive' as portrayed by Dutch and English contemporary propaganda.[35] In the tariff list of 1665, the first issued under the direction of Colbert, import duties on several manufactured products were raised from five to ten per cent.[36] Doubling the duties on wrought woollen cloth, the tariff of 1667 thus raised them up to twenty per cent. Such an import duty was not equivalent to an actual import prohibition, especially not as these goods were mostly luxuries. Their consumption could be restricted to certain echelons of the society, but not entirely be curbed. The tariff of 1667 was intended as a compromise that should shift economic competition from the price to the quality of these products. Colbert wanted to protect French industry while keeping international trade as open as possible in order not to jeopardize France's own agricultural and industrial exports.

There is another aspect, however, which is even more important for the problem discussed here. Contrary to received wisdom, Colbert's tariff list did not apply to the entire kingdom.[37] Until the French Revolution, the different provinces of the

Figure 6.1   The political geography of early modern France (1788).

Source: Bibliothèque nationale de France, Département Estampes et Photographie (map in public domain).

kingdom were divided into three distinct categories: The provinces belonging to the 'five big farms' (*cinq grosses fermes*) roughly comprising the northern half of the hexagon, the 'provinces considered as foreign territories' (*provinces réputées étrangères*) and the 'provinces effectively considered as foreign territories' (*provinces à l'instar de l'étranger effectif*).

The tariff list of 1664 as well as that of 1667 applied only to the *cinq grosses fermes*. In the *provinces réputées étrangères* – to which belonged Brittany, the Guyenne, Flanders, the Artois, the Provence, the Languedoc and others – local duties remained in place. This is very significant inasmuch as the trade relations of those provinces like the Guyenne and Brittany, which depended more than the industrially oriented 'five big farms' on the export of primary or semi-finished products such as wine or salt in return for foreign manufactures, were not directly affected. It is unclear whether Colbert also wanted the 'foreign provinces' to be included in the edict (*arrêt*) of April 1667, which established the new tariff. Probably he did, as the edict's wording suggests. But in any case, protest let to an *arrêt* issued on September 26 of the same year that made it clear that the new tariff would apply only to the 'five big farms'.[38]

Only from the mid-1680s onwards would the central government in France begin to revise its cautious attitude and seriously encroach upon the local direction of trade with regard to national customs duties. The increasing government intervention was partly a consequence of the Treaty of Nijmegen, which had put an end to the Franco-Dutch war in 1678. In an additional *arrêt* issued on August 30 1678, the Dutch were exempted from the tariff list of 1667 with respect to five essential goods including textiles. The exemption was limited to the Dutch, but – as *mémoires* dating from 1686 demonstrate – the Dutch used their exemption to bring English wares to France under the conditions of the 1664 tariff as well. Direct exports of English textiles from London to France reached an extremely high level by the middling years of the 1680s as well.[39] There is only fragmentary evidence available on the economic development of France during that period. But it is reasonable to assume that the strength of English (and Dutch) exports to France led to the breakdown of many French manufactures. At least those in the French government responsible for financial and economic matters had the feeling that the French economy was in dire straits because of foreign competition. A memoir dating from 1686 indicates that there were imported into the area covered by the 'five big farms' alone 2,669 high-quality draperies, as well as 8,000 pieces of *serges de Londres* and 14,000 pieces of other woollens of lower quality such as *bayettes* and *frises*, which can be estimated at a total value of ca. 1.5 Mio. *livres*.[40] At at the toll point of Bordeaux, 200,000 stockings made of wool and cotton entered the Province of Guyenne plus draperies amounting to a value of one Mio. *livres*, in which – as Colbert's son and successor as Secretary of State for the Navy, the Marquis de Seignelay wrote – all peasants and winegrowers were clothed, 'while the manufactures of the surrounding regions languish and the king's subjects are without employment and subsistence'.[41]

To counter this trend the government implemented a series of measures intended to protect industries at home – measures which went far beyond those taken by

Colbert himself.[42] On 8 November 1687, the entry of English draperies was restricted to the ports of Calais and Saint-Valéry-sur-Somme on France's northern coast, thus cutting off the *provinces réputées étrangères* from direct imports of these products. The point of this measure was to make it without further ado impossible for the *provinces réputées étrangères* to import such commodities directly and under the conditions of their regional tariffs, so as to make their inhabitants inclined to buy French products rather than textiles brought from England. In addition, one and a half months later, on December 20, duties on eleven textiles were doubled and raised on others.[43]

These measures immediately provoked the resistance of local communities that wanted to continue their trading relations with England as they had been before. Thereby, they argued in a traditional way remonstrating that their privileges were violated, and that their regional trade with England and the Netherlands would suffer. The provincial Estates of Brittany in early 1688 sent a complaint to Versailles, in which they explained that these laws and prohibitions were 'ruinous to their privileges as well as to their commerce'. Commerce with England was absolutely necessary for the province's subsistence, they maintained, which therefore had always been exempted by royal privileges from (royal) import duties on the Atlantic coast.[44] The syndics of the city of St Malo sent a special complaint in which they insisted upon the fact that the government had cut off the considerable trade of this city by impeding the direct entry of foreign manufactures and that this was against the privileges of the province, adding a lengthy list documenting the rightful possession of such privileges since the beginning of the fourteenth century. They added other reasons why the restriction of imports to the ports of Calais and St. Valery was prejudicial, but all of these reasons concerned the particular interests of the province of Brittany and especially that of the city of St Malo.[45]

This line of argumentation, however, was not apt to make the government change its attitude. Director-general of commerce Jean-Baptiste de Lagny, who together with the Marquis de Seignelay was principally responsible for France's foreign trade policy during this period, countered the Britons' complaints with the dry response that they mistakenly adduced their privileges. These measures, he explained, were intended to re-establish the woollen manufactures in France, which was an issue concerning not only Brittany, but all the provinces of the kingdom, and privileges had to be superseded when the public good was concerned.[46] The point was clear: either resistance against measures taken by the government was founded on the well-being of the entire kingdom, or else there was no hope that complaints from particular provinces would be taken into consideration. The 'common good' had definitely switched from a regional level to that of the whole country, becoming the irrefutable point of reference for any economic argument.[47] This would have important consequences for economic reasoning and future foreign trade theory.

Manufacturing against agricultural interests: merchant lobbying in the Council of Commerce

Director-general of commerce De Lagny was the one who most ardently defended protectionist policies during these years. In his many *mémoires* directed against a tariff agreement with the Dutch eventually concluded in 1699, he tried to hammer home his arguments to anyone in favour of a further opening to Dutch and English imports why this would have serious consequences for the French kingdom. In a memoir written probably in autumn 1696, he explained the economic reason for this, stating that the balance of trade would be unfavourable if France was to exchange its natural products against foreign manufactured goods. For French agricultural products were bulky, whilst foreign manufactures were of lesser volume but of far greater value, wrought goods carrying much more added value produced by human labour:

> The reason for this is easy to discover: nature has a greater part in the production of [agricultural] goods, the art to the contrary makes almost all the products which come out of the hands and the industry of men, who make themselves pay for their time, their nourishment, and their dedication, while nature gives almost all of this free of charge.[48]

This traditional argument in favour of the protection of home industries came under attack, when a French 'Council of Commerce' was created in November 1700.[49] Neither the idea nor the actual establishment of a consultative body composed by merchants was an entirely new development at the beginning of the eighteenth century. Already under Henry IV such a council had been created and Colbert had set up one himself in 1664. But these experiences had not lasted for more than a couple of years, while the Council founded in 1700 would endure until the French Revolution. Also the particular moment of its establishment was significant: after the Nine Year's War (1688–1697), which had interrupted commerce and left the country in a state of financial and economic difficulty, there was a widespread sentiment that things had to change in the direction of commerce. On top of the Comptroller General of Finances, the Secretary of State for the Navy and two *conseillers d'Etat* on the side of the government, there were twelve deputies representing the country's most important provinces and cities called to participate in the Council. Two deputies came from Paris whilst the cities of Rouen, Bordeaux, Lyon, La Rochelle, Marseille, Nantes, Saint-Malo, Lille, Bayonne, Dunkirk and the province of Languedoc sent one deputy each.[50] They were important figures, selected from among the most wealthy and influential traders of their provinces.

On their first assembly in November 24, 1700 the merchant deputies to the Council of Commerce were asked to produce a memoir each on the general state of commerce in France and measures to be taken in order to revive it.[51] With the exception of the famous banker Samuel Bernard (one of the Deputies of Paris), all accomplished their task and handed in their memoirs during the following four months. The interpretation of these memoirs by historians have varied strongly. Pierre Clément and Lionel Rothkrug among others emphasized their 'liberal' character.[52] Others have claimed that the memoirs were rather conservative. Charles W. Cole has spoken of 'random fragments imbedded in a matrix of older ideology' and more recently Thomas Schaeper has insisted on the 'mercantilist' character of the *mémoires*.[53] The inherent fallacy of these interpretations is to assume that the merchants were a homogeneous group, a mistake being already at the heart of Lionel Rothkrug's thesis of a 'merchant opposition' to Colbert. But in the early modern period there actually was no such thing as *the* merchants. Merchants were a very heterogeneous group with a wide range of different interests.[54] And they surely did not derive their policy proposals to governments exclusively from economic theory. The merchant deputies to the Council of Commerce, especially, were not only merchants exposing their theories of the best direction of trade, but also lobbying for the particular interests of their respective provinces.

Not very surprisingly, therefore, the Deputies of Rouen, Paris and Lyon (all from the 'five big farms') defended in principle the protection of French industry.[55] The Deputy of Rouen, Nicolas Mesnager, for example explained that certain trades could benefit a single merchant while being detrimental to the State as a whole. The only advantageous trades for the state were those enhancing production at home and exports to other countries. The only way to make sure that France's balance of trade would be favourable was to reduce the consumption of foreign luxury goods while exporting as many own products as possible. Many of the deputies from the *provinces réputées étrangères* argued to the contrary that this kind of policy had caused intercourse with England and the Netherlands to decay and had damaged dramatically the economic state of the kingdom. Protection of French manufactures by means of high import duties had driven English and Dutch merchants away. They were now turning to other countries and imported from there goods they had previously bought in France. The branch of the economy that was suffering most from this was agriculture. As the Deputy of Bayonne stated:

> We are mistaken if we think that we can do without foreigners and that they cannot do without us. [...]. The provinces of Guyenne, Bourgogne, Anjou, Touraine, Champagne and others groan under it. They have no other principal resource than wine and brandy, which stay in the country and cannot be consumed. Prices are already that low, one can say that in certain cantons the barrel costs as much as the wine itself; we will be ruined if this continues. We will be obliged to abandon agriculture and to rip out the vineyards because of the high costs of cultivation and the low profit one gets from them.[56]

This was all the more deleterious since France was essentially an agricultural country, as the deputies from the *provinces réputées étrangères* claimed. Manufactures were important, the deputy from Nantes, Joachim Descazaux du Hallay conceded. But wine production was of far greater importance and had 'to win it over'. The vineyard was the 'bountiful mother of France', he exclaimed. It not only bolstered the income of several provinces, among whom he listed 'the Guyenne, Languedoc, Provence, Bourgogne, Champagne, Anjou, Poitou, a part of Brittany, of the Saintonge, of the Auvergne, of the Roussillon, of the region of Aunis and the whole region of the Loire'. It made 'the kingdom's wealth'; it was 'France's precious treasure'. The vineyard gave the worker an employment, Descazaux held, and 'almost all peoples [of France] subsist by it and are capable of paying taxes to the State'.[57]

But Descazaux did not limit himself to pointing out the paramount importance of agricultural goods for the French export economy and for certain provinces in particular. In another memoir he submitted shortly thereafter the 'needs' of the said provinces which the Estates of Brittany had upheld some years before as their privilege and the exigencies of their particular region, metamorphosed into a general economic law. In fact, the deputy from Nantes now applied the traditional argument against monopolies, which before had been used only for monopolies excluding fellow countrymen as in the case of exclusive trading companies, to commerce between two countries. Protecting manufacturing by high import duties or prohibitions was, in his eyes, an economically flawed proposition. It only put the manufacturers into a favourable position, which allowed them to neglect the quality of their products 'and to set up the price to the prejudice of the public'. Instead, it would be far better to 'let competition work' by allowing foreign manufactures to enter freely the country while reducing import duties on raw materials.[58] The deputy from La Rochelle (located within the *cinq grosses fermes* but as an Atlantic port with similar interests as the *provinces réputées étrangères*) argued in a similar way for free international competition. He particularly insisted on how the 'common good' was to be defined in economic terms. According to him, it was composed by two elements: The first was revenue from customs for the king. The second was 'to make sure that all things necessary for subsistence and the nourishment of the kingdom's subjects are available at the lowest possible price in order to let the people live with facility and easiness'. In order to achieve this, he explained further, it was necessary:

> to open the doors of freedom to foreigners and to give them an easy entry by making them pay moderate duties proportional to the value of the goods and commodities they want to introduce, whatever nature they may be of, without regard to the manufactures or other particulars which could suffer some prejudice from that; for the good which will arise from this freedom is the public one, which has always to be supported against all particular interests which are directly opposed to it.[59]

If foreign manufactures were excluded from importation, the deputy from La Rochelle underscored, this would ruin both the king's revenues and the common good, 'at the favour of some particulars, trading companies, privileged and manufacturers'. He thereby pushed entirely aside, as Adam Smith would do, the argument of employment: 'Even if in the manufactures one million persons could be employed, one cannot have any regard to this, for the public good, as I have defined it, has to be preferred to anything else'.

Similar statements directed against manufacturers can be found in the memoirs written by the deputies of Lille and Dunkirk. A manufacturer demanding high import duties had to be considered a person who enriched himself at the expense of the public, the former wrote. All import duties were in his favour: 'The higher and heavier they are, the more profit he makes', rising the price of his product proportionally to the protection he received. In addition, the deputies from Lille and Dunkirk hinted more explicitly than their colleagues from Nantes and La Rochelle at the problem of price and production cost, formulating the rule that:

> if one can get commodities from other countries, for which one pays only low duties, transport costs and provisions, with whom the merchant makes profit and which can be sold at a lower price than those, which are produced in our kingdom, it is advantageous for the king and the people to receive them.[60]

Still another twist appeared in the statement by the deputy of the city of Bordeaux, who more clearly than the others emphasized the use of this argument for the establishment of an international division of labour. France should not try to do without the products of foreign nations, he wrote, for the others would only try to do the same in return. Instead, one should specialize on the growth and production of those French products, which other nations were in need of. At the same time, it should be determined which products could be imported from abroad 'in better quality and at a lower price' than if they were grown or produced at home. The import of such commodities had to be favoured. This, according to the deputy of Bordeaux, was the 'only fundament on which commerce between France and the other European nations can be established'. 'The whole mystery' of trade was, he explained, 'to know how to use one's own advantage'.[61]

Conclusion

The memoirs written by the deputies of Nantes, La Rochelle, Lille, Dunkirk and Bordeaux already contain the principal elements of the theory of absolute advantage as we find it in the *Wealth of Nations*. They exist in various manuscript versions. The two most complete were and still are located in the National Library (formerly *Bibliothèque royale*) and the *Bibliothèque de l'Arsenal* in Paris.[62] That an erudite scholar such as Adam Smith who at the time had started to work on a book on political economy would not visit these two libraries and ask for everything regarding this problem, is somewhat unthinkable. Or maybe their arguments had been explained to Smith verbally during his conversations in the Salons at Paris? Difficult to say. There are only few letters conserved in the edition that date from his journey to France. But the lines of argumentation are too similar to be a simple coincidence.

However way Smith came into contact with these ideas, he most probably ignored the precise circumstances under which they had been developed, which gives the story a slightly ironic touch. For he explained to his readers in the *Wealth of Nations* that the French in particular had pursued the wrong policy of favouring their manufactures by imposing restrictions on foreign imports elaborating further that:

> In this consisted a great part of the policy of Mr. Colbert, who, notwithstanding his great abilities, seems in this case to have been imposed upon by the sophistry of merchants and manufacturers, who are always demanding a monopoly against their countrymen.[63]

While suspecting that Colbert had been tricked by merchants' manufacturing interests, he ignored that – in a certain way – he had himself been 'imposed upon' by the 'sophistry' of other merchants opposed to the manufacturing interest who tried to protect the vested agricultural interests of their provinces by advancing certain ideas with claims to universal validity of promoting the common good because the creation of the modern state in France was passing, or threatening to do so, over their local privileges.

Of course, vested interests cannot explain the rise of liberal trade theory entirely.[64] But the example of the theory of absolute advantage shows, I think, that historians of economic thought cannot rely exclusively on intellectual explanations for developments in their domain. They have to look for other, more 'material' factors, too. We should not forget that such factors were at work quite often in the development of economic ideas, and that this probably also extends to other economic 'laws' cherished in the modern economic sciences as eternal principles or 'truths'.

Notes

1 Adam Smith, *An Inquiry into the Nature and Causes of the Wealth of Nations*, ed. W. B. Todd (Oxford: Clarendon Press, 1976), 642.

2 Many economic historians have challenged the argument about the imputed 'Midas Fallacy' of the mercantilists – most of them never conflated money and real wealth. See, e.g. Lars Magnusson, "Is Mercantilism a Useful Concept Still?" in *Merkantilismus. Wiederaufnahme einer Debatte* ed. Moritz Isenmann (Stuttgart: Franz Steiner, 2014), 19–38. Antoine E. Murphy, *Monetary Theory 1601–1758* (London and New York: Routledge, 1997), vol. 1, 15 has qualified this accusation, which holds a very prominent place in Smith's attack on the 'mercantile system', with regard to Thomas Mun as 'both inappropriate and disappointing for a writer of his calibre', and Joseph A. Schumpeter, *History of Economic Analysis* (London: George Allen & Unwin, 1955), 361 even wrote that Smith, 'obviously conscious of the fact that this particular charge cannot be made good', did not strictly speaking make it, but insinuated it 'in such a way that his readers cannot help getting the impression'. For the general debate on the concept of mercantilism see, e.g. Donald C. Coleman, ed., *Revisions in Mercantilism* (London: Methuen, 1969); Philip J. Stern and Carl Wennerlind, eds, *Mercantilism Reimagined. Political Economy in Early Modern Britain and its Empire* (Oxford and New York: Oxford University Press, 2014), and Isenmann, ed., *Merkantilismus. Wiederaufnahme einer Debatte*.

3 The Netherlands are in general less associated with mercantilism. The cloth manufactures of Leiden, however, owed much of their success to an import prohibition on English woollens.

4 Smith, *Wealth of Nations*, 493.

5 Ibid., 660.

6 Ibid., 457–8.

7 See Douglas A. Irvin, *Against the Tide. An Intellectual History of Free Trade* (Princeton: Princeton University Press, 1996), 89–91; David Ricardo, *On the Principles of Political Economy and Taxation*, in *The Works and Correspondence of David Ricardo*, ed. Piero Sraffa (Cambridge: Cambridge University Press for the Royal Economic Society, 1951–73), vol. 1, 133 et *passim*. As Jacob Viner explains in his *Studies in the Theory of International Trade* (London and New York: Harper Bros., 1937), 441, the only difference between the two is that the theory of comparative costs maintains that in certain cases it will be profitable to import goods which can be produced at lesser cost at home, correcting the 'previously prevalent error that under free trade all commodities would necessarily tend to be produced in the locations where their real costs of production were lowest'.

8 As Paul Krugman has put it some years ago: 'If there were an economist's creed, it would certainly contain the affirmation "I Understand the Principle of Comparative Advantage."' Paul Krugman, "Is Free Trade Passé?" *Journal of Economic Perspectives* 1 (1987), 131–144, at 131.

9 Smith, *Wealth of Nations*, 488.

10 See, e.g. Philipp Robinson Rössner, "Mercantilism, Great Divergence and the Reconfiguration of a Productive Landscape: The Case of Scotland," *Annales Mercaturae*, 1/1 (2015), 97–126. Even the balance of trade theory was, considering the essential role played by coined money for pre-modern economies, far from being as 'absurd' as Smith thought. See id. "Mercantilism as an Effective Resource Management Strategy: Money in the German Empire, c. 1500–1800," in *Merkantilismus. Wiederaufnahme einer Debatte*, 39–64.

11 Quite interestingly, Smith does not even enter into a discussion of this point, which he therefore either did not know or else voluntarily ignored.

12 Fernand Braudel, *Civilisation matérielle, économie et capitalisme, XVe–XVIIIe siècle. Vol. III: Le temps du monde* (Paris: Armand Collin, 1979), 36.

13 Erik Reinert, *How Rich Countries Got Rich...And Why Poor Countries Stay Poor* (London: Constable, 2008). See also Ha-Joon Chang, *Kicking Away the Ladder: Development Strategy in Historical Perspective* (London: Anthem, 2002).

14 Reinert, *How Rich Countries Got Rich*, e.g. 19.

15 Terence W. Hutchison, *Before Adam Smith: The Emergence of Political Economy, 1662–1776* (Oxford and New York, NY: Blackwell, 1988); Irvin, *Against the Tide*, 75–86.

16 Reinert, *How Rich Countries Got Rich*, 84–7.

17 Ibid., 247–8.

18 Viner, *Studies in the Theory of International Trade*, 440.

19 See also Andrea Finkelstein, *Harmony and the Balance. An Intellectual History of Seventeenth-Century English Economic Thought* (Ann Arbor: University of Michigan Press, 2000), 94–5.

20 Edward Misselden, *Free Trade or the Means to Make Trade Florish wherein the Causes of the Decay of Trade in this Kingdome are discovered* [1622], reprint New York 1971 (Augustus M. Kelley Publishers), 25.

21 Viner was a founding member of the so-called 'Chicago School' in economics.

22 Henry Martyn, *Considerations on the East India Trade* (London 1701), reprinted in: J. R. McCulloch ed., *Early English Tracts on Commerce* (London: Printed for the Political Economy Club, 1856), 541–629. On Martyn's authorship, see Christine Macleod, "Henry Martyn and the Authorship of Considerations on the East-India Trade," *Bulletin of the Institute of Historical Research* 56 (1983), 222–229.

23 Martyn, *Considerations*, esp. 3–5.

24 David Hume, *Essays Moral, Political and Literary*, ed. Eugene Miller (Indianapolis: Liberty Classics, 1987), 253–267, 308–326 and 327–331. On the concept of 'emulation' in the eighteenth century, see Sophus Reinert, *Translating Empire. Emulation and the Origins of Political Economy* (Cambridge/Ma: Harvard University Press, 2011).

25 Hume, *Essays*, 324: 'All taxes, however, upon foreign commodities, are not to be regarded as prejudicial or useless, [...]. A tax on German linen encourages home manufactures, and thereby multiplies our people and industry'.

26 Raymond de Roover has already pointed out that Adam Smith's argument against monopolies was fairly traditional, reaching back to the Scholastics; see his "Monopoly Theory Prior to Adam Smith: A Revision," *Quarterly Journal of Economics* 65 (1951), 492–524.

27 See Adam Smith, *Early Draft of Part of the Wealth of Nations*, in: *Lectures on Jurisprudence* (Glasgow Edition, vol. V), ed. R. L. Meek, D. D. Raphael and P. G. Stein (Oxford: Clarendon Press, 1978), 562–581, at: 577–8, drawing on his *Lectures* of 1762–3, ibid. 361–368, 388–394.

28 The most recent and detailed account of Smith's journey to France is: Reinhard Bloomert, *Adam Smiths Reise nach Frankreich oder Die Geburt der Nationalökonomie* (Berlin: Die Andere Bibliothek, 2012).

29 Melon's *Essai* can be considered the first tract systematically elaborated on Political Economy published in France. See Jean-Yves Grenier, *Histoire de la pensée économique et politique* (Paris: Hachette, 2006), 159.

30 Jean-François Melon, *Essai politique sur le commerce* ([Dublin: Printed for P. Crampton, 1738] Paris 1936), 132: 'Il est pourtant dangereux d'agir indistinctement selon cette règle, qui souffre bien des exceptions. Car si la marchandise reçüe coûte peu, & que la Nation qui l'apporte prenne de nous une autre denrée surabondante, alors la maxime porte à faux. Nous ne citerons pas pour un exemple décisif le Commerce de vin & de draperie entre la France & l'Angleterre; mais nous le présenterons comme un article qui mérite une discussion applicable à cette maxime'. Cf. Simone Meyssonnier, *La balance et l'horloge. La genèse de la pensée libérale en France au XVIIIe siècle* (Paris: Éditions de la Passion 1989), 69.

31 René Louis Marquis d'Argenson, *Lettre à l'Auteur du Journal œconomique, au sujet de la dissertation sur le commerce de M. le Marquis de Belloni*, in: *Journal Œconomique, ou Memoires, notes et avis sur les Arts, l'Agriculture, le Commerce, & tout ce qui peut y avoir rapport, ainsi qu'à la conservation & à l'augmentation des Biens des Familles, &,* (Paris: April 1751),107–117, at: 113–4: 'Toute l'Europe ne devroit être qu'une foire générale & commune; [...]. L'éloignement et les frais de voiture suffisent à faire préférer les denrées de son pays à celles des autres; là où ces obstacles cessent, l'étranger est préférable à notre compatriote, autrement vous ruinez vos sujets dans le commerce au lieu de le favoriser'.

32 *Select Essays on Commerce, Agriculture, Mines, Fisheries and other useful Subjects* (transl. from the *Journal Œconomique*) (London: D. Wilson and T. Durham, 1754).

33 See, e.g. Charles W. Cole, *Colbert and a Century of French Mercantilism* (Hamden, Conn., Archon Books, 1964 [1939]), vol. I, 428; Simon Elzinga, "Le tarif de Colbert de 1664 et celui de 1667 et leur signification," *Economisch Historisch Jarboek* 15 (1929), 221–273.

34 Lionel Rothkrug, *Opposition to Louis XIV. The Political and Social Origins of the French Enlightenment* (Princeton: Princeton University Press, 1965), 199.

35 Moritz Isenmann, "War Colbert ein 'Merkantilist'?" in: id. ed., *Merkantilismus. Wiederaufnahme einer Debatte*, 143–168.

36 No indication on percentages ad valorem are given in the tariff list. The deputy to the Council of Commerce from Bordeaux, however, stated in 1703 that the 1664 tariff list raised customs from five to ten per cent ad valorem. Archives Nationales de Paris (henceforth: AN), F12 1910.

37 For the opinion that the tariff list applied to the whole country, see the works cited in n. 33 and 34.

38 I have not been able to locate this *arrêt* in the series E of the National Archives in Paris, where most of the *arrêts* are preserved, but this is referred to in a memoir written by the Intendant of the Guyenne dating from the end of the eighteenth century; *Archives du Ministère des Affaires Étrangères, Mémoires et Documents*, France 1587, fol. 265v: 'This difference [between the five big farms and the provinces considered as foreign territories] is established since all times [...] and when with the declaration of April 18, 1667 in form of a new tariff for the raise of import and export duties of the goods there specified with respect to the tariff of September 18, 1664, inadvertently was inserted that these duties would be collected at the entrance and exit of the Kingdom and the *provinces réputées etrangères*, this mistake was corrected by an *arrêt* of the King's Council issued on September 26 of the year 1667 [...]'. Originally it had been intended also that the tariff list of 1664 should be valid for the entire kingdom, but this had equally met with resistance from the *provinces réputées étrangères*. Cole, *Colbert*, vol. 1, 423.

39 See Margaret Priestley, "Anglo-French Trade and the 'Unfavourable Balance' Controversy, 1660–1685," *Economic History Review*, Second Series 4 (1951), 37–52.

40 See the *Memoire sur la quantité de draps fins, qui viennent en France d'Angleterre et d'Hollande*, in: AN, G7 1697, n. 182 and 183.

41 AN, Marine, B7 492, fol. 481.

42 This era has attracted far less attention than the one covering Colbert's ministry. The best study dealing with the economic policy of this period still remains Charles W. Cole, *French Mercantilism 1683–1700* (New York, Octagon Books, 1965 [1943]).

43 Ibid., 12–13. On July 3, 1692 the complete tariff list of 1667 was eventually extended to the whole kingdom, including the Guyenne, the Bretagne and all other *provinces réputées étrangères*. AN, E 1870 (no pagination).

44 AN, Marine, B7 492, fol. 406.

45 Ibid., fol. 454–459.

46 'A l'egard de leurs privilèges, comme l'intention du Roy dans ces establissements, a eu pour objet le retablissement des manufactures, particulierement celles de laine, et l'avantage du commerce de ses sujets, cela regarde autant la Bretagne que les autres provinces du royaume, et les deputez ont mauvaise grace de se deffendre en ce rencontre par leurs privilèges, il n'y en a point qui doivent subsister, quand il est question de l'interest public'; ibid., fol. 403.

47 In general on the importance of the notion of common good for early modern political thought, see e.g. Winfried Schulze, "Vom Gemeinnutz zum Eigennutz. Über den Normwandel in der ständischen Gesellschaft der Frühen Neuzeit," *Historische Zeitschrift* 243 (1986), 591–626, and with particular regard to France Keith M. Baker, "French Political Thought at the Accession of Louis XVI," *Journal of Modern History* 50/2 (1978), 279–303.

48 AN, Marine, B7 497, fol. 426–426v: 'La raison en est aisée à decouvrir, la nature a plus de part dans la production des denrées, l'art au contraire fait quasy tous les ouvrages qui sortent des mains et de l'industrie des hommes, ceux cy se font payer de leur temps de leur nourriture, et de leur aplication, et la nature donne presque tout cela gratuitement'.

49 For a general discussion of the Council of Commerce, see: Thomas J. Schaeper, *The French Council of Commerce, 1700–1750. A Study of Mercantilism after Colbert* (Columbus: Ohio State University Press, 1983). With particular focus on the Council's influence on the formation of a 'public opinion' in France, see David K. Smith, "Structuring Politics in Early Eighteenth-Century France. The Political Innovations of the French Council of Commerce," *Journal of Modern History* 74 (2002), 490–537.

50 J. Cain, "Les mémoires des députés au Conseil du Commerce en 1700," *Revue d'histoire moderne et contemporaine* 18 (1913), 5–20, at 5.

51 Four of the memoirs have been published in Arthur A. de Boislisle, *Correspondance des contrôleurs généraux des finances avec les intendants des provinces, publiée par*

ordre du ministre des finances, d'après les documents conservés aux Archives nationales (Paris: Imprimérie nationale, 1883), vol. 2, 477–504. For all others I have used the Manuscript Ms. fr. 8038 in the Bibliothèque nationale de France (BnF) in Paris, which bears the title *Memoires présentés à M. le Duc d'Orléans Régent par les Députés du commerce.*

52 Pierre Clément, *Histoire du système protecteur en France depuis le ministère de Colbert jusqu'à la révolution de 1848* (Paris: Guillaumin, 1854), 49–58; Rothkrug, *Opposition to Louis XIV*, 416.

53 Cole, *French Mercantilism*, 325–6; Schaeper, *French Council of Commerce*.

54 This point has recently been emphasized also by Guillaume Garner for the case of the German territories at the end of the *Ancien Régime*. See Guillaume Garner, "Le mercantilisme – un faux ami?" in *Merkantilismus. Wiederaufnahme einer Debatte*, 265–288

55 The deputy from Lyon, Jean Anisson, criticized what he (mistakenly) thought had been Colbert's policy, but nevertheless held firm on the principle that the French had to export more manufactured goods to other countries than they imported. Boislisle, *Correspondance*, vol. 2, 479–482.

56 BnF, Ms. fr. 8038, fol. 429v.

57 Boislisle, *Correspondance*, vol. 2, 488.

58 AN, G7 1686, n. 86 (without pagination).

59 BnF, Ms. fr. 8038, fol. 334v–335. Cf. Smith, *Wealth of Nations*, 493–4: 'In every country it always is and must be the interest of the great body of the people to buy whatever they want of those who sell it cheapest. The proposition is so very manifest, that it seems ridiculous to take any pains to prove it; nor could it ever have been called in question, had not the interested sophistry of merchants and manufacturers confounded the common sense of mankind. Their interest is, in this respect, directly opposite to that of the great body of the people'. See furthermore ibid., 266–7.

60 See BnF, Ms. fr. 8038, fol. 112–113 for the Deputy of Lille, fol. 135v for the deputy of Dunkirk.

61 BnF, Ms. fr. 8038, fol. 407–407v: '[O]n doit s'attacher à connoitre les denrées dont les Etats voisins ont besoin et peuvent consommer afin de les cultiver en France pour les leur envoyer. On doit faire attention sur celles dont les étrangers abondent, qu'on peut recevoir d'eux meilleures et à meilleur marché que si on les cultivoit en France afin d'en favoriser l'entrée, puisque c'est l'unique fondement sur lequel on peut établir le commerce entre la France et les autres nations de l'Europe; [...]. Tout le mystère depend de sçavoir user de son avantage'.

62 Bibliothèque de l'Arsenal Paris, Ms. 4395–4396.

63 Smith, *Wealth of Nations*, 467.

64 The present author is currently carrying out a research project financed by the *Deutsche Forschungsgemeinschaft* (DFG) with the title 'The making of the "invisible hand": economic interests, socio-political conflicts and the idea of free competition in the eighteenth century' which seeks to analyse in depth the political and social economic circumstances of the emergence of economic liberalism during the eighteenth century.

7 The demise of regulation and rise of political economy

Taxation, industry and fiscal pressure in Britain 1763–1815

William J. Ashworth

In 1779 William Eden, Member of Parliament for Woodstock and first Lord of Trade, succinctly explained how current fiscal and commercial policy had reached its maximum limit: 'It has hitherto been found in most instances, that our general consumption has gained ground under the pressure of increased taxes; but there is a point beyond which particular duties cannot advance, without the hazard of a fall, from which they may never rise'.[1]

The Scottish philosopher and historian, David Hume, would have concurred. He had prophesised earlier in 1752 that 'either the nation must destroy public credit, or public credit will destroy the nation'. Central to his thinking was the predicted dire consequences to the economy via the apocalyptic debt born of war. The only solution was, he argued, voluntary bankruptcy. The state was now on the verge of consuming the people more than the people were consuming and a new fiscal, industrial and trade policy was desperately needed. The Seven Years War (1756–1763) had greatly increased the National Debt with blame falling upon a perceived corrupt government and state that was in need of significant reform.[2]

The situation became dire in 1776 after the breakout of war with the mainland American colonies, followed quickly by a maritime clash with France and Spain. To add to the woes, it now seemed a real possibility that the West Indies and Ireland would soon follow colonial North America. In general the state finances were in an extremely precarious situation – with yet more money urgently needed for the Royal Navy to modernise.[3] All this would have a profound impact upon the direction of industry and shaping of a new political economy.

Debt and the 1780s

By 1780 the British state was at bursting point and had, somehow, to be radically reduced. This would entail a major dismantling, restructuring and withdrawal from regulatory functions, particularly at first, within the domestic economy. To eventually achieve this would require a supporting creed that would come to be filled by a new political economy, and an alternative source of revenue, namely, the introduction of the income tax. The onus would increasingly emphasise the opposite of past experience and stress an idealised market free of 'unnatural' regulations with individuals efficiently producing, selling and buying.

It was during this decade that a discrete industrial policy took shape on the ground and in the halls of power, which framed the relatively rapid maturation of England's early industrialisation in the 1780s. And this set of policies and practices gave shape to an emerging political economy rather than the reverse. This tension and re-structuring can clearly be seen in the clash between the old protected and excised industries geared predominantly toward the domestic market, and the protected untaxed or lightly taxed export-oriented new industries. This became manifest in the negotiations over the 1786 Anglo-French trade treaty.

It was under William Pitt the younger that a paradigmatic switch in economic policy took place that favoured the newer, export oriented, and less regulated industries (cotton, potteries and iron). Accompanying this was, crucially, a redefining of the state's role in controlling the economy and thus the food and labour markets. This had a revolutionary impact upon the lived experience of the working ranks.

In general, the regulated system that characterised Britain's economic evolution had reached its peak by the close of the Seven Years War and had seemingly become unsustainable in its prevailing form. Consequently, the government's only way out was just that – to shrink from playing a part in adjudicating the interests of the landowner, everyday people, labour and industrialists. The disintegration of a protectionist and paternalist model of food marketing and industrial regulation was mirrored by the retreat of the state, in general, from its close intervening activities in an array of spheres. Attacks upon 'old corruption' and the size of the state were eroding social authority, and something urgently needed to be done.[4]

The various publications of the influential reports made by the Commissioners Appointed to Examine Public Accounts spared nothing, and were damning in their conclusions of administrative waste and malpractice. As always revenue was at the forefront of government concerns and finding new as well as increasing traditional sources was the chief objective. Over the course of the American War of Independence the National Debt had grown from £131 million to an approximate figure of £245 million Sterling. Pitt had a limited number of options to draw upon: the first was simply to cut back on expenditure; the second was to increase the yield from existing taxes; the third was to ensure interest rates stayed low; the fourth was to smash illicit trade and, finally, the fifth option was to introduce new indirect taxes. The creation of an income tax was still politically out of the question. This would all take cautious planning, administrative improvements, and careful timing. There was, however, an area that could be addressed sooner rather than later, and that was a well-advertised gesture at severing administrative waste, cronyism and corruption.

The government had to at least look as if it was seeking ways of economising to subdue the volatile situation. Perceived incompetent administration – especially placement and sinecures, greedy moneyed men feeding off the people's hard earned money and political non-representation – had all combined to leave people feeling powerless. Eden wished for a time 'when all the junto caballing system, which, at the present however, completely triumphs, will wholly be overthrown'.[5]

Frustration started to escalate and increasingly collect into a potentially explosive situation. In an attempt to dilute growing cries for parliamentary reform, politicians started targeting the issue of placemen and abuse of the Civil List. During the early 1780s this List had its independence removed and was brought under closer parliamentary scrutiny (frozen in 1782). Lord North with Lord Shelbourne persistently hounding him, appointed a Board of Commissioners to investigate the state of public accounts and allay 'public' fears that their money was being wasted. Their objective was to cut waste and promote a prudent public ethos in an attempt to improve the efficiency and safeguard the legitimacy of state institutions.[6]

The Board built upon the vast increase of material available concerning the public accounts. This information had been used and worked up by various leading commentators to make such fiscal knowledge much more widely known that, in turn, made a significant impact on the debate. The role of the British Parliament in discussing and legislating upon economic matters, using state collected economic information, tended to make the details accessible to a wider public.[7]

Over the next few years the Commissioners examining the public accounts made a total of fifteen reports that variously condemned sinecures and 'irregular' emoluments, and the idea that offices were private property; a point bolstered by the 'odious system of Fees' in operation within many of the state departments. Importantly, the Excise was the only fiscal department to escape the condemnation of the Commissioners during the 1780s. Indeed it was hailed as the model towards which all branches of revenue (and state departments in general) should aspire.[8]

From Pitt's administration to Robert Peel's, the narrow elite of predominantly landed gentlemen still – despite the rapid rise of the commercially-minded middle classes and increasingly frustrated working classes – governed the country. They were thus under real pressure to find ways of diffusing attacks on 'Old Corruption'. If the government and prevailing social authority were to survive these attacks they had to convince this growing opposition that the state was there to defend everyone's property and interests; that they were prudent and honest in the administration of their public duties. To do this successive Pittite and conservative ministries had to be *seen* reforming the state's administrative structures and financial policy.[9]

Despite Pitt's initial success in casting himself as credible, along with a greater public awareness of economic matters and parliamentary discussion, Britain was still facing financial disaster. Not surprisingly a new fiscal, industrial and trading strategy was paramount and would be defined under Pitt's reign. His government really had no choice but to forge a new pathway with, more than ever, social stability intrinsically tied to economic prosperity. Without the latter, no matter how many political and social reforms were made, they would be lost to empty bellies and an increasingly hostile army of unemployed.

A regulatory and protectionist policy that had roughly carved England/Britain's trading and manufacturing path from the mid-seventeenth century to the late-eighteenth century had served the nation well, but was now severely straining under the ballooning National Debt. An environment of degeneration rather than enlightenment was the main trigger for reform. This context pushed Pitt into building a new fiscal, commercial and industrial pathway but not, of course, without a struggle.

The common economy

Throughout the early-1780s Pitt, like Walpole earlier, concentrated a great deal of his attention on tackling the problem of the illicit 'common economy'. A parliamentary report on the subject in 1783 highlighted Deal, on the south coast, as an 'emporium' of duty-free goods with almost the whole of its population, including the mayor, seemingly aiding smugglers with their work. Events reached a climax in early January 1784, when the government got information that the free-traders had drawn in a large section of their fleet into various creeks and harbours around the vicinity of Deal. They quickly dispatched several hundred soldiers and a number of well-armed cutters culminating in the capture of the whole 'smuggling navy'.[10] The most popular illicit commodities in the common economy were brandy, tobacco and especially tea. The success of free trade in tea was also undermining the finances of the powerful East India Company that resulted in concerted lobbying from this powerful organisation.

The size of illegal trade had recently been investigated under the auspices of Lord Shelbourne's Ministry prior to Pitt's period of power. However, the most extensive investigation was conducted in the summer of 1783, when the coalition government appointed a Commons committee to investigate illicit practices.[11] Eden spoke for many policy advisors in 1780 when he advised that such commodities be transferred from Customs to Excise: 'It certainly appears too, from experience, that the Excise laws confound the operations of the smugglers much more than those of customs'. In addition, he advocated what was fast becoming a primary objective, namely, the removal of drawbacks with an expansion of bonded warehouses and the simplification of duties; no tax would be paid till the stored items were exported or went into domestic consumption. All these policies would be successfully introduced under Pitt's regime.[12]

Pitt's advisors estimated that a mere forty-two per cent of the tea and fourteen per cent of the brandy consumed in Britain had paid tax. These investigations prepared and laid the path for two of Prime Minister's most celebrated tax reforms, namely, the Commutation Act of 1784 and the signing of the Anglo-French trade treaty of 1786. The aim of the former Act was to destroy widespread tea smuggling, and instigate a total monopoly of tea imported by the East India Company through the reduction of duties on tea from 119 to 12.5 per cent *ad valorem*. To enable Pitt to do this required the retail prices of tea to be reduced to a figure that could be compensated by a new Window tax. This was no easy task since the price of such tea was mainly based on its unpredictable availability.[13] Nonetheless for a time the Commutation Act achieved what its instigators had hoped.

In addition, Pitt managed to shift the duties on wines from Customs to Excise in 1786, some fifty-six years after the humiliating defeat of Robert Walpole's tobacco and wine excise Bill of 1733.[14] The government had finally managed to pass most of Walpole's earlier schemes. In addition, they continued to keep the pressure on the common economy by substantially increasing the legal weaponry against such free trade. For instance, the Hovering Act of 1780, in which vessels within two leagues of the coast could be seized, was extended to four leagues in 1784.[15] Free trade was an expensive thorn in the Pitt administration's side and occupied a great deal of their time. It would soon, however, emerge as the perceived solution to socio-economic problems rather than the problem.

The new manufacturers

Despite an ill-fated attempt to implement a new tax upon shops and a concerted attempt to crush smuggling, in the end the only policy Pitt could really pursue was to either introduce new indirect taxes or increase the revenue from existing taxes either by raising them, or improving methods of assessment and making revenue collection more efficient. Not surprisingly such an increase in indirect taxation provoked a number of confrontations. Indeed the extension of excise taxes led directly to the formation of new economic interest groups that quickly impacted upon commercial and industrial policy.

Manufacturing interests were beginning to combine together in an attempt to produce a united manufacturing front. For example, when the coal tax was increased British industry flexed its muscle in such an unexpectedly powerful way Pitt was forced to drop it after just ten days. The iron masters bitterly complained that the increase in coal duties would make it extremely difficult for them to compete with the Swedish. In addition, James Watt and Matthew Boulton were furious and let vent their opposition to the potential impact such a rise would have on their steam engine business.

The Manchester and Glasgow cotton interest, the iron founders of the Midlands and West of England, and the Midland pottery makers combined to establish a General Chamber of Manufacturers, with the objective of being a national body representing industrial interests and influencing Parliament on behalf of all domestic industry.[16] The impact of the new manufacturers on economic policy is extremely significant. Already the cotton industry, led by a petition from 'Richard Arkwright and Company of Nottingham spinners of cotton stuffs', had been given important concessions in 1774 including the removal of prohibitions and, soon after, the go ahead for British people to legally wear or use goods wholly made of cotton. In addition the tax on such British goods would be at the original 1712 rate of 3*d.* per yard putting them on a par with domestic fustians. By this point, too, the government was not so worried about protecting the Scottish and Irish linen industry.[17]

Ten years later an attempt was made to add an additional excise duty upon printed linens, dyed stuffs of cotton, and mixed cotton and linen textiles. In addition, a duty of 15 per cent was to be added to both the old 1774 duty and the new duty, while bleachers and dyers now had to purchase licences. The result was a petition to the House of Commons by an impressive list of vested interests from the Northwest that included both manufacturers and landowners. In April 1785 the House ordered a bill to be constructed that would explain and amend the said Act.[18] It was not just the introduction of these new levies, however, that rattled the cotton manufacturers, but the fact they were collected by the Excise. This was a view that united all the new industries.

One petitioner from Lancashire, John Wright, claimed the increased tax would discourage the growth of the domestic cotton industry and simply encourage Indian cotton textiles. Moreover, the Act would greatly aid Ireland and 'do more harm to England than the persecution of the Huguenots did to France'. Britain's cotton industry had become the country's goldmine and a huge employer of people 'who pay many taxes in the consumption of many articles'. This last point was underlined as a crucial component to the success of the British state: 'If our artists are kept unemployed, can they afford to consume an equal quantity of either the necessaries or luxuries of life, which by various taxes raise the revenue of the State?'[19]

Despite being untaxed the pottery manufacturer and entrepreneur, Josiah Wedgwood, wanted to see the excise tax 'annihilated'. He warned: 'Excise laws are the bane of manufacturers: the officers are spies upon all the operations of the artist: discoveries, which have been the fruit of great labour and expense to him, they convey to his rivals, perhaps foreign nations'. Wright claimed all excise laws struck 'at the root of our freedom, and the basis of British liberty'.[20] This could equally be seen as an indication of just how successful the Excise had been in achieving a nation-wide standardisation of production approaches and standards. These industries still demanded protection from foreign rivals, but they now also wanted to ensure freedom from domestic manufacturing regulation via the potential of being taxed – with Pitt busy trying to tax anything he could the threat of being excised was a real one.[21]

As with all industries taxed by the Excise, production had to conform to a process of manufacturing conducive to the Excise's method of gauging, and spatially it had to have its premises mapped to make visible detailed information on production methods and the precise location of utensils or machinery. Taxing a good frequently required it to be rendered visible both with regard to its ingredients and the way it was produced. This, ultimately, called for attempts to regulate its qualities and for its site of production to be reconfigured to meet the Excise's process of measuring tax. In this sense, the Excise, via administrative needs, encouraged particular areas to specialise in the manufacture of certain excised goods, and instal a dependence upon quantification, instrumentation, and a standardised product. In this sense the state played an important role in the agglomeration and specialisation of Britain's economic geography. Likewise approaches associated with enlightened thinking such as induction, counting, measurement and instrumentation were actually being led by a regulatory state rather than individuals fuelling the rise of public science.[22]

Although the Excise was willing to accept changes concerning the manufacturing process if it did not impact upon the amount of revenue generated, it was now considered far too intrusive by the lightly taxed or untaxed new industries that faced less foreign competition but feared being excised. The new manufacturers (both those excised and those who feared being so) claimed the Excise adversely interfered with the production process. In a familiar tone it was declared by the lightly taxed cotton manufacturers in April 1785, 'such an influx of those gentry [the excise officers] to disturb the harmony and arrangements of their manufacture, to deprive them of personal liberty and the free exercise of their property, is unwise, impolitic and unjust'.[23] Other industries, also fearing a general extension of the excise joined the attack, most notably the untaxed iron founders and manufacturers in the counties of Salop, Worcester, Stafford and Warwick. So too did the Birmingham Commercial Committee who sought the cooperation of other manufacturers.

Thus, despite the incredible pressure upon parliament to find additional revenues, Members of Parliament refused to support increasing or introducing new taxes made upon Britain's well-performing export-oriented newer industries, namely, textiles, potteries and metals.[24] In addition, key imports of certain raw materials, on the whole, remained lightly or untaxed and new labour competing technology also remained free from taxation (and banned from exportation). The latter being an issue that would come to be hotly contested by political leaders of the working classes during the early nineteenth century.

Ireland and the General Chamber of Manufacturers

It was not just the excise that was receiving the wrath of the new industries but, equally, Pitt's policies toward Ireland. By 1779 the situation here seemed to hang in the balance with Irish merchants and gentry arming, furious riots erupting in Dublin, and the economy descending into dire straits. The country's main industry, linen textiles, and its role in the supply of provisions, were both on the brink of collapse.[25] Although legislatively independent from Britain since 1782 the commercial and political relations between the two countries was still obviously far from fair. In 1785 Pitt set about trying to formalise Ireland's place in the British Empire. The aim was to give the country many more trading concessions in return for a change in their constitutional relationship. The idea was to build upon Ireland's increased internal self-government, expand the access of Irish traders into British markets, and for the subsequent increase in Irish wealth to be taxed to aid the defence of the British Empire, especially in shipping.

Meanwhile in Britain manufacturers combined, supported by the Foxite opposition, to prevent the possible threat of Irish competition. The attack in parliament was spearheaded by Eden, now Irish Chief Secretary as well as first Lord of Trade, and John Baker-Holroyd, MP for Coventry and recently made Lord Sheffield. A large momentum was also given by the establishment, touched upon earlier, of the General Chamber of Manufacturers that met for the first time on 8 March 1785. Its chairman, Wedgwood, was in regular contact with Eden and Sheffield. A major mistake by Pitt was not to have first gauged British manufacturers concerns.[26]

Whereas the British woollen textile industry had a monopoly over raw materials, the cotton cloth manufacturers had to compete with Ireland over, at this point, limited supplies. Many English cotton producers seriously considered moving their operations to Ireland. Water was – as it would be well into the nineteenth century – still the most dominant power source in the industry and Ireland provided ideal rivers and streams. In addition, the country had perfect climate conditions for producing cotton textiles, cheaper labour and, of course, without the burden of an excise. Despite an attempt in England to level the playing field by putting countervailing duties on Irish imports, it was the mode of tax collection that the domestic cotton manufacturers were primarily against.

What was also new in this debate, spearheaded by the new export-oriented industries (cotton, potteries and iron), was the view towards the market. Unlike older industries bred upon a culture of preserving and protecting markets, the cotton manufacturers, in particular, wanted to acquire new ones. Unlike the traditional excised industries, cotton was on the verge of eclipsing its Indian rivals and therefore would soon no longer require a protective barrier. This was a unique occasion. The stakes grew and the difference between the Irish and British tax systems took centre stage.

At a meeting in Manchester of the top eighteen British manufacturers, it was resolved that:

> the destructive system adopted towards the manufacturers of this kingdom, and to this town and neighbourhood in particular, renders it incumbent upon them immediately to appoint delegates to go to Ireland for the purpose of treating with any public body, or individual, nobleman or gentleman, respecting a proper situation for conducting an extensive cotton manufacture.

As for their reasons they underlined the 'evil' excise system and compared it to the far more advantageous system in Ireland. The cotton manufacturer, Robert Peel, father of the later Tory free-trade reformer and Prime Minister, claimed the excise tax would mean the end of the British cotton industry. The threat worked. On 20 April 1785 Pitt told the Commons that the additional excise on plain cottons and fustians would be repealed.[27]

The enlightened minds spearheading Britain's Industrial Revolution were liberal free-traders as long as there was no competition. In the midst of these disputes the Lancashire cotton industry continued to rapidly develop and expand mechanised spinning. Unlike other traditional excised industries cotton had been nurtured under a protected system but had never become an important source of revenue. This textile was the world's favourite and, after mechanization and access to raw cotton from the West Indies and subsequently the Southern plantations of the United States of America, the British quickly gained for a time a global monopoly.

The Anglo-French trade treaty of 1786

A decisive moment in Britain's confidence in its new manufacturers and what would later be termed its Industrial Revolution was the Anglo-French Trade Treaty of 1786. The young British Prime Minister was hugely optimistic a few months after the signing of the Anglo-French Trade Treaty in 1786:

I am persuaded that our power and greatness will be extended and increased, and new sources of opulence laid open to the industry, activity, and exertion of this country, which will raise both individuals and the nation to a very high degree of prosperity, such as we have not hitherto known.[28]

The power of the British cotton industry and the other new export oriented industries, most notably potteries and increasingly iron, were surging forward. This was particularly evident in this significant trade treaty with France.

The 1786 Anglo-French trade treaty split British manufacturers roughly in half. Those older industries that had grown up with protection coupled with an emphasis upon the domestic economy and the Excise, were against the treaty. By contrast the newer industries that also developed under protectionism, but would benefit from freer trade with France generally supported the treaty. As the pro-monopoly organ, *The British Merchant*, claimed: One group were keen to conserve control over the domestic markets, while the other faction sought 'an open trade' since 'their present ascendancy of skill, have nothing immediate to fear from competition, and everything to hope from the speculation of an increased demand'.[29] This and other publications identified cotton, pottery and iron as representative of this latter group; other industries such as the silk makers, certain woollen textile producers, ribbon makers, hat makers, paper manufacturers, clock and watch makers, leather manufacturers and glass producers felt they would lose their domestic markets to the French.[30] One woollen draper, probably from the West of England, claimed to foresee the collapse of the old industries. His own industry was being deliberately sacrificed: 'We are told however, that let our *Woollen* trade decline ever so much, our *Cotton* will more than proportionately increase, and our *Iron*, and our *Potteries* become extensive branches of foreign commerce'.[31]

The division between the traditional and new industries was stark within the General Chamber of Manufacturers. This body was dominated by cotton, iron and potteries – all of which fervently supported the 1786 treaty. The leader of the Chamber, Wedgwood, was energetic and vocal in his lobbying. These exponents were also hostile to the domestic regulatory Corn Laws with the quickly expanding Northwest of England needing access to more grain to feed its fast-growing workforce. A clear case of the landed interest clashing with the increasingly powerful provincial manufacturers was rearing its head before the Napoleonic Wars. The cotton industry, especially, was also desperate for raw cotton since the West Indian colonies could not quench its demand. Hence, it now looked beyond the restrictions of the Navigation Acts and would soon rely upon the Southern slave plantations of the new United States of America.[32]

Spearheading the negotiations with the French was Eden. As we have seen he had fervently opposed Pitt's attempt at establishing favourable Irish resolutions in 1784, and was an important supporter of the new industries in general. In the Anglo-French trade negotiations Pitt made it clear to Eden that he was willing to make concessions on glass and other products to aid cotton, some woollens, hardware and earthenware. In addition, the Irish linen industry also became a significant component in the negotiations.[33] Joel Mokyr describes the treaty as 'the first unambiguous sign of Enlightenment influence' and later 'a model of Enlightenment thought'.[34] However, the truth was far more mundane, pragmatic and born of necessity. All that Pitt was advocating were the failed Tory policies of the 1713 Anglo-French Treaty, while the Whig arguments spearheading the attack upon Pitt in Parliament, led by Fox, were simply a reiteration of *The British Merchant* also made some seventy years earlier.[35] However, Britain's industrial base had now significantly changed under regulatory and protectionist policies, while European competition in the new industries was not a huge source of fear. Indeed, these industries would now benefit from freer European trade.

Ephraim Lipson long ago argued that the impetus to the treaty 'was not any theoretical demonstrations of free trade, but the confidence which English industrial interests now felt in their ability to meet foreign competition'. The origins of the free-trade movement in Britain was fuelled 'by practical considerations in which abstract doctrines of economic freedom did not have the influence commonly assigned them'.[36] For the British government it was hoped the treaty would raise more revenue from import duties and greater opportunities for manufacturers to export.[37] Thence create greater employment and therefore more taxpayers. In many ways the 1786 treaty was predominantly about cotton, on which Eden secured a hugely reduced duty from the French of a mere ten per cent duty.[38] The British government knew cotton had no European rivals in terms of technology and production methods, while the French also knew this but thought they would quickly catch up. Leading French advisors to the treaty were convinced the French would soon match and surpass these technological advantages.[39] Fox claimed the trade treaty would be a disaster, 'they may gain our skill, but we can never gain their soil and climate'.[40]

The British woollen textile interests were on the whole furious with the treaty and sarcastically wrote: 'This *wise* scheme is to give power and license to the French to bring in ALL their *woollens* to our market, on proviso of our Manchester Merchants having the same privilege to sell the *French* and their *cottons*, and the Birmingham and Sheffield trades, and the iron branch'. Portugal was also to be sacrificed for French wines, domestic spirits and the West Indies rum for French brandy.[41] In short, the rehash of the originally defeated Tory commercial treaty proposals of 1713 was simply 'a shameful sacrifice of the best trades of Old England, for the worst luxuries of France'. Moreover the French labour force was, according to opponents, much better off than the British due to paying less tax and having cheaper provisions.[42] However, if British manufacturers were split over the treaty, the situation among the French was, if anything, more hostile. When the treaty was signed many manufacturing towns were dismayed; in particular, those areas that produced silk and cotton goods.[43]

The emphasis by the British was upon cotton, iron, steel, metal wares, hardware, pottery and earthenware. By contrast French superiority in areas such as wine, brandy, vinegar, oils, paper, glass (especially plate), and certain textiles such as cambric and silk was acknowledged. Not only would the treaty thus allow certain British goods to enter France at much reduced duties, but smuggled French goods (particularly wine and brandy) would now enter Britain legally and thus help smash illicit trade while increasing customs revenues. In this sense the treaty was also a way for Pitt to put another mighty dent in the 'common economy' and National Debt.[44] This was an objective, as we have seen, close to his administration's policies and he boldly predicted that 'the destruction' of this 'pernicious' trade would create an entirely 'new source' of revenue.[45] Crucially, both countries hoped the treaty would prevent future war.[46] Fear of foreign imports was also being replaced by a confident belief in British exports, thanks to the success of the newer less domestically regulated but still highly protected export-led industries. This selective proto-laissez faire policy, of course, would reach full fruition later in the nineteenth century. The policy of nurturing predominantly non-exporting industries was being eroded and, instead, was now being squeezed to an extremely high level through fiscal demands, which was pushing them to the level of protective custom tariffs.

Of even more immediate concern was the deliberate seduction of skilled French workers into English manufactures. The Normandy Chamber of Commerce reported:

> English travellers are already among our manufactory towns, and are much busier about picking up hints than about getting orders. Manchester has not yet been successful, as we have, in obtaining the fine Indian scarlet dye on cotton, but twenty French dyers have already gone there and from the generosity which has already given 2,000 guineas to a German who produced only a very faint shade, we may rest assured that before a year is out this fine rich colour will be known throughout England.[47]

This is in contrast to much recent historiography that underlines the opposite flow of skilled labour.[48] Thus this represented yet another English gain embedded in the treaty. Whatever way you look at it, the treaty was a huge success and vindication for the new British industries, particularly, cotton textiles

As well as the Anglo-French trade treaty, 1786 was also significant for Pitt's reintroduction of Walpole's earlier sinking fund, established with the aim of paying off the National Debt through surplus revenue. This, for Pitt, was a key policy and one fervently urged by the commissioners examining the public accounts. It had been, of course, for precisely the same reason Walpole had first introduced a sinking fund in 1716. This surplus was to be generated by further tapping domestic industry and especially foreign trade. For a time it seemed a feasible plan with the public revenue increasing by a staggering fifty-six per cent between 1783 and 1792, and government spending slashed by some thirty per cent due to the huge decrease in military spending since the American War of Independence. In addition, despite the fact the National Debt had almost doubled during the war, the cost of servicing it had only grown by 20 per cent. Pitt's government was riding high – but all that was about to change due to events just across the channel. Over the next 23 years the government would have to raise some one and a half billion pounds in taxes and loans to enable the country to effectively fight revolutionary and subsequently Napoleonic France.[49] This would put on hold the reduction of the state's regulatory and protectionist policies, but not severing of food market and labour regulations.

The pre-war reforms came back to the fore after the Napoleonic Wars. A whole array of folk from diverse social backgrounds started voicing their concerns. This ground swell had far reaching political, economic and institutional implications. It was this widespread public hostility that fuelled one aspect of the post-war Liberal Tory rationalising of the state. Ultimately, their administrative reforms would stop government growth and subsequently shrink the state through a dramatic pursuit of deregulation and free-trade. In this sense, too, the emphasis and implementation of values of efficiency and professionalism probably served to secure and melt landed interests into this new guise.[50]

It was only when most British manufactures had become superior in world markets, when government was faced with growing opposition to indirect taxation, when the urgency of near-bankruptcy following the Napoleonic wars created a period of desperation, and with food shortages and innovation increasingly aggravated by market regulation, that the state retreated and adopted a new approach that came to be described by a new political economy. A creed of liberalism and free trade in late eighteenth and early-nineteenth century Britain originally arose out of fiscal, social and political imperatives rather than an enlightened economic doctrine.

Notes

1   William Eden, *Four Letters to the Earl of Carlisle from William Eden to which is added a Fifth Letter* (1779, 3rd. edn., London, 1780), 123.

2   David Hume, "Of Credit," in his *Essays, Literary, Moral and Political* (1777, London: Ward, Lock and Co. Ltd, n.d.), 207–217. Istvàn Hont has masterfully traced Hume's view toward Public Credit and the Scottish thinker's fear of the inevitable dire conclusion of war and debt to Britain, see his *Jealousy of Trade: International Competition and the Nation-State in Historical Perspective* (Cambridge Mass.: Harvard University Press, 2010), 84–88 and 325–353.

3   For a useful overview of the quest for economic reform during this period see Earl A. Reitan, *Politics, Finance, and the People: Economical Reform in England in the Age of the American Revolution, 1770–92* (Basingstoke: Palgrave Macmillan, 2007), 16–113. For the modernisation of the Royal Navy see Roger Knight, *Britain Against Napoleon: The Organisation of Victory 1793–1815* (London: Penguin, 2013), part one.

4   E. P. Thompson, "The Moral Economy of the English Crowd in the Eighteenth Century," reprinted in his *Customs in Common* (Harmondsworth: Penguin, 1993),185–258; Adrian Randall, *Before the Luddites: Custom, Community and Machinery in the English Woollen Industry, 1776–1809* (Cambridge: Cambridge University Press, 1991); Phillip Harling, *The Waning of 'Old Corruption': The Politics of Economical Reform in Britain, 1776–1846* (Oxford: Oxford University Press, 1996).

5   William Eden, *Letter to the Earl of Carlisle from the Right Honourable William Eden* (Dublin, 1786), 26.

6   John Brewer, *Party Ideology and Popular Politics at the Accession of George III* (Cambridge: Cambridge University Press, 1976), 215; J. E. D. Binney, *British Public Finance and Administration 1774–92* (Oxford: The Clarendon Press, 1958), 11; Boyd Hilton, *A Mad, Bad & Dangerous People? England 1783–1846* (Oxford: Oxford University Press, 2006), 41 and 46; William J. Ashworth, *Customs and Excise: Trade,*

Production and Consumption, 1660–1842 (Oxford: Oxford University Press, 2003), chap. 19.

7 Julian Hoppit, "Checking the Leviathan, 1688–1832," in *The Political Economy of British Historical Experience, 1688–1914* eds. Donald Winch and Patrick K. O'Brien (Oxford: Oxford University Press, 2002), 267–294, at 287 and "Political Arithmetic in Eighteenth-Century England," *Economic History Review*, Second Series 49 (1996), 516–540; John Brewer, *The Sinews of Power: War, Money and the English State, 1688–1783* (London: Unwin Hyman, 1989), 221–249; Joanna Innes, *Inferior Politics: Social Problems and Social Policies in Eighteenth-Century Britain* (Oxford: Oxford University Press, 2009),109–175; Christopher A. Bayly, *The Birth of the Modern World 1780–1914* (Oxford: Blackwell, 2004), 74.

8 "Thirteenth Report of the Committee Appointed to Examine the Public Accounts," House of Commons Sessional Papers (HCSP), ed. S. Lambert (147 vols., Delaware, 1975), 1785, vol. 44, pp. 38–39.

9 J. R. Breihan, "William Pitt and the Commission on Fees, 1785–1801," *Historical Journal* 27 (1984), 59–81, at 72–81; Harling, *Waning of "Old Corruption,"* 73–74 and 80; G. E. Aylmer, "From Office-Holding to Civil Service: The Genesis of Modern Bureaucracy," *Transactions of the Royal Historical Society* 30 (1980), 91–108, at 106; N. Chester, *The English Administrative System 1780–1870* (Oxford: Clarendon Press, 1981), 124 and 127; Binney, *British Public Finance and Adminstration*, 14–15. The importance of this argument has been greatly extended by Martin J. Daunton, see his *Trusting Leviathan: The Politics of Taxation in Britain 1799–1914* (Cambridge: Cambridge University Press, 2001) and his essays in *State and Market: War, Welfare and Capitalism* (Woodbridge: Boydell Press, 2008).

10 Ashworth, *Customs and Excise*, 196.

11 John Ehrman, *The Younger Pitt: The Years of Acclaim* (London: Constable, 1969), 240–242; W. O. Henderson, "The Anglo-French Commercial Treaty of 1786," *Economic History Review*, Second Series10 (1957), 104–112, at 105.

12 Eden, *Four Letters to the Earl of Carlisle*, 130–131 and 203–209.

13 H. Mui and L. H. Mui, "William Pitt and the Enforcement of the Commutation Act, 1784–1788," *English Historical Review* 76 (1961), 447–465 and *Shops and Shopkeeping in Eighteenth-Century England* (London: Routledge, 1989), 162; Ehrman, *The Younger Pitt*, 5 and 243–245; J. H. Rose, *William Pitt and National Revival* (London, 1911), 184–185.

14 For Walpole's 1733 scheme see Paul Langford, *The Excise Crisis: Society and Politics in the Age of Walpole* (Oxford: Oxford University Press, 1975); Ashworth, *Customs and Excise*, 67–81.

15 Ehrman, *The Younger Pitt*, 246.

16 Ibid., 252–253; J. M. Norris, "Samuel Garbett and the Early Development of Industrial Lobbying in Great Britain," *Economic History Review*, Second Series 10 (1958), 450–460, at 453 and 458–59; Paul Kelly, "British Parliamentary Politics, 1784–1786," *Historical Journal* 17 (1974), 733–753, at 741–742; Rose, *William Pitt*, 186–187. For Boulton and Watt see Margaret C. Jacob, *The First Knowledge Economy: Human Capital and the European Economy, 1750–1850* (Cambridge: Cambridge University Press, 2014), 39–40. For the ill-fated shop tax see Mui and Mui, *Shops and Shopkeepers*, 34–36 and 73–85. The context, interests and reasons fuelling early industrial lobbying and the formation of manufacturing associations is usefully examined in V. E. Dietz, "Before the Age of Capital: Manufacturing Interests and the British State, 1780–1800" (unpublished Ph.D. thesis, Princeton University, 1991).

17 S. Dowell, *A History of Taxation and Taxes in England: From the Earliest Times to the Present Day* (1884, 3rd ed., 1888, New York, 4 vols., 1965), vol. 4, p. 333; Witt Bowden, "The Influence of the Manufacturers on some of the Early Policies of William Pitt," *American Historical Review* 29 (1924), 655–74, at 656.

18 "House of Commons Committee of the Whole House to Whom it was Referred to Consider of the Petition of the Gentlemen, Clergy, Land Owners, Merchants, Manufacturers, Dyers, Bleachers, and Others Interested in Printed Linens, Dyed Stuffs of Cotton and Cotton and Linen Mixed, and Licenses for Bleaching or Dying," 21 April 1785, Journals of the House of Commons (JHC).

19 John Wright, *An Address to the Members of Both Houses of Parliament on the late Tax Laid on Fustian, and Other Cotton Goods* (London, 1785), 9–10. 12, 19 and 56.

20 Josiah Wedgwood is quoted in Dietz, "Before the Age of Capital," 106–107; Wright, *An Address*, 45.

21 Bowden, "The Influence of the Manufacturers," 656 and, *Industrial Society in England Towards the End of the Eighteenth Century* (New York: The Macmillan Company, 1925), 170.

22 William J. Ashworth, "Manufacturing Expertise: The Excise and Production in Eighteenth-Century Britain," *Osiris* 25 (2010), 231–254.

23 Bowden, "The Influence of the Manufacturers," 656–58 and 665.

24 Patrick K. O'Brien, "The Truimph and Denouement of the British Fiscal State: Taxation for the Wars Against Revolutionary and Napoleonic France, 1793–1815," *Working Papers in Economic History*, LSE, No. 99/07 (2007), 1–56, on 29–30.

25 George O'Brien, *The Economic History of Ireland in the Eighteenth Century* (1918, Philadelphia: Porcupine Press, 1977), 230–233 and "The Irish Free Trade Agitation of 1779 (Part 1)," *English Historical Review* 38 (1923), 564–581.

26 Paul Kelly, "British and Irish Politics in 1785," *English Historical Review* 90 (1975), 536–563, at 534–541; Erhman, *Pitt the Younger*, 206–207; Bowden, "The Influence of the Manufacturers," 663. Lord Sheffield was educated in Dublin as a boy, see J. Cannon, "Holroyd, John Baker, first earl of Sheffield (1741–1821)," DNB, 2004.

27 Bowden, "The Influence of the Manufacturers," 666–72 and *Industrial Society in England*, 172–175; Kelly, "British and Irish Politics," 542–544; O'Brien, *The Economic History of Ireland*, 250–255.

28 William Pitt the Younger, *Speech in the House of Commons*, 12 February 1787, London, 1787, 4.

29 *The British Merchant, for 1787: Addressed to the Chamber of Manufacturers* (London, 1787), p. 8, p. 12 and p. 28 and quoted in Bowden, "The English Manufacturers," 23–24.

30 J. H. Rose, "The Franco-British Commercial Treaty of 1786," *English Historical Review* 23 (1908), 709–724, at 710.

31 *A Woollen Draper's Letter on the French Treaty* (London, 1786), at 26.

32 Bowden, "The English Manufacturers," 24–28. The key importance of raw cotton from the southern North American slave plantations is best described in Sven Beckert's *Empire of Cotton: A New History of Global Capitalism* (London: Allen Lane, 2014).

33 James Kelly, "The Anglo-French Commercial Treaty of 1786: The Irish Dimension," *Eighteenth-Century Ireland/Iris an da Chultur* 4 (1989), 93–111. For the French perspective on the treaty see Marie M. Donaghay, "Calonne and the Anglo-French Treaty of 1786," *Journal of Modern History* 50, issue 3 – supplement (1978): D1157–D1184, and especially "The Exchange of Products of the Soil and Industrial Goods in the Anglo-French Commercial Treaty of 1786," *Journal of European Economic History* 19 (1990), 377–401.

34 Joel Mokyr, *The Enlightened Economy: An Economic History of Britain 1700–1850* (New Haven: Yale University Press, 2009), 153 and 418.

35 See, for example, Anon., *Historical and Political Remarks of the Commercial Treaty* (London, 1787), 56–69.

36 Ephraim Lipson, *The Economic History of England*, 3 vols. (1931, 4th ed., London: Adam and Charles Black, 1947), vol. 3, 114–116; Orville T. Murphy, "DuPont de Nermours and the Anglo-French Commercial Treaty of 1786," *Economic History Review*, Second Series 19 (1966), 569–580, at 575; Oscar Browning, "The Treaty of

Commerce between England and France in 1786," *Transactions of the Royal Historical Society* 2 (1885), 349–364, at 359.

37 W. O. Henderson, *The Genesis of the Common Market* (London: Frank Cass and Co., 1962), 45–46.

38 For a succinct overview of the treaty's contents see W. A. S. Hewins, *English Trade and Finance Chiefly in Ireland* (London, 1892), 147–149 and Rose, "The Franco-British Commercial Treaty," 717–723.

39 Pitt, *Speech*, p. 18; Murphy, "DuPont De Nemours," 577.

40 Browning, "The Treaty of Commerce," 358, Richard Munthe Brace, "The Anglo-French Treaty of Commerce of 1786: A Reappraisal," *The Historian* 9 (1947), 151–162, at 154 and Henderson, *The Genesis of the Common Market*, 50. Fox is quoted in Hilton, *A Mad, Bad & Dangerous People?*, 189. For the physiocrats in relation to the treaty see Jeff Horn, *The Path Not Taken: French Industrialization in the Age of Revolution 1750–1830* (Cambridge Mass.: MIT Press, 2006), 52–53.

41 A Woollen Draper's Letter, *On the French Treaty* (London, 1786), 5.

42 Ibid., 8–14.

43 S H. See, "The Normandy Chamber of Commerce and the Commercial Treaty of 1786," *Economic History Review* 2 (1930): 308–13, on 310; Hewins, *English Trade and Finance*, 156.

44 Pitt, *Speech*, 20–32; Horn, *The Path Not Taken*, 65.

45 Pitt, *Speech*, 43.

46 Horn, *The Path Not Taken*, 65.

47 See, "The Normandy Chamber of Commerce," p. 312. For French cotton and its mechanization see the old, but still informative, article by Arthur L. Dunham, "Development of the Cotton Industry in France and the Anglo-French Treaty of Commerce 1860," *Economic History Review*, First Series 1 (1927), 281–307, especially 281–291.

48 See, for example, J. R. Harris, *Industrial Espionage and Technology Transfer: Britain and France in the Eighteenth Century* (Aldershot: Ashgate, 1998).

49 C. B. Cone, "Richard Price and Pitt's Sinking Fund of 1786," *Economic History Review*, Second Series 4 (1951), 243–251, at 251; Ehrman, *The Younger Pitt*, 260–63; Hilton, *A Mad, Bad & Dangerous People?*, 114–115; Patrick K. O'Brien, "The Political Economy of British Taxation, 1660–1815," *Economic History Review*, Second Series, 41 (1988), 1–32, at 13; Harling, *Waning of "Old Corruption,"* 53–56.

50 Harling, *The Waning of 'Old Corruption'* and Daunton, *Trusting Leviathan*.

Part IV

Knowledge, risk and the idea of infinite growth

8 Development as possibility

Risk and chance in the Cameralist discourse

Marcus Sandl

Cameralism – also labelled the German 'Merkantilsystem', the 'Staats- und Verwaltungslehre' of the German territories in the eighteenth century, or simply a kind of premodern 'Stadtökonomie' (city economics)[1] – has received widespread international attention in the last decades.[2] A number of studies have treated Cameralism as a practice and/or theory[3], as a science or predecessor of a science[4], as an ideology[5] or a poetology[6], a brilliant idea or nonsense.[7] While previous researchers agreed in stressing that Cameralism was an axiomatic and deductive-nomological behavioural theory in the context of enlightened natural law and absolutist exercise of power[8] – a mode of access that prevents irritations –, the actual research situation is more complex, inconsistent and sometimes even contradictory. Obviously Cameralism can be very different things.

This is the point where the following reflections come in. The aim of the chapter certainly is not to reinforce the debate by emphasizing a specific topic mentioned above. Rather it should be pointed out that being different things is a characteristic feature (probably *the* characteristic feature) of Cameralism itself. Therefore, it will be argued that the Cameralists were committed to the principle of change. Change as principle means that two aspects were closely intermeshed: First, change was the perspective governing the Cameralist design of the object – the political economy. Change was, in other words, the mode of being that characterized political economy. Second, change seemed to be, in the Cameralist's view, also the mode of their discourse. Only if the political-economic discourse changed continuously, in order to adapt to the varying modes of its object, could knowledge emerge. So the Cameralist claims of validity were linked with a specific index of temporality. Every intellectual surplus carried with itself, as Joseph Vogl has stated with regard to the temporality of knowledge around 1800, an expiry date marking the limitations of its own historical being.[9] And the Cameralists not only knew this, but made it their principle.

In order to come closer to the dual significance of change in Cameralism it is useful to reinterpret Cameralist knowledge in historic-epistemological terms. In the last decades historic-epistemological modes of access have fundamentally changed the historiography of the natural sciences.[10] Whereas previous science-historical studies were mainly concerned with the knowing subject and its mental capacities, with questions of truth, objectivity, and progress, historical epistemology has stressed the cultural basics of science and turned the focus on the different conditions under which knowledge took different shapes and thus changed over time.[11] The historiography of social und cultural sciences has until recently rarely paid attention to this turn. That means above all that the scientific subject, as well as the scientific object are treated as stable factors; the first initiates changes by formulating (new) ideas and insights into the second factor which functions as a coherent and entrenched scope of statements. A historical epistemology instead refers to a history of numerous and diverse matters and problems, representations, mediations, and communication, practices, events, and changing challenges.[12] In this respect, so the hypothesis of the present essay goes, Cameralism can be described as an 'epistemology of the possible'. This hypothesis will be developed in the following in four areas:

1   The knowledge of the turning point.
2   The mediality of this knowledge.
3   Contingency and probability as its criteria.
4   Risk and chance as its praxeological implications.

Knowing the turning point

Cameralism emerged in the late seventeenth century in the context of the European political situation after the Thirty Years War. Under the hegemony of France an international system arose on the continent that challenged the territories of the Holy Roman Empire in a particular way. The war had not only destroyed many sectors of the economy and nearly halved the population, it had also prevented the formation of a strong central power in the Old Empire.[13] Exactly this situation was reflected in the political-economic considerations of the first Cameralists,[14] and it continued to remain an authoritative principle thereafter. In the eighteenth century one of the most important issues was the backwardness characterizing the Central European economies in comparison to other countries like England, the Netherlands, or France. The Göttingen jurist Gottfried Achenwall, member of the first generation of Cameral scientists teaching at universities,[15] declared clearly and unequivocally that certain states had developed in a way that endangered others: 'If the latter don't wish to loose to much and to become weaker and weaker in relation to the first, if they don't want to fall more and more into a state of decline, they have to change their policy'.[16]

To clarify this point the *topos* of the 'Mächtesystem' (system-of-power) and the balance-of-power-doctrine emerged in the Cameralist textbooks.[17] Both aspects were interlinked, and they reflected a longer-lasting development implementing a territorial principle in the European politics and discourse.[18] Therefore power was no longer derived from personal dependencies but depended on space. A spatially defined category of rule inside the territory corresponded with the spatial structure of power at the European level. And this spatial structure was linked in turn with the European expansion and the discovery and occupation of spaces overseas that had been initially supposed to be mostly empty. The European expansion enabled, in other words, a spatial structure of power in Europe, which also implied a normative order: the 'Ius Publicum Europäum'.[19] This 'Ius' made it first-ever plausible to think of the European states und territories as interrelated, constituting a kind of network or system.

The concept of 'Staatswirthschaft', implemented by the famous Cameralist Johann Heinrich Gottlob von Justi in 1755,[20] synthesized all these aspects.[21] The deciding criterion was no longer the ruler but the comprehensive political and socio-economical connections. *Staatswirthschaft* meant to establish these connections by producing and supporting actively the circulation of money, goods and services.[22] Justi thought the state analogous to the human body in which the ruling class was wedded with its subjects:

> Indeed it is possible to conceptualize a republic very naturally in the image of a body. The wealth is the blood, the businesses are the veins, and the government is the heart in which the circulating commercial wealth through duties levied by the state by and by flows in order to disperse from here again into all parts of the state body through the effort of the government.[23]

The state and not the ruler as single person was consistently the holder of sovereignty. Therefore, the most miserable status of a state was its dependence on foreign powers. So Justi claimed that the state was obliged to take all measures necessary to ensure its own strength and independence.[24] This was the precondition as well as the consequence of a functioning 'Staatswirthschaft'.

Based on this concept other Cameralists in the eighteenth century aimed at enlarging the powers of the state. With the term of 'Staatswirthschaft' in view (often combined with that of the 'gemeinschaftliche Glückseligkeit' as the general state purpose) they composed a system of related policy areas under the signs of an on-going challenge. As Justi had claimed:

> a state without enough strength never could become completely secure in external affairs. [...] And as the external security is exactly related to the internal, and property cannot be gained without external and internal security, a state never can achieve this end use, i.e. the state of general happiness (*Glückseligkeit*), if it is not powerful at the same time.[25]

Accordingly, security, power and prosperity could not be separated from the viewpoint of Justi's colleagues. The disciplines of 'Polizeywissenschaft' (police science), 'Staatskunst', 'Oeconomie' and 'Finanzwissenschaft' (financial economics) stood in all Cameralist textbooks in a close, systematic context.[26] The common aim was, as the influential Cameralist from Mainz, Johann Friedrich Pfeiffer wrote, to give 'all branches of sustenance additional forces and activities, to animate circulation, to consolidate population and to make the state powerful'.[27] The power and strength of the state, however, were a relative factor, seen in relation to the forces and powers of other states; especially those of the neighbours.[28]

What is evident here is that being challenged marked an epistemological principle that organized the Cameralist's concepts in a fundamental way. It effectively meant that every political measure had to be validated in regard to the living conditions of the state. One might perhaps say that the initial situation of policy was defined as a kind of fundamental 'crisis' requiring flexible and effective decision-making.[29] Cameralist knowledge was, in other words, equal to the 'knowledge of the turning point'. That is a crucial difference to the older approaches to it by means of the 'Polizey'-doctrine and the 'Zeremonial-Wissenschaft' (ceremonial science), which emphasized the dominating order and its representation. In contrast, Cameralism focussed on political-economic care and provision combined with increased attention on safety and security needs. The power and strength of the state were no longer identical with the authority of the monarch. Power in the Cameralist sense of the word meant mobilizing all forces and to make the best possible use of available resources. These resources included materials and goods as well as individual human beings and whole populations. All this – 'the nature of things, and of men'[30] – now became an object of policymaking.

A deductive principle or a general normative concept inevitably had to fail here. It rather became imperative to define rules in respect to the political-economic life in its concrete reality encompassing nature, the people and social relations. Achenwall framed this relationship to reality expressly and clearly: 'The state here is the epitome of what can be really (and effectively) encountered in a civil society and its country'.[31] Real and effective were not only the state laws and state institutions but also, and above all, the families and their economies, the cities with their trade and industries, the 'Nahrungsstand' and agricultural production of the farmers, the cultural and religious customs, the health situation of the people, and at least the relations between all these elements. Under a Cameralist perspective the decisive factor therefore was not the 'good order' any more, but its transformation or, in Justi's words, 'the order in the transformation of things'.[32] With this focus Cameralism defined a new level of knowledge that referred to an empirical object in its concrete facticity and variability – an object, which could, therefore, only be recognized in terms of a vast abundance of data.

On the mediality of Cameralist knowledge

'Reality' – that is the second point of the Cameralist epistemology of the possible – does not simply exist but arises out of specific forms of – media-dependent – perceptions. Niklas Luhmann has stated this basic truism, regarding the modern society, clearly and precisely as follows: 'Whatever we know about the society, or indeed about the world in which we live, we know through the mass media'.[33] This is particularly true for that kind of reality that enables us to take decisive action.[34] To recognize different options – to produce 'crises' in the sense of establishing decision-making situations – means to arrange certain kinds of observation and perception.[35] Therefore topics and techniques of perception, including their medial basics, received substantial attention in Cameralist textbooks. It was especially the question of how information could be connected, and which medial forms would play a supporting role in this, which had been addressed frequently.

Considerations about the mediality of governing knowledge had been launched as early as the end of the seventeenth century. Amongst the first voices was Gottfried Wilhelm Leibniz who explored the topic in the context of his writings on state administration.[36] Government, Leibniz was convinced, was not conceivable without information. Information, in turn, consisted of the facts and figures concerning the 'here and now' of the state: the size of population, the quality and number of goods and properties, mortality and birth rates, the volume of exports and imports had, inter alia, to be known. And they had to be made visible at a glance in order to enable the regent and his administration to act quickly and decisively. This became possible, as Leibniz' meant, by specific means of display: the so-called 'Staats-Tafeln' as a 'written short constitution summarizing the heart of all information concerning the government'.[37] Therefore, Leibniz stressed the intrinsic connexion between state and knowledge. Joseph Vogl has rightly pointed out that in Leibniz's 'Staats-Tafeln' the 'state became a function of those empirical data. [...] It collects, selects, renews, systematizes, and compresses information to be used by the regent'.[38]

The eighteenth-century Cameralists followed Leibniz by emphasizing the mediality of politico-economic knowledge. Three medial forms were especially important and highly regarded. The first was the list or the table, which seemed – from the Cameralist point of view – to be of outstanding value in the most parts of government.[39] So Justi proposed, to cite just one example, to record the state of industry by creating tables illustrating any change in the number or composition of work and workers which took place in a given period.[40] These tables should allow policymakers to oversee the current trends and to develop appropriate political principles and strategies. By means of statistical processing of change it was, for example, possible, to draw conclusions about the status, quality and condition of the industry and to initiate appropriate measures of industry promotion. 'Tables have to be the basis', so Justi stated, 'of the whole economic policy'.[41] In this regard, tables represented media of access and manipulation.[42] Or more generally, tables were in line with the Cameralist intention to visualize hidden relations and forces and to make reality compatible with a program of reform and transformation.

This also applied to a second medial form: double-entry bookkeeping. Of course double-entry bookkeeping was closely connected with tables. Using tables, which should be derived from customhouse papers and related files, made it possible for example, to record incoming and outgoing goods.[43] All transactions could be related by account and check-account to recognize whether a country had a positive or negative balance of trade.[44] Therefore bookkeeping facilitated permanent control and the observation of changing relations. This was true not only for the registration of the flows of money and goods but also for the collection of personal data. Here the aim was to compare the number of births and deaths, immigrants and emigrants and thus to get an overview on population trends.[45] In each case the diagrammatical operations produced a field of visibility in which objects were not simply given, but fabricated to become operationalized. The totality of things and facts was made transparent in one moment and, in this way, became available for administration.[46]

The third medial form was, in turn, closely linked with the first two ones: This was scripturality and, last but not least, Cameralism as de-scription of political-economic knowledge itself. Cameralism used not only specified procedures of scriptualization but also reflected on it as an aspect of its conception of statehood. It raised the question of its own practices of data compilation and knowledge processing. Even if, as Justi noted, the 'lessons of the state and their presentation in scholarly writings' were very old, they had been neglected as a science until recently.[47] Only after having been established at universities a few years ago their 'perfect processing' had been initiated. Since then, however, many places appeared where Cameralist knowledge emerged: academic societies and economic associations, bureaus and offices, industries, farms and trading houses. All over now political-economic questions were considered and discussed in written form or scripts such as textbooks, magazine articles, encyclopaedias or reference works. So knowledge circulated in the same way as goods, products and money.[48] A second circuit existed that once again made clear: The state was not placed and given once and for all; in the self-reference of knowledge relationships it was in permanent flux and had to be permanently amended.

Contingency and probability

The fact that the Cameralist link between state and knowledge was a close one should not be conflated with an enclosed self-reference and static solidity. On the contrary, it implied high dynamics for both state and knowledge. To be open, contingent and in a state of flux was characteristic for Cameralist knowledge, as well as for its object of study. That brings us to the third aspect of the epistemology of the possible: *contingency and probability*. In a paradigmatic manner Justi sketched the future as a perspectival space of political thinking and action by pronouncing: 'A wise government has to make provisions for the future and to develop its plans and drafts in advance, in view of the most happy condition which a state might potentially reach'.[49] In the same manner, Johann Heinrich Jung, professor of Cameral sciences in Lautern since 1778, stated that the 'fundamental obligation of a government' was 'to promote the temporal happiness of the state entrusted to it to the highest levels using the most appropriate regulatory instruments'.[50] Pfeiffer saw the ideal of the forward-looking regent realized in Joseph II and commended him for penetrating the present and focussing on the coming future.[51] And Frederick II of Prussia himself regarded politics as an art of forecast.[52]

Particularly because the future was open and had not yet been defined, practical resources emerged in the present. Economy and administration entered here into an intimate connection. In this context, the Cameralists developed the concept of 'Polizey' as an agency sampling all relevant data, devising appropriate plans and ensuring an effective implementation. 'The *Polizey* is', so the Leipzig lawyer and Cameralist Carl Gottlob Rößig stated, 'the agency that orders and organized the inner security, beauty, convenience, population, morality, and the status of sustenance in a state'.[53] Therefore, the task of the 'Polizey' was to take well-informed decisions to improve the economy and to promote stability and prosperity. Decisions had to be made, for example, to minimize or prevent dangers. Among the dangers that threatened prosperity were cases of fire, fraud and moral decline, gambling and other amusements, or floods and draughts.[54] To fight all of these the 'Polizey' had to make provisions for the future by effective means.

But indirect instruments of controlling the time to come should be found as well. This involved for instance trading companies founded to protect merchants and ship-owners from hostile attacks and losses caused by extreme weather and storm.[55] Furthermore plans were drawn up for each kind of other assurances against accidents that could develop into obstacles.[56] 'A wise government has to be aware of such institutions', said Justi,

> which avert the worst impacts of a disaster and to protect the status of sustenance against adverse influences. This goal is achieved particularly well by certain kinds of assurances and insurances. By those institutions a disaster affecting only a few and being in process of throwing them to the ground – to the detriment of the whole economy – is, so to say, distributed equally amongst a larger number of people and thus made more bearable.[57]

In this sense, the 'Polizey' had to create the preconditions for establishing insurances by private persons or companies to deal with the contingent future.

Forward-looking decisive action, however, could also take into consideration the maximum anticipated profit. In this case, the policymaker – who may be a statesman or a private businessman – had to be ready to venture something and to take risks. 'The increase of wealth will make a slow progress if you do not dare [...] something in your enterprises and affairs', Justi proclaimed. This meant, according to Justi, 'to expose a part of our properties to the uncertainty of fortune'. All this, however, should happen 'in a reasonable way'.[58] Even if a deal seemed to be audacious and random, there were nevertheless correct principles and rules waiting to be detected. The most important thing was, on the one hand, to correlate the profit opportunities with the dangers of loss. On the other hand, the 'probability of loss had to be reduced as much as possible'.[59] If one took into account both possibilities and dangers, the 'hazard' could be managed, as Justi announced. Furthermore: 'It is even possible to prove this all by the most correct mathematical calculations'.[60]

Justi's at first sight paradoxical demand to deal with fortune in a reasonable, even mathematical way indicated an important development in the history of the sciences that was crucial for the Cameral sciences in the eighteenth century. This is true both for the insurance business and entrepreneurship. What is meant here is the 'emergence of probability' – a process that was based on the theory of hazard, which had been advanced since the middle of the seventeenth century.[61] In 1654 the French mathematicians Blaise Pascal and Pierre de Fermat developed, in a series of letters in which they dealt with the question of an equitable benefit distribution under the condition of an unfinished game, a method to calculate chance and risk.[62] This method made it possible to rationalize decisions by calculating their preconditions and consequences. Subsequently, generations of mathematicians worked on calculability and probability.[63]

Whilst at the outset, probability was a matter of calculating gambling-chances, it did not take long until it became applied to other contexts such as insurances, lotteries, and literature.[64] In consequence, the emergence of probability implied a development one might call a 'doubling of reality'.[65] This can be illustrated particularly convincingly by the example of Cameralism, which continuously evolved around the difference of facts and fictions. On the one hand, reality was constituted based on the collection of data, as mentioned above. This reality – as a manifestation of the facts – contrasted, on the other hand, with the fiction of a possible reality. While the first reality was 'de facto' true, the second reality was identical with what probably could become true in the future. The second reality was, in other words, defined by what the first reality optionally included and what had to be realized.

'Doubling of reality' therefore means to temporalize politics following the directives of contingency and probability. Although it was impossible to calculate exact probabilities in the area of politics, the probability calculus organized the Cameralist's considerations in a figurative, but nevertheless fundamental sense. This can be demonstrated by the example of the Braunschweig advocate Georg Heinrich Zincke, who already began to systematize the Cameral sciences before Justi. Zincke defined the logic of political-economic activities as a kind of dialectic process, in which on the one hand 'probable reasons' ('wahrscheinliche Gründe') should be found to make transactions, and on the other hand 'probable objections' ('wahrscheinliche Einwürffe') should be made so as to indicate whether the transactions needed to be changed or rejected entirely.[66] So Zincke (and with him other Cameralists, too) utilized recent developments in mathematics for political and economic theory in a fruitful way, thus opening up a new horizon of policy-making. That is what Wolfgang Schäffner described as a 'reinvention of the state which defines itself not any more as territory but as an amount of data making the state of a state body describable and the future calculable'.[67]

Risk and chance

The coincidence of state and knowledge had theoretical effects, which have been referred to above. However, it also left its marks on the practical side, or, more explicitly, in the inseparability of theory and practice. The Cameralists emphasized upheaval as central to their epistemic framework and drew particular attention to figures of dis-quietness. These figures – of risk and chance – should now be stressed as the fourth and last aspect of Cameralist epistemology. Adventurers, entrepreneurs, inventors and speculators were the figures populating the Cameralist textbooks. The most important figure, however, was the project-maker ('Projektemacher'), a figure that had also appeared some time earlier on. As early as 1700 Daniel Defoe dealt extensively with the phenomenon of project-making und the becoming of a project-maker. In his 'Essay Upon projects' (1697) he proclaimed that 'Neccessity, which is allow'd to be the Mother of Invention, has so violently agitated the Wits of men at this time, that it seems not at all improper, by way of distinction, to call it, *The Projecting Age'*.[68] For Defoe, the desolate economic conditions gave rise to new forms of actions: 'These [*the project-makers, M.S.*], prompted by Necessity, rack their Wits for New Contrivances, New Inventions, New Trades, Stocks, Projects, and any thing to retrieve the desperate Credit of their Fortunes'.[69] Project-makers sometimes made the world a better place; normally, however, they were fraudsters, charlatans and profiteers, as Defoe indicated.

The core objects of the early discourse of project-making de facto were adaptability and feasibility independent of customary routines, normative requirements and hierarchical structures.[70] As a kind of non-conformism they manifested themselves especially in the project-maker's dealing with dangers. Like their antecedents, most of Defoe's contemporaries had arranged with fate, destiny and divine providence. They lived in fear of the unpredictable and incalculable lurking everywhere. Dangers were in other words attributed to the environment, and everyone was exposed to them.[71] The project-maker perceived the world quite differently: He was not afraid of dangers because the unpredictable in a strict sense did not exist for him. Every future event could be made an object of calculation. Calculating effectively meant to regard all future possibilities as an outcome of a present decision. If the future, however, was the result of a decision, the nature and type of danger changed: it became a risk one took to create opportunities and chances. So the 'emergence of probability' was linked, as already mentioned above, with the 'emergence of risk and chance' in the sense that acting persons became independent of a *force majeure*.

About 60 years after Defoe had published his essay, project-makers still had not lost their bad reputation. This, however, did not alter the basic fact that Cameralists now considered the project-maker to be the prototypical 'homo oeconomicus'. In 1761 Justi wrote a long article, in which he presented his 'Thoughts about Projects and Project-Makers'.[72] He defined 'a project' as 'an elaborated draft of a certain venture to promote our own and other people's temporal bliss; including the reflection of all instruments and measures to be taken, but also the difficulties and obstacles threatening to arise as well as the nature and manner of dealing with them'.[73] A project was characterized, in other words, as a concept that opened up both chances and risks. Generating future possibilities out of present opportunities was the aim; a comprehensive temporalizing and dynamization was its consequence. Or in the words of Georg Stanitzek: 'We are dealing with an enterprise, an intention, which also considers and demonstrates the conditions of its own realisation and successful implementation and, in this way [...] organizes its own acceptance'.[74]

Consequently, to prepare and implement a project was difficult and required many skills. The project-maker had to combine numerous capabilities and qualities 'to contribute', as Johann Heinrich Ludwig Bergius pointed out, 'to the good of his fellows and human society as a whole'.[75] He should know the country, its state and condition, rights and customs he planned with.[76] He should, in addition, have good reason and imagination to overlook all affairs and facilities and the associated effects and consequences concerning his project.[77] He finally had to be able to present his proposals clearly and concisely in written form.[78] He had to embody, in other words, all aspects of the epistemology of the possible. Conversely the epistemology of the possible had to be practised and made effective in order to exist. Opportunities had to be generated out of crises and the world had to be changed – not always and necessarily for the better – to regenerate development as possibility. So all politicians and human beings had, at least, to be project-makers and they had to change the world by making it a place for further project-makers:

> I actually have to go further; I not only have to assert, that in this respect all human beings are project-makers; I even have to assume that all human beings utterly have to be so; if they want to advance their affairs in an intelligent and reasonable way.[79]

Conclusion

Revisiting the four points raised above it can be noted that it is difficult to determine the very essence of the Cameral sciences. Of course, it is possible to ask for a Cameralist theory, a theorem or a dogma (including questions of their respective validity) as historians of ideas and sciences have done, not only in recent years. The responses, however, precisely demonstrate, in all their diversity and contradictoriness, the limitations of this mode of access. In contrast, a historic epistemology, as it is emphasized here, would focus on the performative and praxeological aspects such as the emerging and processing of Cameral sciences. This approach makes it possible to grasp the unique character and the idiosyncrasy of knowledge with regard to its historical provenance, unfolding and closure. Therefore, the picture of Cameralism changes. It seems that its most characteristic feature was to put things in motion and to establish links between them. Cameralism opposed the existing moral and legal, but also epistemological theories to replace them with a flexible, transferable form of knowledge that was characterized especially by its practical applicability. As has been shown above, this new understanding of politico-economic knowledge was made possible by different scientific and medial circumstances. What changed, however, was not only the interpretation and scientific framing of knowledge. Change itself became the principle of the Cameralists, and knowledge was the way to give change a chance. So every subject of politico-economic thinking – the state, the administration, the population, each single official and private man and woman including the Cameralist himself – became a subject of changing relations and was defined at least not as an essence but as a function that enabled a permanent and universal transformation. More than everything else this aspect – the Cameralist's focus on development as possibility – marks out the notorious and continuous validity of Cameralism that has not vanished today.

Notes

1 E.g. Gustav von Schmoller, "Das Merkantilsystem in seiner historischen Bedeutung: städtische, territoriale und staatlicher Wirtschaftspolitik," in: id., *Umrisse und Untersuchungen zur Verfassungs-, Verwaltungs- und Wirtschaftsgeschichte* (Leipzig: Duncker & Humblot, 1898), 1–60; Hans Maier, *Die ältere deutsche Staats- und Verwaltungslehre (Polizeiwissenschaft). Ein Beitrag zur Geschichte der politischen Wissenschaft in Deutschland* (Neuwied-on-the-Rhine and Berlin: Luchterhand, 1966); Werner Sombart, *Der moderne Kapitalismus. Historisch-systematische Darstellung des gesamteuropäischen Wirtschaftslebens von seinen Anfängen bis zur Gegenwart*, 2 vols., 4th ed. (Munich and Leipzig: Duncker & Humblot, 1921/1928). Heckscher characterized Cameralism as a kind of Mercantilism, although he had difficulties in bringing it into his framework of economic policy and trading relations. See Eli F. Heckscher, *Mercantilism*, 2nd ed. (London: George Allen and Unwin, 1955). Concerning the terminological problems see Thomas Simon, "Merkantilismus und Kameralismus. Zur Tragfähigkeit des Merkantilismusbegriffs und seiner Abgrenzung zum deutschen 'Kameralismus,'" in *Merkantilismus. Wiederaufnahme einer Debatte* ed. Moritz Isenmann (Stuttgart: Franz Steiner, 2014), 65–82.
2 On the background and courses of these developments see Philipp Robinson Rössner, "Heckscher Reloaded? Mercantilism, the State and Europe's Transition to Industrialization (1600–1900)," *The Historical Journal*, 58,2 (2015), 663–683.
3 Guillaume Garner, *État, économie, territoire en Allemagne. L'espace dans le caméralisme et l'économie politique, 1740–1820* (Paris: Editions de l'École des hautes études en sciences sociales, 2005); Marcus Sandl, *Ökonomie des Raumes. Der kameralwissenschaftliche Entwurf der Staatswirtschaft im 18. Jahrhundert* (Cologne and Weimar: Böhlau, 1999).
4 Keith Tribe, *Governing Economy. The Reformation of German Economic Discourse, 1750–1840* (Cambridge: Cambridge University Press, 1988); Justus Nipperdey, *Die Erfindung der Bevölkerungspolitik. Staat, politische Theorie und Population in der Frühen Neuzeit* (Göttingen: Vandenhoeck & Ruprecht, 2012).
5 Andre Wakefield, *The Disordered Police State. German Cameralism as Science and Practice* (Chicago: University of Chicago Press, 2009).
6 Joseph Vogl, *Kalkül und Leidenschaft. Poetik des ökonomischen Menschen* (Munich: Sequenzia, 2002).
7 The last hypothesis is especially supported by the history of economic doctrine that follows a linear model of progress. E.g. Rainer Gömmel, *Die Entwicklung der Wirtschaft im Zeitalter des Merkantilismus, 1620–1800* (München: De Gruyter, 1998); Peter Rosner, *Die Entwicklung ökonomischen Denkens. Ein Lernprozess* (Berlin: Duncker & Humblot, 2012).
8 See particularly Jutta Brückner, *Staatswissenschaften, Kameralismus und Naturrecht* (Munich: C.H. Beck, 1977); Diethelm Klippel, "Naturrecht als politische Theorie. Zur politischen Bedeutung des deutschen Naturrechts im 18. und 19. Jahrhundert," in *Aufklärung als Politisierung – Politisierung der Aufklärung* eds. Hans Erich Bödecker and Ulrich Hermann (Hamburg: Meiner, 1987), 267–293; Hans Erich Bödeker, "Das staatswissenschaftliche Fächersystem im 18. Jahrhundert," in: Rudolf Vierhaus, ed., *Wissenschaften im Zeitalter der Aufklärung* (Göttingen: Vandenhoeck & Ruprecht 1985), 143–162.
9 Joseph Vogl, "Zeit des Wissens," *Dialektik. Zeitschrift für Kulturphilosophie* 2 (2000), 137–148, at 140: 'Man hat es nun [...] mit Aussagen zu tun, die neben ihrem Wahrheits- und Geltungsanspruch den Index ihrer Aktualität und Zeitlichkeit mit sich führen. Jede

Aussage, jeder Satz des Wissens enthält [...] einen zeitlichen Überschuss, der gewollt oder ungewollt die Begrenztheit seiner historischen Seinsweise ausspricht. Alle Begründung des Wissens zieht den Schatten ihrer historischen Kontingenz nach sich [...]'.

10 See *Ansichten der Wissenschaftsgeschichte*, ed. Michael Hagner (Frankfurt am Main: Fischer-Taschenbuch-Verlag, 2001).

11 These developments are especially associated with the name and the works of Hans Jörg Rheinberger. See among others Hans Jörg Rheinberger, *On Historicizing Epistemology. An Essay* (Stanford: Stanford University Press, 2010); id., *Toward a History of Epistemic Things. Synthesizing Proteins in the Test Tube* (Stanford: Stanford University Press, 1997).

12 See in addition to the publications of Rheinberger listed above also the works of Joseph Vogl who pushed an ambitious historic-epistemological program under the banner of 'Poetology of Knowledge'. E.g. Joseph Vogl, "Für eine Poetologie des Wissens," in *Die Literatur und die Wissenschaften, 1770–1930*, ed. Karl Richter, Jörg Schönert and Michael Titzmann (Stuttgart: M & P, 1997),107–127; id., "Einleitung," in: *Poetologien des Wissens um 1800*, ed. Joseph Vogl, 2nd ed. (Munich: Fink, 2010), 7–16; id., "Robuste und idiosynkratische Theorie," *KulturPoetik. Zeitschrift für kulturgeschichtliche Literaturwissenschaft/Journal for Cultural Poetics* 7,2 (2007), 249–258.

13 See, regarding the preconditions and consequences of the Thirty Years War, now *The Ashgate Research Companion to the Thirty Years' War*, ed. Olaf Asbach (Farnham: Ashgate, 2014).

14 As precursors of the 18th century Cameralists were regarded Veit Ludwig von Seckendorff (*Teutscher Fürsten-Staat*, 1656), Johann Becher (*Politischer Discurs*, 1668), and Wilhelm von Schröder (*Fürstliche Schatz- und Rentkammer*, 1686). See Erhard Dittrich, *Die deutschen und österreichischen Kameralisten* (Darmstadt: Wissenschaftliche Buchgesellschaft, 1974).

15 The history of the 'academization' of political economy in Germany is treated in Norbert Wasze, ed., *Die Institutionalisierung der Nationalökonomie an deutschen Universitäten. Zur Erinnerung an Klaus Hinrich Hennings*, 1937– 1986 (St. Katharinen: Scripta Mercaturae, 1988). On the history of the first chairs of 'Oeconomie, Policey und Kammer-Sachen' in Halle and Frankfurt-an-der-Oder see Marcus Sandl, "Die Viadrina und der Aufstieg der ökonomischen Wissenschaften im Zeitalter der Aufklärung," in *Europäische Bildungsströme. Die Viadrina im Kontext der europäischen Gelehrtenrepublik in der Frühen Neuzeit, 1506–1811*, ed. Reinhard Blänkner (Schöneiche-at-Berlin: scrîpvaz-Verlag, 2008), 195–222.

16 Gottfried Achenwall, *Die Staatsklugheit nach ihren ersten Grundsätzen entworfen* (Göttingen, 1761), foreword, pp. 13–14: '[...] die darüber in neuern Zeiten hauptsächlich entdeckten Grundsätze und erfundene künstlichere Einrichtungen gewisse Staaten in solches Aufnehmen, Flor und Ansehen gebracht, daß alle andere Staaten, wenn sie nicht zuviel dabey verliehren, und in Verhältniß mit jenen schwächer werden, und nach und nach in grössern Verfall gerathen wollen, eben diese Maximen und Einrichtungen, so viel eines jeden besondere Verfassung zuläßt, annehmen und nachahmen müssen'.

17 This subject was discussed particularly in textbooks about foreign policy. See inter alia Johann Friedrich von Pfeiffer, *Grundriß der wahren und falschen Staatskunst*, 2 vols. (Berlin, 1778/79); Johann Heinrich Gottlob von Justi, *Natur und Wesen der Staaten als die Quelle aller Regierungswissenschaften und Gesezze*. Annotated and edited by Heinrich Godfried Scheidemantel, 2nd ed. (Mittau, 1771); id., *Gesammlete Politische und Finanzschriften über wichtige Gegenstände der Staatskunst, der Kriegswissenschaften und des Cameral- und Finanzwesens*, 3 vols. (Copenhagen and Leipzig, 1760/61).

18 With regard to the impacts of this development on the German territories see Dietmar Willoweit, *Rechtsgrundlagen der Territorialgewalt. Landesobrigkeit, Herrschaftsrechte und Territorium in der Rechtwissenschaft der Neuzeit* (Cologne: Böhlau, 1975).

19 Carl Schmitt has pointed out this connection impressively in Carl Schmitt, *The Nomos of the Earth in the International Law of the Jus Publicum Europaeum* (New York: Telos, 2003). See Olaf Asbach and Peter Schröder, eds., *War, the State and International Law in Seventeenth-Century Europe* (Farnham: Ashgate, 2010).

20 Johann Heinrich Gottlob von Justi, *Staatswirthschaft oder systematische Abhandlung aller ökonomischen und Cameralwissenschaft*, 2 vols. (Leipzig, 1755).

21 Meanwhile there are a number of recent English works regarding Justi's 'political economy'. See Ulrich Adam, *The Political Economy of J.H.G. Justi* (Frankfurt am Main: Peter Lang, 2006); Jürgen Georg Backhaus, ed., *The Beginnings of Political Economy. Johann Heinrich Gottlob von Justi* (Boston: Springer, 2009).

22 See Justi, *Staatswirthschaft*, vol. 1, p. 59 et seq.

23 Ibid., vol. 1, p. 224: 'In der That kann man sich eine Republik sehr natürlich unter dem Bilde eines menschlichen Körpers vorstellen. Der Reichthum ist das Blut, die Gewerbe sind die Adern und die Regierung ist das Herz, in welcher der in den Gewerben circulirende Reichthum durch die Abgaben nach und nach fließet, und sich von dar wieder in alle Theile des Staatskörpers durch den Aufwand der Regierung ergießet'.

24 Ibid., vol. 1, p. 88.

25 Johann Heinrich Gottlob von Justi, "Rede, von dem unzertrennlichen Zusammenhange eines blühenden Zustandes der Wissenschaften mit denjenigen Mitteln, welche einen Staat mächtig und glücklich machen," in: Justi, *Gesammlete Politische und Finanzschriften*, vol. 2, pp. 128–175, at p. 147 et seq.: '[...] es ist eine Wahrheit, die keiner weitläuftigen Ausführung bedarf, daß ein Staat ohne genugsame Macht niemals eine vollkommene äußerliche Sicherheit genießen kann: und gleichwie die äusserliche Sicherheit mit der innerlichen genau zusammen hängt, eben so wie der Reichthum eines Staates ohne beyde Arten der Sicherheit weder erworben noch erhalten werden kann; so ist es gewiß, daß ein Staat nie seinen großen Endzweck, nämlich die Glückseligkeit, erreichen wird, wenn er nicht zugleich mächtig ist'.

26 See inter alia Justus Christoph Dithmar, *Einleitung in die Oeconomische- Policey- und Cameral-Wissenschafften* (Frankfurt am Main, 1745); Joachim Georg Darjes, *Erste Gründe der Cameral-Wissenschaften, darinnen die Haupt-Theile so wohl der Oeconomie als auch der Polizei und besondern Cameralwissenschaft*, 2nd ed. (Leipzig 1768); Johann Heinrich Jung, *Versuch einer Grundlehre sämmtlicher Kameralwissenschaften zum Gebrauche der Vorlesungen auf der Kurpfälzischen Kameral Hohenschule zu Lautern* (Lautern 1779); Johann Friedrich von Pfeiffer, *Lehrbegriff sämmtlicher oeconomischer und Cameralwissenschaften*, 1764–1765, 3 vols., 2nd ed. (Mannheim, 1773–1778); Joseph von Sonnenfels, *Grundsätze der Staatspolizey, Handlung und Finanzwissenschaft. Zum Gebrauche der akademischen Vorlesungen ausgearbeitet von Franz Xaver von Moshammer*, 2nd ed. (Munich, 1801).

27 Johann Friedrich Pfeiffer, *Natürliche aus dem Endzweck der Gesellschaft entstehende Allgemeine Policeiwissenschaft* (Frankfurt am Main, 1779), vol. 1, p. 290: '[...] alle Zweigen des Nahrungsstandes vermehrte Kräfte und Thätigkeit geben, den Umlauf lebhaft, die Bevölkerung stark, und den Staat mächtig machen'.

28 Justi, *Natur und Wesen*, p. 541 et seq.: 'Damit die Staaten ihre politische Freyheit behaupten können; so müssen sie eine Macht haben, wodurch sie sich dabey zu erhalten im Stande sind. Diese Macht oder Stärke des Staates ist nur ein relativischer Begriff, der sich auf die Kräfte anderer, und insonderheit der benachbarten Staaten beziehet [...]'.

29 The semantic of 'crisis' originates from the legal and medical field in which it defined always situations of decision – decision between conviction and acquittal, life and death. See Reinhart Koselleck, "Krise," in: *Geschichtliche Grundbegriffe, Historisches Lexikon zur politisch-sozialen Sprache in Deutschland*, ed. Otto Brunner, Werner Conze and Reinhart Koselleck, vol. 3 (Stuttgart: Klett-Cotta, 2004), 617–650; id.,

"Krise," in *Historisches Wörterbuch der Philosophie*, ed. Gerhard Ritter, vol. 4 (Basle: Schwabe, 1976), 1235–1240.

30 Johann Friedrich Pfeiffer, *Grundsätze und Regeln der Staatswirthschaft* (Mainz, 1787), p. 7.

31 Gottfried Achenwall, *Vorbereitung zur Staatswissenschaft der heutigen fürnehmsten Europäischen Reiche und Staaten worinnen derselben eigentlicher Begriff und Umfang in einer bequemen Ordnung entwirft und seine Vorlesungen darüber ankündiget* (Göttingen, 1748), p. 5: 'Der Staat heißt hier also der Inbegriff alles dessen, was in einer bürgerlichen Gesellschaft und deren Lande würkliches angetroffen wird'.

32 Johann Heinrich Gottlob von Justi, 'Rede, von dem unzertrennlichen Zusammenhange eines blühenden Zustandes der Wissenschaften mit denjenigen Mitteln, welche einen Staat mächtig und glücklich machen,' in: id., *Gesammelte Politische und Finanzschriften*, vol. 2, pp. 128–175, at p. 151: 'Eine jede Wissenschaft hält Wahrheiten in sich. [...] Eine jede Wahrheit aber gründet sich auf die Ordnung in den Veränderungen der Dinge'.

33 Niklas Luhmann, *The Reality of the Mass Media* transl. Kathleen Cross (Stanford: Stanford University Press, 2000), 1.

34 In regard to Luhmann's theory of decision-making see Niklas Luhmann, *Legitimation durch Verfahren* (Frankfurt am Main: Suhrkamp, 1983), and André Krischer, "Sociological and Cultural Approaches to Pre-Modern Decision-Making," in *Débates Antiques*, ed. Marie-Joséphine Coquin and Fabian Schulz (Nanterre, 2011), 129–140.

35 See among others Fabio Crivellari and Marcus Sandl, "Die Medialität der Geschichte. Forschungsstand und Perspektiven einer interdisziplinären Zusammenarbeit von Geschichts- und Medienwissenschaften," *Historische Zeitschrift*, 277 (2003), 619–654, and Fabio Crivellari, Kay Kirchmann, Marcus Sandl and Rudolf Schlögl, eds, *Die Medien der Geschichte. Medialität und Historizität in interdisziplinärer Perspektive* (Konstanz: UVK, 2004).

36 On this topic Joseph Vogl and Bernhard Siegert are especially prolific researchers. See Bernhard Siegert, *Passage des Digitalen. Zeichenpraktiken der neuzeitlichen Wissenschaften, 1500–1900* (Berlin: Brinkmann & Bose, 2003),156 ff.; Vogl, *Kalkül und Leidenschaft*, 54ff.

37 Gottfried Wilhelm Leibniz, "Entwurff gewißer Staats-Tafeln," in: id., *Sämtliche Schriften und Briefe*, 4th series: Politische Schriften, vol. 3 (Berlin, 1986), p. 341: 'Ich nenne Staats-Tafeln eine schriftliche kurze Verfassung des Kerns aller zu der Landesregierung gehörigen Nachrichtungen, so ein gewisses Land in Sonderheit betreffen, mit solchen Vorteil eingerichtet, dass der hohe Landesherr alles darin leicht finden, was er bei jeder Begebenheit zu betrachten, und sich dessen als eines der bequemsten Instrumente zu einer löblichen Selbst-Regierung bedienen könne'.

38 Vogl, *Kalkül und Leidenschaft*, 59: 'Der Staat, der auf seine eigene Identität reflektiert, ist eine Funktion jenes empirischen Wissens, das er über sich und seine Existenzbedingungen erhebt, auswählt, beständig erneuert, systematisiert und auf einen Extrakt zum Gebrauch durch den Regenten komprimiert [...]. Der Staat ist damit nicht ein für allemal gesetzt und gegeben, sondern im Selbstbezug einer Wissensrelation beständig in Bewegung und beständig zu novellieren'.

39 See on this subject also Rüdiger Campe, "Barocke Formulare," in *Europa. Kultur der Sekretäre*, ed. Bernhard Siegert and Joseph Vogl (Zurich and Berlin: Diaphanes, 2003), 79–96, and – more general – Matthias Bauer and Christoph Ernst, *Diagrammatik. Einführung in ein kultur- und medienwissenschaftliches Forschungsfeld* (Bielefeld: transcript, 2010).

40 Johann Heinrich Gottlob von Justi, *Die Grundfeste zu der Glückseligkeit der Staaten oder ausführliche Vorstellung der gesamten Policeywißenschaft* (Königsberg and Leipzig, 1760), vol. 1, p. 490. Another example would be the Habsburg Cameralist Joseph von Sonnenfels who postulated to create 'jährliche Seelenbeschreibungen' ('annual soul-descriptions') in which information about the inhabitants of a territory

should be collected. See Joseph von Sonnenfels, *Grundsätze der Policey, Handlung und Finanzwissenschaft. Abgekürzet, in Tabellen gebracht, und zum Gebrauche seiner akademischen Vorlesungen eingerichtet vom Hofrathe Moshammer zu Ingolstadt* (Munich, 1787), p. 34.

41 Ibid, p. 491: 'Diese Tabellen müssen der Grund von der ganzen Direction dieser Nahrungsarten seyn'.
42 See also ibid, p. 129.
43 Justi, *Staatswirthschaft*, vol. 1, p. 199.
44 Ibid., p. 200: 'Das was wir hier vorgestellt haben, ist die allgemeine Handlungsbilanz, in welcher nemlich alle eingehende und ausgehende Waaren in Rechnung und Gegenrechnung gebracht werden, um zu sehen, ob die Nation bey der Handlung verliert oder gewinnt'.
45 See Nipperdey, *Erfindung der Bevölkerungspolitik*, 376ff., and Lars Behrisch, ed., *Vermessen, Zählen, Berechnen. Die politische Ordnung des Raums im 18. Jahrhundert* (Frankfurt am Main and New York: Campus, 2006).
46 See for example Sonnenfels, *Grundsätze der Policey*, p. 35ff. The sequence mentioned here gives a good impression of interrelation of tables and bookkeeping: 'Die nothwendigsten Rubriken [...] sind folgende: der Stand der Familie bei der letzten Beschreibung: der Zuwachs von dieser Zeit an Gebohrnen, an aus andern Häusern, aus andern Städten hieher versetzten: an Fremden: der Abgang an Gestorbenen nach den Stufen des Alters, an in andere Häuser, in andere Städte versetzten, an Ausgewanderten. Die Gegeneinanderhaltung dieser beiden Fächer zeigt den gegenwärtigen Stand der Familie, wovon weiters umständlich das Geschlecht, das Alter unter gewissen Stufenjahren, die Religion, die Beschäftigung, und der Stand, die Mitarbeiter, Dienstleute, dann die Ehen, die lebenden Kinder beschrieben werden müssen. Jeder Familienvater beschreibt sich selbst nach einem ihm vom Staate vorgeschriebenen Formular: aus diesen einzelnen Familienbeschreibungen zieht der Hausinhaber, der auf die Richtigkeit der erstern zusehe, und die Familienbeschreibungen beizulegen hat, eine Beschreibung seines Hauses: aus den Haustabellen verfertigen die über die Richtigkeit der Haustabellen wachenden Gassenkommissäre Gassentabellen, oder Tabellen von gewissen kleinern Bezirken, und dann Viertelkommissäre Vierteltabellen [...]. Aus Landes- und Stadttabellen nun wird eine zuverläßige allgemeine Beschreibung eines Staates gezogen, wo die kleineren Untertheilungen hinweggelässen werden. Diese Tabelle ist in den Händen des Staatsmannes die Richtschnur aller Anstalten, und nicht weniger eine Wegweisung das Fehlerhafte in denselben aufzuführen'.
47 Justi, *Staatswirthschaft*, vol. 1, Foreword, p. XI.
48 In regard to the Cameral sciences as a constitutive part of the described circulation process – in the sense of a circulation of money, goods *and* knowledge – see Sandl, "Die Viadrina," 195ff.
49 Johann Heinrich Gottlob von Justi, *Die Grundfeste zu der Macht und Glückseeligkeit der Staaten; oder ausführliche Vorstellung der gesamten Policey-Wissenschaft*, vol. 1 (Königsberg and Leipzig, 1760), p. 65: '[...] so muß doch eine weise Regierung ihre Vorsorge allemal auf das Künftige erstrecken, und ihre Plans und Entwürfe auf den glücklichsten Zustand des Staats, den er möglicher Weise erreichen kann, schon in voraus machen. Sie muß also schon lange vorher überlegen, auf was Art die Commercien in Zukunft immer blühender gemacht werden können [...]'.
50 Johann Heinrich Jung, *Lehrbuch der Staats-Polizey-Wissenschaft* (Leipzig 1788), p. 4: 'Die wesentlich Pflicht der regierenden Gewalt besteht darin: dass sie die zeitliche Glückseeligkeit der ihr anvertrauten Staates durch die besten und zweckgemäsesten Mittel bis zur höchsten Stuffe befördern muß [...]'.
51 Johann Friedrich von Pfeiffer, *Lehrbegriff sämtlicher oeconomischer und Cameralwissenschaften*, vol. 4,1 (Mannheim, 1778), p. 3: '[...] glücklich, und abermals glücklich ist folglich die Nation, die einen Joseph II zum Beherrscher hat, dessen Adlers-Auge das Gegenwärtige durchdringet, und scharfe Blicke auf die Zukunft wirft,

ja dessen herrschende Leidenschaft, das Glück der Menschen, und die wahre Größe Deutschlands zum Endzweck hat'.

52 Politisches Testament Friedrichs des Großen (1768), in *Politische Testamente der Hohenzollern* ed. Richard Dietrich (Munich: Deutscher Taschenbuch Verlag, 1981), 331. See Manfred Schneider, "Die Entdeckung der Zukunft des Staates. Friedrich II. und das Calcul," in *Gutenberg und die Neue Welt*, ed. Horst Wenzel (Munich: Fink, 1994), 327–350.

53 Carl Gottlob Rößig, *Lehrbuch der Polizeywissenschaft* (Jena, 1786), p. 2: 'Die Polizey ist das Ordnungswesen in einem Staate in Rücksicht auf innere Sicherheit, Schönheit, Bequemlichkeit, Bevölkerung, Sittlichkeit und den Nahrungsstand'.

54 See for example Rößig, *Lehrbuch*, p. 215ff., and Jung, *Lehrbuch*, p. 360ff.

55 See Justi, *Staatswirthschaft*, vol. 1, p. 220ff.

56 See Justi, *Grundfeste*, vol. 1, p. 763ff.

57 Justi, *Grundfeste*, vol. 1, p. 764ff.: 'Eine weise Regierung muß demnach auf solche Anstalten bedacht seyn, welchen wenigsten denen äußersten Folgen des Unglücks Einhalt thun, und dessen schädlichen Einfluß in den Nahrungsstand verhintern. Dieses zu leisten sind nun die Assecuranz- und Versicherungsanstalten allerley Arten gar sehr geschickt. Durch diese Anstalten wird gleichsam das Unglück, welches etliche wenige betrift, und sie zum Nachtheil des Nahrungsstandes zu Boden zu schlagen in Begrif ist, unter mehrere verteilet, und dannenhero weit erträglicher'.

58 Justi, *Staatswirthschaft*, vol. 1, p. 465: 'Allein die Vermehrung des Vermögens wird dennoch nur einen ganz langsamen Fortgang haben, wenn man nicht in seinen Gewerben und Angelegenheiten auf eine vernünftige Art etwas waget, und zuweilen einen Theil seines Vermögens den Streichen des Glücks unterwirft'.

59 Ibid., p. 467: 'Eben nach diesen Grundsätzen müssen diejenigen, die dergleichen gefährliche Unternehmungen wagen, die Wahrscheinlichkeit des Verlustes, so viel möglich kleiner machen'.

60 Ibid., p. 466 ff., at p. 468: 'Ja man kann sogar alles dieses durch die richtigsten mathematischen Rechnungen bestimmen'.

61 Ian Hacking, *The Emergence of Probability. A Philosophical Study of Early Ideas about Probability, Induction and Statistical Inference* (Cambridge: Cambridge University Press, 1984).

62 See Keith Devlin, *The Unfinished Game. Pascal, Fermat, and the Seventeenth-Century Letter that Made the World Modern* (New York: Basic Books, 2008).

63 See the overview in Lorraine J. Daston, "The Domestication of Risk: Mathematical Probability and Insurance, 1650–1830," in *The Probabilistic Revolution,* ed. Lorenz Krüger, Lorraine Daston and Michale Heidelberger (Cambridge, Mass.: MIT Press, 1987), vol. 1, 237–260, and the exciting essay of Philipp von Hilgers, "Vom Einbruch des Spiels in die Epoche der Vernunft," in *Visuelle Argumentationen. Die Mysterien der Repräsentation und die Berechenbarkeit der Welt*, ed. Horst Bredekamp and Pablo Schneider (Munich: Wilhelm Fink Verlag, 2006), 205–223.

64 See Rüdiger Campe, *Spiel der Wahrscheinlichkeit. Literatur und Berechnung zwischen Pascal und Kleist* (Göttingen: Wallstein, 2002), and Peter Schnyder, *Alea. Zählen und Erzählen im Zeichen des Glücksspiels*, 1650–1850 (Göttingen: Wallstein, 2009).

65 Niklas Luhmann, *Die Religion der Gesellschaft* (Frankfurt am Main: Suhrkamp, 2000), 58, and id., *Reality of the Mass Media*, 1ff.

66 'Viele neue und besondere Geschäffte und Zwecke in oeconomischen und politischen Dingen sind ohne allen Zweiffel unter denenjenigen, welche zum öfftern viele wahrscheinliche Gründe auf der einen Seite, um solche vorzunehmen und zu suchen vor sich, als auch wahrscheinliche Einwürffe wider sich haben, um solche entweder gar zu unterlassen, oder doch die Mittel und Wege samt der Art und Weise zum Zweck zu gelangen, welche sich bey diesem und jenem Einfall und Vornehmen anfänglich darbieten, zu verändern und zu verwerffen. Beyderley Gründe aber gegen einander zu halten, und das wahrscheinlichste zu finden, ist nicht jeden gegeben'. Georg Heinrich

Zincke, "Vorrede," in: Peter Kretzschmer, *Nunmehrigen Hauß-Vaters im Leipziger Waysen- und Zucht-Hause, Oekonomische Vorschläge* [...], 2nd ed. (Leipzig, 1746), p. 6.

67 Wolfgang Schäffner, "Nicht-Wissen um 1800. Buchführung und Statistik," in: *Poetologien des Wissens*, 123–144, at 128: 'Es handelt sich also um eine Neuerfindung des Staates, der sich nicht mehr als Territorium, sondern als Datenmenge bestimmt, die den Zustand eines Staatskörpers beschreibbar und die Zukunft kalkulierbar macht'.

68 Daniel Defoe, *An Essay on Projects* (London, 1697), p. 1.

69 Ibid., p. 6.

70 For this see the excellent contribution of Christian Reder, "Daniel Defoe. Beginn des Projektzeitalters," in: Daniel Defoe, *Ein Essay über Projekte. London 1697.* Edited and annotated by Christian Reder (Vienna and New York: Springer, 2006), 7–86.

71 See Niklas Luhmann, "Die Moral des Risikos und das Risiko der Moral," in: Gotthard Bechmann, ed., *Risiko und Gesellschaft. Grundlagen und Ergebnisse interdisziplinärer Risikoforschung* (Opladen: Westdeutscher Verlag, 1993), 327–338.

72 Johann Heinrich Gottlob von Justi, "Gedanken von Projecten und Projectmachern," in: Justi, *Gesammelte Politische und Finanzschriften*, vol. 1, pp. 256–281.

73 Ibid., p. 257: 'Meines Erachtens versteht man unter einem Project, einen ausführlichen Entwurf eines gewissen Unternehmens, wodurch unsere eigene oder anderer Menschen Glückseligkeit befördert werden soll; zu welchem Ende alle zu ergreifenden Mittel und Maaßregeln, benebst den zu befürchtenden Schwierigkeiten und Hindernissen und die Art und Weise dieselben aus dem Wege zu räumen, in einem solchen Entwurfe deutlich vorgestellt werden'.

74 Georg Stanitzek, "Der Projektmacher. Projektionen auf eine 'unmögliche' moderne Kategorie," in *Projektemacher. Zur Produktion von Wissen in der Vorform des Scheiterns*, ed. Markus Krajewski (Berlin: Kulturverlag Kadmos, 2004), 29–48, at 33: 'Es geht um ein Vorhaben, eine Absicht, die die Bedingungen ihrer Realisierung, ihrer erfolgreichen Umsetzung mitbedenkt, ausweist und, so kann man hinzufügen, auf diese Weise ihre Akzeptanz mitzuorganisieren sucht'.

75 Johann Heinrich Ludwig Bergius, *Policey- und Cameral-Magazin*, vol. 7 (Frankfurt am Main, 1773), p. 210: '[...] und wenn es die Pflicht eines vernünftigen Mannes ist, zu dem Wohl seiner Mitbürger und der menschlichen Gesellschaft überhaupt alles mögliche beyzutragen [...]'.

76 Ibid., p. 213: 'Ferner muß ein Projectmacher selbst von dem Lande, vor welches er sein Project bestimmet, und von dessen Zustand und Beschaffenheit sowohl, als von den Gerechtsamen und Gesinnungen des Volkes, eine Kenntnis besitzen [...]'.

77 Ibid.: 'Auch muß ein Projectmacher eine gute Vernunft und Vorstellungskraft haben, daß er alle die Angelegenheiten und Einrichtungen, die mit seinem Projecte in Zusammenhang und Verbindung kommen werden, benebst allen daraus entstehenden Wirkungen und Folgen auf einmahl übersehen kann'.

78 Ibid.: 'Endlich muß ein Projectmacher die Fähigkeit besitzen, seine Vorschläge deutlich und kurz schriftlich vorzutragen'.

79 Justi, *Gedanken von Projecten*, p. 257ff.: 'Ich muß so gar noch weiter gehen; ich muß nicht allein behaupten, daß in diesem Verstande alle Menschen Projectmacher sind; sondern ich muß es sogar annehmen, daß es alle Menschen schlechterdings seyn müssen; wenn sie in ihren Angelegenheiten klug und vernünftig verfahren wollen'.

9 The political economy of Sweden's *Age of Greatness*

Johan Risingh and the Hartlib Circle

Carl Wennerlind

Introduction

The Thirty Years' War elevated Sweden to a major world power. Through Gustavus II Adolphus's military conquests, Sweden established control over many strategic regions around the Baltic, sparking dreams of a Swedish *Mare Nostrum*.[1] Enthusiasm about Sweden's unlikely ascent to geopolitical prominence spread quickly. Not only was a bright future envisioned, but Sweden's past was recast to suggest that the present moment represented a return to, rather than a first encounter with, greatness.[2] Yet, in many quarters, a great deal of concern remained about the readiness of the Swedish population, the Swedish economy, and the Swedish state to realize the opportunities that the warrior king had bequeathed to the nation. For the *Age of Greatness* to materialize, a new vision of progress and improvement had to be developed and implemented.[3] While Queen Christina (1626–1689) famously assembled a circle of prominent scientists and philosophers in her court in an effort to elevate the Swedish intellectual climate, the reform movement began in earnest a decade earlier when Lord High Chancellor Axel Oxenstierna (1583–1654), Uppsala University Chancellor Johan Skytte (1577–1645), and merchant and industrialist Louis De Geer (1587–1652) initiated an educational reform, designed to shift the attention away from Aristotle and Luther towards a curriculum centered on utilitarian improvement. Inspired and influenced by the new intellectual currents rapidly spreading throughout Northern Europe, Sweden began to develop its own improvement discourse. This discourse would later provide the foundation for some of Sweden's most illustrious scientists, including the influential chemist Urban Hiärne (1641–1724), the mechanical genius Christopher Polhem (1661–1751), and the famous botanist Carl Linnaeus (1707–1778), all of whom believed that advancement in knowledge was the key to economic improvement.[4] This essay examines the early phase of the Swedish intellectual transformation, focusing on the fascinating figure of Johan Classon Risingh (1617–1672), who articulated the first version of the Swedish improvement discourse.

After concluding his doctorate degree in natural philosophy at Uppsala University in 1640, Risingh spent most of the ensuing decade traveling throughout the Low Countries, France, and England. Risingh was intent upon finding answers to the question of how the Dutch Republic, despite being embroiled in a prolonged war with mighty Spain, was able to prosper so dramatically. Queen Christina, who was desperate for knowledge that might enrich both the state and the nation, provided Risingh with a grant to complete a treatise on this question, which would have been the first treatise on political economy ever written in Sweden. But before he was able to complete his book, Oxenstierna tapped Risingh for service to the state. His unique expertise in political economy qualified him to become the first-ever secretary of the Board of Commerce (*Kommerskollegiet*) and soon thereafter the last-ever colonial governor of New Sweden, Delaware. Unfortunately, his tenure as governor was short-lived, lasting for less than two years (1654–1655). Blamed for the colony's failure, his previously illustrious political career came to a grinding halt. Apart from a brief stint as the inspector of the tolls and excise taxes due to the Swedish crown from Prussia and Pomerelia, Risingh spent the rest of his life, often in poverty, working on his treatise on political economy. Although the full treatise was never completed, he was able to publish two shorter books, one focused on land and the other on commerce.

When his tract on land improvement is read in conjunction with his writings on commerce, a rich political economy emerges that explores the interdependence between agriculture, manufacturing, mining, and trade; the interplay between science and commerce; and the coexistence of liberty and authority. With Risingh's tracts, Sweden now had its own manual for improvement and growth – a political economy fully compatible with the nation's newfound aspiration and self-identity as a great power.

Modern commentators have had a difficult time locating Risingh in the history of political economy. Eli Heckscher proclaimed that Risingh's writings constituted an antiquated version of mercantilism, Anders Fryxell insisted that Risingh was a visionary thinker who laid the foundation for a Swedish free trade tradition, while most recently, Stellan Dahlgren claimed that Risingh fits best in the cameralist camp, an opinion with which Anders Björnsson also seems to agree.[5] While there are certainly parts of Risingh's writings that can be used to assign him to any one of these labels, some more convincingly than others, I find it more fruitful to think of Risingh in the context of *Hartlibian political economy*, or in the broader European universal reformation movement.[6] In exploring Risingh's written work, I suggest that the Swedish improvement discourse was inspired by the ideas of the Hartlib Circle, the pan-European group of scientists and philosophers centered around Samuel Hartlib (1600–1662) in London. While Heckscher noted in passing a link between Risingh and Henry Robinson (1605–1673), one of the key members of the Hartlib Circle, the larger connections between the Hartlib Circle and the development of a new Swedish improvement discourse still remain unexplored.[7]

In tracing the connections between the Hartlib Circle and the Swedish improvement discourse, I am not suggesting that this was a unidirectional transmission of ideas, whereby a dominant English-centered philosophy trickled down to a small and powerless nation. Instead, I hope to capture a salient moment of a complex exchange of ideas that took place within a dynamic, multi-centric, transnational and transcultural network that ranged across northern Europe, and perhaps beyond. While I prioritize the Hartlib Circle in this essay, it should be recalled that while Hartlib was based in London his correspondence network brought together members from all over Protestant Europe. These members and affiliates, in turn, were connected to more local epistemic communities, between which ideas, knowledge, and ideologies flowed back and forth. In depicting how ideas moved between nodal points in this multi-centric intellectual network, I ultimately hope to contribute to the broader project of showing how Sweden's improvement discourse was embedded in and contributed to a broader European reform movement.

The Hartlib Circle in Sweden

Sweden's success in the Thirty Years' War was based on the modernization of its armed forces. Its military ambitions and successes necessitated a major reform of the nation's political institutions. Recognizing that it would be impossible for Sweden to play a central role in European power politics without a serious transformation of the state, Oxenstierna undertook a major reorganization.[8] One of his innovations was to establish a series of councils, designed to provide the state with accurate information and the latest expertise in crucial areas. These included the Board of Warfare (*Krigskollegium*), Naval Board (*Amiralitet-skollegium*), Board of Mines (*Bergskollegium*), and Board of Commerce (*Kommerskollegium*).[9] The state also engaged in various projects designed to enhance the circulation of goods, people, and information, including the founding of new cities, the building of canals, the organizing of a postal system, and efforts to attract prominent Low Country merchants to aid in the modernization of the economy. Economically, the second half of the seventeenth century witnessed spectacular developments in credit and banking, mining and metal works, manufacturing, and shipping.[10] As part of the effort to strengthen the nation's economy, following the examples set by the English and the Dutch, Sweden initiated a campaign to establish colonies throughout the world. They succeeded, if not for very long, in acquiring a fortified presence in Delaware in North America (1638–1655) and in Cabo Corso on the African Gold Coast (1650–1663).[11] If Oxenstierna reasoned that Sweden could indeed establish control over the Baltic trade, its American and African colonies would serve as strategic nodes in a powerful trading network that would bring in riches to the population, strengthen the state, and finance a continued expansion of Sweden's borders. Sweden stood at the doorstep of a glorious age. Given the multiple advantages they enjoyed over both England and the Dutch Republic in terms of access to natural resources, there was no reason why Sweden could not succeed in becoming a world power.[12]

Swedish elites recognized the urgency of modernizing both the state and the economy. While everyone agreed that fiscal and financial mechanisms had to be revamped and the nation's commercial infrastructure developed, ultimately the only way that the nation could improve was if the general population embraced the new spirit of progress. It therefore became essential to conduct a complete reorganization of the nation's educational system. While the utilitarian approach to education advocated by Peter Ramus (1515–1572) had already begun to challenge the prevailing conservative doctrines of Aristotle and Luther, a more systematic redesign of the nation's educational philosophy was launched when Oxenstierna, Skytte, and De Geer invited two important members of the Hartlib Circle – first the Scottish reformer John Dury (1596–1680) and soon thereafter the Moravian scholar, reformer, and theologian John Amos Comenius (1592–1670) – to come to Sweden to remake the nation's curriculum.

Dury came to Sweden in 1636, personally invited by Gustavus II Adolphus and Axel Oxenstierna, whom he had encountered in Elbing a decade earlier. His arrival in Sweden sparked some controversy, as his pansophism and ecumenism were considered too radical by the Lutheran clergy to be compatible with Sweden's aspirations to take a leading role among the Protestant nations engaged in the Thirty Years' War. Dury's controversial presence forced his benefactor De Geer to downplay their relationship. Dury mentioned, in a letter to Hartlib, that:

> Neither shall I appeare to haue anie neere relacon to him but onely be togeather as good acquaintance. His name is Lovijs de Geere, which I would haue yu to keepe to your self, for certeine reasons, because of some relations of State vnder which he standeth.[13]

Dury also reported back to Hartlib that Comenius's name was on everyone's lips in Sweden.[14] Queen Christina's tutor, Johannes Matthiae (1592–1670), had translated a number of Comenius's writings into Swedish and Johan Skytte included two works by Comenius as mandatory reading for all students in his 1637 university reform proposal. His mix of pansophism and ecumenism – focused on the unification of Christianity, the interconnection of the physical sciences, and the interrelatedness of the material and spiritual worlds – combined with his political and eschatological vision, appealed to reform-minded Swedes interested in promoting the formation of a modern, prosperous, and pious society.[15] De Geer first pursued Comenius to come to Sweden to chair the scientific and philosophical reform society he was planning to establish at his newly-acquired demesne of Finspång. Comenius had long been an advocate of the creation of such a 'house of wisdom', arguing that it could serve as a catalyst for universal enlightenment. He insisted that the only way to recapture the knowledge dispersed and scattered by God as a punishment for human folly and hubris was to establish a central location where knowledge from all over the world could be systematically reassembled and wisdom restored.[16] While Comenius never visited Finspång, he arrived in Sweden in 1642 ready to take on the broader mission of modernizing Sweden's intellectual culture. A staunch believer in the Paracelsian prophecy that God had selected Sweden as his instrument on earth and that Sweden was designated as the centerpiece of a united Christian Europe, Comenius enthusiastically accepted the challenge.[17]

Comenius introduced the Swedish intelligentsia to the universal reform program that he and Dury, in collaboration with Samuel Hartlib, Gabriel Plattes (1600–1644), William Petty (1623–1687), Benjamin Worsley (1618–1677), and Henry

Robinson, among many others, were in the process of developing.[18] While it is difficult to do justice to the complexity of the Hartlib Circle's various engagements and undertakings – they wrote no manifesto that all members subscribed to, nor was the membership constant over the years, as a number of people circled in and out – it is plausible to suggest that most of the members shared a similar worldview and subscribed to the same basic principles on the issues of spirituality, natural history, and political economy.[19]

Most fundamentally, the Hartlib Circle believed in humanity's capacity to develop knowledge about nature that would enable them to significantly improve their material conditions. Inspired by Francis Bacon, they insisted that through the proper use of experimental and empirical methods, supported by reason and revelation, mankind could re-create the knowledge lost at the Fall of Man and thus restore human command over nature. Cooperation was essential to the success of the Hartlibian program. People had to collectively and systematically pursue new knowledge and then freely share information about their findings with each other, even across national and religious boundaries – although the latter principle was not always upheld. Knowledge belonged to God and he had given it to mankind in common. No one, therefore, had the right to monopolize God's possession. As scientists uncovered more of nature's secrets, humanity would embark on a self-sustaining journey of improvement, capable of yielding vast material and economic benefits, as well as political, social, and spiritual refinement. For them, the millenarian notion that a paradise on earth was possible, even imminent, was indisputable. As Charles Webster points out, the purpose of the Hartlib Circle was to create the 'conditions for the imminent realization of the Kingdom of God, in the form of the earthly paradise, fulfilling the biblical prophecies of the New Eden and New Jerusalem'.[20]

Hartlib and his collaborators authored, published, and circulated a wide array of proposals for the advancement of humanity. They offered ideas on how to improve knowledge in numerous, and for them interrelated, fields, including linguistics, practical mathematics, mechanics, manufacturing, physics, anatomy, botany, horticulture, husbandry, and alchemy. For many, alchemy played a particularly important role, both as a form of knowledge about nature and as a way of framing mankind's relationship to nature.[21] Consonant with the Paracelsian tradition, they believed that all matter was malleable and that mankind had the capacity to operate on nature. Most of the Hartlibians focused on the improvement of agriculture, offering ways to improve the yield of plants, trees, flowers, grass, meadows, forests, and wastelands.[22] The potential benefits of a systematic implementation of these new ideas were nothing short of remarkable. In summing up his vision for what a properly managed Baconian project might achieve, Hartlib proclaimed:

> that our *Native Countrey,* hath in its bowels an (even almost) infinite, and inexhaustible treasure; much of which hath long laine hid, and is but new begun to be discovered. It may seem a *large boast* or meer *Hyperbole* to say, we enjoy not, know not, use not, the one tenth part of that plenty or wealth &

happinesse, that our Earth can, and (*Ingenuity* and *industry* well encouraged) will (by Gods blessing) yield.[23]

In addition to the improvement of nature and animals, humans could also be improved and transmuted. Through religious instruction, hard work, and proper education, it was possible to transform people, at the very core. William Petty, for example, advocated that all children, regardless of 'poverty and unability of their Parents', should be given proper physical and intellectual training, because 'it hath come to passe, that many are now holding the Plough, which might have beene made fit to steere the State'.[24] While the Hartlibians certainly had no problems with social mobility based on merit, industry, and inventiveness, their overall focus was on improving the character and quality of the entire population, so that everyone became more productive, industrious, and moral.

Ultimately, the spread of useful knowledge would contribute to the irenic aim of uniting Protestant Europe and eventually all of Christianity. By promoting, in Dury's words, the:

> Arts and Sciences Philosophicall, Chymicall & Mechanicall: whereby not only the Secrets of Disciplines are harmonically and compendiously delivered, but also the secrets of Nature are thought to be unfolded, so yt Gods wonderfull power, wisdome and goodness is to be seene more apparently in bodily things than ever heretofore.[25]

As Vera Keller and Leigh Penman point out, the quest for spiritual enlightenment and utilitarian knowledge were inseparably intertwined for the Hartlibians.[26]

Bengt Skytte's *Sophopolis*

Comenius remained employed by the Swedish state until 1648. But because of the reluctance of the clergy to accept him and his ideas, he was forced to undertake most of his work from Elbing. Yet, despite spending limited time in Sweden, Comenius had a significant impact on Sweden's intellectual culture. One of Comenius's most prominent Swedish disciples was the nobleman Bengt Skytte (1614–1683). As the son of Johan Skytte, the influential scholar and Chancellor of Uppsala University, Bengt enjoyed direct access to some of Sweden's most important intellectual circles. The illustrious Georg Stiernhielm served as his mentor during his student years and later ensured that he had access to both the vibrant epistemic communities surrounding Olof Rudbeck (1630–1702) in Uppsala and Queen Christina in Stockholm.[27] The Queen embraced him and trusted him with a position in her privy council. His intellectual interest overlapped extensively with that of the Queen. He was passionately interested in pansophism, ecumenism, natural history, and Paracelsian alchemy and was a keen supporter of the efforts to expose the Swedish public to new ideas through a thoroughgoing educational reform.[28] While Skytte may have encountered Comenius as early as 1642 in Stockholm, their most sustained interactions occurred in Siebenbürgen, in present-day Romania, where they spent a few weeks in each other's company in 1651.[29] They explored their shared interests in the development of a universal language – a project Skytte had been working on for some time with Stiernhielm – and the pursuit of universal knowledge.[30]

After some years of traveling around Europe in search of the latest ideas and knowledge, Skytte moved to London in 1657, a place he had visited a few times before. Charles X Gustav (1622–1660) employed him to report on the political atmosphere in the English capital and to work towards a greater spiritual, political, and commercial partnership between Sweden and England.[31] While he dutifully fulfilled his obligations to the king, he seems to have been mostly focused on meeting and learning from the city's many intellectual authorities. Johan Leijonberg (1625–1691), who later would become the first Swede elected to the Royal Society, introduced Skytte to Samuel Hartlib and his collaborators, including the agricultural improver Cressy Dymock (1629–1660), the prominent alchemist Frederick Clodius (1629–1702), and the great advocate for educational pansophism, John Dury, who had by this time returned to England.[32] Skytte also engaged in a sustained conversation with a group Hartlib referred to as 'the virituosos', which included the 'chymist' Robert Boyle (1627–1691), the experimentalist John Wilkins (1614–1672), the astronomer Paul Neile (1613–1686), the mathematician William Brouncker (1620–1684), and the polymath Christopher Wren (1632–1723).[33] They discussed how to best design a society for the advancement of learning, or more precisely, a *Colledge for the Promoting of Physico-Mathematical Experimentall Learning.* Skytte persistently promoted his plan for a Comenian-inspired *College of the Wise*, or *Sophopolis,* a city of knowledge, replete with libraries, museums, laboratories, printing presses, workshops, hospitals, and botanical garden.[34]

Convinced that Europe's and Christianity's troubles were caused by the loss and fragmentation of true knowledge and learning, Skytte insisted that a place must be established for people from all of the world to come together and weave back together all of the strands of knowledge lost or scattered. In his rationale for the plan, Skytte proclaimed:

> The divisions of Wisdom and of the various Sciences, being distributed between the knowledge and custody of diverse nations and person, will never regain fuller life and vigour and exercise the power of these same among mortals, until from all places, people and nations they are received and perfected in one place, and particular persons in a College and Society of one body, so that what is half-dead in a single person should be more fully revived in the wise conjoined in one location, and should render solid fruit, first to God as Creator, and to all the human race as members of one body, citizens of one city, which along is incumbent upon anyone who desires and hopes to become a citizen in the future eternal universal city of Jerusalem.[35]

Skytte tried valiantly to convince Charles II (1630–1685) that if he were to establish *Sophopolis* in England, he would be 'considered in actual fact the delight of the world'. Indeed, all nations would recognize him, 'not as a foreign, but as their universal king and patron and England . . . as the principal dwelling of Wisdom and of the Wise'.[36] Universal knowledge would unite humanity and by hosting and promoting the College responsible for developing it, the Stuarts would be at the helm of a universal monarchy. To accomplish this lofty aim, he advised the new king to dedicate a set of buildings, dwelling houses, courts, promenades, gardens, pastures, fields, domains, fishing waters, rivers, and hunting grounds to the College and grant it the use of all revenues that might accrue from the estate.[37] Invitations should be extended to experts and devotees of all scientific 'disciplines, arts and extraordinary matters', who would be welcome to take up residence at the College, where they would be free to pursue their projects, individually or collaboratively. They should enjoy 'freedom of Conscience' – as long as they did not practice or preach their religion publically – and in the event that they discovered 'any art or science useful to the public' they should be granted 'freedom to act as they wish in managing, selling, giving away, and disposing of the fruits of their learning and accomplishment and what they have produced'.[38] The only caveat was that they were required to donate a quarter of their proceeds to the College.

Like many of Comenius's and Hartlib's interlocutors, Skytte envisioned a fusion of spiritual and utilitarian knowledge. While he had already outlined the potential geopolitical benefits of locating *Sophopolis* in England, he added that his initiative was also essential to England's commercial vibrancy. In fact, if 'England wished to surpass all nations in Commerce and Wealth', it had no other choice but to go ahead with the implementation of his plan.[39] Direct economic benefits from the inventions produced in the College would be augmented by the commercial prosperity generated by travelers visiting the College. Just as people at some point in life wanted to visit Rome, Jerusalem, Loretta, Mecca, and Medina, so 'all men of all nations, ages and scholarly inclinations' would be drawn to England. They would bring along not only their learning, but also their treasures, which would provide the foundation for 'the most beautiful Emporium'.[40]

Once the Royal Society was formed and received its charter from Charles II in 1662, Skytte, most likely disappointed in his lack of influence on the ultimate institutional design, left England and sought patronage elsewhere.[41] Realizing that his political standing in Stockholm was not what it once was, he instead offered his plan for *Sophopolis* to Frederick William (1620–1688), the Elector of Brandenburg, who supported its launch in 1667. In preparing to break ground in Tangermünde, south-west of Berlin, Skytte interacted with Gottfried Leibniz (1646–1716), as well as Johann Joachim Becher (1635–1682), whose life and projects overlapped at numerous points with those of Skytte. Although Becher portrayed Skytte as a thief and atheist, Becher and Skytte shared many perspectives on learning, reform, and improvement.[42] For a variety of reasons, Skytte's plan ultimately failed to get off the ground, forcing him to move on and seek support from yet another regent, this time Frederick Casimir of Hanau (1623–1685). But once again, little came out of his ambitious plan.

Skytte's project was not only 'unmistakably influenced by Comenius', it was also arguably shaped by his interactions with Hartlib and some of the other members of his circle.[43] It embodied the same Baconian, Pansophist, and Paracelsian spirit that informed not only the Hartlib Circle's program, but also the rest of the northern European intellectual reform movement. Skytte was an important figure in the development of a Swedish improvement discourse. Because of his standing and pedigree he was able to gain access to important intellectuals, scientists, and reformers in England and on the continent. He also disseminated his ideas to students as the longtime Chancellor (1648–1664) of the newly founded Dorpat University. At least one important future contributor to the Swedish improvement project, Urban Hiärne, was enrolled at Dorpat University during Skytte's tenure as Chancellor. Skytte also forged important links between Swedish intellectual elites and their European counterparts, and promoted the project of universal reformation throughout the Protestant world.

Johan Classon Risingh and the formation of a Swedish improvement discourse

At the same time that Bengt Skytte was conducting research together with Comenius in Siebenbürgen, Johan Risingh accepted an invitation from Erik Oxenstierna (1624–1656), Axel's son, to become the secretary of the newly founded Board of Commerce in the summer of 1651. Risingh was the ideal candidate for the job. He was well-versed in natural philosophy, the language in which the new improvement discourse was framed, and he had spent years building up an expertise on commerce. He had come of age intellectually in some of the same circles as Skytte, with both having enjoyed the mentorship of Georg Stiernhielm (1598–1672). Indeed, it is far from unlikely that Rising and Skytte encountered each other on more than one occasion at Queen Christina's court. During his travels, Risingh had observed how the Dutch and English economies were organized, witnessing firsthand the hustle and bustle of the Amsterdam and London ports, and carefully studying the new political economic literature, mostly written by English authors, often focused on the commercial success of the Dutch. The Board of Commerce was founded with the intent of promoting Sweden's navigation, trade, manufacturing, and handicrafts, as well as more generally stimulating the industriousness of the Swedish population.[44] If Sweden were to become a serious contender for political power in Europe, it could not continue to rely on tax revenues from conquered regions, but had to develop a stronger economic base. This meant making better use of its abundant mines and forests, significantly improving its agricultural yield, wresting control of its trade from Dutch merchants, and expanding its trading network to include colonies throughout the world. Confident that Sweden enjoyed far greater natural resources than any other nation – an idea that was firmly rooted in the new patriotic movement, later named *Götisism* – Axel Oxenstierna insisted that the key to Sweden's success was to introduce the most advanced approaches to mining and agriculture and to make sure that the Baltic became a Swedish-controlled *mare clausum*. In his official instructions to the Board of Commerce, he proclaimed:

blessed and enriched from God and nature with many desirable goods, which originate and grow here, in particular all kinds of metals; and the provinces that are now annexed, are so located, that Livonia, Estland, and Ingria, partly by nature, partly by wise and prudent governance, and the population's cooperation, presently attracts, and in the future can attract even further, the most valuable goods out of Moscow and Lithuania; *Pomerania* can attract commerce from Posen, Silesia, Mark, Brandenburg and occasionally some from Mehren [Moravia], Austria, and Italy, *Wismar* from Mecklenburg, Brandenburg, Meissen, Madgeburg, and north German towns, *Stade* from Lüneburg, Brunswick, Magdeburg, Dyringerland [Thuringia] and Westphalia, as well as surrounding counties and towns; So even though everything cannot be reached, these regions are so located that citizens' industry will find their place, or at least be as close as anyone else, in terms of exports and imports.[45]

In order to realize Oxenstierna's vision, Risingh introduced the latest economic thinking to the Board of Commerce. Whereas the economic doctrine that had governed most economic policy in Europe was focused on traditional best practices in agriculture and mining and on trade as an integral part of a carefully balanced hierarchical society, Risingh embraced the Hartlibian idea that it was possible through the development of the right kind of knowledge and the freeing up of commerce, to launch a process of gradual, indefinite improvement.[46] Similar to Skytte's confidence in the capacity of knowledge to transform the world, Risingh believed that a systematic quest to uncover nature's innermost secrets would yield ways to harness nature's inherent powers for the betterment of humanity. While Skytte was confident that the formation of a Salomon's House – or Sophopolis – would suffice to trigger an improvement process, Risingh insisted that knowledge would only emerge and be properly implemented where people lived in freedom and security. Risingh's emphasis on freedom was inspired by Henry Robinson, a central member of the Hartlib Circle, who Risingh studied – and may very well have encountered – during his travels to London. Robinson argued that for an infinite improvement process to take root, people had to enjoy religious, social, entrepreneurial, and commercial freedoms. They also had to be able to count on a soundly organized society, with institutions conducive to commercial prosperity. First, all property rights, not just in land, had to be strengthened. It is absolutely central, he argued, that 'each Improver and Inventor may know what advantages he may expect, and how it is to be determined and secured unto him, without so much attendance and charge.'[47] Second, markets had to be transparent so that buyers and sellers could be easily matched. The labor market, for example, was currently dysfunctional because of a lack of symmetric information. This had led to the highly inequitable situation in which 'the poore mens seeking is rather a begging, than a bargaining for employment; which rich men take advantage of, to the daily more and more undervaluing poore mens paines, and labours.'[48] Third, Robinson firmly believed in the social utility of competition. To him, competition served as a powerful disciplinary mechanism forcing people to be as industrious and productive as possible. While some producers would not be able to survive, society as a whole would still benefit, even if the competition came from abroad. Robinson wrote:

> if some Forreiners be more nimble, ingenious, and industrious in their ways of Trading, than generally the Natives of this Land; may it not be consistent with, nay even a speciall demonstration of the Wisdome of our Governours to encourage such active spirited Forreigners to a cohabitation with us, whom the Fishermen Manifactors and Artificers of Forreign Nations will certainly accompany . . . ? And if by such course any of the lesse ingenious Natives of this Land happen to be outgone in their own Trades and Callings, let them apply themselves unto some other which requires lesse ingenuity and activeness, as they ought to have done at first; and will not the industry and ingenuity of such Forreigners be a good lesson and example to us, and contribute much to the inriching and accommodating the whole Nation in general?[49]

The fourth principle of a soundly organized society primed for a knowledge-driven commercial expansion was a stable and incorruptible monetary mechanism, based both on specie and credit.[50] Robinson's emphasis on freedom and his insistence on a soundly organized commercial order served as central pillars of Risingh's political economy. It was these principles, modified by Sweden's political and geopolitical conditions, that he introduced to the Board of Commerce. While historians have noted his dedication to the Board and his long-term impact on its intellectual trajectory, he himself would later complain in print that those in charge of the nation's economy lacked in expertise and competency.[51]

Having participated in the design of the Board of Commerce and the shaping of its intellectual content, Rising was soon tapped by Axel Oxenstierna for an even more central and prestigious role in his administration – the Governorship of New Sweden. Oxenstierna and Gustavus II Adolphus decided as early as the 1620s that Sweden needed to participate in the colonization of the new world.[52] By establishing a Swedish presence around the world, great honor and wealth would be conferred on the nation. Every estate would benefit:

> The nobility and the clergy would receive more distinguished offices, and churches and schools would flourish. Merchants and craftsmen would profit from the exchange of goods, while the peasants would receive better prices for their grain, and the burden of conscription would be lightened.[53]

Opportunities to find buyers for Swedish products, primarily iron and copper, awaited in the newly discovered world, which would be paid for by some of the most desirable and exotic colonial products, including beaver pelts, spices, tobacco, sugar, dyes, and, of course, gold. Oxenstierna chartered a company in 1637, *The New Sweden Company*, and instructed it to establish a foothold in the Chesapeake region, from which it would export tobacco back to Sweden. This would only be the beginning of Sweden's colonial presence. The plan was to establish a number of colonies in North America, from Florida to Newfoundland, to take advantage of the full array of colonial goods available. Colonies in Africa and Asia were also part of the plan, although only the former materialized. Louis De Geer, the powerful merchant and industrialist, was the key figure behind the creation of *The African Company*. With its headquarters in Swedish-controlled Stade, the company established a fortified presence in Cabo Corso on the African Gold Coast, where they began to trade slaves in 1650. Although *Carolusborg* was soon conquered by the Dutch, the Swedish African Company transported up to 2,000 slaves during its fourteen-year tenure.[54]

The New Sweden Company began its operations in earnest in 1638, when two Swedish ships, commanded by Peter Minuit (1580–1638), who had shifted his allegiance to Sweden after serving as the governor of New Amsterdam, sailed up the Delaware River.[55] Much like he did with the purchase of Manhattan, Minuit negotiated peacefully with the natives and reached an agreement that he regarded as a *purchase* of an area along the Delaware River, south of the Schuylkill River. The first order of business was to start the construction of *Fort Christina*. While this project proceeded well, all of the colony's affairs did not go as planned. Like most other nations' efforts to colonize North America, New Sweden was besieged by numerous troubles, including shipwrecks, poor supplies, diseases, conflicts with natives and rivaling colonists, malnourishment, and harvest failures. Realizing the precariousness of New Sweden, Oxenstierna dedicated greater resources and attention to the colony in the 1640s. Sensing that a greater military presence was required, Oxenstierna named the seasoned military commander Johan Printz (1592–1663) as governor of the colony. In addition to militarizing the colony, Printz was also given strict orders to make the colony profitable. The focus was to remain on the cultivation of tobacco, but many other commodities were mentioned as possible exports. Still, success eluded the Swedish colony. Conflicts escalated with both the natives, who were becoming tired of not receiving agreed upon commodities, and the Dutch, who were increasingly impatient with the Swedish presence.[56] After Printz travelled back to Stockholm to secure more resources, never to return to Delaware, Oxenstierna had to find an appropriate successor.

Intent on finding someone who had the requisite expertise to turn the colony into a source of spectacular profits, Erik and Axel Oxenstierna selected Johan Risingh as the next governor of New Sweden. He was quickly ennobled in 1653 and received his commission from the Queen in December of that year. He set sail towards America and his new job in the ship *The Eagle* on February 2, 1654. He was excited to turn the colony around and ensure that that it would start realizing its potential.[57] In a memorandum published after his tenure as Governor had come to an end titled *The Reasons which most Convinced Me to Undertake the Journey to New Sweden,* Risingh wrote:

> It was pointed out to me in various discussions and deliberations in the Royal Board of Commerce, that the country was rich and prosperous, both for making a living and obtaining some wealth. Not only the mother country, but also individuals could gain great advantage there. It would thus enhance the

reputation and honor of the mother country to have a colony out there as other nations, with ships plying between and with the rise of commerce, for the improvement of seafaring people and the increase of all bounties [i.e. the improvement of the economy in general].[58]

Excited by these prospects, Risingh boarded the ship loaded to the brim with supplies and 350 settlers, many of whom came from Sweden's possessions in the eastern parts of Finland.[59] After a tempestuous crossing, Risingh arrived in New Sweden on May 18, where he quickly began to initiate changes designed to enhance the colony's commercial prospects.[60] He spent a considerable effort trying to make sure relations with the Lenape and Susquehannock Indians were in good standing. He engaged in diplomacy, gift giving, and exchange, capturing in his notebook the dissonance and confusion associated with the clash of North American and European economic cultures.[61] For example, he wrote on June 16:

> Papegoja [acting governor after Printz left the colony] and I traveled to Tinicum, where we had agreed to meet the Indian sachems or chiefs in order to come to a pact of friendship and alliance and, as is the custom, to present them with gifts. On the same day we sent the large yacht to the Horn Kill with a cargo to trade and also to present gifts, thereby confirming the purchase of the land and taking possession of it anew, as it had previously been purchased by our people.[62]

Risingh also launched a number of internal changes. Consonant with his views on improvement, as we shall see in greater detail below, he sought to increase the economic liberty of the settlers, strengthen their property rights, and create the possibility to buy seeds and equipment on credit. He wanted to support a rapid increase in arable land for tobacco cultivation and for the establishment of orchards. He also tried to facilitate the circulation of goods by building roads. Taking advantage of the greater manpower now at his disposal, he initiated the construction of a water-powered sawmill, encouraged the building of sturdier cottages, and planned out a city grid for the intended town next to *Fort Christina*, which would be called *Christinehamn.* Risingh was optimistic about the prospects of his colony; if only Oxenstierna continued to dedicate enough resources, it had the potential to become a jewel in the royal crown.

Unfortunately, the problems facing New Sweden did not go away. Inclement weather, bad harvests, and lack of supplies from Sweden weakened the colonists. Still, Risingh did not give up hope, and neither did Queen Christina in Sweden, even though she was only months away from her famous abdication. On October 3, Risingh gave an account of a meeting at *Fort Christina,* attended by most of the residents, in which 'The letters of Her Royal Majesty and the General Board of Commerce were read to inform them of how her Royal Majesty wanted the territory to be governed'. He noted, 'All were encouraged to have good hope of relief and to diligently plow and cultivate their land'.[63] Yet the problems continued. Increasingly the most disturbing threat was the apparent Dutch preparation for a full-scale attack. Ever since Risingh made the split-second decision on his arrival to conquer the poorly-defended *Fort Casimir,* Peter Stuyvesant (1612–1672) had been planning his retaliation. On August 29, 1655, Stuyvesant attacked New Sweden with seven ships and three hundred men. *Fort Casimir* was reconquered quickly, while Risingh was able to hold out at *Fort Christina* for about two weeks. Although only one person died, Risingh was compelled to capitulate once Stuyvesant's men had 'killed our cattle, goats, pigs, and poultry, demolished our houses, and pillaged the people of their possessions outside of the fort'.[64] By September 15, New Sweden came to an end and Risingh was called back to Sweden. Although he would still work for the Swedish state as a customs official in the occupied territories in Germany for a number of years, the loss of New Sweden, for which he was blamed, spelled the end of his once-illustrious political career.

Risingh's career as a governor of New Sweden was far too short-lived for him to realize his ambitious plans. He had high hopes that the colony could indeed become the jewel in the Swedish trading network that Oxenstierna had envisioned, and thus contribute to making Sweden an economic superpower. But before the colony could become the fountainhead for remarkable mercantile fortunes and the source of Sweden's geopolitical prominence, Risingh insisted that the colony's economy had to be patiently constructed from the ground up. First and foremost, all useful natural resources had to be discovered and the latest methods had to be employed in the transformation of nature. Risingh's notebooks from his time in North America offer plenty of evidence of his preoccupation with the natural abundance of the new world and the opportunities that it provided.[65] For example, he wrote on October 27, 1654:

> our best men were called to Fort Christina, and an ordinance was prepared by us all for the improvement of the land in matters relating to agriculture, fishing, and other things for the best interest of the colonists. The ordinance was thereafter published in New Sweden among the Swedes as well as among the Dutch, but nothing could be put into effect before aid was received from the mother country.[66]

Risingh, like many other colonial governors, was obsessed with improvement. These governors subscribed to the idea, here articulated by the colonial projector Sir Balthazar Gerbier, that 'it would prove more facile to forme a neew World. then to reforme the old'.[67] While they eclectically drew inspiration from many different discourses, Risingh was drawn to the vision promoted by the Hartlib Circle. Much like the governor of Connecticut, John Winthrop Jr. (1606–1676), who was a devout disciple of the Hartlib Circle, Risingh was intent on implementing the Hartlibians' improvement schemes, whether in agriculture, horticulture, mining, commerce, or politics.[68]

In the two books published with the financial assistance of Erik Oxenstierna's successor, Lord High Chancellor Magnus Gabriel De La Gardie (1622–1686), Risingh offered his interpretation of the latest ideas on political economy. These two books, one exploring issues pertaining to land and the other commerce, constituted the first fully-articulated modern statements of political economy in Sweden.[69] Although Risingh was never able to publish the full treatise he had begun writing in the 1640s, he still managed to set the tone and basic parameters of the Swedish improvement discourse. The key to improvement in all of his writings was the development of new knowledge that enabled people to transform nature. Only by better understanding the kingdoms of vegetables, animals, and minerals was it possible to discover and utilize nature's untapped powers and energies. He wrote in *A Land-Book, or a few essays towards the benefit of our homeland (Een Land-Book, eller några Upsattser til vårt Fädernes Lands Nytta),* that only through a systematic study, experimentation, and application of new knowledge in agriculture would it become possible to launch a new era of progress and prosperity, whereby 'the nation will be improved multiple times over and poverty, which so heavily weighs on us, will be alleviated'.[70] He stated unequivocally, '[a]griculture constitutes the basis of wealth in every province'. Not only does it provide the basis for clothes, food, and shelter, it also lays the foundation for commercial prosperity. It is well-known to 'all wise people', he added, that:

> the most dominant nations of Europe have through prosperous agriculture and horticulture reached such a high point in terms of money and commodities, and manufacturing, that city after city filled with rich burghers have been built and fortified [...] enabling them to live free from the violence of foreign potentates.[71]

While the systematic improvement of nature constituted the key to wealth, it was not the only essential ingredient. For a nation to become affluent and prosperous, a number of conditions had to be satisfied. The first and most fundamental component was proper Christian worship, which required pious and learned preachers. Secondly, a highly trained and valiant military had to be available for the protection of the nation's borders. These were absolutely necessary conditions, yet he spent little time exploring religion and defense. Instead, he focused his analytical efforts on the other components on his list, which in order of importance were: agriculture, mining, manufacturing, fishing, commerce, shipping, and ship-building.[72]

Like most other Swedes at the time, in the spirit of *Göticism,* Risingh praised God for having blessed Sweden with a uniquely bountiful nature, in particular in terms of its forests and mines. However, for these natural treasures to bring about the kingdom's 'remarkable enrichment', the nation's 'improvement', and the people's 'advancement', it was necessary to develop the nation's agriculture, horticulture, and fisheries so that food and nourishment could be made more affordable.[73] If fields, meadows, forests, and herb gardens were properly tended and cultivated, foodstuff would become so inexpensive that the country would gain the 'power to eliminate poverty' and the nation's manufacturers and merchants would be in a position to produce goods that would directly contribute to the betterment and honor of the whole nation.[74]

Similar to many of the publications by the Hartlib Circle, including those by Gabriel Plattes, Cressy Dymock, and Hartlib himself, Risingh's book offers a variety of methods of increasing the productivity of land and livestock.[75] He discusses soil-quality, plowing and sowing strategies, irrigation and fertilization methods, and harvesting and storing techniques. He proudly announces that if farmers follow his advice, with God's blessing, they will be able to double the fruits of their land and the whole kingdom will purchase grain at half the former price.[76] He also offers ideas on how to transform infertile land into arable land and pasture, thus 'greatly multiplying grain and livestock, which in turn enables the maintenance of a much larger population'.[77] While there were many agricultural handbooks issued in Sweden around this time, offering tips on all matters pertaining to the management of a manor or farm, what was novel about Risingh's approach was that he focused on the application of science – 'wetenskap' – to agriculture and situated the cultivation of land in a commercial context. The earlier agricultural advice literature had concentrated on pooling traditional expertise and offering advice focused on maintaining order in the household and in the community.[78] Hence, science, which he coupled with terms like 'expertise', 'industriousness', 'art', and 'care', constituted the foundation of the massive productivity improvement he envisioned.[79] Science would not only make orchard gardens flourish; science would also multiply the yield of fields and transform both animal husbandry and fisheries.[80]

In exploring the benefits of productivity enhancements in agriculture and horticulture, Risingh focused on the benefits of lower prices to society in general and on higher profits to the individual farmer. For example, when discussing the importance of proper rotation schemes, he states that it is to 'the farmer's greatest profit, because the faster the fields recover, the lesser his toil and expenses, and the greater the augmentation of his wealth'.[81] Moreover, when exploring the benefits of cultivating coriander, saffron, and 'Lacricia', he mentions that they might yield 'remarkably more profits' than grain, perhaps as much as 'double profits'.[82] He also mentions Burgundian mustard, sold in Paris and throughout the Low Countries, as an example of a grain substitute proven to be capable of yielding many thousands of gold coins. Later, in concluding his discussion of more exotic alternatives to grain, he notes that a good selection of herbs, spices, roots, and tobacco combined with proper 'art and science' have the capacity to yearly bring in significant sums of money.[83]

Risingh was particularly enthusiastic about God's generosity towards Sweden in the realm of metals and minerals, providing an abundance of silver, copper, and iron.[84] While the nation had already begun to exploit these resources, making the mining industry both the largest employer and largest exporter, there were plenty of improvements still to be made. In his writings on metals and mining, he employed the same basic Paracelsian understanding of matter as the Hartlib Circle. In describing how minerals and metals grow in the ground and in the oceans, he informed that:

the Sun, through the powers invested in her by God, [...] together with the power's of the firmament, produces all metals in hard rocks, as well as noble stones in cliffs, pearls and precious stones in oysters and other shells down on the ocean floor.[85]

He explained that it was the angle of the sun that dictates how deep inside the earth the metals grow; he noted 'the greater the angle of the Sun's rays at any place, the more shallow her powers are'.[86] This meant that mines in the torrid zone are much deeper than mines in the temperate zone, and that the closer to the poles the mines are located, the more shallow they are. As an example, Risingh mentioned the silver mines of Lapland, which were only as deep as 50 meters. Risingh also mentioned that metals grow in a tree-like shape inside the earth, a phenomenon that was known in alchemical circles as the *Tree of Diana.* He wrote, 'just like trees above the surface, precious metals grow like trees into the earth in the shape of trunks and branches, which guides each miner in his search'.[87] Skilled miners also had another way to detect the presence of precious metals. Drawing on alchemical practices, Risingh described how the miner can place a pot of mineral water on the fire and let it boil. Then, after distilling the water in a beaker, the metal would end up at the bottom. The metal was then exposed to salt water and once again distilled, at which point the true nature of the metal was revealed.[88]

That Paracelsian philosophy was at the center of Risingh's understanding of the mineral kingdom was further revealed in his discussion of precious metals in his book on commerce. Employing alchemical symbols, he explained the correspondence between the seven planets and the seven metals, and detailed how there is a special 'rapport' between 'Gold and the Sun ☉; Silver and the Moon ☽; copper and Venus ♀; quicksilver and Mercury ☿; iron with Mars ♂; Lead with Saturn ♄; tin with Jupiter ♃'.[89] He further described how gold is the most precious, solid, and expensive of all the metals and like the sun among the planets it 'therefore has a sympathy with human nature'.[90] Silver, he described, in the spirit of the age, as white and pink, cold and wet, just like the moon. Next, he explores the extent to which the different metals can be combined and which alloys would generate the best basis for the minting of coin. In a characteristic passage, he notes that it is preferable to add '⅔☽ and ⅓♀ to ☉, because from only ☽, ☉ is too pale, and from only ♀, it is too dark'.[91] In exploring the composition and compatibility of metals, he references his former mentor Georg Stiernhielm's *Archimede Reform.*[92]

Risingh was clearly inspired by a similar understanding of nature and conception of mankind's ability to transform nature for utilitarian ends as was the Hartlib Circle. Industriousness and knowledge of how to transform nature constituted the key components of improvement and progress. Once agriculture had been refined and developed, it would not take long before the creation of a manufacturing base and the development of a thriving commerce would emerge. This was the ultimate goal. Hence, even as Risingh focused first and foremost on improvements in agriculture, horticulture, and mining as the fundamental building block of prosperity, commerce was never far from his mind.

His intended synthetic treatise on political economy promised to examine the constitutive elements of commerce: the commodity, money, and credit, or what he called, following Gerard Malynes, the body, soul, and spirit of commerce.[93] While he may or may not have concluded it – only fragments of the first part survives – he successfully published a summary of his views on commerce in *Ett Uthtogh om Kiöp-Handelen eller Commercierne* (1669), which he dedicated to his patron Lord High Chancellor Magnus Gabriel De La Gardie.[94] In this book he offers his views on how commerce should be organized to yield the greatest advantage. He also sets out to show what kind of commerce is most compatible with human nature. What emerges is a strong advocacy for free commerce and free enterprise, unencumbered by limitations erected by monopolies, guilds, church, or state. This was not, as I will show below, a simpleminded defense of free trade. Instead, Risingh added numerous twists and turns, reflective of the complexity of the actual world of commerce.

Risingh began his book on commerce by reiterating his ranking of the essential components of the nation's prosperity, starting with proper worship and defense, followed by improvements in agriculture, mining, manufacturing, and fishing, and ending with commerce, shipping, and ship-building.[95] While commerce ranked rather low on the list, it was absolutely instrumental to the vibrancy of all the other components.[96] Therefore it was essential to figure out what made commerce flourish. Risingh began this discussion by exploring the basic motivations behind commerce. He maintained that its success, like that of any other enterprise people pursue in life, is dictated by (1) God's blessing, (2) the extent of people's desires and the level of their industry and diligence, and (3) the command and skill people exhibit in their pursuits. He explained, 'when God approves of your enterprise, he awakens desires in you, which intensifies your industry; industry in turn promotes skill in the art itself and improves your command over the entire enterprise, which ensures that your labor will bring you benefit and honor'.[97] Industry, skill, and success were directly linked. While God, in his infinite goodness, generously poured his blessings onto the merchants, sparking their ambition and industry, multiple problems had arisen that curtailed the flourishing of commerce.

The primary obstacle to Sweden's commercial prosperity was that for a long time its overseas trade had been controlled by foreign merchants. First merchants from Lübeck, as part of the Hanseatic League, dominated Sweden's Baltic trade; later, towards the end of the sixteenth century, merchants from Antwerp and Amsterdam gradually took over the Baltic trades, once again leaving Sweden without control of its own commerce. Now that Sweden had emerged as a strong military power in the Baltic region, commercial independence was possible. As Hugo Grotius had insisted in *Mare Liberum,* God had arranged the world so that every country had an excess of some resource or commodity that could be exported with benefit, as well as needs that could not be fully met locally.[98] Merchants thus carried out an indispensable service to humanity by moving goods around the world. While every nation had to engage in trade to flourish, they should never be compelled to do so through force or violence. Each nation should be able to conduct their own trade, which ensured that each nation was provided with the goods they needed and that the gains from trade were shared throughout the trading world.

A related obstacle that also prevented Sweden's trade from yielding benefits to the general population was the widespread pattern of powerful merchants, foreign and domestic, using their size to exploit others in the marketplace. Smaller merchants, farmers, peasants, miners, and handicraft workers were forced to abide by the conditions and laws set by the powerful merchants, undermining their freedom and autonomy. To Risingh, this was a major violation of the most basic tenet of commerce. Every person should have the right and liberty to engage in negotiations and enter into voluntary contracts with whomever they want. No one, he insisted, 'whether superior, equal, or inferior, out of envy, jealousy, or greed, should be able to obstruct the course of trade'. This freedom, he added, should be 'guarded as an apple in the eye'.[99]

In addition, every person should have the right and liberty to engage in whatever productive pursuit they deem worthy of their time and effort. Thus both monopolies and guilds made him uncomfortable. He complained that when powerful merchants or manufacturers are able to establish exclusionary control over trade in a specific commodity, or to a specific place, a host of deleterious consequences follow. Not only are the skilled and ambitious workmen who are prevented from engaging in their trade hurt, but so are the people producing for the monopoly and the guild. Reminiscent of Henry Robinson's praise for the social utility of competition, Risingh insisted that a lack of competition curtails industriousness and ingenuity, 'because a guaranteed profit makes people both stupid and lazy'.[100] The suffocation of commercial vibrancy damages both the countryside and towns, resulting in 'poverty, distress, dearth, debt, sloth and laziness'.[101] In places where all people enjoy the privilege of commercial freedom, competition will force prices down, improve the quality of workmanship, and compel the rest of the population to become more industrious and obedient.[102] The state therefore must break up monopolies and prevent them from engrossing the profits that rightly should be available to anyone interested in pursuing trade.

Religious freedom was also necessary for commercial success. Risingh added that no one should be barred from engaging in economic or commercial pursuits on the basis of their religious beliefs. He suggested that Sweden ought to follow the example of the Dutch, who had grown rich in people, commodities, and money by allowing people to worship their God of choice. While there were certain limits as to which religions were acceptable and it was strictly prohibited to have no religion at all, Risingh advocated that freedom of religion was an important component of attracting people of expertise and industry to build up the nation's stock of manufacturers.[103]

For Risingh, trade, whether domestic or international, was always natural and voluntary. Trust, confidence, and goodwill – not 'violence and anger' – thus constituted the foundation of trade, and the law spelled out the details of how contracts were made and upheld.[104] Given that all trade was based on mutual interests, forged in amity and protected by law, there were scarcely any reasons for the state to actively intervene, at least not in theory. However, in reality, since trade was a complex organism subject not only to economic considerations, but also to various political and geopolitical interests, destructive patterns sometimes emerged that the state had to rectify. Yet, when suggesting that trade needed some supervision both at home and abroad to make sure that it is properly conducted, Risingh hastens to add that the less people hear and see of such directives the better off trade will be.[105]

Although Risingh advocated for some forms of state intervention, he was not focused on the enrichment and empowerment of the state. Similarly to the Hartlib Circle, Risingh was primarily interested in enhancing the material conditions of the general population, which in extension would yield other benefits, such as social order, moral refinement, and the eventual strengthening of the state. Therefore, the only way to empower the state in a sustainable fashion was to enrich the people. He included a version of the following sentence in both of his published works: 'the government's power and fortune is determined by the good behavior, wealth, and size of its subjects'.[106] Risingh's views were thus reminiscent of Giovanni Botero's (1544–1617) recipe for a strong state with happy subjects and rather similar to David Hume's (1711–1776) famous proclamation some eight decades later:

> The greatness of a state, and the happiness of its subjects, how independent soever they may be supposed in some respects, are commonly allowed to be inseparable with regard to commerce; and as private men receive greater security, in the possession of their trade and riches, from the power of the public, so the public becomes powerful in proportion to the opulence and extensive commerce of private men.[107]

Risingh's insistence that commerce should be free and that the state is better off in proportion to the extent of the nation's commerce led him to advocate that ships and goods should be encumbered with as few fees and tariffs as possible. Customs levied on both incoming and outgoing goods should be set as leniently as possible so that 'trade and shipping can multiply many times over'.[108] Referring to the suffocating effects of high tariffs, Risingh added that 'high customs is like a noose around the neck of trade'.[109] Moreover, when Risingh suggested that the exportation of raw materials, particularly metals from Swedish mines, should be limited, he did not suggest that the state ought to erect trade barriers or artificially increase the prices, but rather that Sweden should through added industry seek to create manufacturers in which the raw materials could be refined and worked-up before – or instead of – exporting them.[110] While later writers following in Risingh's footsteps, such as Christopher Polhem, would use this argument to advocate for the protection of infant industries, Risingh's antipathy towards monopolies precluded him from supporting such policies.[111] Indeed, when discussing how Swedish goods in general should be priced to improve the nation's terms of trade, he presented the discussion as advice to Swedish merchants and manufacturers, not as an instruction to the state.[112]

While Risingh suggested that commerce and trade operate best when free and competitive, he recognized that there are a number of areas in which the state needs to be proactive. Once again echoing the Hartlib Circle, Risingh suggested that the state needs to be responsible for maintaining strict property rights, upholding a stable and incorruptible monetary mechanism, and developing an infrastructure conducive to commerce.[113] In insisting on strict property rights, Risingh wanted to make sure that artisans, merchants, and manufacturers were protected in their property, practice, and profits. They should be allowed to pursue their craft without having to worry about arbitrary obstacles, expropriations, needing to perform public service, or having to pay exorbitant taxes.[114] Moreover, in addition to maintaining strict property rights, the state should also punish those engaged in corruption, sold forged goods, or who neglected to pay their debts. If the state succeeded in instituting laws for the encouragement, freedom, and safety of commerce, Risingh insisted that many 'rich *capitalists*' would be attracted to Sweden.[115]

Risingh also believed that the state had a role to play in managing the nation's balance of trade. Contrary to the long-standing mythology that seventeenth-century political economy fetishized trade surpluses, Risingh, like many of his contemporaries, was primarily concerned that the nation's imports and exports were appropriately balanced, so that destabilizing surpluses or deficits did not arise.[116] Following the reasoning of Malynes, Risingh believed that one of the most important things the state could do to prevent imbalances was to make sure that the nation's currency was properly valued in relation to its silver content and in relation to foreign currencies. Mint officials were thus responsible for making sure that the currency was valued in accordance with its gold or silver content, while the magistrates needed to protect the currency against forgers and counterfeiters. In order to make sure that the currency was not undervalued in the international exchange market it was also essential for Swedish merchants to have access to a sophisticated credit system, consisting both of an exchange bank and a lending bank. Through the judicious management of such a banking system, international bills of exchange could be actively traded and the Swedish currency thus properly valued, which by extension ensured that commodities were properly priced vis-à-vis foreign goods.[117] Risingh's foremost concern was thus that the state, by overseeing both the mint and the banking system, kept the currency stable and thus guaranteed that it properly fulfilled its essential roles as a unit of account and a medium of exchange. Only then could people strike fair and honest contracts based on accurate and transparent information.

While it was certainly the case that Risingh did not want the state to manipulate trade to engineer a trade surplus, he was open to legal restrictions to the importation of certain luxury goods that he thought were unhealthy, excessive, or vainglorious. Such goods included gold and silver brocade, silk, lace, incense, wine, sugar, and foreign fruits – some of which, he argued, could actually be grown in Sweden.[118] Risingh simply could not see the point of bringing in commodities that added little or nothing to the genuine well-being of the population in exchange for either much needed raw materials or ready money. Although this measure qualifies

Risingh's commitment to free trade, the limited scope of his proposed protectionism does not nullify his overall position on free trade and open commerce – it certainly does not mean that his ideas should be characterized as a 'slightly antiquated version of mercantilism', as Eli Heckscher famously proclaimed.[119]

Finally, Risingh argued that the state had to play an active role in the construction of an infrastructure supportive of commerce. This entailed, Risingh suggested, the building and maintenance of a bourse, a chamber of commerce, warehouses, storage silos, merchant houses, harbors, docks, inns, and roads of good quality, safe from 'thieves and highwaymen'.[120] Risingh's most ambitious infrastructural development plan was presented as part of his initiative to create a number of staple towns. If properly constructed and organized, these towns would have a flourishing manufacturing base, a vibrant shipbuilding industry, and merchants from around the world enjoying equal access to free trade.[121] But it required a major effort to establish an entirely new town, something Risingh very well understood after his experience in New Sweden and in his role as a consultant to Magnus Gabriel De La Gardie during the planning phases of the construction of Lidköping.[122]

Conclusion

Risingh played a central role in the development of a Swedish improvement discourse during the *Age of Greatness*. He was dedicated to the importation and adaptation of the latest ideas on political economy; an active participant in some of Sweden's most influential epistemic communities; a central figure in the efforts to turn political economic ideas into practice through his posts as secretary of the Board of Commerce and Governor of New Sweden; and, finally, he was considered to have been Sweden's first published author on political economy. It is indeed rare to come across a figure who has a hand in the authorship, transmission, popularization, and implementation of political economic ideas. Risingh's writings continued to have an important impact on the Swedish improvement discourse long after his passing in 1672, as his writings were often republished, quoted, and referenced.[123]

Unlike the Nco-Aristotelian *Oekonomia* literature that informed most of the thinking in Sweden during the sixteenth and seventeenth century, Risingh did not focus his analytical attention first and foremost on maintaining traditional social order and hierarchy. Instead, in the spirit of the Hartlib Circle, he was interested in the pursuit of growth, improvement, and progress as ways to address Sweden's social, political, and economic challenges. Risingh may not have employed the same radical eschatological and pansophic rhetoric in his discussion of economic growth – exemplified by phrases such as 'infinite improvement' and 'universal reformation' – as Comenius and Hartlib, yet he was clearly thinking in terms of an indefinite multiplication of wealth made possible through a continuous refinement in knowledge and driven by people's desire for greater material comfort.

Risingh's views on the role of science and commerce in the transformation of nature also broke with the earlier tradition. While the Neo-Aristotelians focused on traditional techniques, technologies, and organization, Risingh viewed scientific improvements in agriculture as the kernel of economic growth. Through a gradual refinement of the knowledge of nature and matter, people would be able to transform nature more readily and thus be able to produce more and better commodities. As these goods enter the market, they generate profits for the producers and lower prices for everyone. Risingh's confidence in mankind's capacity to indefinitely improve and refine nature for utilitarian purposes suggests a strong Baconian influence and also an embrace of Paracelsian thinking about nature's malleability.

Commerce also played an essential part in the improvement process, in particular in the way that competition impels industry and promotes liberty. Instead of thinking of the monetized market as a mediation device between people and between classes, the primary purpose of which was to distribute the appropriate amount of wealth to each segment so that they could continue to perform their duties to society, Risingh viewed the market as a mechanism that forces producers to incessantly pursue innovations and intensify their industriousness *and* as a space that facilitates free interactions between people.

Risingh's statement in favor of free trade and open commerce in a society where everyone has the right and liberty to enter any bargain or trade, and where everyone can freely dispose of their property in whatever way they see fit, closely followed Henry Robinson's vision of society. In such a market society, the primary authority over people's economic life should not be the state, nor the master of the household. The application of new knowledge to the production of goods, the unending industry put forth by ingenious farmers, artisans, manufacturers, and merchants, and the risks incurred in the pursuit of new enterprises are not to be forced upon its undertakers, but rather should be the result of their desires and ambitions, mediated by the market. Although he had an unwavering commitment to free trade, Risingh certainly did not offer a naïve free trade ideology, wherein it is assumed that human freedom necessarily generates a thriving and well-functioning society. Instead, he augmented his defense of market liberalism with a set of practical guidelines for how markets should be organized and administered to generate the desired effects. He suggests that the state must intervene to break up monopolies; protect property rights; maintain low tolls, customs, and taxes; and contribute to the formation of a modern commercial infrastructure. While his prescription required a state with the authority to act, he certainly did not have an absolutist, Leviathan-type state in mind, of the kind that scholars traditionally ascribe to seventeenth-century political economic thinkers.

The discourse that Risingh captured in his writings continued to provide the foundation for Swedish improvement writers into the eighteenth century. Writers like Urban Hiärne, Christopher Polhem, Anders Berch, and Carl Linnaeus combined natural philosophy and political economy to create a vision and plan for Sweden's improvement that drew on and further contributed to the broader intellectual movement across northern Europe. This epistemic culture enjoyed a particular flourishing in England, providing what some historians refer to as the critical edge that made England the first nation to enter a self-sustaining process of technological improvement.[124] The Swedish improvement discourse may very well have planted the seeds for the nation's future engineering ingenuity, but it failed, for many different reasons, to spark a productive interplay between invention, innovation, and implementation that would have enabled Sweden to keep up with England, Holland, and France. The Great Northern War may have spelled the end to Sweden's geopolitical power, but the real source of its demise was the nation's lingering economic weakness. In the words of Risingh's first biographer, Ellen Fries, 'our economic weakness became the real Poltava that brought our nation's greatness to an end'.[125]

Acknowledgements

The author would like to thank the following people for helpful comments and discussion, David Armitage, Dan Carey, Vera Keller, Monica Miller, Steve Pincus, Sophus Reinert, Philipp Rössner, John Shovlin, Koen Stapelbroek, Lisa Tiersten, Anders Ögren, and Sophie Wilkowske.

Notes

1 Kerstin Abukhanfusa, ed., *Mare Nostrum: Om Westfaliska freden och Östersjön som ett svenskt maktcentrum* (Stockholm: Riksarkivet, 1999).
2 See Gunnar Eriksson, *The Atlantic Vision: Olaus Rudbeck and Baroque Science* (Canton, M.A.: Watson, 1994). See also chapter five in Michael North, *The Baltic: A History* (Cambridge: Harvard University Press, 2015).
3 The *Age of Greatness* is normally dated between 1611 and 1721, the years between the crowning of Gustavus Adolphus and the Peace of Nystad, which put an end to the Great Northern War (1700–1721).
4 Lisbet Koerner, *Linnaeus: Nature and Nation* (Cambridge: Harvard University Press, 1999), Michael H. Lindgren, *Christopher Polhems Testamente: Berättelsen om ingenjören, entreprenören, och pedagogen som ville förändra Sverige* (Stockholm: Nielsen & Noren, 2011), and Sten Lindroth, *Svensk Lärdomshistoria: Stormaktstiden* (Stockholm: Norstedts, 1975).
5 Eli Heckscher, "Anders Berch och den ekonomiska vetenskapens första steg i Sverige," *Lychnos,* 1942, 36; Anders Fryxell, *Berättelser ur Svenska Historien,* Vol. XVIII (Stockholm: Hiertas, 1852), 124; Stellan Dahlgren, "Johan Risingh," *Svenskt Biografiskt Lexikon* (Stockholm: Riksarkivet, 1917–2013), 233; and Anders Björnsson, "Statsbyggarna – Under Sveriges Modernaste Århundrade," in *Jordpäron: Svensk Ekonomihistorisk Läsebok,* ed. Anders Björnsson and Lars Magnusson (Stockholm: Atlantis, 2011).
6 Scholars have long recognized that there is a great deal of diversity in seventeenth-century economic thought, some to the point of wanting to jettison the category of mercantilism altogether. Lars Magnusson (*Mercantilism: The Shaping of an Economic Language* (London: Routledge, 1994)) recovered and restored the category by showing that there is indeed a discursive coherence, while Steve Pincus ("Rethinking Mercantilism: Political Economy, the British Empire, and the Atlantic World in the Seventeenth and Eighteenth Centuries," *William and Mary Quarterly,* Vol. 69, No. 1 (2012): 3–34) recently pointed out that there are multiple strands of discursive and ideological coherence. Recent work in the intersection between natural philosophy and political economy suggests that a transnational discourse on improvement emerged halfway through the seventeenth century. As Tom Leng (*Benjamin Worsley*

(1618–1677): Trade, Interest, and the Spirit in Revolutionary England (Woodbridge: Boydell & Brewer, 2008)), Ted McCormick (*William Petty and the Ambitions of Political Arithmetic* (Oxford: Oxford University Press, 2010)), Carl Wennerlind, (*Casualties of Credit: The English Financial Revolution, 162–1720* (Cambridge: Harvard University Press, 2011)), and Paul Slack (*The Invention of Improvement: Information and Material Progress in Seventeenth-Century England* (Oxford: Oxford University Press, 2015)) have shown, members and affiliates of the Hartlib Circle played an important role in the formation of this improvement discourse. While the Hartlibians were far from the only ones to work in this capacious tradition, there was enough coherence in their approach to improvement that we can usefully speak of the existence of an *Hartlibian political economy.*

7   Although Heckscher did not pursue the connection, he recognized that Risingh was clearly writing 'under the influence of Robinson'. *Mercantilism, Vol. II* (New York: Macmillan, 1935), 295. Ellen Fries also notes that Risingh was deeply inspired by English thinkers, a fact that he himself acknowledged. Ellen Fries, "Johan Classon Risingh," *Historisk Tidskrift,* Vol. 16 (1896), 58.

8   Gunnar Wetterberg, *Kanslern Axel Oxenstierna* (Stockholm: Atlantis, 2002).

9   Nils Erik Villstrand, ed., *Sveriges Historia: 1600–1721* (Stockholm: Norstedts, 2011), 267.

10   Peter Englund, *Det Hotade Huset: Adliga Föreställningar om Samhället under Stormaktstiden* (Stockholm: Atlantis, 1989), 128–30.

11   Magdalena Naum and Jonas M. Nordin, eds., *Scandinavian Colonialism and the Rise of Modernity: Small Time Agents in a Global Arena* (New York: Springer, 2013).

12   It should be noted that reality did not always match Sweden's lofty aspirations – its geopolitical standing was always precarious, efforts to build a modern state were slow to materialize, and the Swedish economy remained rather undeveloped.

13   Letter from John Dury to Samuel Hartlib, 18/28 May 1636, Norrköping, Sweden. Oxford, Bodleian Library: MS Rawlinson C 911, 269r.

14   Sven Göransson, "Comenius och Sverige 1642–1648," *Lychnos,* (1957–8), 104–5.

15   For a discussion of Comenius's *panshophia,* see introductory essay of Mark Greengrass, Michael Leslie, and Timothy Raylor, eds., *Samuel Hartlib and Universal Reformation: Studies in Intellectual Communication* (Cambridge: Cambridge University Press, 1994).

16   John Lazardzig, "Universality and Territoriality: On the Architectonic of Academic Social Life Exemplified by the *Brandenburg Universität der Völker*" in *Collection, Laboratory, Theater: Scenes of Knowledge in the 17th Century,* ed. Helmar Schramm, Ludger Schwarte and Jan Lazardzig (Berlin: De Gruyter, 2005), 183.

17   Göransson, "Comenius och Sverige," 106. See also Johan Nordström, *De Yverbornes Ö* (Stockholm: Bonnier, 1934).

18   For a discussion of how Comenius contributed in practice and spirit to the Hartlibian project, see Robert Fitzgibbon Young, *Comenius in England: The Visit of Jan Amos Komensky Comenius, Czech Philosopher and Educationalist, to London in 1641–42* (Oxford: Oxford University Press, 1932); Dorothy Stimson, "Comenius and the Invisible College," *Isis* (1935) 23: 373–388; and Anders Grape, "Comenius, Bengt Skytte och Royal Society," *Lychnos* (1936): 319–330.

19   For the most thorough overview, see Charles Webster, *The Great Instauration: Science, Medicine, and Reform, 1626–1660* (Bern: Peter Lang, [1975] 2002); and Greengrass, Leslie, and Raylor, eds., *Samuel Hartlib and Universal Reformation.* See also the middle chapters of Paul Slack, *The Invention of Improvement.* For a discussion emphasizing the diversity in perspectives within the Hartlib Circle, see discussion in Koji Yamamoto, "Reformation and the Distrust of the Projector in the Hartlib Circle," *The Historical Journal,* Vol. 55, No. 2 (2012), 375–9.

20   Charles Webster, "Introduction," in *Samuel Hartlib and the Advancement of Learning* (Cambridge: Cambridge University Press, 1970).

21 See, for example, William Newman, *Gehennical Fire: The Lives of George Starkey, An American Alchemist in the Scientific Revolution* (Cambridge, MA: Harvard University Press, 1994); and Bruce Moran, *Distilling Knowledge: Alchemy, Chemistry, and the Scientific Revolution* (Cambridge, MA: Harvard University Press, 2005).

22 Hartlib, *Samuel Hartlib and His Legacy of Husbandry* (London, 1655), 247–50; and Cressy Dymock, *A Discovery for New Divisions, or Setting out of Lands, as to the best Forme* (London, 1653), 12.

23 Samuel Hartlib, An essay for advancement of husbandry-learning: or propositions for the erecting a colledge of husbandry (London, 1651), 3.

24 William Petty, *Advice of W.P. to Mr. Samuel Hartlib For The Advancement of some particular Parts of Learning* (London, 1647), 4. For a discussion of how humanity could be transmuted and improved, see Ted McCormick, *William Petty and the Ambitions of Political Arithmetic.*

25 John Dury, "A Platforme of the Journeys undertaken for the worke of Peace Ecclesiastical and other profitable ends" (undated), republished in Vera Keller and Leigh T. I. Penman, "From the Archives of Scientific Diplomacy: Science and the Shared Interest of Samuel Hartlib's London and Frederick Clodius's Gottorf," *Isis,* Vol. 106, No. 1 (2015), 42.

26 Keller and Penman, "From the Archives of Scientific Diplomacy," 33–4.

27 See Nils Runeby, "Bengt Skytte, Comenius och Abdikationskrisen 1652," *Scandia* 29 (1963): 360–382.

28 Sten Lindroth, *Paracelsismen i Sverige, till 1660-talets mitt* (Stockholm: Almqvist & Wiksell, 1943), 491–2. For Queen Christina' intellectual influences and interests see Leif Åslund, *Att Fostra en Kung: Om drottning Kristinas utbildning* (Stockholm: Atlantis, 2005) and Susanna Åkerman, *Fenixelden: Drottning Kristina som Alkemist* (Möklinta: Gidlunds, 2013).

29 Grape, "Comenius, Bengt Skytte och Royal Society," 325.

30 For a discussion of universal language, see Gerhard F. Strasser, "Closed and Open Languages: Samuel Hartlib's Involvement with Cryptology and Universal Languages" and Jana Přívratská and Vladimír Přívratský, "Language as the Product and Mediator of Knowledge: The Concept of J. A. Comenius," in Greengrass, Leslie, and Raylor, eds., *Samuel Hartlib and Universal Reformation.* For a discussion of how the curse of Babel interfered with the improvement of Europe, see Sophus Reinert, *Translating Empire: Emulation and the Origins of Political Economy* (Cambridge: Harvard University Press, 2011), 33–8.

31 I am grateful to Vera Keller for pointing out that both Dury and Hartlib played an active role in the negotiations between England and Sweden to establish a closer cooperation. Steve Pincus touches on these negotiations in his *Protestantism and Patriotism: Ideologies and the Making of English Foreign Policy, 1650–1668* (Cambridge: Cambridge University Press, 1996).

32 Grape, "Comenius, Bengt Skytte och Royal Society," 324.

33 Stimson, "Comenius and the Invisible College," 385.

34 Lazardzig, "Universality and Territoriality," 189.

35 Bengt Skytte, "Skytte's Defence of his English College Plan," HP 47/11/2A. Reprinted as appendix B in Finucane, "The Invisible Virtuoso," 146–9.

36 Skytte, "Skytte's Defence," 146.

37 Bengt Skytte, "Skytte's Charter for a College of England," HP47/11/1A. Translated and reprinted as Appendix A in Finucane, "The Invisible Virituoso," 142.

38 Ibid., 143–4.

39 Ibid., 149.

40 Ibid., 147.

41 Grape, "Comenius, Bengt Skytte och Royal Society," 327.

42 Pamela Smith, *The Business of Alchemy: Science and Culture in the Holy Roman Empire* (Princeton: Princeton University Press, 1994), 145–6.

43   Grape, "Comenius, Bengt Skytte och Royal Society," 328.

44   Sven Gerentz, *Kommerskollegium och Näringslivet, 1651–1951* (Stockholm: Nordisk Rotogravyr, 1951), 32.

45   Oxenstierna, quoted in Gerentz, *Kommerskollegium och Näringslivet*, 31.

46   See, for example, Neal Wood, *Foundations of Political Economy: Some Early Tudor Views on State and Society* (Berkeley, C.A.: University of California Press, 1994), Andrea Finkelstein, *Harmony and Balance: An Intellectual History of Seventeenth-Century English Economic Thought* (Ann Arbor: University of Michigan Press, 2000), and Leif Runefelt, *Hushållningens Dygder: Affektlära, Hushållningslära och Ekonomiskt Tänkande under svensk Stormaktstid* (Stockholm: Almqvist & Wiksell, 2001). For a discussion of how commerce could best contribute to the Christian social order, see Philipp Rössner's Introduction to Martin Luther, *On Commerce and Usury*, edited by Rössner (London: Anthem, 2015).

47   Henry Robinson, *Certain Proposalls In order to the Peoples Freedome and Accomodation in some Particulars* (London, 1652), 20

48   Henry Robinson, *Office of Adresses and Encounters: Where all people of each Rancke and Quality may receive direction and advice for the most cheap and speedy way of attaining whatsoever they can lawfully desire* (London, 1650), 4.

49   Robinson, *Certain Proposalls*, 12.

50   For a discussion of how the Harblib Circle conceived of money and credit, see Wennerlind, *Casualties of Credit.*

51   Sven Gerentz suggests that Risingh had a profound long-term impact on the Board of Commerce, in large part through Israel Lagerfeldt, who served as vice Director of the Board from 1654 to 1681. *Kommerskollegium och Näringslivet*, 41–2. Johan Risingh, *Ett Uthtogh om Kiöp-Handelen eller Commercierne, medh Thess Bestånd, Nyttor, och Wesentelige Deelar som äro Warorne, Penningarne, och Wäxelen och om thess Instrument och Redskap, som är Seglationen, sampt hwad mehra som handelen widkommer* (Stockholm, 1669), 9.

52   Gustavus II Adolphus and the 1st Duke of Buckingham (1592–1628) planned to establish a colony in America that followed the design proposal of Sir Balthazar Gerbier. For a discussion of his vision and scheme, see Vera Keller, "The 'framing of a New World': Sir Balthazar Gerbier's 'Project for Establishing a New State in America,' ca. 1649," *William and Mary Quarterly*, Vol. 70, No. 1 (2013): 147–76.

53   "Sveriges Rikes General Handels Compagnie Contract," quoted in Stellan Dahlgren and Hans Norman, *The Rise and Fall of New Sweden: Governor Johan Risingh's Journal, 1654–1655 in its Historical Context* (Stockholm: Almqvist & Wiksell, 1988), 13.

54   György Novaky, *Handelskompanier och Kompanihandel: Svenska Afrikakompaniet, 1649–63* (Uppsala: Uppsala University, 1990). See also the introduction by the editors and the essay by Gunlög Fur in Naum and Nordin, eds., *Scandinavian Colonialism and the Rise of Modernity.*

55   The present discussion about New Sweden draws on information in Fries (1896), Dahlgren and Norman, *The Rise and Fall of New Sweden*, and Bernard Bailyn, *The Barbarous Years: The Peopling of British North America – The Conflict of Civilizations 1600–1675* (New York: Vintage, 2013).

56   New Sweden famously maintained decent relations with the natives. Although a few Swedes were killed in unplanned attacks, New Sweden did not engage in any armed conflicts with the natives. Dahlgren and Norman caution, however, that "there is no reason to create an idyllic picture of the situation." *The Rise and Fall of New Sweden*, 104.

57   Fries, "Johan Classon Risingh," 39.

58   *The Reasons which most Convinced Me to Undertake the Journey to New Sweden*, translated and republished in Dahlgren and Norman, *The Rise and Fall of New Sweden*, 285.

59   Approximately 30 per cent of the population that sailed for New Sweden between 1638 and 1654 were Finns. Sten Carlsson, "The New Sweden Colonists, 1628–1656: Their Geographical and Social Background," in C. E. Hoffecker, R. Waldron, L. E. Williams, and B. E. Benson, eds., *New Sweden in America* (Newark: University of Delaware Press, 1995), 179. Bernard Bailyn suggests that the Finns were perfectly suited for settling North America. He noted that "their way of life was peculiarly primitive by western European standards, and they proved to have a greater affinity to the culture of the native Americans than did any other Europeans in North America." *The Barbarous Years,* 276. For an alternative treatment of the so-called forest Finns, see Fredrik Ekengren, "Materialities on the Move: Identity and Material Culture Among the Forest Finns in Seventeenth-Century Sweden and America," in M. Naum and J. M Nordin, eds., *Scandinavian Colonialism.*

60   Dahlgren, "Johan Risingh," 233.

61   For a discussion that captures the confusion sparked by the clash of economic cultures during the North American colonization process, see Andrew Lipman, *Saltwater Frontier: Indians and the Conquest for the American Coast* (New Haven: Yale University Press, 2015).

62   "Risingh's Journal," translated and republished in Dahlgren and Norman, *The Rise and Fall of New Sweden,* 175.

63   "Ibid., 211.

64   Ibid., 253.

65   Dahlgren, "Johan Risingh," 233.

66   "Risingh's Journal," 219.

67   Quoted in Keller, "The 'Framing of a New World,'" 154.

68   Walter Woodward, *Prospero's America: John Winthrop, Jr., Alchemy and the Creation of New England Culture, 1606–1676* (Chapel Hill: University of North Carolina Press, 2010).

69   Most commentators on Risingh focus exclusively on his writings on commerce. Dahlgren and Norman, for example, disregard Risingh's writings on land and agriculture as a separate project from his political economy. This is a curious analytical choice, considering that these two authors clearly recognize the centrality of land; "it should be remembered that the land and its products formed the basis of economic life and the foundation for the distribution of economic resources." *The Rise and Fall of New Sweden,* 16.

70   Johan Risingh, *Een Land-Book eller Några Upsatter til Wårt Käre Fädernes-Lands Nytta och Förkofring wälmeente om Land-Bruuk och Land Lefwerne* (Wästeråhs, 1671), 4.

71   Ibid., 5.

72   Ibid., 8.

73   Ibid., 5–6.

74   Ibid., 7.

75   There is a palpable similarity between Risingh's *Een-Land Bok* and, for example, Samuel Hartlib's *Cornu Copia* and *An Essay on the Advancement of Husbandry.*

76   Risingh, *Een Land-Book,* 18.

77   Ibid., 18.

78   The English *Commonwealth* literature and the German *Hausväter* literature were represented in Sweden through a series of advice handbooks, all of which shared the term *Oeconomia* in the title. The authors included Laurentius Petri (1499–1573), Per Brahe, d.ä. (1520–1590), Schering Rosenhane (1609–1663), and Åke Rålambs (1651–1718). For intellectual context, see Lars Magnusson, *Äran, Korruptionen och den Borgerliga Ordningen: Essäer från svensk ekonomihistoria* (Stockholm: Atlantis, 2001), 19–21. For a discussion of how the *Oeconomia* tradition conceived of the market as an instrument for social harmony, see Runefelt, *Hushållningens Dygder.*

79   Risingh, *Een Land-Book,* 18–9, 34, 37.

80 Ibid., 34, 38–45.
81 Ibid., 24.
82 Ibid., 33.
83 Ibid., 37.
84 Ibid., 5.
85 Ibid., 81.
86 Ibid., 81.
87 Ibid., 82.
88 Ibid., 82. Elsewhere, Risingh lists alchemists in the same professional category as distillers, apothecaries, and surgeons. *Ett Uthtogh*, 96.
89 Ibid., 35.
90 Ibid., 36.
91 Ibid., 46.
92 Ibid., 38, 48.
93 Ibid., 30. For a list of surviving published and unpublished writings of Risingh, as well as the list of chapter headings of his planned treatise of commerce, see appendix in Fries, "Johan Classon Risingh."
94 Risingh explains that the nearly completed manuscript was lost and destroyed in the Netherlands in 1656 and that he was working hard to restore it. *Ett Uthogh*, 7.
95 Ibid., 5.
96 Ibid., 6, 13, 15–7.
97 Ibid., 8–9.
98 Ibid, 14.
99 Ibid., 18. For a discussion of Risingh's notion of free commerce, see Runefelt, *Hushållningens Dygder*, 198–201.
100 Ibid., 99.
101 Ibid., 10.
102 Ibid., 99.
103 Ibid., 98–99. For a discussion, see Fries (1896), 65.
104 Ibid., 14.
105 Ibid., 25.
106 Ibid., 5 and *Een Land-Book*, 8.
107 Giovanni Botero, *Della Ragion di Stato* (Venice, 1589); David Hume, "Of Commerce," in *Political Discourses* (Edinburgh, 1752), 4.
108 *Ett Uthogh*, 18.
109 Ibid., 21.
110 Ibid., 19–20
111 Ibid., 100.
112 Ibid., 19.
113 For a discussion of Hartlibian political economy, see Wennerlind, *Casualties of Credit*; part I of Philip Stern and Carl Wennerlind, eds., *Mercantilism Reimagined: Political Economy in Early Modern Britain and Its Empire* (Oxford: Oxford University Press, 2013); and the middle chapters of Paul Slack, *The Invention of Improvement*.
114 *Ett Uthogh*, 101–2.
115 Ibid., 23.
116 Risingh clearly did not suffer from belief in the Midas fallacy. In fact, as Lars Magnusson has shown in *Mercantilism*, few seventeenth-century thinkers did. While it is indeed the case that much of the English literature on the balance of trade during the 1620s was focused on ways to bring in more money to the nation, it is a misunderstanding, dating all the way back to Adam Smith, that this implied an advocacy of permanent trade surpluses as the source of wealth. Recent scholarship suggests that the policy prescription to attract more money from abroad was primarily intended as a solution to the devastating scarcity of money that prevailed in England at the time.

117 *Ett Uthogh*, 22, 25.
118 Ibid., 20, 85. *Een Land-Book,* 45.
119 Heckscher, "Anders Berch," 36.
120 *Ett Uthogh,* 29.
121 Ibid., 106.
122 Dahlgren, "Johan Risingh," 232.
123 Ibid., 234. Amandus Johnson reflected on Risingh's legacy, "It is a sad picture to see the former director of New Sweden, the first writer of importance on economy and commerce in Scandinavia, 'ages ahead of his time in his view,' die in a small, miserable garret of a tailor's hut. His books were unsold and his labors unrewarded, but a later age has been more charitable, and his works which could not be marketed during his lifetime are eagerly sought by the collector and often bring a considerable price." "Johan Classon Rising, the Last Director of New Sweden, on the Delaware," *The Pennsylvania Magazine of History and Biography,* Vol. 39, No. 2 (1915), 142.
124 See, for example, Joel Mokyr, *The Enlightened Economy: An Economic History of Britain, 1700–1850* (New Haven: Yale University Press, 2012)
125 Fries, "Johan Classon Risingh," 72.

Part V

Economic growth and the state

From India to Italy

10 State formation and economic growth in South Asia, 1600–1800

Prasannan Parthasarathi

Introduction

This paper surveys the contribution that states made to economic growth in South Asia from the heyday of the Mughal Empire in the seventeenth century to the post-Mughal regional polities of the eighteenth century. It begins with a discussion of agriculture, which was a major arena of state activity. It then moves to trade and manufacturing, for which we possess less information but which was of the utmost concern to rulers. Armaments production, in particular, was essential to the maintenance and exercise of state power. The paper concludes with an examination of knowledge producing activities. While the links to economic growth are not always immediately evident, the accumulation and dissemination of technical knowledge was perceived to be of great political and economic importance and loomed large in the minds of states and their officials in the seventeenth and eighteenth century.

Agriculture

The taxation of agriculture was central to the financial well-being of states and rulers in the seventeenth and eighteenth century. For this reason alone, states involved themselves both in the maintenance and the expansion of agrarian production. Mughal interest in the pushing out of the agricultural frontier is captured in descriptions of Mughal troops accompanied by woodcutters as they added new territories to the empire. According to an early seventeenth-century Mughal document quoted by John Richards, 'From the time of Shah Jahan it was customary that wood-cutters and plough-men used to accompany his troops, so that forests may be cleared and land cultivated'.[1]

Much of the expansion of agricultural production was not done by the Mughal state itself, however, but through intermediaries, who were given financial incentives to do so. Some of these inducements, as well as some examples of direct state actions, are contained in a document from 1665 that has come to be known as Aurangzeb's *farman* to Rasikdas, which, because a number of copies have been discovered, is believed to have been a sort of circular with 'regulations of relevance in general administration'.[2] The document begins with a statement of intent, which declares that the 'entire elevated attention and desires of the Emperor are devoted to the increase in the population and cultivation of the Empire and the welfare of the whole *ri'aya* (peasantry)'. While these goals may have been valued on their own terms, they certainly were a means to a higher end. As the *farman* itself goes on to say, as a consequence, 'the (villages of) *parganas* (administrative subdivisions in Mughal India) will be inhabited and cultivated, the peasantry will be well-off and there will be an increase in the *mahsul* (revenue produce)'. As we shall see both these sentiments were widespread amongst rulers in South Asia in the seventeenth and eighteenth century and formed an integral part of statecraft.

The *farman* goes on to order *diwans*, or high-ranking revenue officials, to:

> direct the *amils* (administrators) that they should at the beginning of the year find out the (number of) cultivators with the number of ploughs and extent of area, village by village. If the peasants are well off, they should arrange that all of them, according to their condition, try to increase (the area under) sowing and so, in comparison with last year, bring about an enlargement in the area cultivated and, while shifting from inferior crops to high grade, not leave waste any cultivable land, so far as they can. If any one from amongst the cultivators has fled, they (*amils*) should find out the reason thereof and try hard in the matter of his return to his native place. Similarly, they should use praiseworthy endeavour and much effort at soothing and conciliation, to gather cultivators from all sides and directions. As for *banjar* (cultivable waste) land, they should impose such *dasturs* (revenue-rates) on it as to enable it to be brought under cultivation.

This passage captures the several ways in which the Mughal officials used the revenue system to promote higher levels of agricultural production. First, the *amil* was to ascertain the quantity of land that could be cultivated on the basis of numbers of cultivators and plows. Second, that same official was to encourage peasants, if they had the means, to expand cultivation and to shift to higher value crops, which would increase the value of the agricultural product and thus the revenue potential of the district. Irfan Habib suggests that by the seventeenth century, the cultivation of high value, commercial crops had reached a considerable extent in the Mughal territories. These included cotton, sugarcane, oilseeds, hemp, dye-yielding crops of various kinds, opium, pepper, fruits and vegetables, and flowers.[3] No doubt some part of this expansion was due to the encouragement of Mughal revenue officials. Third, if any cultivators had fled, the *amil* was to discover why and then endeavor to persuade them to return. The *amil* was also instructed to attract cultivators from neighboring territories (presumably outside Mughal control) and to populate his district. The passage above does not give any details on how the *amil* was to do these things, beyond using his powers of persuasion, but other materials do suggest some means by which Mughal and other state authorities in the seventeenth and eighteenth century attracted cultivators to their realms. Finally, the *amil* was to impose reduced revenue rates on wasteland such as to make them attractive for cultivation. This was a standard feature of pre-British revenue systems in which reduced revenue rates were offered for varying periods to encourage the expansion of cultivation.

The above tasks did not exhaust the work of Mughal revenue officials. The *farman* is full of other instructions, many having to do with the documents to be assembled, the methods by which the work of revenue collection was conducted, but the most important in terms of economic growth was for revenue officials to themselves directly carry out agricultural improvement. In the words of the *farman*, 'Wherever there is a well that is out of repair, he should repair it and also dig new ones'. Such an instruction, which as we shall see was not unique to the Mughal case, directly involved revenue officials in investment in agriculture, presumably using the funds of the state, although the *farman* does not specify that.

Finally, the *farman* issues some limited instructions on how to deal with bad years or poor seasons. The main thrust of these is for revenue officials to assess the extent of the loss peasant by peasant and to protect the poorer peasants from oppression by their superiors. The *farman* orders:

> In no case should they make a collective deduction on account of calamity, whose distribution would be in the hands of the *chaudhris* (head of a 'pargana'), *qanungos* (the chaudri's assistant), *muqaddams*, or *patwaris* (further administrators and officers), so that the small peasants receiving their due, remain safe from injury and loss, and the dominant ones are not able to oppress them.

It is likely that the Mughals, as did their successors in the eighteenth century, did a great deal more to help peasants cope with and recover from disasters, but the document does not address them. Other sources, however, give some idea of the state role at those moments and these will be discussed shortly.

The Mughal state involvement in the maintenance of the agricultural order finds parallels in other parts of the Indian subcontinent and in the eighteenth century after the Mughal heyday. The normative vision of the state as the guarantor of peasant wealth and prosperity contained in the *farman* to Rasikdas finds wide resonance in South India, for instance. The *Rayavacakamu*, a Telugu text on statecraft that is dated to the late sixteenth or early seventeenth centuries declared, 'To acquire wealth: Make the people prosper'.[4]

Similarly, works on statecraft in South India advise rulers to invest in agricultural improvement, particularly in systems for water control. The *Amuktamalyada*, a Telugu work attributed to the Vijayanagar Emperor Krishnadeva Raya (reign from 1509 to 1529), imparted the following words to the sovereign: 'The extent of a state is the root cause of its prosperity. When a state is small in extent then both virtue (*dharma*) and prosperity (*artha*) will increase only when tanks and irrigation canals are constructed'.[5] The *Rayavacakamu* instructed kings to 'beget the sevenfold progeny, which are a son, a treasure, a temple, a garden, an irrigation tank, a literary work, and a village established for Brahmins'. Elsewhere the *Rayavackamu* states:

> A broken family, damaged tanks and wells,
> a fallen kingdom, one who comes seeking refuge,
> cows and Brahman, and temples of the gods—
> supporting these is four times as meritorious.[6]

The following account from the late eighteenth century of repairs conducted on a major dam on the Cauvery River shows that these were not empty words, but shaped state practices. In this case, the king of Tanjore took the leading role in the maintenance of the waterworks in his kingdom:

> When I arrived at the *annacathy* [annicut or dam] I found the Rajah's people employed in repairing the damage the bank and masonry sustained last year. There were at work at this time about 700 coolies and 200 bricklayers or masons, including their assistants and *chunam* (cement or plaster) beaters. All the works in and connected with the *annacathy* are entrusted to the direction of a Bramin, the Rajah's Head Hircar.[7]

Admittedly the annicut was one of the largest and most important structures in the vast South Indian system of water control, but state activities shaped the agrarian landscape in countless less dramatic ways as well, and in many respects similar to the methods used by the Mughals. These are suggested by Tipu Sultan's revenue regulations, which were issued in late eighteenth century Mysore.

Under the rule of Tipu Sultan the Mysore state sought to promote agricultural improvement and expansion. Inducements to invest in agriculture, including reductions in revenue and privileged forms of land tenure such as exemptions from taxation, were offered. The Mysorean revenue regulations instructed revenue officials to grant land tax-free to individuals who 'at his own expence, dig tanks, wells, &c'.[8] New lands brought under cultivation were to 'be delivered to *Reyuts* to cultivate, upon *Cowle*; the first year they shall be exempt from paying any revenue, and the second year they shall only pay half the customary assessment; but the third year the full amount thereof shall be collected from them'.[9]

The Mysore state also supplied capital in the form of *taccavi*, which was widespread in eighteenth-century South India (to cultivators 'who need to purchase ploughs and to cultivate the lands, he shall give *Tucavee*'[10]). In Tanjore, English East India Company officials reported that 'advances for cultivation are made in grain and occasionally in money, and when it does not suit the convenience of the *circar* (government) to make any, the inhabitants are allowed to borrow money, and to charge in their final settlement with the *circar* at the rate of one per cent monthly on the amount of the customary advance'.[11]

Taccavi was also critical for recovery from bad seasons or disasters. In the eighteenth century, the critical importance of taccavi is made evident from the failure of the English East India Company state to provide it in the aftermath of the famine of 1769–70. As Rajat Datta puts it:

The most important dimension of institutional relief is the material help given to support production and the producers both of which are caught in the middle of a severe short-run crisis of survival under famine duress. Here, the Company performed miserably [...]. There was an insignificant amount of financial aid (*taqavi*) provided to help the cultivators to begin production for the next agricultural season. The drought and high prices had destroyed the productive resources of the majority of producers and it was universally acknowledged that they needed cash help on easy terms of repayment (*taqavi*) in order to sustain their future economies.[12]

The location of agrarian activity in eighteenth-century South India and the distribution of zones of highly productive agriculture, neither of which can be explained solely by local initiative, indicate a close correspondence between state formation and agricultural improvement and investment. This was in part a result of medieval activity in agriculture at which time rulers legitimated their power through presentations of land and cash to temples. These institutions then funnelled these gifts into agriculture, especially for rice cultivation, as this was a sure way to receive a high and reliable rate of return on these funds. Less is known on the institutional and political arrangements that promoted agricultural development in post-medieval centuries (after 1600) when temples declined in importance, but this link between political power and agricultural improvement continued to exist, albeit on a different institutional basis. The distribution and location of cotton cultivation in late eighteenth century South India clearly illustrates the continued importance of states in the shaping of the agrarian landscape.

Cropping patterns in South India have most commonly been attributed to geographical and ecological factors such as the location of soils and the availability of water.[13] These factors, however, are not sufficient to explain the pattern of cotton cultivation. Cotton in South India was cultivated under two very different regimes, intensive and extensive, and each form of cultivation was found on very different soils. Intensive cultivation was carried out on heavy, black soils, while extensive was found on thin, red soils. In many parts of South India red and black soils were often found in close proximity, and there was abundant red and black soil throughout South India. Before the nineteenth century, however, intensive cultivation was largely concentrated in two areas, Madurai and the area of the southern Deccan around Bellary. The limited distribution of intensive cultivation becomes even more puzzling given that it was far more profitable than extensive cultivation as it yielded, at a minimum, twice as much cotton per acre.

This pattern becomes explicable when political power is incorporated into the analysis. Extensive cultivation required very little capital. Red soils were easily ploughed and the peasant-cultivator put up his supply of seed. Although intensive cultivation was far more lucrative, it depended upon the availability of abundant supplies of capital. Funds were needed to clear and plough the heavy black soils and to hire the labourers who carried out essential tasks such as ploughing and picking. According to Thomas Munro, who served as the revenue officer in Bellary in the early nineteenth century, political and revenue authorities provided a sizable fraction of the capital necessary for cultivation on black soils, which was extended in the form of taccavi, or advances for the financing of production:

> These lands, after having lain waste eight or ten years, cannot be broken up without a large plough drawn by six yokes of bullocks, and they must afterwards be cleared of the roots of the long grass with which they are overrun, by a machine drawn by seven or eight yokes. The expense of setting a single plough in motion is about 150 *pagodas*, so that it can only be done by substantial *ryots*, or by the union of two or three of those whose means are less. A considerable portion of the bullocks employed are from Nellore, and it is absolutely necessary that the yoke next to the plough be of that breed. It is for the purchase of that yoke, which usually costs from 20 to 24 *pagodas* that the *ryots* require *tuckavi*.[14]

The areas where intensive cultivation was concentrated, Madurai and Bellary, formed the cores of major political entities. Being politically important, they were the focus of state activities to improve agriculture, with the goal of increasing the revenue potential of territories. Outside these two areas, mainly in Coimbatore and Tinnevelly, although black soils were plentiful, they were not brought under the plough until the nineteenth century and the new cotton economy of the colonial period which linked South Indian peasants with China, Bombay, and eventually local cotton mills. Coimbatore and Tinnevelly lay outside major South Indian political centres. Coimbatore was a frontier region from its initial settlement in the medieval period. Its status was to change only from the late nineteenth century when it became a dynamic and booming agricultural, and later industrial, centre.[15] The black soils in Tinnevelly were similarly a frontier zone and until the nineteenth century much of the investment in agriculture in the Tinnevelly region was directed towards paddy cultivation in the valley of the Tambraparni River.[16]

Trade and manufacturing

Although there is evidence that Mughal officials and noblemen engaged in commercial activities as a profitable side-line, the Mughal state cannot be said to have had a trade policy *per se*, save to encourage commerce. In the western Indian Ocean Mughal administrators based in Gujarat strove to maintain trade links with the Persian Gulf and Red Seas open and free of pirates, but beyond this the manipulation of trade or prices were not arenas for state action. This was not due to a lack of interest in trade. Mughal authorities, both at the centre and in the regions, were well aware of the economic importance of trade for imperial power. A thriving commercial sector kept the economy operating at a high pitch; overseas exchange brought in the silver, which was needed for the proper functioning of the monetary system; and internal and external trade was a source of revenue to the state.

The external trade of the empire—bullion for goods, in Om Prakash's memorable phrase—was the source of silver, as well as gold, copper, and other commodities that were used as money and greased the wheels of commerce and the machinery of revenue collection in South Asia. In order to guarantee this inflow of specie imperial authorities granted to European companies the permission to establish factories as well as trade concessions. In 1615, for instance, both the Dutch and the English East India Companies were given the rights to establish trading stations in Surat. Similarly, both the Dutch and the English obtained in the seventeenth century exemptions from the payment of internal transit tolls within the empire. Similar privileges were granted to European traders in seventeenth-century South India. The rulers of Golconda, for instance, allowed the establishment of settlements and lower taxes for Europeans who sought access to the fine chintzes and other cottons of Masulipatnam and its environs.[17]

A flourishing external trade depended upon a thriving internal trade, however, and this fact led Mughal and officialdom from other states to take steps to maintain commercial life within their territories. In the Deccan, for instance, rulers and elites built and maintained caravanserais for the convenience of merchants in cities and towns. Rulers also constructed roads and by the early seventeenth century major arteries crossed the Deccan connecting Masulipatnam with Surat and Hyderabad. These roads were reputed to be extremely well maintained. Similarly, waterways in coastal areas such as the Konkan were constructed to facilitate the movement of people and the transport of goods. Political authorities, up and down the state hierarchy, also took an active role in the founding of markets, whether daily, weekly or on some other schedule in cities, towns, and villages.[18] It is likely that these markets penetrated more deeply into both the urban and rural orders over the course of the seventeenth and eighteenth centuries. Markets, as physical centres for exchange, were founded in smaller and smaller agglomerations of population and the frequency of markets increased. Weekly markets became bi-weekly or daily; periodic markets became permanent. This is certainly a process that Christopher Bayly identified in his study of North India in the closing decades of the eighteenth century and the opening decades of the nineteenth.[19] In addition to supporting external trade, these market places were in themselves a source of revenue as the commodities and the merchants could also be taxed. The growing symbiosis between political power and commercial power in the seventeenth century is captured in a statement attributed to the Maratha king, Shivaji:

> Merchants are the ornaments of the kingdom and the glory of the king. They are the cause of the prosperity of the kingdom. All kinds of goods which are not available come into the kingdom. That kingdom becomes rich. In times of difficulties whatever debt is necessary is available. For this reason the respect due to merchants should be maintained. In the capital market great merchants should be induced to come and settle.[20]

In the eighteenth century the external trade of the maritime regions of South Asia expanded enormously and became even more critical for the survival of states. In 1748, the Court of Directors in London was of the opinion that:

the Nabob cannot but be sensible that his Revenues are supported chiefly by the Immense Sums we yearly import into his Dominions and must know what a stagnation it would create in his Finances, if Calcutta were to be taken by the French and laid waste in the manner Madras hath been.[21]

The new regional states that followed the Mughal era also came under intensified pressure to amass resources. Burton Stein has linked these political changes to new military innovations, perhaps most importantly the rise of standing armies, and labelled these developments military fiscalism. He has also labelled the state-building activities a form of mercantilism.[22]

For Stein, the quintessential mercantilist state in South India was Mysore, which attempted to bring trade in valuable commodities under political control as a means to enrich its coffers. Mysore was preceded by the trading innovations in Malabar under the rule of Martanda Varma, who sought to monopolize the pepper trade within his realm, both to compete against the Dutch and to expand state resources.[23] However, the state trading efforts in Mysore were far more ambitious and ranged from sandalwood to areca nuts, pepper, cardamom, and cotton textiles.

With the extension of state power into commerce, these states also began to insert themselves into the process of production. Mysore, for instance, tried to enlarge its textile manufactures and offered inducements its weavers outside to territories to relocate to the kingdom. In Malabar and Mysore, the state got involved in making advances to growers of pepper and other agricultural commodities, their procurement of these goods, and then the sale and marketing. While many details on these state activities are not available, there is no doubt of their existence. However, this kind of engagement in production had seventeenth century antecedents. The Mughal noblemen who engaged in trade, for example, at times tried to monopolize the labour of producers, including weavers, as they tried to procure goods for shipment.[24]

While the above state interest in the production process was episodic, the manufacture of armaments was an area of sustained state focus in both the Mughal and post-Mughal periods. There are quite a few discussions of the high quality of Indian guns, both small and large, and especially in the late eighteenth and early nineteenth century when East India Company forces directly encountered Indian weapons on the battlefield. There is much less information on how these armaments were produced, however. An important source is a study of the cannon foundry at Jaigarh in the city of Jaipur. The foundry was constructed in the 1580s—the first cannon was finished in 1587—and remained in use into the eighteenth century. The foundry was much altered over its lifetime and what remains now is likely to date from the eighteenth century.

Rajah Man Singh established the foundry in the sixteenth century and he 'obtained the necessary knowledge regarding the casting and manufacture of cannon from captured craftsmen during a six-year campaign in Afghanistan'. Man Singh brought this knowledge of the 'Persian method' of making cannon back to Rajasthan along with 'models of a foundry and lathes, together with examples of barrel cutters and other tools'.[25] This importation of foreign knowledge, as will be discussed shortly, was not exceptional but was an important contribution that states played to economic progress in the seventeenth and eighteenth century.

The foundry was known locally as the Karkhana, which is a state workshop. (In the 1960s Mughal karkhanas were the centre of some historical discussion as they were thought to represent a tendency towards centralized production systems such as the factory and therefore a potential sign of capitalism. These karkhanas were typically set up for the manufactures that used high value items and thus required close supervision of the producers to prevent embezzlement or adulteration). The Jaigarh foundry is in an excellent state of preservation, largely because it remained in the hands of the Maharajah of Jaipur. The facility consists of a furnace where one can still see a channel for the molten metal leading to a pit in which the cannon moulds were placed. The solid casting was then taken to a lathe for boring and in the opinion of T. J. Gander, the 'lathe is perhaps the most remarkable part of the Karkhana to survive'. Gander describes its operation in the following terms:

> The motive power came from eight oxen turning a capstan inside a chamber. A central pole in the chamber turned a large wooden gear wheel below the wooden floor. This wheel used its peg gears to rotate a further and smaller wheel set a right angle to one side, using an (estimated) step-down ratio of about 60–1. The small gear wheel provided rotation to a metal shaft turning through a wall-bearing, on the other side of which was the wood and metal wheel arrangement for holding the cutting and boring tools.

The foundry today contains cutting and boring tools along with their operating rods as well callipers and gauges.

This brief description of the foundry shows the metallurgical and engineering skills that were required to satisfy the armaments needs of South Asian states in the seventeenth and eighteenth century. While the level of skill and knowledge would have varied widely across the subcontinent, state production of arms must have stimulated the creation of knowledgeable individuals. It is likely that some of these individuals would have been connected to private activities, linking these facilities to the broader economy. On the basis of the sources, however, it is difficult (or perhaps more accurately impossible) to gain access to these connections. This, however, brings us to the final state contribution to economic growth, which was the political role in the creation and diffusion of knowledge.

Knowledge

State and elite interest in individuals and institutions that created and diffused knowledge may be identified from the Mughal period to the post-Mughal order of the eighteenth century. As with state contributions to agriculture and state participation in trade and manufactures, the evidence for state knowledge promotion activities increases over the period between 1600 and 1800. This may be an artefact of the greater abundance of source materials for the eighteenth century, but it more likely reflects the greater state participation in the economy by the eighteenth century. Nevertheless, even in the seventeenth century Mughal rulers and political elites exhibited a keen interest in a variety of forms of knowledge. In the discussion that follows, these forms are divided into science, technology, and mathematics, accounting and related fields.

In the late seventeenth century, according to Iqbal Ghani Khan, Mughal officials and elites began to compile manuals of administration. These works contained information on diverse topics and were designed to instruct these individuals on how to manage large households and estates. The manuals contained sections on accounting, inventory-keeping, area calculations, agriculture, crop-yield estimation and crop-sharing techniques. This information would have been essential for the collection of revenue, but some of this knowledge would have aided private individuals as well. The development and diffusion of techniques for area calculations and crop-yield estimation most likely led to advances in geometry and represented a subset of a larger state and official interest in mathematics. In the seventeenth century the ruler of Golconda was famous for having every passing European brought to his court and interrogated for his mathematical knowledge. Mathematics had many practical applications, ranging from ballistics to the creation of accurate calendars, which were critical for the timing of agricultural operations.[26]

Elite interest in accounting would have had broader economic ramifications. As Christopher Bayly has shown, accounting in seventeenth and eighteenth century North India existed at the interface between private merchants and state officials. Therefore any state advances in technique would likely have been transferred to the accounting methods of merchants and bankers, bringing to their operations a more rational outlook and framework.[27] The state interest in advancing accounting continued in the eighteenth century, most strikingly shown in the work of Frank Perlin on the Maratha state where rulers and officials were pushing forward administrative knowledge on a very wide front, including accounting and the standardization of weights and measures.[28]

From the late seventeenth century, the Mughal manuals of the administration began to include more information on agricultural production as well as a variety of crafts, such as metal working, weaving, cotton carding, dyeing, and alchemy. In the eighteenth century, Ghani Khan writes, the information contained in these manuals became more specialized and more technically precise and detailed. A whole host of texts were produced on a range of topics of political, military and economic importance. They included handbooks on cannons and guns, travel literature which told of the lands that lay both inside and outside the Indian subcontinent, and dictionaries of revenue terms that included material on agricultural techniques. Some of these works were indigenous. Others were translations of European and Iranian works. They point, however, to a growing state interest in compiling and disseminating knowledge about techniques of production in a number of areas in order to benefit states and rulers.[29]

States and rulers went beyond collecting knowledge in texts and attempted to directly improve techniques and technology. The Rajput state of Kota, for instance, appears to have conducted agricultural experiments to improve seed strains, grafting methods, oxen breeding, and plough designs. This improved agrarian knowledge was disseminated through the kingdom via the vehicle of state-sponsored fairs.[30] Similar efforts to improve cattle strains took place in Mysore in the late eighteenth century, which has already been identified as the location for far-reaching efforts at economic development under the aegis of military fiscalism or mercantilism.

The Mysore state embarked upon a broad state-sponsored push to expand manufacturing in its kingdom. Needing iron for the manufacture of armaments, in the 1780s orders were issued for the construction of twenty new iron-smelting furnaces within the kingdom. Some of this iron would have fed arms making, which reached very high levels. The Mysore state's interest in improving manufacturing extended to clocks, paper, and glass as well as other goods. Francis Buchanan, who travelled through the region in the early nineteenth century, called the last ruler of pre-British Mysore, Tipu Sultan, a 'wonderful projector'. Buchanan also reported that under Tipu, Mysore had established the manufacture of 'broad-cloth, paper formed on wires like the European kind, watches, and cutlery'.[31] No information is available on to what extent the production of these goods had spread beyond the state manufactories or the links between the skills developed in them and private manufacturing.

Tipu Sultan undertook other efforts to augment the skills and resources of his kingdom. For instance, a diplomatic delegation that was dispatched to the Ottoman Empire, France and Britain was given the task of collecting information on manufacturing and techniques of production in the countries they visited. The delegation was instructed that:

> Industries and rarities of each city and territory [...] should be written down in front of each of you. [...] Requests should be made in the proper and necessary manner to the Sultan of Turkey and the King of France, for obtaining artisans expert in the manufacture of muskets, guns, clocks, glass, mirrors, chinaware, and cannon-balls, and for such other craftsmen as may be there [...] obtaining from them bonds of agreement to come to this Court.

Tipu was particularly interested in carpenters and ironsmiths who were skilled in shipbuilding and gun makers as well as a skilled astronomer, geomancer and physician. Tipu also directed the delegation to send back to Mysore samples of coal as well procure experts who were skilled in recognizing the presence of coal deposits.[32]

These did not exhaust Mysore's efforts to obtain knowledge from outside the Indian subcontinent. Nor was Mysore the only state in the eighteenth century that sought to exploit non-local sources of knowledge. Mysore was one of a number of states in the eighteenth century that sponsored the translation of foreign scientific and technical works into Indian languages, including the vernaculars, which suggests an effort to reach a larger audience for these works. The Mysore state, for instance, financed the translation of French and English works on natural history and botany. This appears to have been part of a larger project of translation in which 'forty-five books on different sciences were either compiled, or translated from different languages, under his [Tipu Sultan's] immediate inspection or auspices', according to Charles Stewart who compiled an inventory of the Mysore library upon the conquest of the kingdom by the forces of the English East India Company. Included among these works were translations of the complete London dispensatory and an English work on electrical and medical experiments.[33]

In addition to these European works, the Mysore state had collected works in arithmetic, mathematics and astronomy in Persian and Arabic. For example, its library contained what Stewart called an 'excellent treatise' on mathematics and geometry written in 1681 by Lutif Allah, who was an engineer in Delhi. Another Mughal work was a compilation of knowledge on diverse subjects, including the manufacture of artificial gems, fireworks, and colours and paints of all kinds, to which was appended a work on the dyeing of cloths, silks, etc. The Mysore library also contained other works from other parts of South Asia. There was a treatise on universal science by the Sufi, Mohammad Ghos of Gwalior, which included material on astronomy, geography, physics, music theology, war, agriculture and horticulture, omens, talismans, chemistry, and the magnet, as well as a Decanni text, *The Complete Equestrian*, which contained information on how to purchase and breed horses, manage the stud and cure the 'disorders to which they are liable'.[34]

In the southern part of India, the state of Tanjore also pursued the compilation and translation of scientific and technical knowledge. The library in that state was founded in the sixteenth century as the Royal Palace Library and expanded in the eighteenth century under the patronage of the Maratha rulers of the kingdom, at some point renamed the *Sarasvati Mahal Library* (the goddess Sarasvati is the patron of knowledge and learning). In the late eighteenth century, the ruler of Tanjore, Serfoji II, purchased substantial numbers of European books on scientific subjects, including works on chemistry, electricity, mathematics, medicine, and veterinary sciences. The king also financed translations of European works. For example, English works on anatomy were translated into Marathi and Tamil, which would have made these works more widely available. He also patronized local scholars in their scientific endeavours. In the late eighteenth and early nineteenth century the library was a centre of study for not only for local scholars and intellectuals but also for Europeans who lived in the region.[35]

In eighteenth-century North India, two of the most notable of endeavours of this sort were found under the rule of Jai Singh in the Rajput state of Amber (1722–1739) and then in the state of Awadh. The astronomical efforts of Jai Singh are well known, not least because of the monumental observatory he left behind in Delhi and several other cities of northern India. Less known was his interaction with European astronomical and other learning. The team of astronomers he assembled consisted of both Europeans and Indians; he commissioned the translation of European astronomical and mathematical works into Indian languages; and he dispatched a team of Indians to Europe to obtain instruments, books, and astronomical tables. Jai Singh's interest in European knowledge was not restricted to astronomy. For instance, he commissioned the translation of a

European book on perspective drawing, which was designed to aid the work of builders, engineers, technicians, artists, and draftsmen. To make the knowledge contained in the work accessible to a broad audience, the translation was made into Hindustani, and more specifically into the dialect used the vicinity of Delhi and Agra. With these translations, Jai Singh may have been emulating Mughal practices.[36] Under Aurangzeb, Francois Bernier was appointed court physician and the texts that he possessed were translated into Indian languages. This commenced a long dialogue between Bernier and North Indians on philosophy and medicine in which Bernier communicated Cartesianism, atomism and other developments in seventeenth-century European thought as well as recent additions to medical knowledge and anatomy, including the circulatory system, to his Mughal counterparts.[37]

Another successor to these Mughal practices was the court in Awadh, which is reputed to have contained in Lucknow the greatest library in eighteenth-century North India. At the end of the century it was reputed to contain some 300,000 volumes. Little is known about the contents of this library. According to one chronicler, only 700 of these volumes were inherited from the libraries of the Mughals. Few details are available on the contents of this library, but others in North India at the same time contained works on geography, travelogues, poetry, medicine, hunting and hawking, and encyclopaedias on natural history, agriculture, veterinary sciences, and alchemy.[38]

The above information indicates that from the Mughal period to the early nineteenth century states and rulers in India collected and compiled knowledge and made it available to the learned men of their territories via translation projects and the creation of repositories such as libraries. We do not know for certain who had access to these but there is information that Serfoji made the Tanjore materials accessible to a number of Europeans. At the same time, a number of states attempted to push out the frontiers of knowledge, as they perceived them. States were patrons to large numbers who were interested in knowledge of the mind as well as the hand. Translators and scientific men received support for their activities. Technical men, who were more interested in the nitty-gritty of agriculture and manufacturing, were similarly supported and encouraged. Although further details on these patronage activities do not exist, the above material certainly suggests a more than passing interest by political authorities in knowledge for the sake of its utility for state power.

Conclusion

This brief chapter has surveyed a range of ways in which states and rulers in seventeenth and eighteenth century South Asia contributed to economic activity. State interests with respect to the economy ranged from agriculture to trade and manufactures and the creation and diffusion of technical knowledge of many kinds. Some of these activities may have been undertaken out of curiosity, a belief in normative ideals of good kingship, and naked self-interest. At heart, however, they were activities that contributed to the power of the state and expanded its political and military reach. Economic life in the seventeenth and eighteenth century were closely connected to the development and formation of states.

Notes

1 John F. Richards, *The Unending Frontier: An Environmental History of the Early Modern World* (Berkeley: University of California Press, 2003), 33.
2 Shireen Moosvi, "Aurangzeb's *Farman* to Rasikdas on Problems of Revenue Administration, 1665," in *Medieval India I: Researches in the History of India 1200–1750*, ed. Irfan Habib (Delhi: Oxford University Press, 1992), 197–208.
3 Irfan Habib, *The Agrarian System of Mughal India, 1556–1707*, 2nd ed. (Delhi: Oxford University Press, 1999), 39–62.
4 Phillip B. Wagoner (transl.), *Tidings of the King. A Translation and Ethnohistorical Analysis of the Rāyavācakamu* (Honolulu: University of Hawaii Press, 1993), 95.
5 A. Rangasvami Sarasvati, "Political Maxims of the Emperor-Poet, Krishnadeva Raya," *Journal of Indian History*, 4/3 (1926), 61–88.
6 Wagoner, *Tidings of the King*, 155.
7 "Some Enquiries into and account of the State of the Annacathy" (May 1777), p. 15, Mackenzie General, vol. 59, Africa, Asia and Pacific Collections, British Library, London.
8 Burrish Crisp, *The Mysorean Revenue Regulations* (Calcutta, 1792), in C. B. Greville, *British India Analyzed* (London, 1793), article 36.
9 Crisp, *Mysorean Revenue Regulations*, article 15.
10 Crisp, *Mysorean Revenue Regulations*, article 2.
11 *Report of the Tanjore Commissioners A.D. 1799* (Tanjore, 1905), 24.
12 Rajat Datta, *Society, Economy and the Market: Commercialization in Rural Bengal, c. 1760–1800* (New Delhi: Manohar Publishers & Distributors, 2000), 259–60.
13 David Ludden, *Peasant History in South India* (Princeton, NJ: Princeton University Press, 1985), 51–67; C. J. Baker, *An Indian Rural Economy 1880–1995: The Tamilnad Countryside* (Oxford: Clarendon Press; New York: Oxford University Press, 1984), chap. 1.
14 Quoted in J. D. B. Gribble, *A Manual of the District of Cuddapah* (Madras, 1875), 201–2.
15 M. Arokiaswami, *Kongunad* (Madras, 1956); Baker, *Indian Rural Economy*, 93–5.
16 Ludden, *Peasant History in South India*, chaps. 1–3.
17 John F. Richards, *The Mughal Empire* (Cambridge: Cambridge University Press, 1993), 196–204.
18 H. Fukazawa, "The State and the Economy: Maharashtra and the Deccan: A Note," in *The Cambridge Economic History of India*, vol. 1, *c.1200–c.1750*, ed. Tapan Raychaudhuri and Irfan Habib (Cambridge, 1982), 202–3.
19 C. A. Bayly, *Rulers, Townsmen and Bazaars: North Indian Society in the Age of European Expansion, 1770–1870* (Cambridge: Cambridge University Press, 1983).
20 Fukazawa, "The State and the Economy," 202.
21 Quoted in K. N. Chaudhuri, "Foreign Trade: European Trade with India," in *Cambridge Economic History of India*, vol. 1, 382–407, at 407.
22 Burton Stein, "State Formation and Economy Reconsidered," *Modern Asian Studies*, 19 (1985), 387–413.
23 Ashin Das Gupta, *Malabar in Asian Trade* (Cambridge: Cambridge University Press, 1967).
24 Tapan Raychaudhuri, "The State and the Economy: The Mughal Empire," *Cambridge Economic History of India*, vol.1, 172–192, at 182–3.
25 T. J. Gander, "The Cannon Foundry at Jaigarh," *Journal of the Ordnance Society*, 12 (2000), 49.

26 See two important articles by Iqbal Ghani Khan, "Technology and the Question of Elite Intervention in Eighteenth-Century South India," in *Rethinking Early Modern India*, ed. Richard B. Barnet (New Delhi: Manohar Publishers & Distributors, 2002), 257–88 and "The Awadh Scientific Renaissance and the Role of the French: *c.*1750–1820," *Indian Journal of the History of Science*, 38 (2003), 273–301.

27 C. A. Bayly, "Pre-Colonial Indian Merchants and Rationality," in *India's Colonial Encounter: Essays in Memory of Eric Stokes,* eds. Mushirul Hasan and Narayani Gupta (New Delhi: Manohar, 1993), 3–24.

28 Frank Perlin, "State Formation Reconsidered," *Modern Asian Studies*, 19 (1985), 415–80.

29 See the two essays by Iqbal Ghani Khan cited previously.

30 Norbert Peabody, *Hindu Kingship and Polity in Precolonial India* (Cambridge: Cambridge University Press, 2003), 131–2.

31 Francis Buchanan, *A Journey from Madras through the Countries of Mysore, Canara and Malabar*, 3. Vols. (London: T. Cadell and W. Davies, 1807), vol. 1, 70. For additional information on Mysore see the documents in Irfan Habib, ed., *State and Diplomacy under Tipu Sultan. Documents and Essays* (New Delhi: Tulka, 2001).

32 Ibid.

33 Charles Stewart, *A Descriptive Catalogue of the Oriental Library of the Late Tippoo Sultan of Mysore. To which are Prefixed, Memoirs of Hyder Aly Khan, and His Son Tippoo Sultan* (London: Sold by Longman, Hurst, Rees, and Orme, 1809).

34 Ibid.

35 Savithri Preetha Nair, "Native Collecting and Natural Knowledge (1798–1832): Raja Serfoji II of Tanjore as a 'Centre of Calculation," *Journal of the Royal Asiatic Society*, series 3, 15 (2005), 279–302, at 285, 291; R. Jayaraman, *Sarasvati Mahal: A Short History and Guide* (Thanjavur: Tanjore Maharaja Serfoji's Sarasvati Mahal Library, 1981).

36 Virendra Nath Sharma, *Sawai Jai Singh and His Astronomy* (Delhi: Motilal Banarsidass Publishers, 1995).

37 Khan, "Awadh Scientific Renaissance," 276–7.

38 Khan, "Awadh Scientific Renaissance," 281.

11 Economic reasons of state in Qing China

A brief comparative overview

Peer Vries

The Qing economy and the idea of economic growth

In this chapter, I will discuss the political economy of Qing China (1644–1912). I will focus on 'practices' more than on abstract 'theories' and will systematically compare Qing China's case with that of Western Europe in the early modern era. As an economic historian of Western Europe in that era I will certainly even with my ever-increasing interest in the history of East Asia have a certain Eurocentric bias in the sense that my knowledge of the European case is deeper and broader than that of the Chinese case for which I have based myself on quite general literature. I nevertheless hope the text will be interesting and relevant for scholars of both regions. The bulk of the text will deal with roughly the first 200 years of Qing rule till the 1840s, in which China's rulers could basically implement their ideas unchallenged. The much smaller second part deals with roughly the last half century of their rule in which they had to confront the challenge of 'modernization'.

Economic growth in the sense of modern economic growth as economists define it means an increase in real income per capita that is sustained and substantial and accompanied by structural economic transformations. Up until far into the nineteenth century it definitely never was a goal of any Qing government to create such growth. As such that is not surprising. Till the take-off of Great Britain's economy with industrialization such growth was not known anywhere in the world, not even as a concept. Even economists like Adam Smith and David Ricardo still considered a lasting increase of productivity and wealth to be impossible.[1] Qing China's rulers never looked at the economy in terms of overall growth but rather in terms of a zero-sum game. Feuerwerker writes about a 'traditional Chinese preoccupation with dividing a static economic pie' and misses a 'recognition of the need for and possibility of increasing the size of the pie'.[2] The principle of 'preserving the wealth among the people' was considered very important: 'the realm has only so much wealth. If it is not accumulated with the sovereign, it will be dispersed among the subjects'.[3] What the state takes, is taken from the people, or as the Qianlong emperor put it: 'If the quantity of grain held by the government is too large, then that held by the people must be too small'.[4] As we will see later on this idea had a big impact on thinking about taxation, expenditure and government debt. High incomes and profits outside agriculture easily aroused the fear that agriculture would be neglected, which was considered dangerous, whereas, to quote Hsu Tzu, a nineteenth-century local official: 'When the profits of commerce are small, those who plow and weave will be numerous'.[5] Economic problems could best be solved by frugality.

But even if the concept of modern economic growth would have been known: such growth can only exist in an environment that is quite incompatible with the kind of society that Qing rulers advocated. Modern economic growth is characterised by 'creative destruction'. It involves permanent, structural change and 'development', which usually is regarded as a form of progress. A strong resistance to change, however, has always characterized imperial China's civilization. Qing China in this respect was no exception. Harmony and stability counted as paramount and the idea of progress was almost universally rejected. Two Westerners with first-hand and extensive knowledge of the country were convinced that this was still the case as late as 1869. In that year missionary Griffith John wrote about China: 'The idea of establishing a new order of things, which shall be an improvement on the old, never enters the mind of anyone [...]'. Robert Hart, Inspector-General of China's Imperial Maritime Custom Service in that very same year claimed: 'To the mass of Chinese officials the word improvement would convey no idea corresponding to that which is in the Western mind'.[6] Overall Qing rulers were fascinated with – and constrained by – precedent and did not think that the future would have better things in store than Golden Ages in the past.

Interventions in the economy therefore, at least until way into the second half of the nineteenth century, were not meant to lead to major transformations, but to 'put things in order'. It is misleading when Peter Perdue writes: 'The capabilities of the Qing to manage the economy were powerful enough that we might even call it a "developmental agrarian state."'[7] The term 'developmental state' as a rule is reserved for states that promote structural change and modern economic growth. I would even be hesitant to claim that Qing rulers were striving for *any* kind of growth.[8] There are no indications that they wanted to rule over a society in which productivity and standards of living would steadily improve. The essence of their policies was that people should be able to live their decent lives in security and wealth, as they were traditionally defined. They certainly were more oriented toward preservation than towards change and lifting the entire economy to a new, higher level.[9]

A moral economy

In Qing China thinking about 'economic' affairs was deeply embedded in conceptions of what would be the 'right' moral, social and political order. There certainly existed a notion of what we nowadays describe as the 'market mechanism'. Overall – in contrast to what has always been claimed in literature that emphasized the interventionist tendencies of China's rulers – there existed a willingness to not intervene in its workings. One can even find many examples where they used that mechanism or even enforced it, but they always did so on the condition that there would be no consequences that were unwanted from a moral, social or political perspective. If that was the case or suspected to be the case, rulers did not hesitate to intervene.[10]

Qing China's economic order to a very large extent was determined by the fact that China was an agricultural country in which the overwhelming majority of the population consisted of peasants. It was the peasants who fed the country; who, to the extent that they were landowners, paid the bulk of the taxes and who provided the bulk of the soldiers, that, moreover, often also continued to live on and from the land. The word 'peasant' was not considered a term of abuse. In a way even the emperor was considered to be a peasant. During the so-called Tilling Ritual, he symbolically, as part of the yearly spring ritual, plowed the first three furrows of the new farming season. Several emperors were proud to know a lot about agriculture. The same goes for many officials. The number of them with a peasant background was not negligible. The Manchu rulers, whose background was quite different from that of the Han Chinese and who in several respects were anxious to continue distinguishing themselves from the Han population, in this respect were no different. They, too, considered agriculture as the basis of the people's livelihood and the government's resources and they too knew that 'The ruler is a boat; commoners are the water. The water can carry the boat; the water can capsize the boat'. They were aware that they were held responsible for 'people's livelihood' under the penalty of losing the 'mandate of Heaven' and certainly felt responsible.[11]

As such, having an agricultural basis of course was not something special. All major societies before the Industrial Revolution were agricultural societies. But Qing China was a society with a specific kind of agriculture. Almost without exception its agriculturalists were free, landholding peasants, whether they owned the land or held it in leasehold. There were hardly any landless people employed in agriculture. This agricultural reality had an agricultural 'mentality' or even cult to match. Landed property was considered a solid foundation for family fortunes that secured the household economy and the propriety of family ritual practices. Farming and a rural lifestyle were highly esteemed because they were assumed to play a positive role in undergirding orderly social relations and fostering good moral character. The possession of arable land was considered the precondition for establishing a home. A 'real' member of society had a stake in the ground. Landholding might be less profitable than trade and moneylending, but counted as more reliable, honest, and dignified as a means of securing a livelihood.[12]

It was considered an essential task of government to protect the property of peasant owners and leaseholders and as a rule peasants indeed were protected in their status. Forms of fixed and secured tenure were general. Most leaseholders actually had permanent tenancy rights. There was an almost universal rejection of primogeniture: in principle all male sons inherited.[13] Male children were allowed to make claims against their parents, which was very exceptional in Chinese law, when they were excluded from the inheritance. Peasants without land often received free land, seed or implements from government that also supported agriculture and agriculturalists in other ways for example by low taxes, regular tax holidays, and substantial famine and disaster relief. Government saw to it that many books on agriculture were published and spread. There of course were limits to this peasant-friendly approach. Those who owned the land paid land taxes. Government could not afford to weaken the position of landowners who rented out their land so much that they no longer could or wanted to pay taxes. At times there were debates whether relief did not also support 'undeserving' and 'indolent' poor who abused the system, which strikingly enough never led to the massive efforts to *force* people to work that we see in early modern Western Europe.[14] Peasant-friendly policies certainly were a major fact of Qing China's economic life.

The provision of food, 'people's God', was considered the main preoccupation for every government. In recent literature about famine relief in particular the role of government's 'ever-normal' granaries tends to be highlighted. These granaries, stocking grain bought by government in order to distribute it in times of scarcity, certainly were important and often effective. But one must be careful not to exaggerate their importance and make them more unique than they were.[15] At their height, in the second half of the eighteenth century, their total reserves amounted to, very roughly, a couple of per cents of total grain production. Roughly one third of total stocks were distributed annually. That is certainly substantial but official spending on poor relief in Qing China was not exceptionally high. In Britain in the period from the 1750s to the 1850s, it, for example, was far higher in absolute terms per capita as well as in terms of percentage of GDP.[16]

It is a well-known fact that Confucianist thinking was much less positive about merchants and about their place in society. In the Confucianist' worldview merchants – and that actually almost exclusively means 'big merchants' – held the lowest position of the four recognised social groups. They counted as 'low fellows who aim at profit'[17] and tended to be associated with profit seeking and speculation, both of which easily endanger public order. We have to realize though that such a negative image is almost universal in agricultural societies where many people regard trade as unproductive and traders as people who, while not producing anything themselves, try to profit from existing scarcity; that is, if they are not actually creating it. The Confucianist motto 'Exalt agriculture, disparage commerce' continued to be popular under Qing rule. In practice it of course was obvious to everyone that a huge, complex society like China at the time simply could not function without merchants and that their activities could very well have positive effects. In daily life the anti-merchant ideology therefore did not necessarily have much impact. Many merchants managed to become wealthy and acquire important positions in society (see below). Probably the best way to describe the attitude towards trade and traders would be 'ambivalent'.

Livelihood of full-time professional merchants was not always easy. Those dealing in ordinary goods often had to enter into competition with huge numbers of peasants who did some trading on the side and who could drive down prices to levels that made wholesale trade unprofitable. Many merchants, moreover, regularly had to deal with meddling, regulation or extortion by officials. It is easy, though, to come up with a picture that is too negative. Here too the famous proverb applied: 'The mountains are high and the emperor is far away'. Central government often had hardly any knowledge of what was going on at the local level – let alone that it would have a firm grip on it – and the merchants' money could of course give them substantial leverage. Merchants certainly were not just helpless puppets. Many of them managed to accumulate a large fortune. Let me just refer to two examples, both of licensed traders. The aggregated profits of the salt merchants of Yang-chow in the second half of the eighteenth century have been estimated at some 250 million *taels*. By way of comparison: the total sum of taxes levied annually for central government at the time, including so-called surcharges, amounted to somewhere between fifty and eighty million *taels*. The official *tael* had a value of some 37 grams of silver, about one third of the silver value of a pound sterling. The second example deals with the Hong merchant Howqua, of whom it is claimed that in 1834 he had amassed the equivalent of some seventeen million taels. According to contemporaries, that probably made him the owner of the largest mercantile fortune on earth. But the merchants' way of earning money and their lifestyle did not fit in easily with Confucianist views. They often were under pressure to provide gifts to officials or contribute to the costs of government activities and investments. At times some of them had their wealth confiscated. Many of them apparently felt they would be well advised to (also) find other sources of income and adopt a more respectable lifestyle. Therefore they often, to spread their (sources of) income and wealth, tried to find entries for themselves or their family in officialdom and almost without exception acquired large tracts of land. They strikingly enough hardly ever challenged the status quo.

Manufacturing as a rule received little specific attention as a distinct economic activity. Many activities that we normally describe as 'handicraft' or as a form of 'manufacturing' took place inside the household, in particular the production of textiles. This was the case to such an extent that 'Men plow and women weave' was considered the canonical, state-supported gender division of labor inside the household in imperial China. At least parts of the processing of tea, sugar and tobacco (in China all grown by peasants) also often took place in a context of, surprisingly efficient, family labour. Officials often insisted on self-sufficiency of family and village production, which hampered the development of large-scale manufacturing. There existed a fear that (too many) people would leave agriculture to look for employments that provided them with higher incomes. It was assumed that this in the end would have unwanted consequences like lower food production, less tax income and an increasing number of people on the move. In this context it is striking that guilds were not protected against competition by cheap (female) labour working at home.[18] The main exceptions to the predominance of a household mode of production in manufacturing were the producing of silk and porcelain that simply were too capital intensive to be carried out at home.

There was no 'mercantilist' focus on promoting the production of goods with a high added value for export.[19] Foreign trade was fairly irrelevant for Qing China's economy as a whole. That would still have been the case if the country had known a successful policy of export promotion. The domestic market was simply too big for foreign trade to have any major overall impact before the emergence of new means of transportation and a more integrated global economy in the second half of the nineteenth century. Policies of import substitution were unknown. For the period up until the first decades of the nineteenth century during which silver formed the bulk of Qing China's import that need not come as a surprise. In that period, strikingly enough, the country, without any systematic effort, managed to do what mercantilist countries were all very keen on: to collect a huge amount of bullion, in this case silver.

The Qing state: structure and policies

In an article that is supposed to deal with 'economic reasons of state' one of course has to discuss what is meant by China's state at the time. What did it look like and what did it do? The answers given to these questions could hardly be more different. One can find texts in which the Qing state is pictured as a clear instance of 'oriental despotism', omnipresent and even totalitarian, next to texts in which it emerges as practically absent and 'under-governing'. Some scholars describe it as all intrusive, some as not interfering at all. To a certain extent – but definitely not entirely – these differences of opinion are a matter of definition and emphasis. My position is that Qing China's state formally and when it comes to hard power was fairly weak whereas it actually was very strong informally and when it comes to soft power.[20]

It certainly was not a modern, formalistic-bureaucratic and legal-rational state in the Weberian sense of the word. Let me here just point at several striking differences. It was personal and moral to such an extent that it has been claimed that in Qing China on many levels the state did not actually exist as an organization. Magistrates at the lowest level of government were called 'father-mother officials'. Good rule meant 'good rulers' i.e. rulers with the right moral standards and behaviour. It was assumed that whether government flourished simply depended on the availability of the right men.[21] These men were generalists, 'universalists' and 'morally superior', not specialists. Till 1905 the main road to the best government positions continued to be passing the official exams in which the more technical aspects of administering a huge state in a modernising world continued to receive very scant attention as compared to learning how to be a 'good' ruler. The country's legal system, in line with Confucianist convictions, was not based on formal, abstract law but on 'moral codes' and 'rules of proper behaviour' that had to be interpreted on a case-by-case basis and that were constantly adapted to local circumstances. The Qing state, to make one final comment, moreover, in many respects, e.g. when it comes to taxes or monetary affairs, was far less centralized than a focus on Beijing and its officials might suggest.

One can certainly adduce good arguments for the thesis that the Qing state was 'thin', 'absent' and 'weak' as compared to most European states at the time. In terms of hard power its presence was anything but impressive. Revenue of central government, even including so-called 'voluntary contributions' and 'recruited investments', was very low. In real terms it decreased over time. Two-thirds to even three-quarters of tax income consisted of land taxes. Official expenditure also was very low, as a rule even lower than official revenue. Up until the second half of the nineteenth century, the country never knew any public debt. The Qing state never employed more than some 30,000 officials. Its armed forces were relatively small. A large number of those who in name were soldiers, moreover, had hardly any professional military experience and training and looked more like a group of rentiers or part-time farmers than like soldiers. As compared to what was normal in these respects in Europe, the Qing state in any case looked extremely weak. It was certainly unable to steer Chinese society in any specific new direction.

But up until as late as the 1880s, that was not what the overwhelming majority of its rulers actually wanted. To a certain extent those rulers explicitly wanted their state-apparatus to be small and their state 'distant'. To put it quite succinctly, in the words of Li Yesi, a seventeenth-century writer: 'The hallmark of good ruling is to keep the number of officials low; the hallmark of good government is to keep the burden of taxation light'.[22] Chen Hongmou (1696–1771), a Grand Secretary of the Qianlong Emperor and still very influential as a thinker after his death, claimed, that: '[…] the good official is constantly attentive to keep taxes to a minimum' and thought that 'In managing wealth on behalf of the state, restraint and care are vital'. It was considered obvious that government expenditure should adapt to government revenue, not the other way around, as was the rule in most of Europe. Chen Hongmou regarded it as the 'naturally correct doctrine' to determine expenditure on the basis of income.[23] The idea that government might make debts or raise 'new' taxes in order to invest and thus improve and develop the economy was strange to most rulers and officials. Chen Hongmou personally thought that extra funding of investments in, for example, waterworks would in the longer run be positive to people's livelihood but the Qianlong emperor was opposed to extra spending and very keen on showing how 'frugal' and 'benevolent' he was. He only followed in the footsteps of the Kangxi Emperor who in 1713 basically fixed the land and labour taxes at the level of 1712 and set a standard of 'eternally not increasing levies', at least officially. The Qing would try and abide abide by this principle as long as possible. As late as 1868 a censor and an official were punished by the Grand Council for coming up with a plan that involved an increase in taxes und thus lacked 'love of the people'.[24]

Qing rulers wanted to be considered 'benevolent rulers' who confined themselves to 'controlling from afar' and have a policy of *wu-wei* or rather *wu-wei erzhi*, literally: 'Order and equilibrium will be achieved without the ruler's intervention'. This principle even became the appropriate description of the ideal Confucian ruler: 'One who reigns but does not rule'.[25] In the prevailing political philosophy, government and administration should consist of a small group of people who broadly define the rules, competences and resorts and leave the actual implementation of policies and the details to those locally responsible. Local administrators in turn were supposed to delegate and take local conditions into consideration, which meant that at their level administration and politics were almost indistinguishable. Next to these ideological reasons for having 'lean government' there also were practical ones: the realm was simply too big and too populous to be actually and effectively ruled from one central point. Trying to do so, on top of that, would mean that the ruling Manchus had to involve many more non-Manchus in their ruling, something they were not really keen on. Those who already had a job as official normally also were not fond of getting many new colleagues, never mind their 'ethnicity'.

But one must be wary to not identify the realm of the Chinese state too closely with a formal 'public sphere' as we tend to do in modern states. In Qing China the distinction between 'public' and 'private', whether it comes to resources, people or tasks, was anything but clear-cut. Government often collected extra revenue on an ad-hoc basis in the form of 'voluntary contributions' or 'recruited investments' that were asked of wealthy subjects. The salaries of officials normally only were a tiny part of their total income. Several hundreds of thousands (!) of people worked as 'semi-officials', e.g. so-called clerks and runners and private secretaries. They executed public tasks without formally being state-employees and without formal payment. Public works were often executed via corvee and/or paid for by officials or local gentry from their private pockets. It will not come as a surprise that corruption in the broadest sense of the word was rife and, in contrast to most West-European countries, became worse.[26]

Particularly interesting and relevant in the context of 'political economy' and 'reasons of state' is the fact that many public tasks were delegated to private persons in a broad variety of systems of 'mutual responsibility', 'brokerage' and 'guaranteeing' in which specific people who were *not* state officials were held responsible by the state for the correct implementation of state regulations or demands. Such arrangements were quite prominent in the sphere of the preservation of law and order, tax collection and the regulation and controlling of economic activities. What also kept the official state small is the fact that there was strong pressure on the population *not* to appeal to state officials but to try and find solutions for conflicts via mediation or conciliation.

All this implies that the state actually was much more present and much stronger in Qing China than it may look if one only looks at its hard infrastructure. Its incredible longevity of course also points in that direction. That certainly is related to the fact that more than in the West the state was a moral institution or as Pines describes it 'an extraordinarily powerful ideological construct'.[27] Thornton claims it was '*the* moral agent [...] in modern Chinese history' and argues that 'in modern China, state-making strategies [...] have been shaped at least as decisively by normative agendas as they were by military goals'.[28] Those normative agendas had predominantly been set by Confucianism. All those who had ever prepared themselves for the official exams were thoroughly 'indoctrinated' with that worldview. The main active support for the existing state, or rather the existing *status quo*, was provided by the tiny group of government officials and the much larger so-called 'gentry', a term referring to what best can be called 'local notables', an amalgam of those who held a degree, some form of wealth, a relevant pedigree or some other source of power and who ran daily affairs at China's grassroots level. Between this gentry and officialdom many forms of co-optation and cooperation evolved. Gentry and officials normally had more to loose than to win in destroying the status quo in which they were privileged. The peasants, by far the biggest group of the population, often were rebellious, but in their rebellions always strove to restore the system that in principle supported them.[29] As indicated, merchants also never mounted strong opposition. It was only with the Taiping Rebellion (1850-1864) that broad protest movements developed that strove for revolution instead of restoration.

Let us now focus more on the direct, concrete impact of China's state on the country's economy and begin with the question to what extent it had a direct grip on the means of production. Adherents of the thesis of Chinese 'oriental despotism' have always claimed the country would know no or in any case very little private property. That is simply untrue. The Qing state never owned much of China's land: estimates vary from three to a maximum of eight per cent.[30] The claim that it would have been a hydraulic empire that permanently mobilised huge amounts of unfree labour to execute major irrigation projects – an idea popular in circles of adherents of the oriental despotism thesis – also has to be rejected. As a rule, irrigation works were organized on a local or regional basis. The big hydraulic projects that were executed mostly were for transport or flood control, not irrigation.

For those who consider or considered Qing China an instance of Oriental despotism with an overwhelming coercive and possessive state the country simply could not be a market economy. In this respect too a lot of revisionism has taken place. When it comes to consumer goods, markets definitely were very important in Qing China. As long as 'people's livelihood' was not endangered they were normally left to themselves. Large parts of China Proper were covered by dense networks of (local) markets. The country as a whole was so big that it actually consisted of a number of macro-regions with their own trade circuits. Those, however, were not unconnected. Some scholars even claim that the economy of China Proper was as integrated as that of continental Europe.[31] There was a market for labour, but that was relatively small. The number of people who were fully dependent on wage income relatively speaking was quite low. If the height of interest rates is a trustworthy indicator, which I think it is, Qing China must have had an underdeveloped money market.[32] Its land markets certainly were not functioning as smoothly as perfect markets in economics textbooks but overall the situation in that respect was not 'worse' than in most other economies at the time.

There were some state monopolies e.g. the production and trade of ginseng or jade. There were several state factories. Two examples immediately come to mind: imperial silk production and the production of porcelain in the Imperial Kilns in Jingdezhen. Imperial silk production, however, lost much of its previous importance under the Qing. Government, the largest single consumer of silk, tended to buy its silk below market price and at times intervened in the sector by, for example, prohibiting silk exports because it thought they endangered domestic supplies. But one certainly cannot claim that silk production was a state enterprise.[33] Porcelain production at the imperial factories in Jingdezhen certainly was impressive but it amounted to less than one per cent of total production in the eighteenth century.[34]

In several sectors there was substantial government intervention. A well-known example is copper mining in Yunnan. That took place under a system of licensing, in which the licence-holders had to deliver a substantial fixed part of the copper they mined to the state, often at prices below market prices. On top of that they paid a tax levied as a percentage of their output. Government had a tendency to control and intervene in all sorts of mining, for economic but also social reasons, as it feared large gatherings of unruly people. Two other well-known examples of the use of licenses would be the producing and trading of salt and the trade with Westerners by the Hong merchants in Canton, who often were more or less forced to take up their job. In the tea trade there also was a system of licensing. That, however, only covered a small part of total trade.[35]

Government also used several other arrangements to try and control economic life without direct massive involvement of officials and resources. At times it simply commanded people to make contributions or invest in certain projects. It often used systems of licensing – as already pointed out above for several sectors – or co-optation. In many sectors it established the principle of holding so-called head merchants personally responsible for a collective of merchants they were held to represent. Another arrangement was the quite common, obligatory use of government brokers or guarantors. In this context one can also refer to the *lijia* and *baojia* systems in which groups of peoples and their representatives were collectively responsible for tax collecting and local 'law and order' and to several forms of tax farming.

In foreign trade intervention was rife, almost always for political reasons although the prohibition to export silver had a clear economic rationale. Government did not want to lose overview and feared foreign influences. Sometimes it went as far as to entirely block foreign trade, but normally interventions were much less rigorous.[36] What is striking in the context of our comparison with the situation in Europe is that till far into the nineteenth century there have never been systematic efforts to *increase* foreign trade and that for very long nobody seemed to really care about the country's balance of trade. It was in any case not discussed and no statistics were collected to try and determine it. Revenue from customs was small as compared to total tax income and completely negligible as compared to national income.[37] As always it is dangerous to generalize: There were differences in the way Qing rulers dealt with foreign trade, depending on time and especially place. They tended to be much more cautious and restrictive in their policies concerning the maritime trade of the coastal regions than concerning the overland trade with Mongolia, Russia, Inner Asia or Tibet. What was common to all their trade policies is that political considerations in the widest sense of the word, again including people's livelihood', always were decisive.

To be able to better oversee foreign trade in particular with Western barbarians government preferred to keep it concentrated in specific places. From 1757 onwards till the opening of the so-called treaty ports after the First Opium War 1839-1842, overseas foreign trade with Westerners in principle was concentrated in Canton. China's exports to the West in that period became increasingly dominated by tea grown in Fujian. It was very expensive, complicated and time consuming to transport it from there overland to Canton, but government stuck to its decision that this was the way to proceed. Fuzhou, a port that was located much better in this respect, was only officially declared open to foreign trade in 1842, to no immediate effect. Trade with Russia too was concentrated in one place,

Kiakhta. Till 1848, the Grand Canal had to be used for transporting tribute grain to Beijing, whereas transporting it by sea turned out to be much cheaper. In the West, especially in Western sea powers, there was a tight connection between trade and empire. The Kangxi, Yongzheng and Qianlong emperors more than doubled the size of their realm and added huge non-Chinese territories to it. In that sense they certainly were imperialists. But they never intended to create peripheries that one could then exploit in the way Western European powers did with their peripheries. Their main goal was to create natural and safe borders.

Whatever else it may have been about, mercantilism in Europe certainly was about trade, trade balances and the permanent benchmarking of countries against other countries. It was the economic theory of states operating in a fiercely competitive states-system. Until the Opium Wars other states did not play a prominent rule in China's worldview, certainly not as entities to compete with. The economic policies of the Qing rulers showed none of the preoccupations we have just referred to. Those rulers certainly were aware of the economic importance of bullion – another major element in many varieties of mercantilism – but their policies relating to it were quite un-mercantilist. For them bullion in essence meant silver and copper. Those were of huge importance as they were used as means of payment, in contrast to gold for which that was *not* the case. Till the beginning of nineteenth century huge amounts of silver entered the country. That was not the result of any conscious policy. Imported silver was even taxed and silver mining in the country itself often hampered. Surprisingly enough, given its great importance as means of payment, silver was not coined. It functioned as a means of payment on the basis of purity and weight and the tael referred to earlier on was just a money of account. Government – which could mean central government but in many cases also local government – closely watched the production of copper *and* of copper coins, which they tried to fully keep in their own hands, but their policies in this respect often were not exactly effective. When it came to 'the people's money', i.e. copper cash that was the means of payment in ordinary transactions, rulers certainly did care. Government, again central but often also provincial, tried, to little avail, to monopolize its production and control its quality. It did levy seigniorage on copper. All in all government was not very effective in controlling the supply and demand of neither copper nor silver. It did not manage to keep the silver-to-copper rate fixed at the official rate of 1000 to 1. Over the period between the 1640s and the 1850s the actual rate could vary as widely as from 700 to 1 to some 2500 to 1, with quite disturbing effects on the economy.[38] Monetary sovereignty apparently was not a big issue for government, as foreign dollars circulated more of less freely in several parts of the country. Only in the second half of the nineteenth century did government start to issue paper money. A central bank was only founded in the first decade of the twentieth century. The silver drain during the first half of the nineteenth century caused many debates on monetary and financial issues but it brought no stable viable solutions.

To modernize or not to modernize[39]

Up until far into the nineteenth century, Qing China had a very different political economy from Europe. It existed in a very different setting. These two facts were not unrelated. With the two Opium Wars of 1839-1842 and 1856-1860 that forced China to open up to the outside world, its international situation changed fundamentally. It now became a vulnerable part of a fiercely competitive state-system and saw its sovereignty increasingly impaired by countries like Great Britain, France, Germany, Russia and Japan. Industrialization in the West and Japan and increasing global economic integration intensified global economic competition and exchange. Even a country as big as China could no longer ignore what was going on in other countries and how their economies developed. A global development race was emerging in which falling behind could have very serious consequences. The Chinese model increasingly came under pressure. It was now obvious that something had to be done to cope with the many new challenges. Till the very end of Qing rule, however, no clear, coherent and effective strategy prevailed. Two main 'strategies' can be distinguished that both strove at 'self-strengthening'.

The first one could be described as conservative. The essence of this strategy was to keep 'the Barbarians' in check by preserving the essence of China and only borrow the methods of the West. The 'Tongzhi Restoration', 1862-1874, so called after Emperor Tongzhi, can be considered a clear example of that strategy. There was a willingness to take over certain elements of Western technology and, if need be, Western institutions, with a focus on technology and institutions that might strengthen China's governments international position, but only to the extent that the borrowing and adopting did not endanger China's culture. The 'Tongzhi Restoration' indeed was meant to be a real restoration, i.e. a return to China's 'better days' and a 'putting things in order'. Conservatives were hesitant, half-hearted innovators at best because in their view – and correctly – creating a full-blown modern economy would mean destroying traditional society.

Those who wanted to radically modernise China till the very end of Qing rule were never in control of government. Modernizers seemed to be more aware of the fact that creating an economy and a state strong enough to compete with the West meant industrializing and creating a modern, as we would now say, 'Weberian' state. They also realized that this was impossible without fundamentally changing institutions and ways of thinking and they were more willing to also abandon revered traditions. The disastrous defeat in the war against Japan in 1894-1895 provided yet another and very clear sign that drastic changes were necessary. Efforts were made to indeed push through some radical measures during the Hundred Days' Reform of 1898. That attempt to renovate China, however, ended in failure, only to then re-emerge in 1901 with the beginning of the so-called New Policies, which in 1905 led to the highly symbolic abolishing of the imperial civil examination system. We will never know in what direction Qing China may have developed. Rather unexpectedly the Qing Empire came to its end in 1911. As of January 1912 the Republic of China was proclaimed.

Basically Qing China's modernization during the last half century of its existence was a stop-and-go process with ups and downs and conflicts between modernizers and conservatives, between central government and regional governments, and between different factions, towards the very end of Qing rule increasingly including conflicts between Manchu and Han. There was ambivalence and hesitation because thoroughgoing modernization would imply a break with tradition and pose a fundamental threat to the livelihood and cultural convictions of many people. But also because at the time modernization meant 'westernization', including opening up the country to Western (here including Russian and Japanese) people, money and influences which of course was not exactly popular in the heydays of imperialist intervention. It would moreover imply a different role of government that was not terribly keen on giving up its traditional controlling role as shows in the 'official-supervision and merchant management' enterprises that it created and that were operated by merchants but controlled and directed by government officials. Overall they were not a success.[40]

Qing China's 'self-strengthening movement' essentially was a top-down phenomenon in which government – very often actually *provincial* government – played a crucial role. As such that of course need not be a problem. No economy ever successfully caught up without substantial state support and guidance. In this case, however, government did not have much money and expertise. When it comes to expertise the role of technology and science and thus also education became increasingly important. Government did take initiatives in that respect but as compared to, for example, Japan these certainly were not impressive.

But even if Qing China would have had a ruling elite during its last half century of rule that had been united in an effort at modernization – which was never the case –, it still would in all probability not have been strong enough to fundamentally modernize the country's economy. On the one hand one can only endorse Perkins' claim that for promoting economic development, in my view already from the last decades of the eighteenth century onwards, '[…] the Chinese government was an almost unbelievably weak instrument'.[41] On the other hand one has to realize that this government ruled over an enormous country with some thirty per cent of the world's population and was confronted with huge challenges. In several regions population pressure on resources had become very intense. Not unconnected to that there was ecological degradation. The Yellow River shifted its course northwards in the 1850s, which caused enormous floods. The Imperial Canal had been silting up for decades and for that reason could not be used for some ten years after 1855. There were some very severe droughts and floods. There were the enormous havoc, destruction and loss of lives caused by many rebellions, first and foremost the Taiping Rebellion of 1850-1864. These internal problems of course to some extent were symptoms of China's predicament but in their effects they certainly worsened it. There was the continuing confrontation with the imperialist foreign powers that permanently infringed on China's sovereignty. That confrontation culminated in several costly wars that were all lost by China and that entailed loss of territory and huge reparations. Several innovations would certainly have been adopted earlier and with less resistance if they hadn't been associated with the 'imperialists'.

Over time, nevertheless there did develop a 'political economy' and a way of thinking in terms of 'reasons of state' that resembled what was current in the West. With some success China's governments now also tried to create a stronger, 'fiscal-military' state. We see successful efforts to collect more revenue via taxes on trade, domestic as well as foreign. But even with those increases China's state continued to be severely under-funded in comparison to states in the West. There were efforts to create a new military apparatus. 'Enrich the country, strengthen the military' has become famous as a motto of Meiji Japan's Restoration but the idea certainly was also popular in Qing China. Strengthening the state now increasingly received priority over people's livelihood because it became increasingly clear that taking care of that livelihood without a strong state was becoming impossible. The importance of the military in efforts to develop shipping, railways, mining, and telegraphy is obvious. When Qing rule ended in 1911, China certainly was quite different from half a century earlier. Changes in Japan in that same period of time had been much more impressive but Japan's development was very exceptional and Japan's 'modernizers' in several respects certainly had an easier job. With the end of Qing rule in 1911 China entered a new phase in its history that turned out to be very turbulent and in which its growth rates and its political economy went through very drastic changes. But that is another story.

Notes

1　E. A. Wrigley, "The Classical Economists and the Industrial Revolution," in id. *People, Cities and Wealth* (Oxford and New York: Blackwell, 1987), 21–45.

2　Albert Feuerwerker, *China's Early Industrialization. Sheng Hsuan-Huai (1844–1916) and Mandarin Enterprise* (Cambridge Mass.: Harvard University Press, 1958), 242. See for similar comments e.g. Gang Deng, *The Premodern Chinese Economy. Structural Equilibrium and Capitalist Sterility* (London and New York: Routledge, 1999), 87, and 95–96 and Mary Clabaugh Wright, *The Last Stand of Chinese Conservatism. The T'ung-Chih Restoration, 1862–874*, second edition (Stanford: Stanford University Press, 1972), 148 and 156.

3　For the principle of 'preserving the wealth among the people', see e.g. Yingcong Dai, *The Sichuan Frontier and Tibet. Imperial Strategy in the Early Qing* (Seattle: University of Washington Press, 2009), "Epilogue." The quote is taken from Helen Dunstan, *State and Merchant. Political Economy and Political Process in 1740s China* (Cambridge Mass.: Harvard University Asia Center, 2006), 445.

4　William T. Rowe, *Saving the World. Chen Hongmou and Elite Consciousness in Eighteenth-Century China* (Stanford: Stanford University Press, 2001), 260. Cf. ibid., 191 and 332 and Helen Dunstan, *Conflicting Counsels to Confuse the Age: A Documentary Study of Political Economy in Qing China, 1644–1840* (Ann Arbor: Center for Chinese Studies, University of Michigan, 1996), 189.

5　Wright, *Last Stand of Chinese Conservatism*, 156.

6　For both quotes see Wright, *Last Stand of Chinese Conservatism*, 63–64.

7　Peter Perdue, *China Marches West. The Qing Conquest of Central Eurasia* (Cambridge Mass.: Belknap Press of Harvard University Press, 2005), 541.

8　This means I certainly do not endorse the claim by Rosenthal and Wong that 'early modern Chinese political economy was more explicitly intended to foster economic growth than European political economies'. See Jean-Laurent Rosenthal and Roy Bin Wong, *Before and beyond Divergence. The Politics of Economic Change in China and Europe* (Cambridge Mass. and London: Harvard University Press, 2011), 209.

9 They at best strove for 'static efficiency; that is, spreading the best techniques available across a vast area.' See for this expression Roy Bin Wong, *China Transformed. Historical Change and the Limits of European Experience* (Ithaca and London: Cornell University Press, 1997), 280. For similar comments see Pierre-Étienne Will, "Développement Quantitatif et Développement Qualitatif en Chine à la Fin de l'Époque Impériale," *Annales. Histoire, Sciences Sociales* 49/4 (1994), 863–902.

10 See William T. Rowe, "State and Market in Mid-Qing Economic Thought. The Case of Chen Hongmou (1696–1771)", *Études Chinoises* 12/1 (1993) 7–40.

11 The quote is by Xunzi, a Chinese thinker living in the third century B.C. I found it in Yuri Pines, *The Everlasting Empire. The Political Culture of Ancient China and its Imperial Legacy* (Princeton and Oxford: Princeton University Press, 2012), 134.

12 In this paragraph I have strongly paraphrased Yiqun Zhou, "Honglou Meng and Agrarian Values," *Late Imperial China* 34/1 (2013), 28–66.

13 That of course could easily lead to a tendency of average plots to become smaller.

14 Dunstan, *State or Merchant*, passim.

15 For that tendency see in particular the publications by Wong and by Wong and Rosenthal. For comments on their points of view, see my *State, Economy and the Great Divergence. Great Britain and China, 1680s–1850s* (London: Bloomsbury, 2015), 190–200.

16 For some calculations see ibid., 190–200, and Dunstan, *State or Merchant*, 6–12 and 152–164. The claims by Roy Bin Wong, presented time and again in his publications, in this respect simply seem to have no empirical basis.

17 Wright, *Last Stand of Chinese Conservatism*, 175.

18 Susan Mann, "Household Handicrafts and State Policy in Qing Times," in *To Achieve Security and Wealth. The Qing Imperial State and the Economy, 1644–1911* ed. Jane K. Leonard and John R. Watt (Ithaca, New York: Cornell University Press, 1992), 75–96.

19 See for that emphasis e.g. Erik S. Reinert, *How Rich Countries got Rich ... and why Poor Countries stay Poor* (New York: Carroll & Graf, 2007), under 'mercantilism/ mercantilist'.

20 That at least I regard as the outcome of the extensive analysis in my *State, Economy and the Great Divergence*. I refer to that text for literature on the subject.

21 Wright, *Last Stand of Chinese Conservatism*, 69.

22 Dunstan, *Conflicting Counsels*, 151.

23 Ibid., 189.

24 For details about Kangxi's measure see Immanuel C.Y. Hsü, *The Rise of Modern China*, sixth ed. (Oxford and London: Oxford University Press, 2000), 59–61. For the punishment by the Grand Council see Wright, *Last Stand of Chinese Conservatism*, 155–156.

25 See for these notions Christian Gerlach, "Wu-wei in Europe. A Study of Eurasian Economic Thought," London School of Economics, Department of Economic History. Working Paper no 12/05, 2005, passim. I here paraphrase and quote from pp. 3 and 4.

26 There are ample references in almost all books dealing with the Qing period. For literature specifically dealing with it see Edgar Kiser and Xiaoxi Tong, "Determinants of the Amount and Type of Corruption in State Fiscal Bureaucracies. An Analysis of Late Imperial China," *Comparative Political Studies* 25 (1992), 300–331; Shawn Ni and Hoang Van Pham, "High Corruption Income in Ming and Qing China," *Journal of Development Economics* 81/2 (2006), 316–336, and Nancy E. Park, "Corruption in Eighteenth-Century China," *The Journal of Asian Studies* 56 (1997), 967–1005.

27 Pines, *Everlasting Empire*, 3.

28 Patricia M. Thornton, *Disciplining the State. Violence and State-Making in Modern China* (Cambridge Mass.: Harvard University Asia Center: Distributed by Harvard University Press, 2007), 1–2.

29 For a quote about the (non) revolutionary character of the Chinese people in general under imperial rule, see Pines, *Everlasting Empire*, 134, where he cites British interpreter and intelligence officer Thomas Meadows who lived in China in the early stages of the Taiping Rebellion and wrote: '[…] of all the nations that attained a certain degree of civilization, the Chinese are the least revolutionary and the most rebellious'.

30 Deng, *Premodern Chinese Economy*, 54, 77–79 and 89, and my *State, Economy and the Great Divergence*, 93, note 108.

31 G. William Skinner, "Marketing and Social Structure in Rural China," *Journal of Asian Studies* 24/1 (1964), 3–43; 24/2 (1965), 195–228; 24/3 (1965), 363–399; and Carol H. Shiue and Wolfgang Keller, "Markets in China and Europe on the Eve of the Industrial Revolution," *American Economic Review* 97/4 (2007), 1189–1216.

32 See Jan Luiten van Zanden, "The Road to the Industrial Revolution: Hypotheses and Conjectures about the Medieval Origins of the 'European Miracle'," *Journal of Global History* 3, 3 (2008), 337–360, at 342–345.

33 Lillian M. Li, *China's Silk Trade: Traditional Industry in the Modern World 1842–1937* (Cambridge Mass.: Council on East Asian Studies, Harvard University: Distributed by Harvard University Press, 1981).

34 Christine Moll-Murata, "Guilds and Apprenticeship in China and Europe: The Jingdezhen and European Ceramics Industries," in *Technology, Skills and the Pre-Modern Economy in the East and the West* ed. Maarten Prak and Jan Luiten van Zanden (Leiden and Boston: Brill, 2013), 225–257.

35 Robert P. Gardella, "Qing Administration of the Tea Trade: Four Facets over Three Centuries," in *To Achieve Security and Wealth*, 97–118, at 100.

36 See Part V of Dixin Xu and Chengmin Wu, eds., *Chinese Capitalism, 1522–1840* (Basingstoke: Macmillan, 2000), written by Fang Xing, with several examples on pages 395–399.

37 See e.g. for total customs income my *State, Economy and the Great Divergence*, 169–175 and for a concrete example of the revenue of tea taxes Gardella, "Qing Administration of the Tea Trade," 100. For a comparison with the situation in post 1688 Great Britain see my *State, Economy and the Great Divergence*, 166.

38 For monetary policies of Qing China till the 1850s, see my *State, Economy and the Great Divergence*, 250–266. For silver to copper ratios see *ibid.*, 112, Graph 6.

39 My comments in this 'chapter' are very general. For further background and explanation I refer to the relevant literature in the works cited.

40 Feuerwerker, *China's Early Industrialization*, Conclusion.

41 Dwight Perkins, "Government as an Obstacle to Industrialization: the Case of Nineteenth-Century China," *The Journal of Economic History* 27 (1967), 478–492, at 492.

12 Infant industry protectionism and early modern growth?

Evidence from eighteenth-century entrepreneurial petitions in the Austrian Netherlands

Ann Coenen

Introduction

Today, the idea of government intervention seems to be slowly recovering from the surge of bad press it had been receiving in both the scientific and the public debate ever since the early seventies. Especially during the eighties, neoliberal theory discredited all sorts of market regulation.[1] The so-called 'infant industry' theory is one of the rare economic arguments in defence of interventionist, protectionist policies that remained fairly widely accepted throughout the twentieth and twenty-first centuries. Indeed it is the only argument that – through the protection of budding national industries, usually by imposing restrictive import tariffs on competing goods – actually claims increased long-term economic prosperity for all parties involved, and not just for the domestic economy or the targeted sector.[2] However, even the infant industry approach has, from its conception, caused major controversy among economists and more recently also within history departments, where uncovering the causes of economic development remains one of the leading challenges.

The prevailing definition of an infant industry states that it is an activity for which the necessary technology is not yet available or still insufficiently mastered. Some economists add that it should also be an industry for which the region has a potential comparative advantage, but opinions on this criterion diverge strongly.[3] The infant industry approach that advises government protection for sectors that match the aforementioned criteria was officially introduced by an American, Alexander Hamilton (1791), and further developed by Daniel Raymond. They aimed their recommendations specifically to the fledgling economy of the United States.[4] These ideas were quickly picked up and disseminated by Friedrich List (1841) in Germany. These authors advocated massive import substitution, which indeed proved successful in a number of industries such as iron and steel. But in fact, such ideas had already been explicitly expressed much earlier, in for example Austria and Italy.[5] During the twentieth century the approach became known as Import Substitution Industrialisation (ISI) and was especially promoted by economists in the Global South.[6] Many authors agreed that this type of protectionism could prove useful for economies in developing regions, and merely criticise the height of some protective tariffs (in modern economies we see rates of twenty to even thirty per cent) and the fact that trade barriers are not always abrogated at the end of the catch-up period.[7] However, according to its adversaries the approach eventually caused a net welfare loss, as many of the supported industries possessed no intrinsic comparative advantage. In the end, protective measures only helped the infant industries involved, and did nothing for national – let alone international – economic prosperity.[8] Consequently, a number of authors raise the objection that tariff policies, especially those in the past, are not devised because of industrial considerations, but in the context of strategic trade policy and, primarily, because of the financial requirements of the government.[9] Jeffrey Williamson goes even further and states that because of the aforementioned arguments there can be no question of actual infant industry protectionism before the beginning of the twentieth century:

> Looking at the same history that Eli Heckscher and Bertil Ohlin did to produce their famous theorem, or that Alexander Hamilton and Frederick List did to produce their equally famous infant industry argument, I find that the latter is pretty much irrelevant until the 20th century [...].[10]

Williamson's statement is surprising because both within the field of economics as in historiography there is by no means a lack of research on cases from the nineteenth century; and of course Alexander Hamilton's policy recommendations already date back to 1791. Historians are now starting to look more closely at even earlier periods. And they have every reason to do so. With the empirical case that will be discussed in this chapter, I will show that List and Hamilton's infant industry argument is built upon the philosophy and empiricism of predecessors from the eighteenth century, in this case: the local administrators in the Austrian Netherlands. Also, I will claim that applying the concept in analysing the period that preceded the Industrial Revolution yields valuable new insights for the wider research on government interference and economic development.

My earlier research on the tariff policy of the Austrian Netherlands during the second half of the eighteenth century suggested that the region's economic policy did not fit the stereotype of an approach solely aimed at accumulating bullion.[11] Instead this policy, which had been completely redesigned in 1749, focused on the protection of domestic industries, expressing the explicit hope that these would become able to counter foreign imports with a local substitute.[12] Historians and economists have an interesting track record of questioning all kinds of dogmatic free-trade policy that disdained mercantilism, among them are esteemed scholars such as Paul Bairoch, Patrick O'Brien, Joseph Stiglitz and Ha-Joon Chang.[13] The recent surge in literature on mercantilism and economic growth corroborates Peer Vries' dictum that mercantilism cannot simply be dismissed as an 'historiographical "zombie"' and that the state should again be granted a larger role in economic history.[14] Vries describes mercantilism as a form of economic nationalism, consisting of a wide range of measures to protect the nation's economy.[15] Of course, commercial and naval power were very much entwined during the eighteenth century, so the large players still considered trade a zero sum game.

However, the Austrian Netherlands's new trade policy was not in the first place concerned with encouraging exports – ergo with predominance in international trade – but emphasised primarily import substitution, meaning domestic or internal industrial development. Like List, who had begun by pointing out the obvious shortcomings of the laissez-faire doctrine, the ideas of director Henri Delplancq and his colleagues at the *Bureau de la Régie* (the customs administration) in the first place bear witness of an 'ultra-empiricist attitude'.[16]

In this chapter I will explore whether the Austrian Netherlands's administrators were indeed trying to develop an economic policy that favoured new industries and I will use this new perspective to gauge the wider significance of government interference for the economic development of the Southern Netherlands. This involves a number of questions. First of all, were policymakers aware of some kind of infant industry argument, and did this concept weigh in on economic decision-making? Why did officials and administrators opt for certain changes in tariffs during the second half of the eighteenth century? Were the industrial and mercantile arguments they used in fact only subterfuge to generate state revenue? Was the degree of protection reduced whenever possible, or did powerful industrial or political lobbies stand in the way? To answer these questions, I will not only use known sources such as tariff books, but will also analyse the large collection of petitions by entrepreneurs, a primary source that has not been systematically used and analysed before.[17] In the end, it will be possible to identify some potentially positive effects of mercantilist policies and discuss the extent to which a protectionist policy can serve as an explanatory factor in the history of an economy that would soon become one of the most successful ones worldwide.[18]

The finance council: architects of an enlightened economic policy?

After the Treaty of Aix-la-Chapelle (1748), the Austrian Netherlands entered a period of relative political stability for the first time in decades. Moreover, under the rule of Empress Maria Theresa the region was granted a larger degree of self-government than the Habsburg hereditary lands. Helped by a number of highly competent technocrats, the Habsburg government grabbed the opportunity to develop its own economic policy with both hands.[19] The influence of international politics on domestic economic affairs obviously had not disappeared; competition between neighbouring nations was fierce, and larger states had more powerful means to influence the international economy.[20] At the same time, Maria Theresa had to deal with the enormous debt that she had inherited from her father, Charles VI, due to the War of the Spanish Succession. Especially during the first half of the eighteenth century that debt had rendered the search for tax revenue a prominent motif in trade policy, and it is possible – as Williamson argues – that it would remain one until the end of the century.[21] Nonetheless, the Finance Council in Brussels managed to develop a cautious ad hoc policy to support a number of its industries.[22] At first glance this policy undoubtedly seems incoherent, given the many obscure rules and exceptions. Yet in practice, it may have led to import substitution in a number of sectors, and – according to some – even to export-led growth.[23]

With the economy looking up and entrepreneurs benefiting from the less chaotic political context, more or less anyone seized the opportunity to plea for government support. Representatives of regions, cities, abbeys, industrial branches and individual companies, or even the most insignificant rag-and-bone man would send their appeals and views on international trade to the Finance Council. The vast collection of sources from the Finance Council contains both government decrees as well as petitions by various stakeholders, and it covers more or less the entire second half of the eighteenth century. For this chapter I have used the files concerning entrepreneurs in five nascent industries,[24] namely: coal mining, cotton production, textile printing, salt and sugar refining.[25] Salt refining was in fact not new, but it was closely attached to some incipient chemical industries that caused a huge increase in the amounts of salt required during the second half of the eighteenth century.

Before we go deeper into the analysis of the sources, it is important to be clear about the range of policy options available to eighteenth-century administrators. Policy makers in the Austrian Netherlands could theoretically rely on a number of tactics if they wanted to protect and/or encourage a certain sector. Import tariffs on competing goods and 'subsidies' (in this case mostly one-off allowances in cash or kind) are the two measures that contemporary economists typically classify among infant industry protectionism. Other possibilities included a ban on the export of certain commodities that a competing sector needed,[26] the reduction of all kinds of fees for domestic entrepreneurs, travel restrictions for skilled labourers,[27] or even granting a monopoly. Since starting a company was relatively inexpensive at that time (much cheaper than, say, the construction of a ship), such supportive policies may have been more important than the availability of seed or investment capital.[28] Furthermore, we should probably not underestimate the importance of the fact that entrepreneurs quite effortlessly received permission to start a business (and as mentioned not seldom with some kind of active government support), which indicates that the government was favourably inclined towards free (internal) markets and private enterprise.[29]

Before going into the details of these petitions and assessing to what degree these measures proved successful in encouraging infant industries, we must first of all scrutinize the arguments the Finance Council drew on, in order to determine whether the use of the term 'infant industry protection' is not just blatantly anachronistic. To establish whether they were aware of the possible significance of supporting burgeoning industries, I have searched for cases where administrators used the protection of a young industry as an explicit argument for a particular measure. Such cases are actually quite rare in the sources on our key sectors. When statements and decrees tackle the topic of industrial protectionism, they mostly focus on the traditional sectors that were under pressure from foreign competition, wool in the first place,[30] but linen and salt as well.[31] However, there are at least three important exceptions – particularly regarding coal mining, cotton printing and sugar refining – where the measures were indeed framed in a protectionist discourse focussing on the need to develop a nascent industrial sector.

The first product, coal, was in fact not new. From the thirteenth century onwards, sporadic examples of coal mining can be found in the Southern Netherlands,[32] but it was only during the second half of the eighteenth century, that its use became widely accepted and mining thus became large-scale.[33] At that time the government also began to expand its measures to reduce the imports of foreign coal.[34] At the same time however, many manufacturers that required foreign coal as a resource in their factories were granted exceptions from the higher import duties (see Table 12.1), because there were still many internal obstacles to transport Walloon coal to firms in Brabant or Flanders. Still, in a reaction to some of the complaints, finance councillor Paradis does his best to explain the government's motives in raising import duties:

> In short, the patriotic spirit that governs the national economy can, with equal fairness, maintain or even impose new duties on foreign goods to further our domestic productions and encourage those who risk their fortunes to support this.[35]

The cotton sector was also identified by the Finance Council as a promising new industry that held opportunities in terms of import substitution and even prospects for industrial innovation. Innovation is explicitly mentioned as a motive in a letter promising support to a man named Schepers who wanted to import a machine from Britain.[36] Several examples show that entrepreneurs who wanted to start a spinning mill for cotton yarn were supported with a loan, because in time, their

Table 12.1 Merchants granted exception from the higher import duties.

Source	Date	Suppliant
NAB, FC, 5024	August 5,1762	Van Schorel
5025	March 2, 1763	Manufacturers of Ostend
5025	August 16, 1763	Joseph Peeters, Jean Van Eersel, J.B. DeClerck
5027	April 22, 1764	Brewers
5027	May 11, 1764	N. Deheyder
5026	August 2, 1764	Manufacturers of Antwerp
5026	September 17, 1764	Manufacturers of Mechlin
5027	July 17, 1768	Textile printers of Antwerp
5027	August 8, 1768	Manufacturers of Antwerp
5027	August 27, 1768	N. Deheyder
5028	October 23, 1769	Manufacturers of Ostend
5028	December 4, 1769	Manufacturers of Antwerp and Mechlin
5029	January 13, 1770	Manufacturers of Lier
5029	March 12, 1770	N. Deheyder
5029	October 24, 1770	Manufacturers of Mechlin
5029	February 16, 1771	Manufacturers of Bruges, Ostend and Newport
5029	March 11, 1771	La Motte
5030	July 8, 1772	Manufacturers of Antwerp
5030	April 12, 1773	Manufacturers of Antwerp
5031	March 1, 1777	Jean Basteyns
5033	August 6, 1781	Manufacturers of Antwerp
5032	July 26, 1783	d'Hooge
5033	August 6, 1783	Manufacturers of Antwerp

activities might reduce foreign yarn imports.[37] In one case, the Finance Council not only provided protection against foreign competition (by for example French *siamoise*) but it also granted a monopoly. Jean Beerenbroeck of Dambrugge near Antwerp, the first cotton printer in the region, received such a privilege. The Council expressed hopes that the monopoly would ensure the development of a very important activity, for which they until then had depended almost entirely on imports from abroad. Unfortunately, it held domestic supply at an insufficient level to meet the fiercely increasing need for cotton. Import substitution therefore did not occur immediately after the change in tariff rates (instated in the form of individual patents reducing import tariffs on resources for textile printers, instead of a general decree for the sector) but was delayed until the expiry of the monopoly in 1778, when new printers popped up all over the country.[38]

In the case of sugar refining the customs bureau conducted a much more general (and by consequence more overt) tariff change.[39] On 2 March 1765, after pleas from sugar refiners using similar arguments as the coal miners, import duties on refined sugar were raised, and this appears to have kept imports stable despite the strongly rising demand for finished sugar.[40] Also, exports of domestically refined sugar were exempted from tariffs and tolls.[41] Sources from a sugar refinery in Antwerp show that its yearly profit averaged around 15 per cent – due to a large extent to the high import tariffs – and this in a time when commerce was perilous and agriculture offered few opportunities for investors.[42] The same also happened in a fourth, albeit still very insignificant, sector: chocolate production. Here the import duty on the finished product, chocolate, was almost tripled in 1764 and at the same time the cost of importing the required raw materials, cocoa in the first place, was reduced.[43] Later, councillors Tomboy and de Libeau even advised to free raw cocoa for chocolate producers entirely from duties.[44]

Another important question is: was the protection of the above-mentioned sectors reduced when a certain degree of 'self-reliance' had been achieved? In some cases, the government did in fact already slightly revise its policy during the period that these sources cover (circa 1750–1790). They refused to extend the monopoly of cotton printer Jean Beerenbroeck, and in the case of coal they increasingly allowed exemptions from the high import duties. However, during the period investigated here, Habsburg rulers mostly continued their protectionist measures such as the ban on various types of textiles.

A new path towards development? Evidence from petitions

Table 12.2 gives an overview on the requests that manufacturers and producers from the abovementioned sectors sent to the Finance Council. It shows that overtly protectionist measures such as a general import ban were still only rarely wielded for new sectors. There are only a few examples of instances where an official and general import ban was issued; in 1744 imports of *siamoise*, *calmande* and *molton* cloths coming from France had been forbidden for a short period and in 1767 silk manufacturer Adrien Metdepenningen was able to enforce a ban on the imports of foreign silk fabrics (namely muslin and tripe).[45] For the newer sectors discussed

Table 12.2 Supportive measures requested in entrepreneurial petitions (sectors: production of dyestuffs, sugar refining, textile printing, coal mining and salt refining, 1756–1791).

Nature of the request		Granted	Rejected	Partially granted	Unknown	Total
Supportive measures*	Coal	13	0	2	0	15
	Dyestuffs	7	4	5	2	18
	Salt	5	7	8	4	24
	Sugar	1	1	0	1	3
	Textiles	21	12	8	5	46
	Total	46	23	23	11	103
Monopoly	Dyestuffs	0	1	1	0	2
	Total	0	1	1	0	2
Permission to start a manufactory	Dyestuffs	8	0	3	1	12
	Salt	3	7	8	1	19
	Sugar	4	1	0	0	5
	Textiles	16	4	6	0	26
	Total	31	12	17	2	62
Warehouse access	Salt	4	1	1	1	7
	Textiles	1	0	0	0	1
	Total	5	1	1	1	8
Increase of import duties	Coal	1	1	3	0	5
	Salt	1	3	0	0	4
	Textiles	0	2	3	0	5
	Total	2	6	6	0	14
Diminution of duties	Coal	31	4	5	0	40
	Salt	6	1	1	0	8
	Sugar	3	2	0	0	5
	Textiles	1	1	2	0	4
	Total	41	8	8	0	57

Exemption from duties	Coal	14	3	3	0	20
	Dyestuffs	89	4	4	1	98
	Salt	7	1	0	0	8
	Sugar	0	1	0	0	1
	Textiles	132	9	4	1	146
	Total	242	18	11	2	273
Exemption from import duties on resources and machinery	Coal	10	0	1	0	11
	Dyestuffs	0	0	0	1	1
	Sugar	1	0	0	0	1
	Total	11	0	1	1	13
Unknown	Coal	3	1	0	0	4
	Salt	2	3	1	0	6
	Sugar	0	1	0	1	2
	Textiles	2	1	2	0	5
	Total	7	6	3	1	17
Total	Coal	72	9	14	0	95
	Dyestuffs	104	9	13	5	131
	Salt	28	23	19	6	76
	Sugar	9	6	0	2	17
	Textiles	173	29	25	6	233
	Total	386	76	71	19	552

Sources: NAB, FC, 4504–4517, 4520, 4522–4524, 4556–4559, 4570–4571, 4585, 4588, 4590–4592, 4602, 4614–4616, 4618–4635, 4639–4643, 5022–5034, 5221–5226, 5228–5234, 5260–5265, 5328.

Note: Applications relating to errors by the customs officers (resulting in the reimbursement of taxes or confiscated goods) were not included in this table.

*For example, forms of subsidization such as government grants for starting businesses, but also infrastructure projects, or a mitigation of administrative obligations.

here the administration never went that far. However, import duties on foreign products were raised a few times due to appeals to the customs sources. In eight cases the demands of producers to ward off their foreign competitors were at least partially met. Yet the increase never amounted to a restrictive level (it was usually not more than three to five per cent of the product's value) and another six similar applications got rejected entirely.[46] The tariff books contain several other examples of rising import tariffs, but unfortunately both the alleged rationale for such a decision as well as the arguments used by suppliants are absent there.[47] Moreover, it is clear that the vast majority of such cases concerned traditional textiles, particularly broadcloth, serge, *camelot* and woollen blankets, but also flannel, (mixed) cotton velvet and various printed fabrics.[48] The trade measures taken for new industries in fact rarely shielded these industries from foreign competitors through higher import tariffs, but they did favour domestic producers via an exemption from or reduction of domestic taxes (330 of the 552 applications, with a 86 per cent approval rate), or through other supportive measures such as subsidies or infrastructure projects (106 cases).[49]

When we look at the evolution of these requests over time, we see that the number of petitions was increasing (Figure 12.1) as was their success rate (Figure 12.2). In other words, the government seems to have been responsive to the rise in petitions and was increasingly flexible in altering its policies, as was the case in Britain.[50]

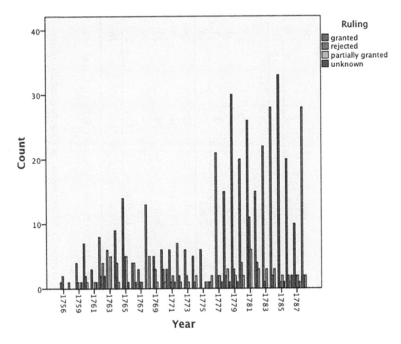

Figure 12.1 Number of rulings, 1756–1791.

Source: NAB, FC, 4504–4517, 4520, 4522–4534, 4556–4559, 4570–4571, 4585, 4588, 4590–4592, 4602, 4614–4616, 4618–4635, 4639–4643, 5022–5034, 5221–5226, 5228–5234, 5260–5265, 5328.

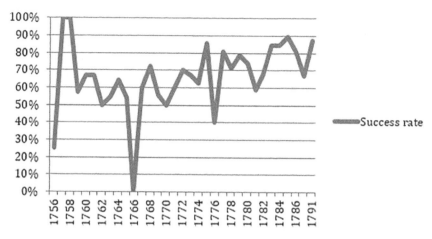

Figure 12.2 Success rate of petitions, 1756–1791.

Source: NAB, FC, 4504–4517, 4520, 4522–4534, 4556–4559, 4570–4571, 4585, 4588, 4590–4592, 4602, 4614–4616, 4618–4635, 4639–4643, 5022–5034, 5221–5226, 5228–5234, 5260–5265, 5328.

It is clear that the central government of the Austrian Netherlands actively intervened in economic life and tried to encourage and protect its domestic industry in various ways. That its approach still appeared fairly liberal compared to contemporary Britain[51] was due to the fact that nearly all tariff barriers were subject to frequent exceptions. These were probably for a large part the consequence of the precarious international diplomatic situation of the region, and not of free choice. For example, the Barrier Treaty of 1699 contained a clause that stipulated that the Austrian Netherlands were not allowed to tax tea and coffee imports to an amount of more than five per cent ad valorem, as this trade was particularly profitable for the great naval powers at that time.[52] In the case of salt, it remained prohibited to tax the import of refined salt more heavily than that of crude salt until well into the eighteenth century; in order to safeguard the exports of the Dutch Republic.[53] The customs administration had to abide by such restrictions imposed by neighbouring states and could only circumvent some of the unfavourable conditions by ad hoc decisions.

However, while it is striking that the Finance Council's approach was highly time and space specific, I do not think that this was merely a consequence of having its hands tied by international politics. The multitude of individual actions sometimes raised the impression of arbitrariness,[54] but as the available evidence studied for the present purpose suggests there was in fact a thoroughly thought-out rationale behind them.[55] First, it was based on a surprisingly large and detailed collection of trade and census data.[56] Examples in the sources show that this statistical material was effectively used to justify certain decisions on tariffs. In the years before the start of the *Relevé Général* in 1759 the call for a list of goods entering and leaving the region – following the example of France – became louder and louder.[57] When they had finally been created, the annually published statistics were indeed used for economic decision-making.[58] Second, research on Britain shows that other governments had a very similar *modus operandi*. This type of ad hoc policy making was comparable to the development of British estate, statutory authority, and enclosure acts at the opening of the eighteenth century, as described by Bogart and Richardson.[59] Bogart and Richardson assume that:

> piecemeal actions that address specific problems facing individuals and communities may be easier to implement than widespread reforms that address general problems. Overtime, a piecemeal process may reveal general patterns that could serve as the foundation for nationwide reforms.[60]

According to them, this type of policy making was rapid and affordable and thus enabled entrepreneurs to exploit opportunities that could not be accommodated by the inflexible rights regime inherited from England's past.[61]

The efforts of the Finance Council to develop an evidence-based and case-driven strategy clearly reveal a strong parallel with the approaches of infant industry theorists. There can be no doubt that the government considered it its task to actively promote its industries, and that entrepreneurs often made use of the available supportive measures, but this protectionism was not limited to infant industries. The government also tried to shield traditional sectors such as wool from foreign competition when the entrepreneurs involved sounded the alarm. Certainly, many of the manufacturers benefited from this, but it did not necessarily lead to greater public prosperity, because the producers of (often expensive) domestic substitutes not always made the effort to improve the quality of their products in order to stay one step ahead of the competition, and even more so because most of the workers' wages in the region remained very low.[62] While the underlying rationale might have been sound – although, as Philipp Rössner has written on the Scottish case, it is hard to disentangle 'crony economics' (lobbyism or private interests) from 'development economics'[63] – the results were not always successful.

Protectionism as the key to industrialisation?

The preceding paragraphs show that there are clear parallels between the eighteenth-century Austrian Netherlands's policy and the infant industry theory written out around the subsequent turn of the century. It is thus not surprising that in his *magnum opus* on the *National System of Political Economy*, List expresses his admiration for the meticulously designed customs policy in the Austrian Netherlands. Yet List does not seem to have made up his mind on whether the Habsburg policy contributed to the rapid growth of the Belgian industry in the nineteenth century.[64] He does, however, describe the positive effects of infant industry protectionism in Germany and the United States, and he even praises the success of Colbert's policy – in spite of his aversion towards the French.[65] So we have to continue looking for the answer to the question whether the embryonic (and, because of the pressure of surrounding states, only partially carried-out) form of infant industry protection may have had a positive net effect on the economic development of the Austrian Netherlands. Did the benefits for some companies outweigh the disadvantage of increased tariffs for consumers? Did the stimulating of certain industries boost long-term growth or did it in fact slow it down? Is it true that protected companies were not inclined to increase their efficiency? And was the interventionist discourse not merely a fallacy in order to feed the treasury?

The optimal way to go about this would be to measure the potential effects of tariffs and the other measures listed in Table 12.2 on the performance of the abovementioned industries. Unfortunately we only have limited data on trade, and few to none on productivity and profits. New research is definitely needed, but we can draw some preliminary conclusions from the trade flows. A seemingly heterogeneous approach such as that of the Finance Council not surprisingly yielded heterogeneous results. Not all measures were successful. And they certainly were not universally beneficial. First of all, there were some sectors where the extensive government intervention made very few alterations to the status quo, especially for the older textile branches (mainly wool) that were suffering from waning popularity and declining economic significance.[66] The government obviously could not 'save' an industry when there was no longer sufficient demand for its products. And in the case of the printed cotton trade flows the protection against foreign competition had no effect as long as the domestic market was not liberated. However, from the perspective of nascent industries, it is more important to observe that the supportive measures were first of all designed to seal off the internal market for the purpose of import substitution. And they did so with some success. Data on the region's international trade flows show that it became next to autarkic when it came to its salt and sugar supply, and it might have done the same for coal if it would have reacted more fiercely against internal obstacles and tolls.[67] No successes were achieved in the field of exports by these new sectors, but that was never the administration's goal. On the other hand, the government weakened its own policy with numerous exceptions that were needed to keep certain stakeholders satisfied. Also, the possible objection remains that some of the measures taken actually would have entailed a welfare loss in the long run. First of all, the government sometimes chose to encourage sectors that already enjoyed very stable demand, particularly the linen industry, which is seen as one of the culprits for the region's economic underdevelopment in the nineteenth century.[68] The protection of infant industries that would become very prosperous later on was also criticised by some contemporaries. In the case of the coal industry, complaints came mostly from city governments and small manufacturers, who claimed that the import duties on foreign coal rendered this resource too expensive, and thus stood in the way of imports of higher quality coal which would further their industries.[69] In the case of salt, one of the finance councillors expressed concerns on the lack of quality improvement of inland salt.[70]

One kind of criticism, however, turns out to be much less applicable on this case study than many would expect.[71] Even though Maria Theresa's government was burdened by the debt she had inherited from her father,[72] the high level of autonomy that she had granted her administration in the Low Countries seemed to allow the policymakers to be little concerned with fiscal troubles.[73] On one hand, decisions were based on large quantities of empirical data from customs statistics and industrial censuses,[74] and on the other hand they have proven to have been constantly (and increasingly) influenced by the lobbying of stakeholders. Here – not surprisingly – the manufacturers with strongest leverage on the authorities (such as companies with many employees or the large coal mines) most often won the battle.[75] Note also that the government in the Austrian Netherlands repeatedly took measures against the vested interests of established institutions such as guilds or merchant houses and improved domestic market performance and efficiency.[76] Also, by exempting some goods from tax that did not pose a threat to domestic producers (as was often the case for raw materials or for colonial commodities for which no local alternative existed) a significant potential source of income was left aside.[77] In those cases in which an explicit request by an importer was needed to renounce the customs revenue from the imported commodity (such as coal, crude salt or cotton fabrics) this had less to do with financial concerns than with international diplomacy.

Of course, this chapter does not wish to claim that government policy can take all the credit for the modest success stories we have seen above. In the cases where import substitution proved to be a success one should also take into account a number of favourable circumstances, such as the changing international political climate and – especially – the greatly increased internal demand for finished products such as sugar, or an industrial resource such as coal. It is possible in the latter three cases that domestic production would have boomed even without public aid. Yet a well-considered government policy did exist and contributed to their success. Without such a protectionist policy, the increased demand for refined sugar, printed cotton and other light fabrics could just as well have led to an increase in imports, as Britain and France supplied cheaper versions of these products, and local businesses might not have had the guts to launch a company without government support. The effect of the import-substitution policies might even, to some extent, have been psychological – giving entrepreneurs the feeling that the government was supporting them and in that way encouraging economic activity – but maybe that was sufficient.

Conclusion

Research into the eighteenth-century Austrian Netherlands has shown that Williamson has been too quick to cast off the early modern period. By employing a very narrow interpretation of the term infant industry protection and benchmarking it against contemporary standards, and even worse: by tarring all forms of early modern economic policy with the same brush, he reached the conclusion that governments before 1900 could have only been guided by fiscal concerns, not by more advanced economic theories.[78] It is clear that even though the region lacked the means and power of a country such as Britain – or in earlier decades the Dutch Republic – a strongly interventionist central government emerged in the Austrian Netherlands.[79] Research into its economic policy shows that it was a dynamic tool to support the industry. The administration operated on the basis of a number of overarching economic goals, specifically tailored to the local economy. The Austrian Netherlands's economic policy did not offer a universally valid economic model, but was regularly adapted to the changing needs of individual entrepreneurs and that was indeed its strength.

In the end, we cannot speak of generalized success or failure of the proto-ISI-approach in the Austrian Netherlands – at least not as long as we do not have sufficient data on the long-term development of its developing industry – but it is in any case clear that the active role that the new economic administration played had a major impact on almost all sectors and stakeholders involved. Its economic policy did not always have the desired effect, but it was rarely without consequences. The results of this specific type of government intervention are certainly diverse, but the claim that mercantilist, protectionist policy only hindered economic development clearly cannot be held. This chapter thus illustrates once more the influence of economic and political institutions, with a key role for the central government. Recent research increasingly bears out this conclusion. In other regions the government also became actively involved so as to improve domestic competitiveness. Indeed, we can probably find exactly the same type of policies in contemporaneous Scotland, Prussia, Spain, Portugal and Sweden. Again, they were not always successful (especially in later, neoliberal theoretical terms), but given the times and age they were anything but irrational.

Notes

1 David Harvey, *A Brief History of Neoliberalism* (Oxford: Oxford University Press: 2005), 5.
2 At least in case of non-strategically important industries. Ludo Cuyvers et al., *Internationale economie* (Antwerp: Garant, 2002), 218–219.
3 Ha-Joon Chang and Justin Lin, "Should Industrial Policy in Developing Countries Conform to Comparative Advantage or defy it? A Debate Between Justin Lin and Ha-Joon Chang," *Development Policy Review* 27 (2009), 483–502. More on the technical criteria to opt for infant industry protection can be found here: Marc Melitz, "When and How Should Infant Industries be Protected?" *Journal of International Economics* 66 (2005), 177–196.
4 Alexander Hamilton, *Report on Manufactures* (London: 1791); Ha-Joon Chang "Kicking Away the Ladder," *Post-autistic Economics Review* 15 (2002) (internet resource).
5 See for example Philipp Wilhelm von Hörnigk's *Austria Supreme/Oesterreich über alles* (1684), in the upcoming translation by Keith Tribe, with an introduction by Philipp R. Rössner (London and New York: Anthem, 2016); or the Italian author Giovanni Botero's *Delle Cause della Grandezza delle Città*.
6 Raúl Prebisch, "Commercial Policy in the Underdeveloped Countries," *American Economic Review* 49, No. 2, Papers and Proceedings of the Seventy-first Annual Meeting of the American Economic Association (May, 1959), 251–273.
7 Partha Dasgupta and Joseph Stiglitz, "Learning-By-Doing, Market Structure and Industrial and Trade Policies," *Oxford Economic Papers* 40 (1988), 266; Douglas Irwin, "Did Late Nineteenth Century U.S. Tariffs Promote Infant Industries? Evidence from the Tinplate Industry," *NBER Working paper* 6835 (1998): 30; Béla A. Balassa,

"The Process of Industrial Development and Alternative Development Strategies," *Essays in International Finance* 141 (1980), 5.

8 Irwin, "Did Late Nineteenth Century U.S. Tariffs."

9 For an overview, see: Jeffrey Williamson, "Was it Stolper-Samuelson, Infant Industry or Something Else? World Tariffs 1789–1938," *NBER Working paper* 9656 (2003), 2.

10 Williamson, "Was it Stolper-Samuelson," 2.

11 Bruno Bernard, *Patrice-François de Nény: portrait d'un homme d'état* (Brussels: Editions de l'ULB, 1993); Hilda Coppejans-Desmedt, "Aspecten van de industriële politiek in de Oostenrijkse Nederlanden," in *Overheid en Economie. Economische Aspecten van der Overheidspolitiek in en met Betrekking tot de Oostenrijkse Nederlanden*, ed. Helma De Smedt et al. (Antwerp: Universiteit van Antwerpen, Universitaire Faculteiten Sint-Ignatius, 1989).

12 Catharina Lis and Hugo Soly, "Different Paths of Development Capitalism in the Northern and Southern Netherlands during the Late Middle Ages and the Early Modern Period," *Review: A Journal of the Fernand Braudel Center for the Study of Economics, Historical Systems, and Civilizations* 20 (1997), 211-242.

13 Paul Bairoch, *Economics and World History – Myths and Paradoxes* (Chicago: University of Chicago Press, 1993), 44–55; Joseph Stiglitz, *Towards a New Paradigm for Development: Strategies, Policies, and Processes* (Geneva: UNCTAD, 1998); Ha-Joon Chang, *Bad Samaritans – Rich Nations, Poor Policies, and the Threat to the Developing World* (London: Random House, 2007).

14 Peer Vries, "Replies to my Commentators," *Tijdschrift voor Sociale en Economische Geschiedenis* 12, 1 (2015) 105–120, at 116–117.

15 Peer Vries, *Escaping Poverty: The Origins of Modern Economic Growth* (Göttingen: Vandenhoeck & Ruprecht, 2013), 371.

16 Friedrich List, *National System of Political Economy* (London: Cass, 1983) original: Friedrich List, *Das nationale System der politischen Ökonomie*, in: *Friedrich List's gesammelte Schriften*, ed. Ludwig Häusser, Vol. III (Stuttgart and Tübingen: Cotta, 1851), 9; J. Pricken, *Delplancq, l'oublié* (Brussels: s.n., 1967); National Archives Brussels (NAB), Finance Council (FC), nr 8580, *Dictionnaire de Commerce*, by Henri Delplancq, 1776.

17 For this, I will make use of the methodology developed by Bogart and Richardson. More on this below.

18 Jan Dhondt and Marinette Bruwier, "The Industrial Revolution in Belgium and Holland, 1700–1914," in *The Fontana Economic History of Europe*, ed. Carlo M. Cipolla, vol. IV, part 1 (London: Fontana, 1973), 329–69.

19 Some of the most influential functionaries have been researched by Bernard, *Patrice-François de Nény*, 113–115.

20 For literature on the possible beneficial influence of the use of violence and warfare, see the overview in Peer Vries, *State, Economy and the Great Divergence Great: Britain and China, 1680s–1850s* (London: Bloomsbury 2015).

21 Bernard, *Patrice-François de Nény*, 116.

22 This hypothesis has been put forward in among others: Catharina Lis and Hugo Soly, "Living apart together: overheid en ondernemers in Brabant en Vlaanderen tijdens de tweede helft van de 18e eeuw," in *Arbeid in veelvoud. Een huldeboek voor Jan Craeybeckx en Etienne Scholliers*, ed. Jan Craeybeckx (Brussels: VUB Press 1988); Alfons Thijs, "Aspecten van de opkomst der textieldrukkerij als grootbedrijf te Antwerpen in de achttiende eeuw," *Bijdragen en mededelingen betreffende de geschiedenis der Nederlanden* 86, 2 (1971), 200–217; Christiaan Vandenbroeke, *Agriculture et alimentation dans les Pays-Bas autrichiens* (Gent and Leuven: Centre belge d'histoire rurale, 1975).

23 Lis and Soly, "Different Paths," 211–242.

24 The list is not exhaustive of course: the eighteenth century witnessed among others the birth of new industries for potash, vitriol, litmus, and the establishment of several gin distilleries, paper factories and blast furnaces.

25 National Archives Brussels, Finance Council, 4503–4537 (dyestuffs), 4556–4560 (mixed fabrics), 4610–4644 (cotton printing), 5019–5033 (coal), 5215–5245 (salt and chemicals) and 5256–5267 (sugar).

26 Etienne Sabbe, *De Belgische vlasnijverheid* (Kortrijk: Nationaal Vlasmuseum, 1975), 22.

27 Erik Reinert, "The Role of the State in Economic Growth," *Journal of Economic Studies* 26, 4 (1999), 268–326. In the Austrian Netherlands, we know that for example *cloutiers*, or nail makers, were obliged to pay a tax when crossing borders.

28 Vries, *Escaping Poverty*, 235–239; Hervé Hasquin, "Nijverheid in de Zuidelijke Nederlanden: 1650–1795," in *Algemene Geschiedenis der Nederlanden* (Haarlem: Fibula-Van Dishoeck, 1979): 159; Robert Duplessis, *Transitions to Capitalism in Early Modern Europe* (Cambridge: Cambridge University Press, 1997), 236.

29 The importance of such an entrepreneur-friendly government is highlighted among others by Daron Acemoglu and James Robinson, *Why Nations Fail: The Origins of Power, Prosperity, and Poverty* (New York: Crown Publishers, 2012), *passim*.

30 Ann Coenen, *Carriers of Growth? International Trade and Economic Development in the Austrian Netherlands* (Leiden: Brill 2014), 117; NAB, FC, 4571, memoir (presumably 1762) concerning higher import duties on woollen fabrics, to protect the domestic wool industry; 4278, *commerce en général 1752*, memoir on the need to protect textile products from Flanders; 4579, on 4 September 1769 the import duty on woollen fabrics is raised in order to 'boost production' (*l'augmentation des Manufactures de ces Païs*); this is also mentioned in the request by Dotrenge and a group of Antwerp merchants (March 9 1770, FC, 4581); 4564, letters about the 'ruinous' French camel cloth imports, September 30 1752; 4576, documents on the potential increase of the import duty on woollen blankets and frisades, comments by Delplancq, February 13, 1766.

31 For salt the approach is admittedly very ambiguous. Sometimes an increase in the import tariff is approved, but in other cases the Finance Council declined it. NAB, FC, 5221, a request by Joseph Pieters to increase the import duty on refined salt was granted, August 16 1760; 5239, a similar request by C. D. Block, the widow Vandenvelde and P. Saeys (refiners from Dendermonde) was rejected (without explanation), July 17 1782.

32 Jean Vercleyen, *Histoire du charbon* (Brussels: 1965), 65–74.

33 NAB, FC, 4999, mining applications. Developments in the coal sector have been thoroughly documented by Roger Burt, "The Extractive Industries," in *The Cambridge Economic History of Modern Britain*, ed. Roderick Floud and Paul Johnson (Cambridge: Cambridge University Press, 2004), 417–450, at 436.

34 NAB, FC, 5022, letters concerning the increase of import duties on British coal, 17 December 1760; 5027, request to increase the import duties on coal (August 8 1768) and requests to be exempted from these duties (November 10 1767, Antwerp).

35 'En un mot, l'esprit patriotique qui préside à l'économie du commerce national peut avec une égale équité laisser subsister ou même imposer de nouveaux droits sur les denrées du crû étranger afin de favoriser nos productions internes et encourager ceux qui exposent leur fortune à les faire valoir.' NAB, FC, 5027, response to complaints from Antwerp, 1767.

36 NAB, FC, 4558, letters, June 26 and July 6, 1776.

37 NAB, FC, 4559, note from Delplancq, De Cazier and Dewitt, 1782.

38 Ann Coenen, "Katoen en economische groei. De katoenhandel in de Oostenrijkse Nederlanden tussen politieke ambities en economische realiteit 1759–1791," *Tijdschrift voor Sociale en Economische Geschiedenis* 8 (2011), 32–64, at 41.

39 NAB, 5258, patents for refiners Denis Ryckaert and Antoine Joseph Latteur, September 10 1749; 5260, patent for Pierre Joseph De Quesne, March 6 1760; 5262, patent for Albert Goddyn, September 16 1765 and Jacques de Kersmaecker, March 20 1766; 5260, letter to all customs offices, March 20 1756.

40 Coenen, *Carriers*, 188.

41 NAB, FC, 5606, tariff book: *sucre raffinée de ces pays - libre de sortie, tonlieu et de convoi* ('refined sugar from this country: free from export duties and fees'), June 15, 1761.

42 Harald Deceulaer, "Een 'siroopoorlog' in de tweede helft van de achttiende eeuw? Comerciele conflicten rond een vergeten ersatzprodukt uit de volksvoeding," *Bijdragen tot de geschiedenis* 74 (1991), 47–67, at 58.

43 NAB, FC, 8580, *Dictionaire de commerce* (by Delplancq, 1776); 5606, tariff book; 4507, letter from De Beelen about the import duty on chocolate, August 18 1764.

44 NAB, FC, 4526, memoir from the customs bureau, June 8 1782.

45 NAB, FC, 4601, request by Adrien Metdepenningen, September 24 1767; 4564, letter by camel cloth producers from Brussels, September 30 1752.

46 Granted requests: 5022, December 17, 1760 (coal miners from Hainaut); 5221, August 16, 1760 (salt producer Joseph Pieters). Partially granted requests: 4616, November 1, 1767 (mixed textile manufacturer Pierre De Heyder); 4642, 28 September, 1779 (two requests by textile manufacturer Adrien Janssens); 5025, 16 May 1763 and 5033, 7 June 1784 (coal miners from Mons); 5027, 8 August 1768 (coal miners from Namur). Rejected requests: 4642, 29 January 1780 (Adrien Janssens); 4557, 14 March 1769 (Pierre De Heyder); 5030, 2 August 1773 (coal miners from Charleroi); 5226, 4 December 1764 (States of Flanders, concerning salt); 5234, 30 December 1769 (salt refiner Jean Michel Poncelet); 5239, 17 July 1782 (salt refiner C.D. Block).

47 NAB, FC, 5606 and 5608, passim.

48 NAB, FC, 4556, printed decree on the increase of the import tariff on foreign flannel, March 29, 1758; 4556, letter by Vanoverloope on the increase of the import tariff on *velours de coton et fil,* September 3, 1762; 4586, letter by Delplancq about higher tariffs on serge and woollen blankets, August 30, 1775; 4569, request by Cornelius tKint to raise the import tariff on broadcloth (granted), April 18, 1761; 4884, broadcloth manufacturers from Hodimont request higher import tariffs (granted), October 15 1778; Secretariat of State and War, 2149/2, *Extrait de la feuille hebdomadaire intitulé: Esprit des Gazettes*, Tome 10 n°1°, Vienna, September 15, 1784, wool and printed cotton from the Dutch Republic may not be imported as from November 1st 1784.

49 In the following sources an allowance or loan is granted to an entrepreneur: NAB, FC, 4556, to Jean-Baptiste Lefebvre on 17 May 1760; 4582, Antoine Roussel and N. Motte, 19 June 1771; 4620, Platteau, 16 December 1771; 4631, Jacques François Delvingne, 30 March 1786; 4642, various cotton printers, 13 March 1780, François Faveers, 16 and 22 June 1781; 5232, Charles Levasseur, 3 June 1766; 4557, Denis Aubert, 12 September 1764 and Antoine Sergeant, 6 November 1768; 4559, Jean Schreiner, 29 January 1787; 4593, Soumagne, 26 October 1785; 4634, John Lever, 6 April 1791.

50 Dan Bogart and Gary Richardson, "Institutional Adaptability and Economic Development: The Property Rights Revolution in Britain, 1700 to 1830," *NBER Working Papers* 13757 (2008), 28.

51 Vries, *Escaping Poverty,* 364.

52 Vandenbroeke, *Agriculture,* 567.

53 NAB, FC, 5228, letter from the States of Brabant, 14 May 1765.

54 G. Van Dievoet, *Patrice de Nény (1716–1784) et le gouvernement des Pays-Bas Autrichiens* (Kortrijk: UGA, 1987), 76.

55 Catharina Lis and Hugo Soly, "Restructuring the Urban Textile Industries in Brabant and Flanders during the Second Half of the Eighteenth Century," in *Textiles of the Low Countries in European Economic History*, ed. Erik Aerts and John Munro (Leuven: 1990), 105–113.

56 Hubert Van Houtte, *Histoire économique de la Belgique à la fin de l'Ancien Régime* (Ghent: Van Rysselberghe & Rombaut, 1920), 317–318; Lis and Soly, "Living apart together," 133.

57 NAB, FC, 5853, Folder 1; 5854, *Commerce en general* 1755 and *Commerce en général* 1757; letter calculating the amount of work that would go into the creation of such statistics, August 9, 1755.

58 Explicit examples can be found in: NAB, FC, 4281, letter by councillor de Mullendorff, September 16, 1762; 4640; 4303, *Extrait du Protocole du Committé établi pour les affaires du Commerce Réciproque des provinces allemandes & Belgiques*, October 25, 1770.

59 Dan Bogart and Gary Richardson, "Property Rights and Parliament in Industrializing Britain," *Journal of Law and Economics* 54 (2011), 241–274, at 248.

60 Bogart and Richardson, "Institutional Adaptability," 36.

61 Ibid., 269.

62 Duplessis, *Transitions*, 236; Vandenbroeke, *Agriculture*, 482.

63 Philipp Robinson Rössner, "Mercantilism, Great Divergence and the Reconfiguration of a Productive Landscape: The Case of the Periphery," *Annales Mercaturae*, 1/1 (2015), 97–126.

64 List, *National System*, 109. However, List does explicitly point to the restrictions on raw material exports as an impediment for the region's development (154).

65 Ibid., 66,141. Habsburg officials and the members of the Finance Council were also very impressed by Colbert's realisations: Natalie Briavoinne, *De l'industrie en Belgique, Sa situation actuelle. Causes de décadence et de prosperité* (Brussels: s.n., 1839), 83.

66 Ann Coenen, "The International Textile Trade in the Austrian Netherlands, 1750–1791," in *Selling Textiles in the Long Eighteenth Century*, ed. Jon Stobart (Basingstoke: 2014), 67–84, at 67.

67 For detailed data on the international trade flows, see Coenen, *Carriers*, Appendix.

68 NAB, FC, 4287, consult of 27 August 1753; Sabbe, *De Belgische Vlasnijverheid*, 94. It is interesting to note the similarities between the linen policy in this region and in Scotland (see Rössner, "Mercantilism, Great Divergence and the Reconfiguration of a Productive Landscape"), suggesting that many contemporaries considered this a very logical choice for government support.

69 NAB, FC, 5025, letter by the city of Ostend, 2 March 1763; 5027, city of Antwerp, 10 November 1767; 5029, request by J.S. Toebast, 5 March 1770; ARA, Conseil du Gouvernement Général, 821, 10 September 1787.

70 NAB, FC, 5223, report by Van Heurck, 11 July 1761. Much has been written on the influence of conflicting interests of domestic lobby groups. See for example the notes in: Williamson, "Was it Stolper-Samuelson," 27; Chang and Lin, "Should Industrial Policy," 484.

71 Williamson, "Was it Stolper-Samuelson," 2. Herman Coppens (1992) also assumed that state finances remained a constant concern within the customs policy.

72 Briavoinne, *De l'industrie*, 83.

73 Coppejans-Desmedt, "Aspecten," 72.

74 NAB, FC, 5748–5805, *Relevés Généraux Des Marchandises, Manufactures et Denrées Entrées, Sorties et Transitées*; Philippe Moureaux, *La statistique industrielle dans les Pays- Bas autrichiens à l'époque de Marie-Thérèse. Documents et cartes* (Brussels: Palais des académies, 1974–1981).

75 A comparison of the percentage of approved applications for various stakeholders (producers, consumers, merchants and officials) shows that the first category was most successful in influencing trade policy. This supports the presumption that eighteenth-century 'industrialists' possessed relatively efficient lobbying channels. Coenen, *Carriers*, 129.

76 Joseph II's measures against the guilds are well known, but there are also earlier examples. NAB, FC, 4505, December 22 1760.

77 The members of the Finance Council believed that many goods could be imported without damaging domestic production, and should therefore not be taxed. The list of goods that the region could import without posing a disadvantage to its industry included: dyestuffs, spices, tea, coffee, cocoa, crude Indian silk, tobacco, sugar from the West Indies, wood from the North, tin and lead. NAB, Manuscripts, 850 A, memorandum by councillor Van Heurck (1754), 292; NAB, FC, 4506, circular from councillor De Beelen, 23 June 1761; 4522, memorandum by councillors Paradis and Delplancq, 29 November 1779.

78 Williamson, "Was it Stolper-Samuelson," 29.

79 Sven Beckert, *Empire of Cotton. A New History of Global Capitalism* (New York: Alfred A. Knopf, 2014), 182.

13 *Achtung! Banditi!*

An alternative genealogy of the market

Sophus A. Reinert

Introduction

In one of the opening scenes of Carlo Lizzani's 1951 neo-realist masterpiece *Achtung! Banditi!*, the first great Italian World War II epic, the heroic *partigiani*, or anti-fascist partisans, descend from the Appennines to sabotage a munitions-factory towards the war's end. Passing around a bombed-out and still smoldering farmhouse on their way down the mountainside, they come across one of the numerous road signs put up by the German army across Italy wherever it felt uncertain of its territorial control: *'Achtung! Banditen'*: *'Beware! Bandits'*. Defiantly, the partisans strike the sign with their weapons, tear it down, and throw it towards the cloud-shrouded valley below. The short scene encapsulates the movie's moral message by underlining the historical polyvalence of banditry; for who were really the bandits in the Appennines? The sign clearly referred to the partisans themselves, dubbed bandits by the occupying forces, but in appropriating it the partisans expressed a warning to the real bandits in the movie's moral economy: the Fascist regime itself; 'Beware, bandits', their stern faces seem to say, 'we are taking our rightful lands back'.[1] One man's bandit, to repeat a tired yet lucid cliché, is often another man's freedom fighter.[2]

In fact, though often marginalized or approached from a 'social' and frequently utopian perspective, bandits have historically occupied the very core of political philosophy and political economy alike. And they naturally occupy a fault line in Max Weber's classic definition of 'the state' as 'that human community which (successfully) lays claim to the *monopoly of legitimate physical violence* within a certain territory, this "territory" being another of the defining characteristics of the state'.[3] Not only do bandits by their mere presence disrupt successful governmental monopolies on violence, they destabilize territories and challenge the very legitimacy of states. Taking this argument one step further in light of recent scholarship on the historical development of commercial societies, bandits were by definition their nemeses. As scholars from a remarkably wide variety of theoretical, ideological, and empirical perspectives have argued, 'markets' are eminently social and political historical constructions, not the teleologically necessary manifestations of behaviors immanent to human nature.[4] Annabel Brett has recently explored the tension between 'nature and the city', in early modern political philosophy, arguing that the '*civitas*', meaning human 'commonwealth' rather than simply built urban environment, was 'a metaphysical, not a physical place', the borders between which were a site of 'tense negotiation' at the time.[5] And though this undoubtedly is true to a great extent, the metaphysical *civitas* itself in turn depended on the actual territoriality of civilization. Indeed, bandits played a significant yet often ignored role in the processes of early modern state formation and in concomitant debates of political economy during the so-called age of state-building mercantilism.[6] Unveiling how requires a more careful excavation of what Henri Pirenne long ago defined a 'territorial economy' and Saskia Sassen more recently has referred to as 'the political economy of urban territoriality', terms themselves closely related to Michael Mann's notion of a state's 'infrastructural power'.[7]

Few regions offer a richer history of banditry and state building than the Italian peninsula. And it is noteworthy, in light of this history, that Antonio Genovesi, Italy's first professor of anything like 'political economy' and a man who is often referred to as a 'mercantilist', never called his discipline by either of those names. Rather, the Neapolitan abbot first chose 'commerce and mechanics', a decision doubtlessly influenced by his mentor Bartolomeo Intieri's statement that 'physics is the foundation of the economy of politics', then '*economia civile*' or 'civil oeconomie', in more modern terms 'civil economics'.[8] Today, the phrase 'civil economics' has come to be identified largely with a tradition of Catholic economic thought focused on the importance—and ostensibly revolutionary possibilities—of a 'Third Sector' of voluntary associations related to but distinct from states and markets. The expression was, however, rather more inclusive in Italy during the long eighteenth-century, reflecting a historical context in which the discipline of political economy was still searching for an identity.[9] Considering the case of Enlightenment Lombardy, for example, 'Cameralism', 'civil economics', 'political economy', 'public economics', and 'the sciences of Finance, Commerce, etc.' were all used, seemingly interchangeably, by the same historical actors to refer to essentially the same thing: aggregate analyses of the economic dimension of civil life.[10]

It is, however, important to note that 'civil society' at the time seldom if ever was contrasted to the state, the way Western political philosophy has habitually done since the works of Immanuel Kant and Georg Wilhelm Friedrich Hegel.[11] Because of Europe's unique developmental trajectory, in other words, analyses of the emergence of governmental state capacity that assume it to be something imposed on a presumed pre-existing society are of only limited analytical relevance.[12] Rather, a civil society was understood historically to by necessity have a government and be disciplined by an array of laws that, although weak by contemporary comparison were upheld by recognizably state-like structures such as courts, legislators, and law-enforcing institutions. The meaningful contrast with civil society was as such less the state than the state of nature.[13] '*Economia civile*' was a quintessentially political, legal, *and* social economy, in that it engaged with the economy of the *civitas*, the Roman philosopher and politician Marcus Tullius Cicero's venerable concept of a 'social body of citizens united by law [*concilium coetusque hominum jure sociati*]' that Thomas Hobbes would equate with 'that great Leviathan called a Common-Wealth, or State, (in latine [*sic*] *Civitas*)'. And though grounded in, and expanding across, the natural world such a civil society was dramatically distinct from it.[14] The 'civile' part of eighteenth-century political economy was, in short, hardly a Catholic prerogative, though Catholicism of course deeply influenced thinking on the matter at the time, and was less antithetical than synonymous with the state as such, however embryonic by modern standards. The 'civilizing process', around which so much has been written in wake of German sociologist Norbert Elias' eponymous book of 1939, can after all easily be seen to take form in the emerging communes of Medieval Italy, where mercantile, classical, and religious influences came together to domesticate elite behavior and discipline urban life.[15] Civil society, as opposed to savagery in the state of nature, required the government of the self and of others, and '*economia civile*' was the discipline of its material organization.[16]

Yet the example of '*economia civile*' highlights the inherent problems of applying modern conceptions of political economy, such as 'states' and 'markets', to earlier historical periods. There were of course 'states' in existence in the eighteenth century, theorized as such in terms remarkably similar to many of those we would use today. Similarly, the economic imagination of early modern Europe allowed not merely for markets in the physical sense of marketplaces and fairs, but also today's more abstract principle of exchanging goods as such, without immediate referent to people and places. Widely conceived, political economy operated on the tacit and sometimes explicit assumptions that states had territories in which there were marketplaces, that sovereignty over the former did not by necessity entail dominance in the latter, whatever formal dominion might suggest, that both marketplaces and territories were actively competed for by states involved in shifting constellations of alliances, and that some greater commercial principle united these different locations through the production and exchange of goods across the myriads of borders still dismembering the European continent, not merely political but also of customs and religions.[17]

That said, the state was far from the only locus of sovereignty at the time, and what Weber would have liked to be monopolistic claims to legitimacy and violence really took the form of competing spectrums of authority.[18] James Scott is certainly right to point out the extent to which 'the premodern state' was 'partially blind', in that it lacked the capacity to monitor, regulate, and administer the people, things, and concepts it would have liked to.[19] States seldom had a clear idea of where their own borders were, of who lived within them, and what passed between them internally and with regards to other states, and a central concern of the tradition of '*economia civile*' lay precisely in remedying this situation— through everything from cartography to cadasters—in expanding the civil sphere of governance over ever larger areas and harness controlled resources to fruitful ends. As a Milanese cadasteral instruction for surveyors put it already in 1549, minute descriptions and assessments of the most varied terrains and people of the state were necessary to ensure 'true news' of the 'quality and quantity of goods' in the dominion, a strategic necessity guiding many of the key attempts to codify economic statecraft in early modern Europe, from French '*économie politique*' through German '*Kameralismus*' to English 'political arithmetick'.[20] Cadasters had, of course, been part of political economy broadly conceived since antiquity, but it is undeniable that the eighteenth-century gradually saw their increased sophistication, theoretization, international emulation, and purposeful application for policy purposes.[21] And, not surprisingly, Enlightenment cadaster was often justified in relation not merely to state power but to the 'public good' of 'peoples' in terms of how a more complete territorial awareness and assessment would improve revenues and the 'dignity' of the 'State' and thus 'the administration of justice, defence, and the peace of all'.[22]

One of the founding works on the historiography of the unhappy phenomenon known as 'mercantilism', Gustav von Schmoller's *The Mercantile System and its Historical Significance*, can still be helpful in illuminating this process.[23] Schmoller saw the origins of early modern political economy in the economic policies of medieval towns, and discerned 'the soul of that policy' in 'the putting of fellow-citizens at an advantage, and of competitors at a disadvantage'. The period saw, in other words, the spatial demarcation of competing lines of exclusion, in which 'territorial institutions' sought to 'shut themselves off from the outer world, and to harmonize and consolidate their forces at home' to produce 'an independent territorial unit' ultimately based on the 'territorial harmonizing of production and consumption'.[24] This territoriality of state power eventually transcended its urban origins, and:

> what, to each in its time, gave riches and superiority first to Milan, Venice, Florence, and Genoa; then, later, to Spain and Portugal; and now to Holland, France, and England, and to some extent, to Denmark and Sweden, was a *state* policy in economic matters, as superior to the territorial as that had been to the municipal.[25]

As this territorial impulse of governance extended, Schmoller argued, it came to define European history in global terms, in relation to both the internal and external relations of states as they emerged and solidified. 'Questions of political power' were essentially 'questions of economic organization', and 'what was at stake was the creation of real *political* economies as unified organisms, the centre of which should be, not merely a state policy reaching out in all directions, but rather the living heartbeat of a united sentiment'.[26]

> Only he who thus conceives of mercantilism will understand it; in its innermost kernel it is nothing but state making—not state making in a narrow sense, but state making and national-economy making at the same time; state making in the modern sense, which creates out of the political community an economic community, and so gives it a heightened meaning. The essence of the system lies... in the total transformation of society and its organization, as well as of the state and institutions, in the replacing of a local and territorial economic policy by that of the national state.[27]

And, strikingly in light of eighteenth-century debates, Schmoller emphasized the crucial importance of internal 'circulation' and external 'commercial competition' for the process of early modern state building.[28] The need to defend the former, and the seemingly uncontrollable escalation of the latter, paradoxically gave rise to para-governmental preoccupations with the nature and fate of humanity as such.

> The very idea of international law is a protest against the excesses of national rivalry. All international law rests on the idea that the several states and nations form, from the moral point of view, one community. Since the men of Europe had lost the feeling of community that had been created by the Papacy and Empire, they had been seeking for some other theory which might serve to support it; and this they found in the reawakening 'law of nature.' But the particular ideas for which in the first instance men strove, and for which they sought arguments *pro et contra* in the law of nature, were mainly products of the economic and commercial struggle then proceeding.[29]

There was, then, a deep tension at the very core of early modern political economy in Schmoller's analysis. On the one hand, human circulation and communication depended on the expansion of civil spheres of government civilizing and pacifying ever-greater areas and bringing them under the ordering institutions born from urban life; the territorialization of civilization, no less. On the other, in the absence of the unifying sense of community previously offered by the Holy Roman Empire and the Papacy, these competitive regional projects of state-expansion and spatial socialization ended undermining the circulation and subsequent socialization of humanity as such. The great Renaissance realist Niccolò Machavelli might, perhaps unsurprisingly, have encapsulated this mindset when he instructed Iuliano Lapi in a Florentine chancellery dispatch of 27 August 1503 to 'have an eye to everything that regards the good of our city and the conservation of these places and of our men'.[30] The paradigm of the common good was, contrary to what its semantics might suggest, rigorously circumscribed in spatial terms, and the sublimation of city-state good into territorial, and ultimately universal good was by necessity a painful and ironically paradoxical process. And though less interested in the underlying philosophy of this mechanism than their Prussian predecessor, the basic historical process laid out in *The Mercantile System and Its Historical Significance* was influentially adopted by economists, sociologists, and historians along the lines of Eli F. Heckscher, Karl Polanyi, Henri Pirenne, and Fernand Braudel in the subsequent century.[31]

Indeed, Schmoller's account in many ways still represents our principal way of understanding the nature and consequences of European state-formation in the early modern period and the nature of economic competition today. We might even call it the Schmollerian Moment. He saw 'natural law' as the attempt to again impose coherence on this anarchic world, swaddling humanity with ideas rather than with empires of the sword or of the soul. And, in doing so, he put his finger on a set of problems that had preoccupied early modern political philosophers and economists and that has again become a fixation of the historiographical mainstream, namely the sociability question and the overarching problem of pacifying a world at once economically interconnected and politically dismembered, a world in which individual states linked by treaties, by shared customs, and by commerce often were at war and always were locked in a struggle for supremacy, whether military or economic.[32] A world, in short, much like our own. The logic of each state might be domestic peace in their expanding, often contested territories, but the outcome of their interaction could become quite the opposite internationally. This was the perennial tragedy of '*economia civile*', the tradition of Enlightenment political economy practiced in the region in which this process had gone on for the longest, but which also, by contemporary standards, seemingly had stopped at the level of city-states and minor territorialities. As Verri noted late in life, 'Italy' lacked 'a centre of reunion' of its own, a peninsular capital, and its only 'common fatherland' remained the Roman Catholic Church.[33]

The perhaps most interesting question, however, is not what went into such civil economics but rather what it excluded, and what it *had* to exclude and even eradicate, an issue that relates the micro and macro dynamics of Schmoller's analysis and further helps elucidate the *Accademia dei pugni*'s project, Enlightenment debates over commercial society, and the vexing role of crime— and particularly banditry—therein.[34] To better contextualize the longer history of commercial sociability in the age of 'mercantilism', in short, and indeed the politics of what eventually would be known as Enlightenment 'socialism', it is worthwhile turning to this idea of 'civil economics' and, importantly, its threshold, its boundaries, and its emergence in light of that timeless agent of civil and economic discord: Cicero's old 'common enemy of all', the pirate, and more broadly, bandit and the outlaw, whose very existence undermined civil society and what early modern Italians conceived of as the '*viver Politico*', the politicized or civic life.[35] *Achtung! Banditi!* indeed.

Good and bad government

Somewhat curiously from a longer historical perspective, such 'enemies of mankind' are today increasingly eulogized, whether in the form of actor Johnny Depp or celebrity chef Anthony Bourdain, Wikileaks' Julian Assange or the hacktivist collective Anonymous, not to mention more generally through an ever-increasing volume of academic publications, from Eric Hobsbawm's foundational work on 'social bandits' through Peter Leeson's libertarian buccaneers to Rodolph Durand and Jean Philippe Verone's piratical organizations spearheading capitalism, plausibly inspired by Steve Jobs' famus slogan 'it's better to be a pirate than to join the navy'.[36] One could even argue that this is merely a particularly flamboyant expression of a general critique of governments and governmentality fielded across the political spectrum in recent years, from the libertarians of the left to those of the far right.[37] Whatever the complex political and institutional causes, it remains that we live in a world that has become remarkably enamored with the outlaw aesthetic, from the vigilante to the villain, and more specifically with its creative and indeed productive potential.[38] Compared to the great and widely emulated Italian *giallo* and *polizieschi*-movies of the 1970s and 80s, for example, in which redoubtable crimes were resolved by dedicated and often underdog police detectives representing the state's judiciary branch, today's crime aesthetic frequently favors corrupt and inept law-enforcement officials, revenge fantasies, and wrongdoings ultimately avenged by extra-legal vigilantes, often in the form of disillusioned police officers taking matters into their own hands.[39] Needless to say, things have not always been this way, and the tradition of '*economia civile*' can perhaps remind us of why.

Though for many historical sources they were essentially interchangeable, others were careful to differentiate between outlaws.[40] From one perspective that is rather easy to adopt, pirates are simply bandits in boats. From a more nuanced legal perspective, however, they are engaged in admittedly analogous yet dissimilar activities: bandits tend to corrode the territorial sovereignty of political communities; pirates assault the relations between them. Banditry is a landlocked activity, by default occurring in a territory claimed by one or more sources of authority the lawfulness of which they challenge or, at the very least, momentarily disregard. Pirates literally operate in a no-man's land, at sea, where they challenge not only territorial rights but the existence of rights at all. Cicero defined 'pirates' as 'common enemies of all' by virtue of their acting without 'good faith' by threatening the channels of commerce—understood to be both trade and communication—and thus of sociability itself, purposefully operating outside of the 'immense fellowship' of humanity and therefore outside of the parameters of that most basic 'obligation' human beings, even warring competitors, owed each other. Pirates were not simply foreigners to society, they were antibodies of society, and as such, antinomious to it and not owed anything, by anyone.[41] For practical purposes, however, piracy and banditry were often expressed in the same breath in early modern Europe, and with good reason.

As long as there have been polities, said polities have contained members who were unwilling to peaceably partake in them. From the Roman Emperor Tiberius, who dispatched four thousand Jewish troops to Sardinia to fight bandits there, to Adolf Hitler, rebranding partisans as bandits during World War II, the sovereigns of very different polities have historically come to violent terms with the problem of 'banditry'.[42] It is often argued that banditry resurges in periods of duress, and early modern Europe saw many kinds of duress, not merely material, in terms of subsistence anxieties and failed harvests, but also social, in terms of rapidly changing laws and norms, of veritable 'regime changes' in contemporary parlance.[43] At a hitherto unknown speed, early modern rural communities— proverbial 'traditional societies'—were not simply incorporated into ever larger and more *present* state organizations, they were simultaneously brought into connection with each other in often less than peaceful ways. It was perhaps, in David Armitage's terms, not yet a globalized age, but it was certainly one of globalization.[44] The history of banditry is, from this perspective, also a counter-history of the consolidation and increasingly institutionalized legitimacy of state power in early modern Europe, and an underappreciated aspect of its impact lies in its violent rebuttal of the very essence of commercial sociability as it began spreading outwards from the Italian city states of the Middle Ages. Modern proponents in the tradition of 'civil economics' often emphasize its medieval origins, and there can be no doubt that the problem of banditry, trade, and good government in early modern political economy also benefits from being considered from such a deeper historical perspective.[45]

In effect, this problem was a veritable theme in late Medieval and Renaissance political art in Italy, already present in Giotto's monochromatic fresco depictions of the virtue of *Justice* and the vice of *Injustice* on the walls of the Scrovegni Chapel in Padua (c. 1303–1305). The female figure of *Justice* is adorned with a crown, seated on a throne, and holds scales supporting, on her left, an angel about to smite a villain with a sword, and, on her right, an angel about to crown a sage. Her gaze is calm and directed straight at the viewer, a way for Giotto to communicate truthful honesty. Underneath her, Giotto depicted the joys of civil life under justice and good government in a mock bas-relief, including dancing, hunting, safe travel, even for women, and, crucially, trade. Though the inscription below her has long faded, the phrase 'mercat[ori]... itur' is still legible. Under justice, 'merchants' 'do' '[something]', presumably trade, in any case something understood to be positive given the larger moral economy of the fresco. The parallel figure of *Injustice* on the opposite wall is more striking. An elderly, blind man in a ruined castle, with a judge's cap placed backwards and long, demonic fingernails, he holds a sword down by his side and seems caught on his throne, unable to move, held in place by large, wildly growing forest that litereally emerges from the wall itself, Dante's 'selva oscura' triumphant. In the mock bas-relief underneath him, women are raped and killed, armed brigands haunt the roads and the woods, and trade and travel are impossible.[46]

As the Victorian art historian John Ruskin read the seeming inactivity of *Injustice* itself, this 'is, indeed, the depth of Injustice: not the harm you do, but that you permit to be done [...]. The baronial type exists still, I fear, in such manner, here and there, in spite of improving centuries'. The agency of the fresco is, in this reading, human, in that civilization is a question of active legislation and governance while trusting nature and spontaneous events leads only to chaos. This was a truism Ruskin found reflected in the precarious and threatened nature of civil life as such, when he noted that 'in Giotto's time woods were too many, and towns too few'.[47] It was a sentiment echoed by the elderly Pietro Verri, who argued that 'the oldest and most common art of despotism is to introduce a reciprocal diffidence between men', for 'like ideas, the sentiments of men cannot develop and become whole if not through commerce and reciprocal communicaiton'. The 'art of tyranny', he concluded, 'is that of keeping men isolated like so many grains of sand, detached and discomposed, that remain very close to each other but do not form a mass and an entirety'.[48] Beccaria would repeatedly express the very same preoccupation, even casting it in explicitly sylvan terms in a poem on commerce he penned in 1760. 'Commerce', he rhymed, was the only force able to overcome the 'forested mountains [*selvosi gioghi*'] that 'divided distant lands'.[49]

Figure 13.1 Giotto, 'Justice', Scrovegni Chapel, Padua, c. 1305, *public domain.*

Figure 13.2 Giotto, 'Injustice', Scrovegni Chapel, Padua, c. 1305, *public domain.*

A very similar aesthetic, and a very similar legal and political-economic argument is evident in the most picturesque and justly famous expressions of the problem posed by enemies of mankind for the nexus of states, markets, and sociability, namely Ambrogio Lorenzetti's famous fresco cycle in the Palazzo Pubblico of Siena, his 1338–1339 *Allegory of Good and Bad Government*.[50] Doubtlessly inspired by Giotto, and among the most sophisticated and most commented upon expressions of political art in world history, Lorenzetti's work defies singular explanations. But from our present perspective, the relationship between banditry and civil society in effect emerges as the very axis around which his fresco cycle turns. Contemplating, as intended, the work from left to right, one first encounters the effects of *Bad Government in the Countryside*, with burning fields and villages, and bands of heavily armed bandits and brigands stalking the roads. They are depicted as soldiers really, less of fortune than of anarchy. The scene of utter devastation is only explained when one reaches the gate to *Bad Government in the City*, over which the harrowing undead figure of *Timor*, or *Fear*, flies with a brandished black sword and a banner explaining:

> Because each seeks only his own good, in this city, Justice is subjected to Tyranny; wherefore along this road nobody passes without fearing for his life, since there are robberies outside and inside the city gates.[51]

Figure 13.3   Ambrogio Lorenzetti, 'Allegory of Good and Bad Government' (detail), Siena, 1338–1339, *public domain.*

Figure 13.4   Ambrogio Lorenzetti, 'Allegory of Good and Bad Government' (detail), Siena, 1338–1339. DEA/A DE GREGORIO / age fotostock.

One then enters the urban expression of *Bad Government*, in which houses are falling down, only the arms dealer's shop remains open (bandits too, after all, have their business needs), and people are raped and murdered in the streets with abandon by armed outlaws. Bad government is essentially *depicted* through—and quintessentially *characterized* by—the existence of bandits and brigands, by those not yet or no longer civilized in the Ciceronian sense. Their very existence desocialized territories by threatening trade and travel, commerce and communication, galvanizing civic vices of fear and selfishness.

Continuing the eye's march rightward across Lorenzetti's masterpiece, one sees the courts of *Bad Government*, where the Devil has *Justice* bound at his feet, and *Good Government*, where *Justice* reigns supreme, respectively, before entering the vibrant and developing (tall buildings are being constructed in the background) merchant metropolis achieved under *Good Government in the City*, a scene characterized by trade, education, and civic happiness, and in which, though the city itself is heavily fortified, no trace of violence can be found.

The explanation can again be found outside the city gates, this time in the shapely form of a female angel, named *Securitas*, in one hand holding a gallows aloft with a hanged corpse dangling from it, in the other holding a banner stating:

> Without fear every man may travel freely and each may till and sow, so long as this commune shall maintain this lady Justice as sovereign, for she has stripped the wicked of all power.[52]

Figure 13.5   Ambrogio Lorenzetti, 'Allegory of Good and Bad Government' (detail), Siena, 1338–1339, *public domain.*

Figure 13.6   Ambrogio Lorenzetti, 'Allegory of Good and Bad Government' (detail), Siena, 1338–1339, *public domain.*

Figure 13.7   Ambrogio Lorenzetti, 'Allegory of Good and Bad Government' (detail), Siena, 1338–1339, *public domain.*

Figure 13.8   Ambrogio Lorenzetti, 'Allegory of Good and Bad Government' (detail), Siena, 1338–1339, *public domain.*

Figure 13.9   Ambrogio Lorenzetti, 'Allegory of Good and Bad Government' (detail), Siena, 1338–1339, *public domain.*

Figure 13.10 Ambrogio Lorenzetti, 'Allegory of Good and Bad Government' (detail), Siena, 1338–1339, *public domain.*

Across the plastered walls of the Palazzo Pubblico in Siena, Lorenzetti gracefully depicted one of the most enduring questions, and tensions, of political philosophy: that of the nature of *justice* in civil society. Proverbially speaking, what Lorenzetti offered was not 'our way or the highway', for in theory the highway was precisely where the political leaders of Siena did not want their adversaries. The right dichotomy was our way or the gallows, a rather more finite destination, though in practice medieval Italian jurisprudence tended to be remarkably nonconfrontational, falling back on a politics of exile and bans to expel unwanted persons and fractions.[53] *Justice* unbound contributed to extraordinary riches in the fresco, visualizing core features of the Italian tradition of '*economia civile*' as it developed out of late medieval political humanism.

The female figure of unbound *Justice* is assisted by *Wisdom* in Lorenzetti's fresco, a heavenly figure suggesting the necessity of divine inspiration, and emanates two personal incarnations derived from late medieval readings of Aristotle also present in Giotto's earlier masterpiece: *Distributive Justice*, engaged in beheading and crowning citizens at her leisure, and *Commutative Justice* in charge of funding and arming the worthy. A rope in turn connects these two aspects of the 'divine virtue' to *Concord*, who hands the rope on to a group of twenty-four representative male citizens of Siena. Order and concord were medieval dreams, and one should be careful about reading Lorenzetti's vision of Siena as anything more than a utopian reverie. Yet it projected an ideal of a remarkable longevity in the canon of Italian political philosophy, also as it eventually interacted with the development of more succinctly economic thinking on the peninsula. And in spite of all the Thomistic influences on Lorenzetti's vision, the iconography of *Good Government* betrays a fundamental difference in its view of human nature. For St. Thomas Aquinas, peace was simply the absence of discord, it was the normal state of affairs from which one could deviate unless careful.[54] War was, as such, accidental and to be resisted. Lorenzetti's imagery aligned with, and contributed to, a far more Ciceronian vector for Italian political economy that would come to profoundly influence thinking on these matters throughout the early modern period.

War, in this 'civic' tradition, was endemic, spontaneous, sudden, and though peace could be achieved and human relations socialized through political means, it represented a fragile exception to, and momentary victory over, the violent rule of nature. It was not order but disorder that was spontaneous, and inaction, as both Giotto and Lorenzetti depicted so clearly, lay at the core of injustice. *Peace* was one of the central themes of both their fresco cycles, which in Lorenzetti's version took physical form at the very center of his *oeuvre*, a beautiful woman holding an olive branch and reclining, pensively, on a massive suit of armor. The parallel to the city under *Good Government* is striking. There should be no need for fortifications and city walls, given there are no bandits or armies on the other side, but a deep knowledge that discord could—and by necessity *would*—return justified their continued presence, just like *Peace* knew better than to discard her plate mail.[55] There was also a deeper issue that remained unresolved in Lorenzetti's political vision, for though 'good government' in Siena seemingly had succeeded in socializing *people* in the polity, and exterminating or exorcizing deviants from its hinterlands, the problem of socializing *peoples* remained. However well a polity was regulated, it could still succumb to greater and more aggressive powers, as the case would be when Siena herself fell to Florentine and Spanish troops in 1555.[56] It was a tension that would haunt thinkers and statesmen in Italy into the era of the Risorgimento, and Pietro Verri himself would ponder, in one of his last dialogues written in the wake of the French Revolution and Napoleon's invasion of Italy, about the relationship between 'good' and 'bad government', 'social order', 'justice', and how international conflicts and consequent warfare destroyed 'humanity'. They were all terms through which approach the overarching question of human sociability.[57]

A similar vision of peace was encapsulated by Sandro Botticelli's triumphant c. 1482 *Pallas and the Centaur*, depicting Pallas Athena, also known to the Ancient Greeks as *Athena Polias* or 'Athena of the City', goddess of wisdom and civilization, among other things, restraining the beastly centaur. Subdued, even remorseful, man's animalistic side incarnated in the centaur looks to Athena for guidance, the background—replete with fences demarcating and territorializing

Figure 13.11 Ambrogio Lorenzetti, 'Allegory of Good and Bad Government' (detail), Siena, 1338–1339, *public domain.*

Figure 13.12 Ambrogio Lorenzetti, 'Allegory of Good and Bad Government' (detail),
Siena, 1338–1339, *public domain.*

civil and civic life as well as merchant ships—reinforcing the impression that the
mountainous wilderness was being domesticated by the civil sphere. Awesome
Athena herself, dressed like the Spring of Botticelli's contemporary *Allegory of
Spring*, holds his hair like a Judith might hold that of a beheaded Holofernes, but
her complex visage is not without compassion, even pity as she considers the
wretched beast by her side.[58]

Figure 13.13 Sandro Botticelli, 'Pallas and the Centaur', Uffizi, Florence, 1482, *public domain*.

Strikingly, the equation of forests with banditry would become so pervasive in Renaissance Lombardy that even crime-ridden urban spaces would be described as 'forests' full of 'homicides, wounds, and assassins' by legislators.[59] The metaphorical fight against such urban forests found its real-world equivalent in widespread deforestations in early modern Italy also to civilize the land by removing the Sherwoods of the world.[60] Yet by the early years of the nineteenth century, the tradeoff between the threat bandits posed to commerce and the economic potential of forests had become evident enough that the Brindisian naturalist Teodoro Monticelli could lament the irony that deforestations 'to destroy, as one thinks, the asylums of brigands, and of assassins... in reality destroy the first source of salubrity and wealth in a country, adding a new cause of desperate brigandage to those already known'.[61] Banditry was, in Monticelli's eyes, an essentially economic phenomenon related to popular poverty, a tradition of interpretation of which Cesare Beccaria might have been the most eloquent exponent.

The political economy of banditry

Italian polities waged wars on banditry—and each other—throughout the Renaissance and early modern periods. By the time Tommaso Garzoni penned his extraordinary 1587 *La piazza universale di tutte le professioni del mondo*, or *Universal Marketplace of all the World's Professions*, 'Bandit' was a career option listed like any other, identified in a now venerable phraseology primarily in terms of the danger they posed to communication and commerce, to the arteries, in short, of the body politic. Just as 'broken bridges' and 'mud' impeded travel, 'bandits' and 'assassins' aborted interactions and the circulation of people and goods within and between countries.[62] In the reason of state tradition, Giovanni Botero would explain how the population of Ancient Rome had exploded because it was able to offer security 'at a time when the neighbouring towns were oppressed by tyrants and the nearby lands were consequently full of bandits', thus rendering the connection between bad government and banditry explicit in terms not unlike those depicted visually by Giotto and Lorenzetti. For Botero too, banditry was at its core a threat to human commerce broadly conceived, and a ruler should 'judiciously' maintain the infrastructure not merely of trade but of humanity:

> for instance protecting the harbor with breakwaters, facilitating the loading and unloading of cargo, keeping the sea free of pirates, making the rivers navigable, building suitable warehouses big enough to contain large stocks of merchandise, strengthening and repairing the roads, both over the plains and over the Mountains.[63]

The problem of banditry continued to be conceptualized in these terms into the eighteenth century, when a liminal figure like Ludovico Antonio Muratori, a baroque humanist librarian as well as Enlightenment reformer, bemoaned that bandits threatened 'the security of the roads' and presented them as one of the greatest dangers to 'public happiness' and the 'glory of a government' alike.[64] An anonymous 1749 Venetian treatise on *General Maxims Regarding Commerce*, plagiarized a little more than a decade later in Genoa, followed suit, presenting banditry as a symptom of economic decay and civil inertia, the violent manifestation of a worldview according to which people could 'live on the shoulders of others'.[65] Banditry remained, in short, the antithesis not only of medieval notions of 'common good' and 'public happiness', but of a particularly modern form of commercial order and sociability forged in the city-states of the Italian peninsula. Far from avatars of capitalism, bandits were originally their very antithesis.

But this was of course not merely an Italian preoccupation, though Italian thinkers might have had a longer perspective on the phenomenon than others. Indeed, the centrality of banditry to eighteenth-century political economy widely understood has long been neglected. The *abbé* de Saint Pierre was among those who noted, in his seminal *Plan for Perpetual Peace in Europe*, the 'bands of bandits' that from time to time arose to terrorize the Italian countryside, 'rendering the roads and the canals unsafe, and the houses in the countryside dangerous to inhabit', strongly diminishing 'the interior Commerce of the land'. It is therefore noteworthy that among the primary benefits that he foresaw would result from a 'permanent union' of the 'system of European societies', that is, from his plan for a perpetual peace, would be allowing countries to 'promise that their merchants would no longer need to fear bandits on land, nor their ships pirates on the sea'.[66] And as the English deist Matthew Tindall put it, in words often attributed to Daniel Defoe, 'the pirate...destroyeth... all Government and all Order, by breaking all those Ties and Bonds that unite People in a Civil Society under any Government'.[67]

But though evocative, these engagements were far less intense than that offered by Genovesi, who engaged with the problem at length in what was arguably the most influential work of political economy published in eighteenth-century Italy, his translation of the Bristol merchant John Cary's 1695 *Essay on the State of England*.[68] To Genovesi, perhaps the most crucial aspect of economic development lay in the promulgation of a 'persuasion', a sentiment, animating economic life as such, based on the certainty that '*fatica*' or 'labor' paid off, that work and the output it created were rendered sacred. It was the very essence of commercial society itself, of a world order based on something recognizably 'capitalist' in nature. It was only:

> born from removing all the reasons why the use and enjoyment of our goods are, or can be, impeded, and why we have fear for our property. Because if, for example, thieves and brigands are left to run with impunity in a nation... in this nation, I say, it being convenient for proprietors to remain in constant and cruel war to defend what is their own, what industry, and what spirit of industry can take root and spread?[69]

It is striking that the danger Genovesi saw for private property was not government interference or taxation but bandits, an argumentative choice that makes further sense in a context in which private property anyway is a civil rather than natural invention and right. Private property ultimately existed only because of the laws of civil society, and as such taxation, again emanating from civil laws, was inherently lawful. Banditry, of course, represented an entirely different problem for private property as it took the form of an extra-legal tax. For a commercial society to flourish, it had to unfold on a civil basis of legal security of property grounded not in the absence of government but in its increasing capacity and territorial saturation. Only thus could individuals, connected to each other by solidifying avenues for commerce and communication, feel safe in pursuing their ventures. Genovesi elsewhere equated this sentiment with the act of contemplating the world 'with the eyes of a merchant', the only attitude conducive to the production of an individual, and ultimately social 'surplus', giving 'movement and vigor' to internal as well as external trade.[70] This emotional foundation for commercial society was as powerful as it was fragile, being entirely dependent on a sense of social trust and security; on life, in short, having been socialized. It was a problem he returned to in the final essay he added to the three-volume work, his '*Ragionamento sulla fede pubblica*' or *Discourse on Public Trust*.[71]

Activities such as banditry, Genovesi argued, were the greatest of all crimes, that is, a 'crime against public trust', acts seeking to 'destroy the foundations of the reciprocal familiarity between men, and their security, which in civil nations are many, and varied'. Bandits were, in short, enemies of the 'empire of civility', agents of anarchy and, through that, retrograde savagery.[72] This was why, in Genovesi's opinion, 'in all nations, even those, which only have a mere shadow of a Government, such crimes are ordinarily punished with death'. For, echoing the moral message of Giotto and Lorenzetti's frescoes, were such crimes 'allowed to happen, by necessity society will either dissolve or convert entirely into a band of brigands'.[73] The state of savagery was a political artifact, commercial society depending completely on the vigilant regulation and maintenance of civic trust. Commercial society, or rather 'the good faith, which is the spirit of Commerce', was entirely contingent on the endless regulations to which 'internal and external Commerce' were subject for the cause of the 'common good'. But Genovesi remained adamant that the only 'great, stable, and internal foundation of true virtue' in the world was 'religion'.[74]

The greatest legal theorist of political economy in Enlightenment Europe was undoubtedly the Milanese reformer and later professor of Cameralism Cesare Beccaria, who, though certainly building on Genovesi's work on the topic of sociability and commercial society in the tradition of '*economia civile*', resolutely went beyond it, with his epochal 1764 *On Crimes and Punishments* forcing him to engage with the practice of banditry in a fashion that was both more nuanced and more immediate. But just as pirates and bandits were not the same, so bandits themselves came in many stripes and colors in early modern Italy, and an exploration of their spectrum of appearances, and the shifting politics of their activities, can serve to contextualize Beccaria's unique take on the phenomenon and its role in the Schmollerian Moment.

Political bandits

Among history's many failed states, Montferrat was one of the happier, sharing many similarities—territorially as well as gastronomically—with Burgundy.[75] A hilly, truffled landscape historically wedged between the Republic of Genoa and the Duchies of Savoy and Milan, the area still known as Montferrat stretches from the Po River southward to the Appennine watershed between Piedmont and Liguria. A longtime Margravate of the Holy Roman Empire, it was briefly controlled by Spain in the period 1533–1536 before coming under the control of the Gonzaga of Mantua, from which it passed, in a piecemeal fashion, to Savoy until its complete incorporation in 1708. Historically among the wealthiest and, as its late eighteenth-century chronicler Giuseppe Antonio de Morani put it, 'most fertile' areas of Italy, it remains one of the world's premier wine-producing regions and was an early exporter of high-value agricultural produce in the form of cured meats and cheeses.[76] Naturally, Montferrat was among the more contested territories of early modern Italy, its political vicissitudes telling with regards to the longer history of the Schmollerian Moment.[77]

In particular, a forgotten Montferrine criminal process against 'bandits' caught in Verolengo in 1569 can shed useful light on the multifaceted role of banditry in the economic and political formation of early modern Italy, the emergence of international markets, and the larger question of socialization between people and, crucially, between peoples. In the historiography of modern Italy 'banditry' has largely come to be equated with armed resistance to the expanding central state following national unification, taking on anti-capitalist and anti-statist aspects in Eric Hobsbawm's famous formulation of the 'social bandit'. This is particularly emphasized in treatments of traditionally ungovernable pastoral areas such as Sardinia.[78] The problem, of course, is that more Robin Hoods populate the literary than the historical record, and mainland forms of early modern banditry could take on conceptually related yet distinct forms speaking directly to the 'civil' preoccupation with pacifying human interactions and the means of achieving it.[79]

The sleepy town of Verolengo, nested North-East of Turin near where the glacial Dora Baltea coming down through Aosta flows into the Po River, was once a thriving Roman settlement on the main road from Pavia to Turin and on across the Alps to Gaul. In the early modern period it became an increasingly important, and disputed, commercial center with about 1,000 inhabitants on the border between Mantuan Montferrat and Savoy, officially granted to Guglielmo Gonzaga of Mantua at the 1559 Peace of Cateau-Cambrésis.[80] Still, Verolengo seems to have remained rather somnolent until, on the evening of Saturday 15 February 1569, shouting 'bandits' stormed its fortress. Though they quickly were routed and hounded by Mantuan authorities, the deeper significance of the bandits' acts, and their role in the longer process of socialization with which we are dealing, is revealed by the surviving legal procedures against them.

Resistance had been growing across Montferrat since most of the region passed from the dying Paleologus dynasty—cadet branch to the former Emperors of

Constantinople—to the Gonzaga of Mantua in 1536, and in 1565 the long-time capital city of Casale Monferrato revolted yet again 'to defend its ancient privileges' and, joining that venerable tradition of righteous rebellion, to resist 'arbitrary' taxation.[81] This local incident immediately came to affect the balance of powers between the larger states of Northern Italy and, through their roles in the larger system of Europe, the great imperial powers themselves. News of the revolt and its consequences reached even the ears of Philip II on the one hand, who at the time was King of Spain, Portugal, and England, as well as Duke of Burgundy and Lord of the Seventeen Provinces of the Netherlands, and the Habsburg Holy Roman Emperor Maximillian II on the other; none of whom wished to see regional intestinal conflicts in Italy ignite another continental war. The climate remained tense, however, and with Guglielmo openly blaming Emanuele Filiberto of Savoy for instigating the resistance, Spanish, French, and Savoy troops were all thought about to descend on Casale. Yet the great powers continued to favor diplomatic solutions, and Guglielmo Gonzaga was finally made to agree on Casale's terms to exchange ancient priviledges for sole lordship over their land. Casale had to dismember its fort and disband its militia, and if the terms of the pact were ever broken, Gonzaga would have to pay the city 50,000 scudi while disobedient Casalese automatically would be deemed guilty of '*lèse-majesté*', the terrible crime of violating the majesty and authority of a ruler or a state.[82]

Therein lay the rub, for though the city of Casale was allowed to retain the 'ancient priviledges' of a medieval commune in terms of local decision-making capacities and economic administration, these ultimately proved ephemeral in light of the city's incorporation into the larger political sphere of the Gonzaga. As Quentin Skinner and others so influentially have argued, a powerful current of Renaissance and early modern republican political philosophy equated liberty with the state of being subject to one's own laws and freedom from arbitrary power.[83] Within this paradigm, the history of Montferrat represented an eloquent justification for this line of thought. For the very fact that disagreement with the Gonzaga was equated with the greatest political crime ever codified—the tremendous capital crime of *lèse-majesté*—in effect made the Casalese slaves to the shifting sentiments of an at times arbitrary foreign ruler who, in the parlance of the day, had succeeded in 'giving laws' to them. Having lost their fortress and their militia, and thus their capacity for civic protection—understood to be the communal defense of a civic ideal[84]—the polity of Montferrat simply ceased to be political as such. For all their 'ancient priviledges' were ultimately trumped by the Gonzaga's overwhelming power of sovereignty, and, as so often in history, the principal area of contestation came to rest on questions of taxation. Many would simply not accept a new regime they considered *unjust*, and took up arms against their new sovereign.[85]

Equally infuriated, Emanuele Filiberto of Savoy threatened military action against Mantua and solemnly took the Casalese rebels, now quite literally outlaws, under his wing.[86] During the next few years, rebels would strike at Casale and particularly its Gonzaghesque elements with surgical precision, engaging in both assaults and assassinations, even making an attempt at the life of Guglielmo

Gonzaga himself. In retaliation, he risked justified retribution by chasing Casalese rebels into Savoy territory, an endemic problem of international relations in the early modern period, and by poisoning rebel leaders and plausible sympathizers, including Flaminio Paleologus, the last natural heir of the Dukes of Montferrat.[87] The remaining rebels, pushed into a corner by a war of attrition they did not have the resources to win, made a final, desperate gambit by occupying Verolengo, a strategic town from which, ideally under Savoyard protection, they could harass Gonzaga territories. Nearby Chivasso had been in Savoyard hands since 1435, and Verolengo itself had been a source of extreme contention at the 1559 Peace of Cateau-Cambrésis, making it a natural beachhead in Gonzaga lands. This was the complex context in which 'bandits' stormed Verolengo that fateful winter's eve of 1569, proclaiming a 'republic' that never would be. Upon hearing news that Gonzaga had directed three hundred troops to Verolengo, and with Emanuele Filiberto having withdrawn his support for Casalese rebels involved in the endeavor already the previous night, doubtlessly in the face of pressure from greater powers than himself, the 'bandits' merely sacked the place before disbanding, a large number of them soon arrested by Gonzaga's troops.[88]

As criminal proceedings began against the attackers of Verolengo, they were systematically described as 'bandits' from Mantua and Montferrat who acted with the 'help and succor of many foreigners and from other dominions', but it soon became clear that this had been no normal act of banditry. Not only had more than *one hundred* 'bandits' stormed Verolengo, but they had charged '*mano armata et bandiere spiegate a modo de soldati',* that is 'with weapons in hand and banners flying like soldiers'. Soon, in fact, as the proceedings unfolded they were branded 'rebelli e banditi' by the court, and it was eventually revealed that their war crimes had been more politically loaded than first expected; witnesses soon attesting that the bandits in question ostensibly had stormed the fortress 'shouting Savoy, Savoy, Liberty, Liberty'. We will probably never know whether they had meant that liberty lay with the Savoy or that the Savoy could help them reclaim their liberty, but their explicit—if possibly imputed—aim of establishing a 'republic', however chimerical, might suggest the latter. In the end, the 'criminals' were found guilty of having with '*insegna spiegata',* that is with 'flying banner', entered 'Verolengo in the dominion of Montferrat shouting the name of another Prince and provoking the people to depart from their due obedience to their true supreme and natural ruler'. In short, they were found guilty of '*robbaria forza pubblica, rebellione et delicto di offesa maestà',* that is robbery, the venerable Roman crime of *vis publica* or violent acts against the integrity of public institutions, rebellion, and *lèse-majesté.* A perfect criminal cocktail for which it seems at least 23 Montferrine 'rebels' were hanged and 19 foreign 'bandits' sent to the galleys for life after having their goods confiscated.[89]

There are endless ways in which the archival classification of the 'bandit' in this case becomes problematic. Against the stereotype of the rugged rural bandit dressing the part of an untamed outsider to social conventions, these 'bandits' and 'rebels' attacked Verolengo with all the trappings of an official army, 'with weapons in hand and banners flying like soldiers'. Symbolically, the difference was immense, and their cries for 'liberty' were quite specific in their social and political content. This was not the vague longing for halcyon days of Hobsbawm's 'revolutionary traditionalist' bandits, but a concrete equation of capitalized 'Liberty' with the recent rule of the 'Savoy'.[90] Far from 'pre-political', in Hobsbawm's famous formulation, banditry was in this case a vehicle of territorial aggrandizement closer, certainly, to covert military and mercenary operations than to freebooting in the classical sense.[91] The siege was manifestly not an act of resistance against 'modernizing' processes, though the moniker of '*banditi*' technically was quite correct, etymologically the past principle of '*bandire*' or banish (though their name also might have derived from their punishment having been 'announced' by an official decree or '*bando*', or from the very fact that they acted against such a decree).[92] Bandits were literally outlaws, banished from the political sphere of law itself, and in this meaning at least correctly equated with 'rebels', understood to mean people waging war on their own polity with the aim of changing it fundamentally, from the Latin *rebellare*, or 'wage war against'. A politicized bandit was by default a rebel, but the real question arises of whether all bandits, by virtue of their very acts, are not in a Ciceronian sense political precisely by virtue of their anticivic and indeed antisocial telos.[93]

The motley crew of Verolengo is striking in this context for several reasons. It was comprised of rebels banished from Casale, unwilling to accept the yoke of the Gonzaga and resorting to common acts of banditry, as well as sundry Savoy sympathizers, and they attacked, with the aim of conquering, a nearby town which also was in the process of negotiating its new civic identity at the exact border between competing and frequently hostile polities seeking, in a Schmollerian sense, to solidify their territorialities. They ultimately did not enjoy the support of the Savoy authorities, and were indeed expelled from their lands when they sought to retreat to nearby Chivasso after their plans unraveled, but consciously adopted the symbolic trappings of officialdom to combat political processes operating above their proverbial heads and to which they had remained powerless observers. There are in the end ways in which they *were* tragic 'social bandits' of the Hobsbawmian type precisely in their attempt to proclaim they were not bandits at all. Their calls for a 'republic' were, as such, a way of formulating, however vaguely, the need to be active participants in their own political lives. They might simply have been attempting to exchange one semi-absolutist ruler for another, but their choice nonetheless amounted to a lethal vote of civic identity.

But the line between 'bandit' and 'rebel' in Montferrat, and the ultimate futility of the vote at Verolengo—not only in terms of the conquest failing but in the larger Schmollerian sense that both competing polities ultimately would disappear anyway as civil spheres were consolidated—had in the final instance been decided not by local protagonists but by the distant sovereignties of Philip II and Maximilian II. There is in the end something vaguely Pirandellian about this band of bandits in search of historical actors willing to play them in the European theatre of war.[94] Their numbers were after all considerable, given that Pizarro after all had conquered the whole Inca Empire a few decades earlier with a mere 160 men, but the point was that while both Emanuele Filiberto of Savoy and Guglielmo

Gonzaga sought to give laws to Montferrat, they themselves had come to operate in a grander context in which even greater powers gave them the law in turn. It was a notable chapter in the Schmollerian process of European unification, in which ever larger territories slowly and often painfully were integrated, pacified, and socialized—one is tempted to say disciplined or normalized—by increasingly centralized but still competing sovereignties. This process of course occurred unevenly, haphazardly, and not, as the case of Verolengo illustrates, without cost, both human and political, but the ultimate tragedy of solidifying state territorialities—with concomitant commercial socializations—in Europe undermining the social coherence of the continent itself would only increase in intensity. Verolengo was, as such, a late convulsion of that first transition explored by Schmoller, from Lilliputian states based on the territorial claims of medieval communes to the increasingly larger regional states of the Baroque.

Economic bandits

Indeed, such mechanisms of imperial competition and painful geographic consolidation elucidated by the events at Verolengo were by no means merely a Renaissance phenomenon. They remained all too evident throughout the long eighteenth-century, though inflected by changing circumstances and by the process of territorial amalgamation itself. The most intensely Machiavellian period of territorial flux in Italy was in effect over by the mid eighteenth-century, a relative calm that would be overturned only in wake of the French Revolution. Key regions in Northern Italy had consolidated, with varying degrees of geographic and political coherence and independence, in wake of the War of Austrian Succession under the aegides of Austrian, Spanish, and French powers. Italy's relative decline simultaneously secured its integrity and safeguarded it from potentially explosive confrontations such as that over Casale Monferrato. Yet, the borderland politics of the North Italian hinterlands continued to dominate political and economic thinking throughout the age of reason, and banditry remained a constant source of exceptions and challenges to contemporary logics of centralized territoriality.[95]

During the harsh winter of 1725, for example, the citizenry of Valsesia, an Alpine valley on the border between Lombardy and Piedmont under Savoy control since 1703, were finally allowed to carry firearms 'by Measure of the Damages that said Valley suffers for bordering on diverse foreign states, exposed to Thieves, Vagabonds, and Bandits and infested, and hurt by Wolves, Foxes, Bears, and other ferocious beasts'. And it was particularly the 'assassinations' committed there by 'people from foreign States and jurisdictions' that caught the attention of central authorities. Where the state could not protect its citizens, citizens were given the right to protect themselves, a long-established political practice in early modern Italy.[96] Not surprisingly, foreign bandits, agents not merely of foreign jurisdictions but of ochlocracy, preyed upon the Valsesians where they were most vulnerable. They struck at night, and particularly during the long winter-months of increased darkness, and they struck marketplaces and the roads leading to them, posing 'a grave danger to the people competing in the markets'. Not only that, but they were well informed enough to follow the scheduled market-day throughout the valley, striking localities precisely on the days in which they hosted merchants and traders.[97]

Like elsewhere in Europe, roads in northern Italy were fragile investments that were monitored, contested, and of course often taxed heavily, and regulations for their use—such as a common prohibition to carry arms while traveling—were simultaneously socializing *and* sources of increased vulnerability to beasts and bandits of the Valsesian kind. Roads were understood to be the means by which commerce and communication could unify and crucially socialize territories, contributing to peace, economic development, and spatial sovereignty, but there was nothing automatic about this process. And, contrary to certain ideological shibboleths, early modern roadbuilding and infrastructural maintenance—not to mention canal-bulding—was not simply the achievement of enlightened self-interest.[98] Individuals lobbied for roads and for protection to peddle their wares where they found good prices, and governments sought to help them do so as a means of promoting welfare, tranquility, and territorial security alike. There would seem to be few areas of contemporary civil economy where private and public interests overlapped more synergetically than with regards to infrastructure, but where recent literature has explored tensions in the infrastructure state with regards to whether roads should be private or public, toll-driven or 'free', it is easy to forget that lives were lost in early modern Europe over a very different kind of roadside liberty: namely the freedom to trade without being robbed and killed.[99]

The Norwegian-American economist Thorstein Veblen would, much later, employ terms such as 'interstitial disturbance' and 'sabotage' to describe acts of destructive rent-extraction at nodal points of capitalism, and banditry is perhaps the very oldest form of such behavior, and at times posed such threats to trade and to make regional systems of trade inoperative.[100] Bandits were, of course, in this sense entrepreneurs, but resisted ongoing attempts to clarify, codify, and normalize what sorts of rent-seeking activities were deemed fruitful to society as a whole. Thinking geographically about Steven L. Kaplan's differentiation between the 'marketplace' and the 'market principle' in early modern Europe, banditry in Valsesia was implicitly recognized to be one of the gravest threats to the peaceful transition from one to the other, from the market understood to be a policed site of exchange to the market understood as a form of social organization, a mindset reflecting Genovesi's concept of seeing 'the world with the eyes of a merchant'.[101] You might still be able to exchange goods on Tuesdays in the Valsesian township of Borgo d'Ale with bandits roaming the countryside, but the arteries connecting this to the rest of the economy—and importantly to the wider social tissue of the body politic and even other polities—were weakened, if not severed, by the very threat of lawlessness.[102] And, as Adam Smith would argue, 'as it is the power of exchanging that gives occasion to the division of labour, so the extent of this division must always be limited by the extent of that power, or, in other words, by the extent of the market'.[103] What precisely Smith meant with this oft-quoted argument is of course debatable, for though he evidently did not merely intend the physical extent of a given marketplace when referring to 'the market', he cannot

realistically have aluded to twenty-first century conceptions of a self-regulating
economy either. Perhaps he intended something in between—not unlike what the
Accadèmia dei pugni referred to with phrases such as '*il mercato*' and
'*l'economia*'—referring to the actual territoriality of political economy. In his
Meditations on Political Economy, Verri would similarly explain the territoriality
of commercial society thus:

> Cities are in the country what marketplaces are in a city. They are the point of
> reunion, where sellers and buyers meet. The capital is in turn to the cities
> what they are to the country.[104]

Markets, in short, were geographical and even sociological metaphors for political
communities themselves. But what did such marketplaces look like?

Giovanni Michele Graneri was one of the greatest painters of so-called
Bamboccio-scenes in the eighteenth century, a tradition born from the popular
paintings of the seventeenth-century Dutch painter Pieter van Laer, known as '*Il
Bamboccio*', and his hyper-realistic depiction of an Enlightenment marketsquare
might be illuminating in this regard. As the baroque painter and art-critic Giovanni
Battista Passeri described the work of van Laer and his 'imitators', they were
'unique in representing the quintessence of truth', so that their 'paintings appear
to us like an open window [...] without divergence or alteration'.[105] Graneri's
1752 *Market in San Carlo Square* today hangs in the museum of Palazzo Madama
in Turin, and depicts one of the central market squares of the old Savoy capital.[106]
Between gamblers, monks, inspectors, soldiers, priests, playing children, and
public orators, market stalls offered everything from coal, firewood, textiles, and
pottery through a wealth of meat and produce to cheese, bread, and grain,
and surrounding it were Turin's traditional porticoed streets lined with more
permanent shops and cafés. Donkeys, cows, and horses have brought goods from
afar, and people from all walks of life, from nobles to street urchins, have been
drawn to the scene. Significantly, a minor brouhaha unfolds next to an armed
official in the bottom right corner, thus underscoring the simultaneously
carnivalesque and deeply regulated nature of early modern economic life; a melee
of arms both visible and invisible.[107] In the background loom not only a regiment
of Savoy troops but also the twin churches of Santa Cristina and San Carlo,
powerful reminders that trade was embedded in a civic as well as spiritual world.
Graneri's painting envisioned the market as a civic site, a locus of commerce, but
it was far from exhaustive of its own meaning, extent, and importance for
eighteenth-century life, or for that matter of Smith's definition.

For 'the market' so realistically rendered by Graneri was a nodal point of an
increasingly complex economic system of production and exchange, drawing on
and connecting Alpine pastures and coastal free ports; the Po river and the Indian
Ocean; local urban labor and transoceanic goods and resources, from coffee beans
to the South American metals used as currency throughout Europe.[108]
Simultaneously, however, such markets emanated norms and legal practices
through the prism of policing and regulation in relation both to time and space;

Figure 13.14 Giovanni Michele Graneri, 'Market in San Carlo Square', Palazzo Madama, Turin, 1752. DEA/A DE GREGORIO / age fotostock.

passports were issued for the movement of grain and other goods in relation to such markets, and the rhytms of life were adapted to its clock. In both cases, the Smithian 'extent of the market' depended on the undisturbed territoriality of economic life, on functioning roads and navigable seaways connecting ever more distant producers and consumers, and ultimately on the civilization of expanding territories in the sense of the spatial subjection of nature to one or more *civitates*. Far from capitalist champions of creative destruction, bandits and pirates were agents of entropy in this context, causing Valsesia to suffer a breakdown of commercial society and of civil economy, limiting not merely social territorial cohesion but also the extent of the market and therefore avenues for economic development.

The symbolic effects of rearming the citizenry were, in this context, powerful, and, in light of the venerable principle of political philosophy according to which subjects owed sovereigns allegiance in exchange for physical protection, could only be conceptualized as a devolution, a resolute step backwards on the accepted trajectory of civilization. As Beccaria would write regarding the temptation to offer 'bounties' to encourage vigilantism in his *On Crimes and Punishments*, by empowering his citizens to take the law into their own hands a 'sovereign' only 'shows his weakness', for 'those who have the power to defend themselves do not seek to buy it'. Such measures were 'the expedients of weak nations, whose laws are nothing but hasty repairs to a building in ruins that is crumbling on all sides', a sign that the polity was not 'enlightened' and lacked 'good faith and mutual trust;' that it lacked, in short, the basic building-blocks of a civil economy, the 'faith' and 'trust' threatened by the so-called enemies of mankind.[109] The Valsesian case was a painful reminder not merely of the incongruence between states and markets but also of that between the ambitions of developing states and the very real limits to their capacity for enforcement in the eighteenth century. For if it is easy to imagine an idealized process in which expanding states galvanized banditry to the point where they had to strengthen their territorial capacity, only to further expand and encourage banditry and so on ad infinitum, it was, to the extent that such a progression reflected a historical reality in which the state needed bandits and vice versa, as violent as it was slow, partial, and haphazard, not to mention deeply dependent on spatial and geographical factors. As Thomas W. Gallant has argued, 'bandits helped make states, and states made bandits'.[110]

Some of the greatest preoccupations of Northern Italian statesmen during the years in which Beccaria penned his celebrated work indeed involved very similar problems of banditry, commercial society, and state territoriality, and in precisely the Appennine areas that later would host Lizzani's *Achtung! Banditi!*[111] Though the borders between French-backed Savoy and Habsburg Milan with some exceptions were reconsolidated in wake of the end of the War of Austrian Succession in 1748, this cannot be appreciated outside of a context in which major powers such as the French and Austrian Empires really did not wish to risk continental warfare because of contested townships on the Po plain. The main problem in the region was facilitated, if not caused, by the small Republic of Genoa, whose diehard independence and mercenary approach to international allegiances made territorial disputes increasingly problematic at the time. Important passes through the Appennines, like Serravalle Scrivia, which in the past repeatedly had changed hands between Genoa, Savoy, and Milan, and furthermore hosted numerous feudal domains of the Holy Roman Empire, were particularly contested for political as well as economic reasons, and entire borderland villages like Pozzolo became renowned as havens for smugglers, bandits, and 'villains' in general, landlocked Tortugas at the core of the Old World.[112]

These outlaw enclaves were particularly damaging for regional and long-distance trade because the Appennines represented a nodal point of commerce between the Tyrrhenian Sea and the Alps, connecting the Mediterranean to Northern Europe. Territorial integrity had been high on the list of diplomatic concerns for the Piedmontese ambassador to Genoa at the time, and Gabriele Verri, father of Beccaria's sometime mentor and nemesis Pietro Verri and a leading statesman heading numerous territorial negotiations, considered the state's failure to neutralize this threat to be the most manifest sign of contemporary Milanese decline.[113] Much like the Gonzaga had once risked reprisals for tracking bandits out of their own jurisdiction, international scandals were in fact frequently caused in eighteenth-century Italy when authorities arrested bandits across often remarkably porous, not to mention shifting, borders, whether Milanese, Genoese, or Savoyard, most famously when a special regiment of French troops kidnapped the great smuggler and bandit Louis Mandrin across the border in Savoy Rochefort in 1755.[114]

The problem intensified markedly around the time of Beccaria's writings in the early 1760s, however, and literally hundreds of letters passed, sometimes daily, between the Habsburg Plenipotentiary of Milan Count Firmian, the Savoy Plenipotentiary of Turin Count de Viry, and the Austrian State Chancellor Wenzel Anton von Kaunitz in Vienna regarding the problem, the dangers it posed, and the means of resolving it. The tax represented in terms of time and resources by what they came to call '*l'affare de' malviventi*' was staggering.[115] 'Bandits', the synonym for which no longer was 'rebels' but 'villains [*malviventi*]' in official documents, were 'infected', outsiders to the body politic to be 'extirpated', 'destroyed', and 'exterminated' to secure 'public tranquility'. The basic problem was simple. Writing to Firmian, Kaunitz undermined his commitment to pursue by 'all means, both ordinary and extraordinary, as well as economic, the great object of assuring the security and tranquility of the state'.[116] By occupying the mountainous, liminal lands in the Appennines where Piedmont, the old Montferrat, Lombardy, and Genoese Liguria intersected, outlaws were able to safely harass the populations of Savoy and Milan, scuttling across the border to enjoy voluntary exile in Genoa whenever attempts were made to persecute them.[117] In Firmian's words, these attacks amounted to 'scandalous atrocious incursions' challenging the sovereignty of their territories.[118] The obvious solution was suggested by the Count of Viry, who proposed a 'Convention with the Republic of Genoa' to 'remove' the 'asylum of Genoese lands', which bandits 'abuse to keep themselves safe and within reach of performing new crimes', a situation which rendered Savoy and Milan 'dependent on the arbitrariness and caprice of the government of Genoa' to the point where it was 'salutary' and 'necessary' to do something.[119] In the political vocabulary of the day, Genoa's support for the bandits in the area posed a clear and present danger to the sovereignty and independence of its neighbors.

Both the Savoy and Milan governments deployed reinforcements to the borderlands, and experts were called in to provide the respective governments with 'the desired enlightenment' regarding how to act.[120] Nothing less than a 'cordon of troops' was laid across the Appennines to 'arrest, or at least keep away' the bandits 'infesting the Societies' and 'the peace of the Subjects'.[121] Though these bandits superficially had a politically more limited scope than their Casalese antecedents, terrorizing merchants and looting priestly abodes with equal exuberance, the consequences of their actions themselves remained profoundly political.[122] Bandits broke into houses with skeleton keys and by leveling walls; bound people up by the dozens, including children and pregnant women, sometimes so roughly that they died; they maimed and they slew; and they stole everything from cash and gold through commercial merchandize to furniture, clocks, and ladies' underwear. They could move in armed bands of more than twenty, wounding and killing soldiers they encountered. And, to the great consternation also of the Genoese, they particularly haunted 'merchants' along the 'public roads', taking their funds, their goods, and at times their lives.[123]

The gravity of the situation is evident from contemporary descriptions of particular incidents, including one in July of 1764 in which ten bandits occupying a bridge along one of the commercial arteries across the Appennines opened fire on a contingent of 16 grenadiers, the military elite of the Enlightenment. As the officials reported in parenthesis, this was 'an evident sign that they [the bandits] believed themselves to be in a secure place'.[124] Banditry, in short, was usurping the territorial security of the solidifying states of Northwestern Italy. Military campaigns themselves were in the end deemed insufficient unless they were able to 'cut the root of the evil', the 'source of which' was 'the free retreat and security such people [bandits] enjoy in the Dominion of Genoa'.[125] By the spring of 1764, Vienna itself got involved in pressuring Genoa to rethink its asylum policies in talks with Savoyard and Milanese officials, but the problem seemed to merely increase in intensity.[126]

A venerable tradition of diplomatic relations, and an important origin of practical international law, can be traced to early conventions to mutually expel wanted criminals and to collaborate in struggles with bandits, and progressively so during the early modern period through formalized standing extradition agreements.[127] That said, it was certainly not the only way to think about the international ramifications of banditism at the time. As the great reason of state theorist Scipione Ammirato wrote against the long tradition of Machiavellianism in political theory in his 1594 *Discourses on Cornelius Tacitus*, because of 'reason of State, a Prince must favour the bandits of another Prince'. Bandits, in short, could be strategic weapons in international competition, and though they could undermine one's interests, hope was that they would weaken neighbours more.[128] Mutual agreements to extradite bandits were, as such, keystones in the gradual construction of robust international institutions to facilitate trade, communication, and, ultimately, an expanding sphere of civility. Diplomats knew that Lombardy and Savoy had enjoyed precisely such a treatise for more than a decade already, and the example of a comparable treatise between Lombardy and Genoa dating back to 1598 was dusted off for good measure as well.[129] A similar pact was suggested again with Habsburg involvement in the form of a 'Convention for the Reciprocal Delivery of Bandits and Villains' between all the States of Northern Italy on 18 May 1765, a bold document proposing and codifying this limited, but crucial sphere of international law.[130] Its main impetus and force can neither be reduced to facilitating rehabilitation and vengeance, nor to apprehensions regarding territorial integrity, though both these concerns certainly played a part in the process. The pact was, strikingly, deemed necessary because of the dangers posed by banditry 'to the public peace, to life, and not the least to the support of the subjects and the liberty of trade [*libertà del Commercio*], which equally benefits their interests', in other words which were equally important to their welfare.[131] International penal law was here conceived of as a tool for creating, by projected civic and importantly *civil* force, a space in which trade could be 'free' (though, needless to say, heavily taxed), with a remarkably economic vocabulary of 'interests' and 'benefits' to regulate the sorts of profit-seeking deemed acceptable in civil society; the sorts, in short, mirroring Verri's contemporary identification the roots of 'public happiness' in the alignment of 'private and public interests'.[132]

The problem with the proposed treaty to end banditry, however, and the reason why it lay dead in the water from the outset, resulted form the incommensurability of legal orders and the territorial tensions of the Schmollerian moment. Different sovereign polities ranked the same crimes differently, and a uniform exchange of criminals, even if limited only to those demanding capital punishment, would collapse different criminal taxonomies in inopportune ways. Genoa had namely suffered its own interstitial problems in recent years, resulting in a territorial fragmentation that was supported de facto by both Savoy and Milan. The ancient port city of Sanremo had revolted against Genoese rule and declared allegiance with Savoy in 1753, mostly as a result of heavy duties and taxes levied on the territory at a time of economic turmoil following the British naval bombardments of 1745, and though Genoa had ruthlessly reimposed its dominion over the city numerous Sanremese rebels remained at large in Northern Italy.[133] Similarly, Genoa had lost control of the island of Corsica when, under the revolutionary Pasquale Paoli's influence, the island began its independent republican experience in 1755, a dramatic experiment which gained European fame for vaunting the first ever constitution based on 'Enlightenment' principles.[134]

Initially, Genoese envoys were in effect positively inclined towards the suggested treaty, sharing many of the preoccupations of their neighbors. They too worried about the 'infestation', how it might 'perturb the public peace', and what 'bandits' prowling along the main 'public roads' would do to the 'liberty of commerce', in some documents even underlined for emphasis as *'libertà del Commercio'*.[135] In a secret, numerically coded missive, Genoa's agent in Turin further noted the 'benefits' that might result from a state of perpetual friendship' between the states of Northern Italy, yet realpolitik stood resolutely in the way.[136] Genoa namely had ulterior reasons to fear for what their envoys repeatedly would refer to as their 'domestic affairs' and the 'unbendable principles of domestic rights', protected by the 'full, free, and independent Sovereignty of our city and district', that is the territorial claims of the Genoese Republic.[137] For while these negotiations were underway, Genoa's agent in Turin was hunting down Sanremese spies in the Piedmontese capital and even sending coded rumors that Savoy troops clandestinely might be headed to San Remo to support its rebels with the help of Habsburg 'intelligence'.[138] The *'Affare dei Malviventi'*, in short, seemed able to precipitate an all out war over the tension between sovereignty and spatial socialization. All the states involved sought to 'civilize' their territories, but the interplay between them rendered the process both more contentious and more fragile both locally and globally.

A convention between Savoy, Milan, and Genoa securing the exchange of capital crimes would in the final instance exchange Genoese bandits for political exiles from Corsica and Sanremo who lived outside of Liguria under the protection of the Holy Roman Emperor, but who in Genoa were guilty of *'lèse-majesté'*.[139] In fact, Genoa would only pardon the surviving Sanremese rebels in 1775.[140] Though negotiations would continue for more than a year, it was already evident by the late summer of 1764 that the *'Affare dei Malviventi'* would not be resolved diplomatically within the parameters of existing territorial sovereignties. In an official dispatch, the Genoese agent described a meeting with the Viennese ambassador to Turin who told him the inclusion of 'the crime of rebellion' among those qualifying for reciprocal extradition had 'put fire' to the entire project, but in a coded letter he could be more frank:

> In the above described discussion I had with the Viennese Minister regarding the reasons why the Negotiations over the Treaty collapsed, he added that he had been told that the King of Sardinia [ie. of Savoy] as '*Vicario dell'Impero*' could never have considered the men of San Remo to be rebels.[141]

The convention therefore failed, after numerous 'vain conferences', and a later Savoyard analyst put the blame for this squarely on Genoa's shoulders for not differentiating between simple banditry and political misdeeds of 'Rebellion and *lèse-majesté*' within the category of capital crimes. That said, even he accepted that the Genoese objections remained 'well founded' in the still rigorously lupine world of international relations, a stance even Kaunitz came to adopt in private correspondence with Firmian in the summer of 1766.[142]

Legal scholars have traced the long and rich history of extraditions to the second millennium BCE, when a pattern first clearly emerged of sovereigns in the Middle East exchanging bandits as well as political and religious criminals—the ones which, given the technology of the time, were deemed most disruptive to authority—and generally agree that the extradition of non-political crimes only appeared and gradually was normalized in wake of the French Revolution.[143] What today is known as the 'political offence exception', that is a clause in extradition treatises specifically exempting crimes of a political nature from extradition, was first codified in Belgium in 1833, an event that ostensibly overturned the millennial history of extraditions by shifting their purpose from safeguarding political and spiritual authority to one of enforcing domestic law.[144] The history of extradition-treatises in early modern Italy suggests that the use of international diplomatic and legal measures to legalize domestic territories and thereby 'provide to the public peace' preceded the French Revolution by decades, and that states on the Italian peninsula actively sought to introduce a political offence clause already at mid-century to safeguard international trade and infrastructure.[145]

These treatises lie at the conceptual core of the tragedy of '*economia civile*', ever torn between the competing civilizing policies of territorial polities and the larger goals of peaceful international interaction. By its very nature, Genoa's sovereignty trumped measures that risked debilitating its authority, even if the Doge and Senate were all too aware of the advantages of peaceful international trade and collaboration in the region. With their interests in this sphere aligned, Savoy and Milan continued to sign criminal extradition treaties throughout the century, and all three states began committing greater resources to the fighting bandits in their territories. Genoa increased not only the salaries of their policing forces and appointed a '*capitano contro banditi*' or 'Antibandit Captain' in all their communal militias in these years, they also established rich bounties for the capture of such outlaws.[146] Even so, the problem of banditry in the Appennines would only be durably resolved in the wake of World War II, and would occur

CONVENZIONE

Per l'arreſto dei Banditi, e Malviventi frà lo Stato Pontificio per una parte, e gli Stati della Lombardia Auſtriaca dipendente da S.M.R.I. per l'altra.

PER provvedere alla pubblica quiete non meno dello Stato Eccleſiaſtico, che delli Stati Auſtriaci della Lombardia turbata dalle Perſone Malvagie, e Facinoroſe, fino dal Meſe di Luglio dell'Anno 1750. la Santità di Noſtro Signore Papa BENE-DETTO XIV. felicemente Regnante, e la Maeſtà della Imperatrice, e Regina ſtabilirono una Convenzione, colla quale ſi determinava il modo di procedere alla conſegna delli reſpettivi Sudditi con i Capitoli ſeguenti ſottoſcritti dal Signor Cardinal Valenti Segretario di Stato di Sua Santità, e dal Signor Cardinal Millini Miniſtro Plenipotenziario di Sua Maeſtà in queſta Corte, autorizati ſpecialmente à queſto atto da loro reſpettivi Sovrani.

I. I Banditi per ſentenza di pena capitale, che li dichiara eſpoſti alla pubblica vendetta, dagli Stati di Sua Santità, o della Lombardia Auſtriaca, non poſſano in modo alcuno abitare, nè dimorare in alcuna Città, Terra, Luogo, e Diſtretto di eſſi Dominj, e ſe ſaranno ritrovati dentro di eſſi, debbano eſſer preſi dagli Ufficiali di Giuſtizia, o Milizia, e Comandante, che ſi troverà ſopra luogo, e conſegnarſi reciprocamente à Miniſtri del Dominio, onde ſono, e ſaranno banditi, e non ſolamente potranno eſſere impunemente offeſi, ed anche ucciſi, quando nell'atto della Cattura ſi opponeſſero alla medeſima con Armi, mà ancora quando foſſero ritrovati alla Campagna; e chi li ammazzerà, oltre l'impunità, potrà conſeguire anche i premj, che ſi ritrovaſſero allora per Grida propoſti contro tali Banditi, ed all'incontro chi darà a' medeſimi albergo, ajuto, ſoccorſo, ò favore, incorrerà le pene impoſte dal-

le

Figure 13.15 'Convention for the Arrest of Bandits and Villains between the Papal States on the One Hand and Austrian Lombardy on the Other', 1750. Scan of document from private colllection, made by author.

only within a radically different regional context in which the sovereignties involved in the '*Affare dei Malviventi*' (with the exception of distant Habsburg Vienna, itself undergoing a parallel process of realignment) had been absorbed into a larger national unit of authority encompassing the Italian peninsula. And, as the Schmollerian Moment would have predicted, this national unit itself soon gave way to an even greater territorial form of sovereignty in the European Union, the growing pains of which will remain evident for years to come.

Beccaria's bandits

In Beccaria's formulation of the social contract discussed elsewhere, individuals invoked sovereignty by investing it with a part of their natural liberty, in the process creating an authority in turn devoted to defending the liberties of its individual constituents and, importantly, terrestrial justice, which the Milanese reformer equated explicitly with sociability itself.[147] Yet this partial sublimation of individual liberty into the greater liberty offered by subjection to their sovereign was not enough, for men were not angels. The need for punishment arose for Beccaria to combat 'the despotic spirit of every individual' and the universal instinct to 'withdraw not only his own share but also to usurp that belonging to others'.[148] So pessimistic was indeed Beccaria's anthropology—which took criminal behavior to be inevitable in a rather Ciceronian fashion—that he resolutely rejected the idea that such a balanced system could have emerged voluntarily: 'No man ever freely surrendered a portion of his own liberty for the sake of the public good; such a chimera appears only in fiction' for 'every man sees himself as the center of all the world's affairs'.[149]

It is therefore all the more striking how Beccaria, who praised Antonio Genovesi on many other occasions, resolutely took his distance from the ways in which the tradition of '*economia civile*' he represented had dealt with enemies of mankind, outsiders to its paradigm. True, Beccaria agreed with Genovesi, citizens had given up parts of their liberty to imbue a sovereign entity with the power to maintain justice and thus, ultimately, sociability, but they had crucially not given it power over life and death. As such, the 'death penalty is not a *right*', he argued, but rather 'the war of a nation against a citizen'. The only case in which Beccaria could accept an execution was, again, in the hypothetical case in which someone 'retains such connections and such power that he endangers the security of the nation even when deprived of his liberty, that is when his very existence can provoke a dangerous revolution in the established form of government'.[150] Needless to say, the Genoese bandits harassing trade routes across the Appennines into the Po Valley posed no such existential threat to society, whatever their crimes against sociability and 'free trade'. And even though Beccaria favored 'banishment' as a punishment for serious misdeeds, he again resisted traditional logics of retributions by suggesting—extraordinarily influentially, one might add in hindsight—that the property of outlaws should not be confiscated by the state because most such crimes usually were born from conditions of poverty in the first place, and confiscations, hurting the innocent relatives of bandits, would merely serve to aggravate the cycle of destitution, crime, and injustice. The only way to structurally resolve the problem of banditry—even crime more generally— identified by Beccaria was to ensure more sociable ways of subsistence through popular enlightenment and a more equitable distribution of wealth, within and between nations.[151]

An early commentary Beccaria wrote on the fifth volume of Jean Le Rond D'Alembert's *Mélanges* supports this reading of *On Crimes and Punishments*. 'Experience' D'Alembert wrote, 'has convinced me that this world is a sort of forest invested by brigands. History further assures me that it has always been so'. To this Beccaria commented that these 'reflections' were 'in truth interesting', for they 'read in history the crimes of men, and discover their evil; from this he learns to forgive his contemporaries many defects which he sees deeply rooted in human nature, and which are a necessary consequence of the situations in which men find themselves'.[152] The task of Beccaria's legislator was to manipulate men's environments, to civilize the dark forests of the world and of the mind and make illegalities both more difficult and more consequential, maintaining proportionality between crimes and punishments but simultaneously assuring the 'certainty' of the latter.[153] In the important chapter of *On Crimes and Punishments* devoted to 'Public Peace', he wrote:

> Lighting the streets at public expense; guards posted in the various quarters of the city; the plain and moral discourses of religion confined to the silence and sacred peace of temples protected by the public authority; public speeches in support of public and private interests delivered in the nation's assemblies, in parliaments, or wherever the majesty of the sovereign resides—these are all effective means of preventing a dangerous clustering of popular passions.[154]

Banditry and religious extremism were, in Beccaria's scheme, enemies of civil and civic life to be fought with the enlightenment of roads as well as of minds. The 'certainty' of establishing such crimes of course required a notable capacity to monitor individual activity and enforce laws, which, at the time, often found itself diluted in line with the territorial expansion of early modern states. As he defined 'internal police' in his lectures on political economy, it 'covered all rules that contribute to good order and the ease of all the economic affairs of a state: cleanliness, security, and low prices [*buon mercato*] are the principal objects of every civil police'. As such, 'the custody of public roads and the security of the borders' were key preoccupations of said 'science', well-lit roads the vehicles for expanding the civic and economic sphere across dark territories; an ethos that appropriately found its apotheosis in the railway-linkages of Italian national unification in the nineteenth century.[155] Building on a prevalent metaphor at the time, Beccaria further emphasized the importance of a truly capillary distribution of roads to connect the lands of a polity:

> The roads are like canals in which fluids run in living bodies; and as in these it is not enough that they are devoid and free of any obstacles, but the minimal

and invisible channels have to be open and easy for the animating liquid to run through, so must not merely roads that lead indefatigable travelers to the dominant cities in political bodies be solid and durable, but also those which serve the entire distribution of marketable goods in all the diverse parts of a province. Taking care only of the so-called master roads while neglecting lateral roads, which are those which more than others serve to transport all things throughout the interior, is the greatest, but not therefore the least frequent political incoherence.[156]

Beccaria would, in effect, frequently return to the problem of infrastructure in his lectures, to 'difficult and scabrous roads', to 'defective canals', to the need to 'render transportation easier' by 'enlarging and consolidating roads' and building 'canals' in 'all possible directions'. These were 'immortal works that render sovereigns conquerers of their own nation: conquests consecrated by the thanks and prosperity of future generations, not cemented with the blood and laments of desolate provinces'. The territorialization of a political economy, in short, depended on its successful 'conquest', an argument that stood at odds with the classic dichotomy between conquest and commerce in the history of political economy. Commerce in effect required conquests, not only of nature but of people, such as bandits and Firmian's *malviventi*, resisting the expansion of a civil sphere over the land. In a discarded draft of his lectures, Beccaria similarly wrote of how the human condition itself, to escape the most primitive state of nature at the very beginning of civilization, required man's need 'to arm himself and defend himself against the assaults of ferocious beasts'.[157] Political economy was, for Beccaria, not an abstract discipline but one deeply grounded in the actual physical territory of a political community, much like he developed his theory of commercial sociability in a context of acute warfare on bandits. The *affare dei malviventi* was not a tangential preoccupation in Enlightenment Lombardy; it lay at the very core of its theory and practice of *economia civile*. As Verri put it in his *Meditations on Political Economy*, 'guai se la fede pubblica s'oscuri!'[158] 'Industry', he argued, could be 'animated' by 'bringing man closer to man', for:

> The further man is isolated from his similars, that much closer is he to the savage state; reversely, the closer he is to the state of industry and of culture, the closer he is to a larger group of people; and one must study every way possible of accosting man to man, village to village, city to city… Wherever there are taxes on internal transportation within the State, if the Legislator removes them he will effectively have accosted the cities among which the tax fell… Wherever there are roads that are difficult for transportation or dangerous for security, if a good government [*buon governo*] smoothes them and makes them easy and safe, it will have accosted between them all the lands and cities that communicate by way of that road.[159]

'Roads' had the unique power to 'multiply internal circulation' and therefore 'increase annual reproduction' or output. Infrastructure was a way to internal security, to economic development, and ultimately to power in international relations and to territorial socialization.[160] 'Roads' and 'bridges' were, Verri would reiterate as late as in wake of the French Revolution, the only way to connect 'the economy of the community' to 'the economy of the provinces' and finally to the 'general economy' of a State.[161]

But neither was this somehow a Lombard phenomenon. Geographical size has been a thorn in the side of political theorists for millennia.[162] Indeed, similar mechanisms by which the territorialization of political economies characterizing the expansion of central state organizations into formerly 'feudal' or simply unregulated regions generated banditry that in turn both necessitated increased centralized control and engendered a Manichean language of animalistic savagery and sociable civilization can be identified across cases as diverse as the Nile Delta at the time of the Roman Empire, Baroque Valencia, the thuggee in eighteenth and nineteenth-century British India, the *rampoks* or armed robberies plaguing Dutch Batavia a century later, and, of course, the Sicilian Mafia.[163] And though some such cases took the form of Hobsbawm's 'social banditry', most were far more opportunistic and haphazard in nature.[164] This was certainly the case in the early modern Appennines, and the *Accademia dei pugni*'s project to define a science of political economy and delineate forms of rent seeking amenable to social relations must be read in its context.

Similarly, these mechanisms do not merely pose a historical problem, as evident from the experiences of contemporary states still very much involved in expanding their presences internally such as Indonesia as well as from the birth of entirely new categories of criminal activity in wake of the most recent spatial, if digital and thus virtual, expansion of civil society.[165] As the elusive New York internet entrepreneur and owner of the legendary hacktivist website 4chan Chris Poole for example explained in a rare interview, 'manners are learned over a lifetime', and the problem posed by the new space of the internet was that 'easier to fall down the wrong path' because there were so few restraints and such a short history of instilling and enforcing appropriate manners. 'I've never been in a fight in real life. It's a lot of effort and hassle. On the net you need 55 seconds and you make trouble. It's just so easy', a general sentiment shared by the likes of Wikileak's Julian Assange.[166] Then, as today, the mechanism of state formation and its concomitant development of Ciceronian civil society demanded the tortuous socialization of individual activity across expanding territorial spaces, a process both galvanized and thwarted by the existence of competing loci of sovereignty.

Banditry and piracy are not, in the West, the problems they once were. But the ways that our forebears dealt with them, and the language of enmity to the human race, lingers on. American legal scholar John Yoo, the author of George W. Bush's infamous torture memos, has recently argued that even the Christian just war tradition would consider 'terrorists to be *hostis humani generis*, the enemy of all mankind, who [merit] virtually no protections under the [law]'. And, on another occasion, he mused that the status of 'illegal enemy combatant' was not new at all; 'what', he asked, after all, 'were pirates?'[167] Intending no offense to Genovesi, he and Yoo (and even Lorenzetti) share a fundamental notion about the bandit, the pirate, the outlaw. Indeed, the still-thriving notion that banditry (or piracy, or terrorism) and a just civil-economic order are true opposites has long been part of the Western tradition. Given our infatuation with the symbolically piratical, however, we have come to find ourselves in the tragic situation in which real-life cases of contemporary piracy like that in Somalia are refused the ennobling moniker of 'piracy', because, as leading business theorists have argued, simply 'committing an illegal act at sea does not make one a pirate'.[168] Having ennobled the symbolically piratical, we seem to have entirely lost touch with the reality of the crime, Somali pirates apparently being so bad they are not merely expelled from humanity but from human language as such.[169]

But another view has also persisted, one in which these polar opposites are not as far apart as we might believe or hope. We need only think of St. Augustine's justly famous remark in the early fifth century *City of God*: 'Remove justice and what are states *but* gangs of *bandits* on a large scale? And what are *bandit* gangs *but kingdoms* in miniature?'[170] It was in this tradition that the Milanese writer and revolutionary adventurer Count Giuseppe Gorani would complain that 'the finances of Joseph II were nothing but brigandage'.[171] Without justice, power could not be legitimate, opening for a penumbral world in which enlightened absolutist sovereigns and common bandits roamed the land with equal claim on moral authority. On the one hand, the bandit is the complete outsider, the threat to the commercial and civil order, the danger lurking at the edge of society. On the other, he is part of that order, the product of it, demanded by the economic and political ideas and practices at its core, and in many ways its mirror image.

For Beccaria, although the bandit is to be punished, reformed, or banished, he is not truly pushed outside humanity—indeed, he is imbued with inalienable rights by virtue of belonging to it, no matter his ostensible crimes. Rather than the antithesis of sociability and commerce that we saw in Genovesi, or the antithesis of good government we saw in the frescoes of Lorenzetti, Beccaria's bandit (or today's Somali pirate) is a product of society and of the Schmollerian Moment, a criminal but also a victim of poverty and social structures that themselves are *unjust* from the greater perspective of human sociability. Unlike Genovesi, who thought banditry the worst of crimes against society and rightly deserving of death, in Beccaria we ironically see something very much like a true Christian reciprocity, though of a wholly secular sort, a real sociability and nascent 'socialism' that makes the bandit an enemy of civil society (and, indeed, banishment is nothing else than civil death) but not an enemy of the human race. As such, Beccaria can ultimately be seen to represent a refinement, rather than a rejection, of these central tenets of 'civil economics', and a theorist of a veritable political economy based on human rights.[172]

Banditry was, in this sense, a neglected but important context for understanding not only the tradition of '*economia civile*' in Enlightenment in Italy but also the tortuous relationship between solidifying states, long-distance trade, and the international sphere at the time. Bandits were important, if often ignored, protagonists of the 'mercantilist' period, not merely practically but theoretically and conceptually. Whether explicitly political, as in Verolengo, or more privately rapacious, as in the Appennines, they were core symptoms at the margins of what might be called the Schmollerian Moment, in which the competitively expanding economic, social, and political spheres of once urban polities simultaneously facilitated and undermined the socialization of the world as such. And this was why any *just* project for perpetual peace, socializing the relations not merely between people but between peoples, had to begin with the basic rights of individuals rather than those of political authorities communal, regional, or national. For until the world becomes just and, in Beccaria's terms, 'socialized', the warning is that we might all be bandits.

Notes

1   *Achtung! Banditi!*, directed by Carlo Lizzani, Genoa: Cooperative Spettatori Produttori Cinematografici, 1951, on which see Eligio Imarisio, ed., *Achtung! Banditi!: Parole per film* (Recco: Le Mani, 2010).
2   See, for the venerable nature of this expression, Michael Broers, *Napoleon's Other War: Bandits, Rebels and their Pursuers in the Age of Revolutions* (Oxford: Peter Lang, 2010), 8; for its use in the context of Nazi Europe see Philip W. Blood, *Hitler's Bandit Hunters: The SS and the Nazi Occupation of Europe* (Washington, DC: Potomac Books, 2006), xvi.
3   Max Weber, "The Profession and Vocation of Politics," in id., *Political Writings*, ed. Peter Lassman and Ronald Speirs (Cambridge: Cambridge University Press, 1994), 309–369, at 310–311.
4   See the immense arc from Karl Polanyi, *Great Transformation: The Political and Economic Origins of Our Time,* ed. Fred Block with a foreword by Joseph E. Stiglitz (Boston: Beason Press, 2001), 60, 66, 71 and *passim* to Bernard E. Harcourt, *The Illusion of Free Markets: Punishment and the Myth of Natural Order* (Cambridge, MA: Harvard University Press, 2011), 242 and *passim* and Bruce R. Scott, *Capitalism: Its Origins and Evolution as a System of Governance* (Heidelberg: Springer, 2011), 178–179.
5   Annabel S. Brett, *Changes of State: Nature and the Limits of the City in Early Modern Natural Law* (Princeton: Princeton University Press, 2011), 1, 3, 5.
6   See, on Enlightenment banditry through the lens of smuggling, Michael Kwass, *Contraband: Louis Mandrin and the Making of a Global Underground* (Cambridge, MA: Harvard University Press, 2014). On banditry and borders, see also Rosario Villari, "Conclusioni," in Francesco Manconi, ed., *Banditismi mediterranei: Secoli XVI–XVII* (Rome: Carocci, 2003), 413–415, at 415.
7   Henri Pirenne, *Economic and Social History of Medieval Europe* (New York: Harcourt, Brace & Company, 1937), 216–217; Saskia Sassen, *Territory, Authority, Rights: From Medieval to Global Assemblages* (Princeton: Princeton University Press), 53 (for a fleeting reference to the existence of pirates and robbers, see p. 57); Michael Mann, "The Autonomous Power of the State: Its Origins, Mechanisms and Results," *Archives européennes de sociologie* 25 (1984), 185–213 and id., "Infrastructural Power Revisited," *Studies in Comparative International Development* 43/3–4 (2008), 355–365.
8   Bartolomeo Intieri to Antonio Cocchi, Napoli 8 August 1752, Archivio Baldasseroni Corsini, Florence, 290/4, 1r. On Genovesi see Sophus A. Reinert, *Translating Empire: Emulation and the Origins of Political Economy* (Cambridge, MA: Harvard University Press, 2011), 186–232. On the concept of 'economia civile' in contemporary Italian and more widely Catholic economics, see, for a foundational statement, Stefano Zamagni and Luigino Bruni, *Economia civile: Efficienza, equità, felicità pubblica* (Bologna: Il Mulino, 2004).

9   That said, the identification of this current with a refusal to accept the dichotomies of libertarianism and Marxism, and the 'state-market' antinomy valuably paves the way for a more historical and indeed realist approach to political economy, see Stefano Zamagni interviewed by Nicola Curci, *Economia ed etica: La crisi e la sfida dell'economia civile* (Brescia: Editrice 'La scuola', 2009), 72, 76.

10 For one particularly clear case of conceptual and terminological overlap, compare the various definitions of Beccaria's university chair in Wenzel Anton von Kaunitz-Rietberg to Karl Joseph von Firmian, 16 November 1767, in Barbara Costa, "'Un regolare sistema per la progressione degli studi': il ruolo di Gian Rinaldo Carli nella riforma degli studi e della censura (1765–1775)," in *Con la ragione e col cuore: Studi dedicati a Carlo Capra,* ed. Stefano Levati and Marco Meriggi (Milan: FrancoAngeli, 2008), 263–288, at 272 and Kaunitz-Rietberg to Firmian, 5 December 1768, in the voluminous Haus-, Hof- und Staatsarchiv, Österreichisches Staatsarchiv, Vienna, Austria, *Korrespondenz Lombardei 124,* 5r. Compare further to Gian Rinaldo Carli, "Piano per la cattedra di *Scienze Camerali* o sia di *Economia Civile*," 14 April 1768, in Angelo Mauri, "La cattedra di Cesare Beccaria," *Archivio storio italiano,* vol. 60, 1933, 199–262, at 233–235, but see now also Antonio Trampus, "Riforme politiche e 'pubblica felicità' negli scritti di Carli sul problema dell'educazione," *Quaderni Istriani: Contributi per la storia contemporanea della Venezia Giulia,* no. 5–6 (1991–1992), 13–40, at 32–34. Not that there were not clearly articulated arguments that Beccaria's chair was in one thing rather than another; see the famous example of Giuseppe [Joseph von] Sperges to Cesare Beccaria, 27 March 1769, in *Edizione Nazionale delle Opere di Cesare Beccaria,* vol. V: *Carteggio (parte 2: 1769–1794),* ed. Carlo Capra, Renato Pasta, and Francesca Pino Pongolini (Milan: Mediobanca, 1996), 47–48, suggesting Beccaria did not really teach 'cameralism' at all, on which see Franz Pascher, 'Freiherr Joseph von Sperges auf Palenz und Reisdorf', PhD Dissertation, University of Vienna, 1965 [e-dissertation with altered pagination, 2009], 109.

11 See among others Pasquale Pasquino, "Theatrum Politicum: The Genealogy of Capital – Police and the State of Prosperity," in *The Foucault Effect: Studies in Governmentality; with Two Lectures by and an Interview with Michel Foucault,* ed. Graham Burchell, Colin Gordon, and Peter Miller (Chicago: University of Chicago Press, 1991), 105–118.

12 See, among many others, Joel S. Migdal, *Strong Societies and Weak State: State-Society Relations and State Capabilities in the Third World* (Princeton: Princeton University Press, 1988).

13 A point that is often easy to forget in light of Hegel's subsequent work, see Stuart Elden, *The Birth of Territory* (Chicago: University of Chicago Press, 2013), 1 and *passim.*

14 Cicero, *Somnium Scipionis c3*; Thomas Hobbes, *Leviathan,* ed. Richard Tuck (Cambridge: Cambridge University Press, 1996), 9; Annabel Brett, *Changes of State* (Princeton: Princeton University Press, 2009), 1.

15 John M. Najemy, "The Medieval Italian City and the 'Civilizing Process,'" in *Europa e Italia/Europe and Italy: studi in onore di Giorgio Chittolini/Studies in Honour of Giorgio Chittolini,* ed. Paola Guglielmotti, Isabella Lazzarini, and Gian Maria Varanini (Florence: Firenze University Press, 2011), 355–369, meditating on Norbert Elias, *The Civilizing Process: Sociogenetic and Psychogenetic Investigations* (Oxford: Blackwell, 2000 [original German edition 1939]). Najemy's evidence also suggests the problems of investing the Protestant Reformation, or more particularly Calvinism, with as much transformative power as has been done in recent historiography, see for example Philip S. Gorski, *The Disciplinary Revolution: Calvinism and the Rise of the State in Early Modern Europe* (Chicago: University of Chicago Press, 2003). For caveats with regards to much literature on this 'civilizing process', see Andre

Wakefield, "Butterfield's Nightmare: The History of Science as Disney History," *History and Technology* 30/3 (2014), 232–251.

16 On the related Stoic tradition of political philosophy in early modern Europe, see Christopher Brooke, *Philosophic Pride: Stoicism and Political Thought from Lipsius to Rousseau* (Princeton: Princeton University Press, 2012).

17 On contemporary 'territoriality' see Elden, *The Birth of Territory*, 322–330.

18 I have previously referred to the multiplicity of vectors of economic and political sovereignty in the early modern world with the moniker '*baroquepunk*', see Sophus A. Reinert, "Rivalry: Greatness in Early Modern Political Economy," in *Mercantilism Reimagined: Political Economy in Early Modern Britain and its Empire*, ed. Philip Stern and Carl Wennerlind (Oxford: Oxford University Press, 2014), 348–370.

19 James Scott, *Seeing Like a State: How Certain Schemes to Improve the Human Condition Have Failed* (New Haven: Yale University Press, 1998), 2.

20 'Ordini stabiliti dal sig. governatore don Ferrando Gonzaga l'anno 1549 da osservarsi nel fare la misura generale dello Stato di Milano', Archivio del Comune di Cremona, *Misc. A, b. 146, cc. 124–125*, published in Ircas Nicola Jacopetti, *Il territorio agrario-forestale di Cremona nel catasto di Carlo V (1551–1561)* (Cremona: Annali della biblioteca statale e libreria civica di Cremona with the Camera di commercio industria artigianato e agricoltura, 1984), 192–194, quote from 192. On these themes in the respective traditions, see Antoine de Montchrestien, *Traicté de l'économie politique*, ed. Théodor Funk-Brentano (Paris: Plon, 1889), 34, quoted slightly differently and discussed in Pasquino, "Theatrum Politicum," 114; Alix Cooper, "'The Possibilities of the Land': The Inventory of 'Natural Riches' in the Early Modern German Territories," in *Oeconomies in the Age of Newton*, ed. Margaret Schabas and Neil DeMarchi (Durham: Duke University Press, 2003), 129–153; Ted McCormick, *William Petty and the Ambitions of Political Arithmetick* (Oxford: Oxford University Press, 2009).

21 On eighteenth-century changes, see among others Costanza Roggero Bardelli, "Fonti catastali sabaude: l'editto di Carlo Emanuele III per la Perequazione generale de' tribute del Piemonte (5 Maggio 1731)," in *La figura della città: I catasti storici in Italia*, ed. Angela Marino (Rome: Gangemi Editore, 1996), 49–59, 51–55. On their emulation, see for example Christine Lebeau, "Exchanging Taxation Projects in Eighteenth-Century Europe: The Case of Italian Cadasters," in *Global Debates about Taxation*, ed. Holger Nehring and Florian Schui (Basingstoke: Palgrave Macmillan, 2007), 21–35; Antonella Alimento, *Finanze e amministrazione: Un'inchiesta francese sui catasti nell'Italia del Settecento (1763–1764)*, 2 vols. (Florence: Leo S. Olschki, 2008). On the longer history of cadasters, see for example Federick Mario Fales, ed., *Censimenti e catasti di epoca neo-assira* (Rome: Tipografia Don Bosco, 1973); Roger J. P. Kain and Elizabeth Baigent, *The Cadastral Map in the Service of the State: A History of Property Mapping* (Chicago: The University of Chicago Press, 1992).

22 'Regio editto per la perequazione generale dei tribute nelle provincie del Piemonte [5 May 1731]', reproduced in Bardelli, "Fonti catastali sabaude," 49.

23 Gustav von Schmoller, *The Mercantile System and its Historical Significance* (New York: The Macmillan Company, 1897). On mercantilism and its historiography, see among others Lars Magnusson, *Mercantilism: The Shaping of an Economic Language* (London: Routledge, 1994) and now *Mercantilism Reimagined*.

24 Schmoller, *The Mercantile System*, 8, 14, 30.

25 Ibid., 48

26 Ibid., 48–50.

27 Ibid., 50–51.

28 Ibid., 51, 64.

29 Ibid., 70–71.

30 Niccolò Macchiavelli, "Instructione ad Iuliano Lapo," in id., *Legazioni, commissarie, scritti di governo*, ed. Fredi Chiappelli with Jean-Jacques Marchand, 4 vols. (Bari: Laterza, 1971–1985), vol. III, 32. Emphasis added.

31 Eli F. Heckscher, *Merkantilismen: Ett led i den ekonomiska politikens historia*, 2 vols. (Stockholm: Norstedt, 1931); Polanyi, *Great Transformation*, particularly 66–73; Henri Pirenne, *Economic and Social History of Medieval Europe* (New York: Harcourt, Brace & Company, 1937), 216–219; Fernand Braudel, *Afterthoughts on Material Civilization and Capitalism*, transl. Patricia M. Ranum (Baltimore: Johns Hopkins University Press, 1977), particularly 99–104. Scholars have noticed Schmoller's influence on these authors on different grounds. See, for the case of Heckscher, Lars Magnusson, "Eli Heckscher and His Mercantilism Today," in *Eli Heckscher, International Trade, and Economic History*, ed. Ronald Findlay et al. (Cambridge, MA: MIT Press, 2006), 231–246, at 236; for Polanyi, Fred Block and Margaret R. Somers, *The Power of Market Fundamentalism: Karl Polanyi's Critique* (Cambridge, MA: Harvard University Press, 2014), 230–232; for Braudel, see Immanuel Wallerstein, "Fernand Braudel, Historian, '*homme de la conjuncture*,'" in id., *Unthinking Social Science: The Limits of Nineteenth-Century Paradigms*, 2nd ed. (Philadelphia: Temple University Press, 2001), 187–201, at 188.

32 This is part of the 'Enlightenment Narrative' explored by J. G. A. Pocock, *Barbarism and Religion*, 5 vols. to date (Cambridge: Cambridge University Press, 1999–2010), for a lucid statement of which see vol. IV, 206. For a wide-ranging analysis of the problem of states and international markets, see Istvan Hont, *Jealousy of Trade: International Competition and the Nation State in Historical Perspective* (Cambridge, MA: Harvard University Press, 2005).

33 Verri, "Pensieri sulla corte di Roma," 477–479.

34 See also recently Christopher J. Berry, *The Idea of Commercial Society in the Scottish Enlightenment* (Edinburgh: Edinburgh University Press, 2013).

35 Cicero, *De officiis*, III, p. 29; 'Del viver Politico, et Cristiano [9 April 1583]', in *Compendio di tutte le gride, et ordini publicati nella Città, et Stato di Milano* (Milan: Malatesti, 1609), 1, on which see Luigi Lacchè, *Latrocinium: giustizia, scienza penale e repressione del banditismo in antico regime* (Milan: Giuffrè, 1988), 40. Though only in furtive notes, Istvan Hont identified this original meaning of the term 'socialists' with 'society-ists', see *Jealousy of Trade*, 45 and 159n–160n, building particularly on Franco Venturi, "Contributi ad un dizionario storico: 'Socialista' e 'socialismo' nell'Italia del Settecento," *Rivista storica italiana* 75 (1963), 129–140, truncated in id., *Italy and the Enlightenment: Studies in a Cosmopolitan Century*, ed. Stuart Wolf, transl. Susan Corsi (London: Longman, 1972), 52–62, on which see Luciano Guerci, "Gli studi venturiani sull'Italia del '700: dal *Vasco* agli *Illuministi italiani*," in *Il coraggio della ragione: Franco Venturi intellettuale e storico cosmopolita*, ed. Luciano Guerci and Giuseppe Ricuperati (Turin: Fondazione Luigi Einaudi, 1998), 203–241, 218–219, and Giorgio Spini, *Le origini del socialismo: Da utopia alla bandiera rossa* (Turin: Einaudi, 1992), 347–349, developed in id., "Sulle origini dei termini 'socialista' e 'socialismo,'" *Rivista storica italiana*, 105 (1993), 679–697, republished in id. *Dalla preistoria del socialismo alla lotta per la libertá* (Milan: FrancoAngeli, 2002), 31–49.

36 See, among many, many examples, the Hollywood franchise *Pirates of the Caribbean*, Burbank: Walt Disney Pictures, 2003–; Anthony Bourdain, *Kitchen Confidential: Adventures in the Culinary Underbelly* (London: Bloomsbury, 2000), the cultural impact of which influenced even the children's movie *Ratatouille*, directed by Brad Bird, Burbank: Walt Disney Pictures, 2007, though its culinary advisor was the rather unpiraty Thomas Keller, whose Weberianly perfectionist approach to bureaucratic cooking is evident from id., *The French Laundry Cookbook*, New York (Artisan Books, 1999) and *Chef's Story: Thomas Keller*, directed by Bruce Franchini, New York Soho Culinary Productions, 2007; Micah Sifry, *Wikileaks and the Age of*

Transparency (New Haven: Yale University Press, 2011); Parmy Olson, *We are Anonymous: Inside the Hacker World of LulzSec, Anonymous, and the Global Cyber Insurgency* (New York: Little, Brown and Company, 2012); Eric Hobsbawm, *Primitive Rebels: Studies in Archaic Forms of Social Movement in the Nineteenth and Twentieth Centuries* (New York: W.W. Norton, 1959); Peter T. Leeson, *The Invisible Hook: The Hidden Economics of Pirates* (Princeton: Princeton University Press, 2009); Rodolphe Durand and Jean Philippe Verone, *The Pirate Organization: Lessons from the Fringe of Capitalism* (Boston: Harvard Business Review Press, 2013), perhaps inspired by Steve Jobs' influential maxim, quoted among other places in Walter Isaacson, *Steve Jobs* (New York: Simon & Schuster, 2013), 144.

37   The gamut is neatly represented by a conjoined reading of James C. Scott, *The Art of Not Being Governed: An Anarchist History of Upland Southeast Asia* (New Haven: Yale University Press, 2009) and Terry L. Anderson and Peter J. Hill, *The Not So Wild, Wild West: Property Rights on the Frontier* (Stanford: Stanford Economics and Finance, 2004).

38   For an incisive if irreverent take on the problem, see Chuck Klosterman, *I Wear the Black Hat: Grappling with Villains (Real and Imagined)* (New York: Scribner, 2013).

39   The examples are too many to cover, but compare, for example, *Banditi a Milano*, dir. Carlo Lizzani, Rome: Dino de Laurentiis Cinematografica, 1968 to *The Departed*, dir. Martin Scorsese, Burbank: Warner Bros. et al., 2006. On these genres see Roberto Curti, *Italia odia: il cinema poliziesco italiano* (Turin: Lindau, 2006); Mikel J. Koven, *La Dolce Morte: Vernacular Cinema and the Italian Giallo Film* (Lanham, MD: The Scarecrow Press, 2006). See also recently Ulrike Kreger, *Genrespezifische Untersuchung des US-Slasher-Films im Vergleich zum italienischen "Giallo"* (Munich-Ravensburg: Grin Verlag, 2009). Admittedly, though it has heuristic value, this argument can easily be taken too far given the richness of recent cinema.

40   See, for example, Janice E. Thomson, *Mercenaries, Pirates, & Sovereigns* (Princeton: Princeton University Press, 1994), 156, n.19; Durand and Verone, *The Pirate Organization*, 13–14, 56.

41   Cicero, *De officiis*, III.107; I am here indebted to Daniel Heller-Roazen, *The Enemy of All: Piracy and the Law of Nations* (New York: Zone Books, 2009),13–18; Harry D. Gould, *The Legacy of Punishment in International Law* (Houndmills: Palgrave Macmillan, 2010), 84–89.

42   Christopher J. Fuhrmann, *Policing the Roman Empire: Soldiers, Administration, and Public Order* (Oxford: Oxford University Press, 2012), 156. On bandits in Ancient Rome, see also Brent Shaw, "Bandits in the Roman Empire," *Past & Present*, 105, no. 1 (1984), 3–52; Thomas Grünewald, *Räuber, Rebellen, Rivalen, Rächer: Studien zu Latrones im römischen Reich* (Stuttgart: Franz Steiner Verlag, 1999); Werner Riess, "The Roman Bandit (Latro) as Criminal and Outsider," in *The Oxford Handbook of Social Relations in the Roman World*, ed. Michael Peachin (Oxford: Oxford University Press, 2011), 693–714. On Nazi approaches to banditry, see Blood, *Hitler's Bandit Hunters*.

43   A culmination of this tension between change and armed resistance was recently explored by Broers, *Napoleon's Other War*.

44   David Armitage, "Is there a Pre-History of Globalisation?," in id., *Foundations of Modern International Thought* (Cambridge and New York: Cambridge University Press, 2013), 33–45.

45   On the Medieval origins of Genovesi's 'civil economics', see among others Zamagni and Bruni, *Economia civile*; Oreste Bazzichi, "Il modello socio-economico nel pensiero e nella predicazione di San Bernardino da Siena," in San Bernardino da Siena, *Antologia delle prediche volgari: Economia civile e cura pastorale nei sermoni di San Bernardino da Siena*, ed. Flavio Felice and Mattia Fochesato (Sienna: Edizioni Cantagalli, 2010), 205–226, at 222; Luigino Bruni and Stefano Zamagni,

"Introduzione," in Antonio Genovesi, *Lezioni di economia civile*, ed. Francesca Dal Degan (Milan: Vita e Pensiero, 2013), vii–xxii, p. x.

46 On Giotto see Francesca Flores d'Arcais, *Giotto,* translated by Raymond Rosenthal (New York: Abbeville Press Publishers, 2012). For different but enlightening interpretations, see Péter Bokody, "Justice, Love and Rape: Giotto's Allegories of Justice and Injustice in the Arena Chapel, Padua," in *The Iconology of Law and Order*, ed. Anna Kerchy (Szeged: JATE Press, 2012), 55–66 and Judith N. Shklar, *The Faces of Injustice* (New Haven: Yale University Press, 1990), 46–48. On the dichotomy between the city and the woods in Giotto's fresco see also Martin Warnke, *Political Landscape: The Art History of Nature* (London: Reaktion Books, 1994), 43. For Dante's phrase see id., *Inferno*, I, 1–2.

47 See for his reading John Ruskin, *Giotto and His Works in Padua; Being an Explanatory Notice of the Frescoes in the Arena Chapel* (London: George Allen, Sunnyside, Orpington, 1900), 188–190.

48 Verri, "Primi elementi per somministrare," in *ENOPV*, vol. VI, 631–632, 634–635.

49 Cesare Beccaria, "Della relazione che hanno l'osterie con il commercio," in *ENOCB*, vol. II, 246–248, at 247.

50 On this fresco, and its immense literature, see Reinert, "Introduction," 18–19. See, however, particularly Nicolai Rubinstein, "Political Ideas in Sienese Art: The Frescoes of Ambrogio Lorenzetti and Taddeo di Bartolo in the Palazzo Pubblico," *Journal of the Warburg and Courtauld Institutes*, vol. 21, no. 3–4 (1958), 179–207; Quentin Skinner's "Ambrogio Lorenzetti and the Portrayal of Virtuous Government" and "Ambrogio Lorenzetti on the Power and Glory of Republics," both in id., *Visions of Politics*, 3 vols., (Cambridge: Cambridge University Press, 2002), vol. II, 39–117. The similarity between the dancers in Giotto's *Justice* and those in Lorenzetti's *Good Government* has been noticed before, see for example Randolph Starn and Loren Partridge, *Arts of Power: Three Halls of State in Italy, 1300–1600* (Berkeley: University of California Press, 1992), 52.

51 For a transcription and translation, see Starn and Partridge, *Arts of Power*, 264.

52 Starn and Partridge, *Arts of Power*, 266.

53 See, on the politics of exile and banditry, among others Giuliano Milani, *L'Esclusione dal commune: Conflitti e bandi politici a Bologna e in alter città italiane tra 12. e 14. Secolo* (Rome: Istituto storico italiano per il Medio Evo, 2003); Christine Shaw, *The Politics of Exile in Renaissance Florence* (Cambridge: Cambridge University Press, 2000); Fabrizio Ricciardelli, *The Politics of Exclusion in Early Renaissance Florence* (Turnhout: Brepols, 2007), for caveats regarding which see John M. Najemy's review in the *English Historical Review* 124 (2009), 1474–1476. For the problem's classic origins see Sara Forsdyke, *Exile, Ostracism, and Democracy: The Politics of Expulsion in Ancient Greece* (Princeton: Princeton University Press, 2005).

54 Skinner, "Ambrogio Lorenzetti," 68–69, developed also in John T. Hamilton, *Security: Politics, Humanity, and the Philology of Care* (Princeton: Princeton University Press, 2013), 158.

55 Hamilton, *Security*, 158. See also, for a similar analysis with reference to Immanuel Kant's *Perpetual Peace* and piracy, Heller-Roazen, *The Enemy of All*, 188–189.

56 John M. Najemy, *A History of Florence 1200–1575* (London: Blackwell, 2006), 484.

57 Pietro Verri, "Primi elementi per somministrare al popolo delle nozioni tendenti alla pubblica felicità," in *ENOPV*, vol. VI: *Scritti politici della maturità*, ed. Carlo Capra, 629–677, particularly 631–635, 650, 655, 662, 664.

58 For this painting, see still E. H. Gombrich, "Botticellis's Mythologies: A Study in the Neoplatonic Symbolism of His Circle," *Journal of the Warburg and Courtauld Institutes* 8 (1945), 7–60, at 50–53.

59 Letizia Arcangeli, "'Come bosco et spelunca di latroni': Città e ordine pubblico a Parma e nello stato di Milano tra Quattrocento e Cinquecento," in Livio Antonielli, *Le polizie informali* (Soveria Mennelli: Rubbettino, 2010), 65–89, 80.

60   On this locus classicus of outlawry and its modern incarnations, see Oren Barak and Chanan Cohen, "The 'Modern Sherwood Forest': Theoretical and Practical Challenges," in *Nonstate Actors in Intrastate Conflicts*, ed. Dan Miodownik and Oren Barak (Philadelphia: University of Pennsylvania Press, 2014), 12–33.

61   Teodoro Monticelli, *Memoria sulla economia delle acque* (Naples: Stabilmento tipografico dell'quila, 1841 [1809]), 13. On which see Bruno Vecchio, *Il Bosco negli scrittori italiani del Settecento e dell'età napoleonica* (Turin: Einaudi, 1974), 224–227 and Giuseppe Foscari, *Teodoro Monticelli e l'economia delle acque nel Mezzogiorno moderno: storiografia, scienze ambientali, ecologismo* (Salerno: Edisud, 2009).

62   Tomaso Garzoni, *La piazza universale di tutte le professioni de mondo* (Venice: Giovanni Battista Somasco, 1587), 447–8, 812–814.

63   Giovanni Botero, *On the Causes of the Greatness of Cities*, ed. Geoffrey Symcox (Toronto: University of Toronto Press, 2012), 31, 49–50.

64   Lodovico Antonio Muratori, *Della pubblica felicità oggetto de' buoni principi* (Lucca: No Publisher, 1749), p. 66.

65   Anonymous, *Massime generali intorno al commerzio ed alle sue interne, ed esterne relazioni; o sia Principj universali, per ben coltivarlo per terra, e per mare: a linea di buon governo* (Venice: Albrizzi, 1749), 36–37, copied verbatim in Giuseppe Antonio Costantini, *Elementi di commerzio, o siano regole generali per coltivarlo, appoggiate alla ragione, alla pratica delle nazioni, ed alle autorità de' scrittori* (Genoa: Novelli, 1762), 40, published in a place and at a time when bandits were particularly harrowing.

66   Charles Irénée Castel de Saint-Pierre, *Projet pour rendre la paix perpetuelle en Europe*, 3 vols. (Utrecht: Schouten, 1713–17), vol. I, 265; vol. III, 215–216.

67   Matthew Tindall, "An Essay Concerning the Laws of Nations, and the Rights of Sovereigns," in *A Collection of State Tracts Publish'd during the Reign of King William III*, 3 vols. (London: No Publisher, 1705–1707), vol. II, 462–475, at 471, emphasis added. This passage is frequently quoted, but attributed to Daniel Defoe without further reference. For the perhaps earliest attribution to Defoe see Anne Pérotin-Dumon, "The Pirate and the Emperor: Power and the Law on the Seas, 1450–1850," in *The Political Economy of Merchant Empires: State Power and World Trade 1350–1750*, ed. James D. Tracy (Cambridge: Cambridge University Press, 1991), 196–227, 215.

68   Reinert, *Translating Empire*.

69   Antonio Genovesi, *Storia del commercio della Gran Brettagna*, 3 vols. (Naples: Benedetto Gessari, 1757–8), vol. II, 16n.

70   Genovesi, *Storia del commercio della Gran Brettagna*, vol. I, 11n.

71   Antonio Genovesi, "Ragionamento sulla fede pubblica," in id., *Storia del commercio della Gran Brettagna*, vol. III, 473–505.

72   Genovesi, "Ragionamento sulla fede pubblica," 495. On the problem of trust in Genovesi, and for further references, see Reinert, *Translating Empire*, 226–227.

73   Genovesi, "Ragionamento sulla fede pubblica," 496.

74   Ibid., 498–499.

75   Strangely, it does not make an appearance in recent works on the phenomenon, among which Norman Davis, *Vanished Kingdoms: The Rise and Fall of States and Nations* (London: Allen Lane, 2011); Daron Acemoglu and James Robinson, *Why Nations Fail: The Origins of Power, Prosperity, and Poverty* (New York: Crown, 2012).

76   Giuseppe Antonio de Morani, *Memorie istoriche della città e della chiesa di Casale Monferrato* [1800], Biblioteca Civica Casale Monferrato, 091 73, p. 11.

77   On the historiography of frontiers in the area, see Giuseppe Ricuperati, "Frontiere e territori dello stato sabaudo come archetipi di una regione europea: fra storia e storiografia," in *Lo spazio sabaudo: Intersezioni, frontiere e confine in età moderna*, ed. Blythe Alice Raviola (Milan: FrancoAngeli, 2007), 31–55.

78   The literature on Sardinian banditry is infinite, but see recently Alberto Ledda, *La civiltà fuorilegge: Storia del banditismo sardo* (Milan: Ugo Mursia, 2009). On the

longer history of banditry in the Piedmontese highlands, see Tavo Burat [Gustavo Buratti], "Il tuchinaggio occitano e piemontese," in *Achtung Banditen: Contadini e montanari tra banditismo, ribellismo e resistenze dall'antichità ad oggi*, ed. Anonymous (Novara: Millennia, 2005), 18–32.

79   See, for bandits, among others Anton Bok, "The Peasant and the Brigand: Social Banditry Reconsidered," *Comparative Studies in Society and History* 14/4 (1972), 494–503. On the relationship between literature and reality with regards to piracy, see Neil Rennie, *Treasure Neverland: Real and Imaginary Pirates* (Oxford: Oxford University Press, 2013). For a survey of early modern European banditry, noting the limitations of Hobsbawm's paradigm, see Julius R. Ruff, *Violence in Early Modern Europe 1500–1800* (Cambridge: Cambridge University Press, 2001), 217–239.

80   Felice De Gioanni, *Verolengo: Cenni storici–coreografici* (Casale Monferrato: Stabilimento Arti Grafiche, 1932), 134–136, 156–157; on the town's earliest history, still an active battlefield of contemporary Italian politics preoccupied with Ligurian and Celtic influences, see Fabrizio Spegis, "Origini di Verolengo," monographic issue of *Quaderni verolenghesi*, 5 (1997), 1–95; on the Peace treaty and its intense focus on border disputes, see Joycelyn G. Russell, *Peacemaking in the Renaissance* (Philadelphia: University of Pennsylvania Press, 1986), 133–223. For the contested case of Verolengo in particular, see Romolo Quazza, *Emanuele Filiberto di Savoia e Guglielmo Gonzaga (1559–1580* (Mantova: Società Tipografica Modenese, 1929), 17. As to the economic fortunes of Verolengo, a pithy insert by the town's local historian in a discussion of the place around 1600 is telling: 'Il mercato di Verolengo aveva allora importanza e vi affluivano genti del Monferrato, del Vercellese, e del Canavese. Il ponte sul Po a Chivasso, indi quello sul Po a Crescentino distolsero ogni ulteriore concorso al nostro mercato che gia aveva ricevuto un fierissimo danno dalle ferrovie affluenti a Chivasso. Ora colla soppressione dei porti, e tagliato fuori perfin dalla prossima collina'. De Gioanni, *Verolengo*, 135.

81   On the Gonzaga and the Paleologus see Stefano Davari, *Federico Gonzaga e la famiglia paleologa del Monferrato*, Genoa: Tip. Sordo-Muti, 1891. The first anti-Gonzaga rebellion in Casale was tellingly already in 1533 at the mere *prospect* of a transition, see for this and for context Roberto Oresko and David Parrott, "The Sovereignty of Monferrato and the Citadel of Casale as European Problems of the Early Modern Period," in *Stefano Guazzo e Casale tra Cinque e Seicento*, ed. Daniela Ferrari (Rome: Bulzoni, 1997), 11–86, at 22. For an entertaining list of such tax revolts, see David F. Burg, *A World History of Tax Rebellions: Encyclopedia of Tax Rebels, Revolts, and Riots from Antiquity to the Present* (London: Routledge, 2003).

82   Blythe Alice Raviola, *Il Monferrato Gonzaghesco: Istituzioni ed èlites in un micro-stato (1536–1708)* (Florence: Olschki, 2003), 56; Fabrizio Spegis, "'Giunti colà, si sciolsero e si sparpagliarono': fuoriusciti casalesi tra Monferrato, Savoia e Francia (febbraio 1569)," *Bollettino storico vercellese*, A. 39, n. 2 (2010), 155–169, at 158–160. On the evocative crime of '*lèse-majesté*', see Mario Sbriccoli, *Crimen laesae maiestatis: Il problema del reato politico alle soglie della scienza penalistica moderna* (Milan: Giuffrè, 1974).

83   Quentin Skinner, *Liberty before Liberalism* (Cambridge: Cambridge University Press, 1997); id., *Hobbes and Republican Liberty* (Cambridge: Cambridge University Press, 2008).

84   For an examination of the complex role of the militia in Renaissance political and military life, see John M. Najemy, "'Occupare la tirannide': Machiavelli, the Militia, and Guicciardini's Accusation of Tyranny," in *Della tirannia: Machiavelli con Bartolo*, ed. Jérémy Barthas (Florence: Leo S. Olschki, 2007), 75–108. See also John Rigby Hale, "The End of Florentine Liberty: The Fortezza da Basso," in id., *Renaissance War Studies* (London: Hambledon, 1983), 31–62 and, for Casale in particular, and for caveats regarding the actual efficiency of fortifications, see Oresko and Parrott, "The Sovereignty of Monferrato," 25–27 and *passim*.

85   Raviola, *Il Monferrato Gonzaghesco*, 56. On the question of sovereignty and rights at the time, see Kenneth Pennington, *The Prince and the Law, 1200–1600: Sovereignty and Rights in the Western Legal Tradition* (Berkeley: University of California Press, 1993).

86   Romolo Quazza, "Il Monferrato nei centosettanta anni di dominio gonzaghesco," *Convivium*, IV (1932), 383–391, at 385–386.

87   Spegis, "'Giunti colà, si sciolsero e si sparpagliarono,'" 163–166.

88   Quazza, *Emanuele Filiberto di Savoia e Guglielmo Gonzaga*, 17, 108–110; Spegis, "'Giunti colà, si sciolsero e si sparpagliarono,'" 167–169.

89   'Processo contro vari Banditi di Casale li quali avevano tentato di occupare la Fortezza di Verolengo, 1569,' Archivio di Stato di Torino, Turin, Italy [henceforth AST], *Monferrato, Materie Economiche ed altre, Mazzo 10, Criminale, n. 3*, 2r, 56v, 57v, 58r, 71r–73r. For context, and though they overlooked this document, see the summary of a contemporary chronicle in Vincenzo de Conti, *Notizie storiche sulla città di Casale e del Monferrato*, 11 vols (Casale: Mantelli, then Casuccio, then Casuccio e Bagna, 1838–1842), vol. V, 616–624; Spegis, "'Giunti colà, si sciolsero e si sparpagliarono.'" Legal documents are, needless to say, not always perfect reflections of past events, and such overly convenient episodes should clearly be read with a grain of salt. See still Natalie Zemon Davis, *Fiction in the Archives: Pardon Tales and Their Tellers in Sixteenth-Century France* (Stanford: Stanford University Press, 1990).

90   For these ideal types, see Eric Hobsbawm, *Bandits* (New York: The New Press, 2000), 31, 41.

91   Eric Hobsbawm, *Primitive Rebels: Studies in Archaic Forms of Social Movement in the 19th and 20th Centuries* (New York: W.W. Norton, 1959), 6 and *passim*.

92   Desiderio Cavalca, *Il bando nella prassi e nella dottrina medieval* (Milan: Giuffrè, 1978).

93   On the technical differences between bandits and rebels at the time generally, see Sbriccoli, *Crimen laesae maiestatis*, 117–148.

94   Luigi Pirandello, *Sei personaggi in cerca d'autore*, ed. Guido Davico Bonino (Turin: Einaudi, 2005 [1921]).

95   On the territorial history of Lombardy in the period, see Roberto Mainardi, "Milano e la Lombardia alle soglie della 'modernità'," in *Lombardia: Il territorio, l'ambiente, il paesaggio. L'età delle riforme*, ed. Carlo Pirovano (Milan: Electa, 1983), 7–36; for Piedmont, see Blythe Alice Raviola, "Sabaudian Spaces and Territories: Piedmont as a Composite State (Ecclesiastical Enclaves, Fiefs, Boundaries)," in *Sabaudian Studies: Political Culture, Dynasty, & Territory 1400–1700*, ed. Matthew Vester (Kirksville: Truman State University Press, 2013), 278–297. On the tenuous territorial centralization of Savoy, see also the masterful Christopher Storrs, *War, Diplomacy and the Rise of Savoy, 1690–1720* (Cambridge: Cambridge University Press, 1999).

96   On the tensions of armed citizenries in relation to banditry in late Renaissance Italy, see Arcangeli, "'Come bosco et spelunca di latroni,'" 78. On Valsesia, its geography, and its history between Lombardy and Piedmont, see Gian Paolo Garavaglia, "Un Confine 'fluido', Sesia e Valsesia in età napoleonica," in *Alle frontiere della Lombardia: Politica, guerra e religion nell'età moderna*, ed. Claudio Donati (Milan: FrancoAngeli, 2006), 227–256.

97   AST, *Paesi nuovo acquisto Valle di Sesia, Mazzo 2, #22*, 'Memoriale a capi, rispote ad esso, supplica, esame, e lettere concernenti diverse dimande fatte da Regenti della Val Sesia,' particularly the 1725 'Esame Sommario', 2v–5r. Such valleys had, of course, been victims of banditry since time immemorial, see for a readable account from an earlier century Emilio Podestà, *I banditi di Valle Stura: Una cronaca del secolo XVI* (Ovada: Accademia Urbense, 1990). For an extended meditation on the problem of marauding beasts in early modern states, see, though for a different context, Jay M. Smith, *Monsters of the Gévaudan: The Making of a Beast* (Cambridge,

MA: Harvard University Press, 2011), with references also to bandits on pp. 17–18, 130, 347–348, n99. On the timing of Savoy control, see Cristophe Gauchon, "Le cadaster d'un état Alpin: L'espace, les frontiers, les institutions," in Andrea Longhi, ed., *Cadastres et territoires/ Catasti e territori: L'analyse des archives cadastrales pour l'interprétation du paysage et l'aménagement du territoire/ L'analisi dei catasti storici per l'interpretazione del paesaggio e per il governo del territorio* (Florence: Alinea editrice, 2008), 34–45, at 36.

98 Marco Battistoni, *Franchigie: Dazi, transiti e territori negli stati sabaudi del secolo XVIII* (Alessandria: Edizioni dell'orso, 2009), 158 and *passim*. For a contemporary Sovereign theorization of this principle, see Carlo Emmanuele III, *Regie Patentii d'approvazione dell'annesso Regolamento per la manutenzione, e riparazione delle Strade Reali, e pubbliche. in data de' 11. Settembre 1771* (Turin: Stamperia reale, 1771). On the importance of roads for trade, proto-industrialization, and economic development in the area see among others Mortarotti, *L'Ossola nell'età moderna*, 297. On Lombard roads as vehicles of trade and military territorialization, see Alessandra Dattero, "Percorrere il territorio nel Settecento: militari asburgici in marcia tra Domini ereditari e Stati italiani," in *Alle frontiere della Lombardia*, 201–225, 204. On the importance of roads for territorial unification see Eugen Weber, *Peasants into Frenchmen: The Modernization of Rural France, 1870–1914* (Stanford: Stanford University Press, 1976), 195–220. For the case of roads in relation to unification and socialization in eighteenth-century Italy, see still Borlando, *Il problema delle communicazioni*, 154. On the emergence of the infrastructure state and the extraordinary importance of public roads for territorial integration and economic development see now Jo Guldi, *Roads to Power: Britain Invents the Infrastructure State* (Cambridge, MA: Harvard University Press, 2012), particularly 194–197, who throughout strongly emphasizes the state-led nature of roadbuilding but engages with highwaymen only in passing, though see 174–177 and, for the New World, John Lauritz Larson, *Internal Improvement: National Public Works and the Promise of Popular Government in the Early United States* (Chapel Hill: The University of North Carolina Press, 2001), who, however, neglects crime entirely. For the case of canals, see also Chandra Mukerji, *Impossible Engineering: Technology and Territoriality on the Canal du Midi* (Princeton: Princeton University Press, 2009).

99 Economic works emphasizing the importance of infrastructure were, in effect, legion at the time, for an eloquent example of which see Gregorio Pedro Pereira, *Dissertazione sopra la giusta valuta della moneta,* (Faenza: Per Gioseffantonio Archi, [1757]), 97–98.

100 Thorstein Veblen, *The Theory of Business Enterprise* (New York: Charles Scribner's Sons, 1904), 31; id., *The Engineers and the Price System* (New York: B.W. Huebsch, 1921), 1. For the current resurgence of interest in this aspect of Veblen's work, see recently the essays in Erik S. Reinert and Francesca Lidia Viano, eds, *Thorstein Veblen: Economics for an Age of Crises* (London: Anthem, 2012).

101 Steven L. Kaplan, *The Bakers of Paris and the Bread Question, 1700–1775* (Durham: Duke University Press, 1996), 14–15 and now his *Stakes of Regulation: Historiographical Reflections on Bread, Politics, and Political Economy in the Reign of Louis XV* (London: Anthem, 2015), chapter I; Antonio Genovesi, *Storia del commercio della Gran Brettagna*, 3 vols. (Naples: Benedetto Gessari, 1757–8), vol. I, 11n.

102 AST, *Paesi nuovo acquisto Valle di Sesia, Mazzo 2, #22*, 'Esame Sommario', 4v.

103 Adam Smith, *An Inquiry into the Nature and Causes of the Wealth of Nations*, ed. Edwin Cannan, 2 vols. (Chicago: University of Chicago Press, 1976), vol. I, 21.

104 Verri, 'Meditazioni,' 495.

105 Giovanni Battista Passeri, *Vite de pittori, scultori ed architetti che anno lavorato in Roma morti dal 1641 fino al 1673* (Rome: Gregorio Settari, 1772), 55. On the movement, see Giuliano Brigani with Ludovica Trezzani and Laura Laureati, *The*

Bamboccianti: The Painters of Everyday Life in Seventeenth-Century Rome, transl. Robert Erich Wolf (Rome: U. Bocci, 1983).

106 Giovanni Michele Graneri, *Mercato in piazza San Carlo*, 1752, Palazzo Madama, Turin, Italy, 540/D.

107 See, again, Kaplan, *Stakes of Regulation*.

108 See for example Carlos Marichal, "The Spanish-American Silver Peso: Export Commodity and Global Money of the Ancien Regime, 1550–1800," in *From Silver to Cocain: Latin American Commodity Chains and the Building of the World Economy, 1500–2000*, ed. Steven Topik, Carlos Marichal and Zephyr Frank (Durham: Duke University Press, 2006), 25–52.

109 Cesare Beccaria, *On Crimes and Punishments and Other Writings*, ed. Aaron Thomas, transl. Aaron Thomas and Jeremy Parzen (Toronto: University of Toronto Press, 2008), 72–73.

110 For variations on this theme, see Thomas W. Gallant, "Brigandage, Piracy, Capitalism, and State-Formation: Transnational Crime from a Historical World-Systems Perspective," in *States and Illegal Practices*, ed. Josiah Heyman (Oxford: Berg, 1999), 25–61, at. 25, 40–41, 50–52; Eric Tagliacozzo *Secret Trades, Porous Borders: Smugglig and States Along a Southeast Asian Frontier, 1865–1915* (New Haven: Yale University Press, 2005), 369–370.

111 The problem of banditry in liminal lands had, of course, been a trope of political philosophy, see for example Scipione Ammirato, *Discorsi sopra Cornelio Tacito* (Florence; Filippo Giunti, 1594), 140–148. On banditry in the period, see among numerous others Enzo Ciconte, *Banditi e briganti: rivolta continua dal Cinquenteco all'Ottocento* (Soveria Mannelli: Rubbettino, 2011), 23–61. In the case of nearby Piedmont, this was perhaps most clearly evident in the case of Sardinia, see Maria Lepori, *Faide: Nobili e banditi nella Sardegna sabauda del Settecento* (Rome: Viella, 2010), 171–196.

112 Gabriella Solavaggione, "Brigantaggio e contrabbando nella campagna lombarda del Settecento," *Nuova rivista storica*, 1970, vol. I–II, 23–49 and vol. III–IV, 46–49 and 374–419; Battistoni, *Franchigie*, 182, 209–213, 229–240; Andrea Zanini, "Soldati corsi e famegli: la forza pubblica della Repubblica di Genova nel XVIII secolo," in *Corpi armati e ordine pubblico in Italia (XVI–XIX sec.)*, ed. Livio Antonielli and Claudio Donati (Soveria Mannelli: Rubbettino, 2003), 141–180, emphasizing how feudal jurisdictions undermined territorial law-enforcement on p. 178; Vittorio Tigrini, "Giurisdizione e transito nel Settecento: I feudi imperiali tra il Genovesato e la pianura Padana," in *Lungo le antiche strade: Vie d'acqua e di terra tra Stati, giurisdizioni e confine nella cartografia dell'età moderna*, ed. Marina Cavallera (Busto Arsizio: Nomos, 2007), 45–94, particularly at 50; Andrea Zanini, "Feudi, feudatari ed economie nella montagna ligure," in *Libertà e dominio. Il sistema politico genovese: le relazioni esterne e il controllo del territorio*, ed. Matthias Schnettger and Carlo Taviani (Rome: Viella, 2011), 305–316. On banditism and 'Feudal values,' see Villari, "Conclusioni," 414. These problems themselves were, however, ancient, occurring precisely at the intersection of Savoy, Milan, and Genoa, see, for mid-seventeenth-century occurrences, the many incidents collected in AST, *Incidenti con Genova, Mazzo 1, fasc. 1*. On pirate utopias, see the anarchist writer Peter Lamborn Wilson's *Pirate Utopias: Moorish Corsairs & European Renegados* (Williamsburg: Autonomedia, 2003); for the case of Tortuga see the mention in Hakim Bey [id.], "The Temporary Autonomous Zone," in *Crypto Anarchy, Cyberstates, and Pirate Utopias*, ed. Peter Ludlow (Cambridge, MA: MIT Press, 2001), 401–434, at 420. For a more historical analysis exploring also the dysfunctionality of such places, their role in early modern political economy, and the concentrated state action to get rid of them, Niklas Frykman, "Pirates and Smugglers: Political Economy in the Red Atlantic," in *Mercantilism Reimagined*, 218–238.

113 For the ambassador's orders, see AST, *Materie Politiche, Negotiazioni con Genova, Mazzo 9, n. 2*, 'Istruzioni di S.Mta al Conte [Giuseppe Maria] Ferrero di Lauriano per la sua Commissione di Ministro presso La Repubblica di Genova', 30 January 1753, 3v–5r. For Verri on this, see Battistoni, *Franchigie*, 232.

114 See the numerous cases collected in those years in AST, *Incidenti con Genova, Mazzo 5*. On the illegal capture of Mandrin see Kwass, *Contraband*, 204–216.

115 For the Milanese side of this correspondence see particularly the collections in Archivio di Stato di Milano, Milan, Italy [henceforth ASM], *AG 30, Potenze estere post. 1535, 44 Genova 1733–1801; AG 30, 210 Torino e Savoia 1761–1770; AG 28, Arresto e consegna di rei, convenzioni... (Genova), 1581–1799; AG 37 (Torino) 1761–1773*, particularly Kaunitz to Firmian, 24 September 1764 and Kaunitz to Firmian 1 October 1764. For the rich and varied spectrum of humanity covered by this term at the time, see Giacomo Todeschini, *Visibilmente crudeli: Malviventi persone sospette e gente qualunque dal Medioevo all'età moderna* (Bologna: Il Mulino, 2007). On the territorial policing of the Milanese state at the time, see Livio Antonielli, "Polizie di città e polizie di campagna in antico regime: il caso dello Stato di Milano a metà Settecento," in *Polizia, ordine pubblico e crimine tra città e campagna: un confront comparativo*, ed. Livio Antonielli (Soveria Manelli: Rubbettino, 2010), 17–48.

116 Note accompanying Kaunitz to Firmian, 15 April 1765, 1r in ASM, *AG 28, Arresto e consegna di rei, convenzioni... (Genova), 1581–1799*. The use of such beastly, medical, and pathological metaphors for bandits was of course venerable, see for example the great reason of state theorist Ammirato, *Discorsi sopra Cornelio Tacito*, 148 and Cosimo I to Pope Pius IV, 7 July 1563, Archivio di Stato di Firenze, *Mediceo 327*, ff. 173r–175r, particularly 174v.

117 ASM, *AG 28, Arresto e consegna di rei, convenzioni... (Genova), 1581–1799*, and particularly Firmian to Kaunitz of 4 August 1764, 1v–2r, Viry to Firmian, 8 May 1765, Viry to Firmian 18 May 1765, and Kaunitz to Firmian, 1 [5?] April 1765; AST, *Milano, Lettere diverse, 1751 in 1765, Mazzo 12, #1, Lettere dei Conti Cristiani, e di Firmian...* See particularly the letters bound in a volume entitled *1754 Milano, 1754... 1765*, and, for particularly purple prose, Viry to Firmian, 4 August 1764, 11 August 1764, 8 September 1764, 12 September 1764, 22 September 1764, 3 October 1764, 26 January 1765, 27 March 1765, 18 May 1765, 53r–55r, 55v–56r, 59v–60r, 65v–67v, 74r–76v, 83r–84v, 86v–93v and the unbound Firmian to Viry, 2 February 1765, 1r–1v. This is, needless to say, not to suggest that the Genoese themselves did not worry about domestic banditry. On their relentless war on the phenomenon, see among others Maria D. F., "La repressione della criminalità organizzata nella Repubblica di Genova tra Cinque e Seicento: Aspetti e cronologia della prassi legislative," in *Bande armate, banditi, banditismo e repressioni di giustizia negli stati europei di antico regime*, ed. Gherardo Ortalli (Rome: Jouvence, 1986), 87–106 and Zanini, "Soldati corsi e famegli."

118 AST, *Milano, Lettere diverse, 1751 in 1765, Mazzo 12, #1, Lettere dei Conti Cristiani, e di Firmian...*, Firmian to Viry, 2 February 1765, 1r.

119 AST, *Milano, Lettere diverse, 1751 in 1765, Mazzo 12, #1, Lettere dei Conti Cristiani, e di Firmian...*, volume entitled *1754 Milano, 1754... 1765*, Viry to Firmian, 4 August 1764, 53v–56r.

120 AST, *Milano, Lettere diverse, 1751 in 1765, Mazzo 12, #1, Lettere dei Conti Cristiani, e di Firmian...*, volume entitled *1754 Milano, 1754... 1765*, Viry to Firmian, 3 October 1764, 67r–67v.

121 AST, *Materie Politiche, Negotiazioni con Genova, Mazzo 9, 1753 al 1798*, no. 5, manuscript beginning 'Alle rappresentanze,' 1r.

122 AST, *Materie Politiche, Negotiazioni con Genova, Mazzo 9, 1753 al 1798*, no. 5, manuscript beginning 'Alle rappresentanze,' 2r.

123 See the lengthy report on incidents dating back to 1762 submitted alongside the letter from Girolamo Gastaldi to the Doge and others, 25 January 1764, Archivio di Stato di Genova, Genoa, Italy [hereafter ASG], *Archivio Segreto, 2505, Torino Anni 1764–1765*, Mazzo 18, particularly 2r–2v.

124 AST, *Materie Politiche, Negotiazioni con Genova, Mazzo 9, 1753 al 1798*, no. 5, manuscript beginning 'Alle rappresentanze,' 2v.

125 AST, *Milano, Lettere diverse, 1751 in 1765, Mazzo 12, #1, Lettere dei Conti Cristiani, e di Firmian...*, volume entitled *1754 Milano, 1754... 1765*, Viry to Firmian, 26 January 1765, 76r–76v.

126 AST, *Milano, Lettere diverse, 1751 in 1765, Mazzo 12, #1, Lettere dei Conti Cristiani, e di Firmian...*, volume entitled *1754 Milano, 1754... 1765*, Viry to Firmian, 27 March 1765, 83r–84v.

127 On the Bronze Age origins of such conventions, see Stephen C. Neff, *Justice Among Nations* (Cambridge, MA: Harvard University Press, 2014), 14, and, for a diverse roster of such conventions in Italy dating back to the mid-fifteenth century, ASM, Atti di Governo, 26, *Giustizia Punitiva, Parte Antica*.

128 Ammirato, *Discorsi sopra Cornelio Tacito*, 146, on which see also Lacchè, *Latrocinium*, 76, 78. Though she ignores the phenomenon of banditry, this supports some of the general arguments in Thomson, *Mercenaries, Pirates, & Sovereigns*, 149–152.

129 See the anonymous 'Pro Memoria' dated 10 April 1764 attached to Gerolamo Gastaldi to the Doge and others, [29?] February 1764, 1v, as well as Gastaldi's own 'Riflessioni sopra la minuta consegnata dal S. Conte Bogino,' 1r for the argument that times had changed too much to imitate such old models, both in ASG, *Archivio Segreto 2505, Torino Anni 1764–1765, Mazzo 18*. On such agreements in general, see Lacchè, *Latrocinium*, pp. 73–80 and Pagano, "Questa turba infame," 98–101.

130 AST, *Milano, Lettere diverse, 1751 in 1765, Mazzo 12, #1, Lettere dei Conti Cristiani, e di Firmian...*, volume entitled *1754 Milano, 1754... 1765*, Viry to Firmian, 18 May 1765, 86v–93v, particularly 91v. For one of endless examples, see AST, *Ducato di Monferrato, Mazzo 17, n. 24*, 'Promessa del Marchese Guglielmo di Monferrato di far rimettere al Duca Carlo di Savoja li banditi, che si rifugieranno nei suoi stati pendente un anno' [4 September 1516]. Lombardy had recently signed such agreements not only with Piedmont but also with the Papal States and Venice, see among other instances *Convenzione per l'arresto dei Banditi, e Malviventi frà lo Stato Pontificio per una parte, e gli Stati della Lombardia Austriaca dipendente da S.M.R.I per l'altra*, Rome, 1 Jaunary 1755, renewing a 1750 agreement again renewed also in *Convenzione per l'arresto de banditi, e malviventi, fra lo Stato Pontificio e gli Stati della Lombardia Austriaca*, Rome, 1 January 1767.

131 AST, *Materie Politiche, Negotiazioni con Genova, Mazzo 9, 1753 al 1798*, no. 5, manuscript beginning 'Progetto di Convenzione colla Repubblica di Genova per gli Stati di Terraferma', 10 April 1764, 1v. This language of banditry and 'free trade' was evident in Italy already in the sixteenth century, see Lacchè, *Latrocinium*, 47.

132 On customs duties in the area, see again Battistoni, *Franchigie*. Pietro Verri said similar things over and over again, but see his *Meditazioni sull'economia politica* (Livorno: Stamperia dell'Enciclopedia, 1771), 41. This theme has been explored, among others, by Pier Luigi Porta and Roberto Scazzieri, "Pietro Verri's Political Economy: Commercial Society, Civil Society, and the Science of the Legislator," *History of Political Economy* 34/1 (2002), 83–110. On the tradition of public happiness in particular, see Antonio Trampus, *Il diritto alla felicità: Storia di un'idea* (Rome-Bari: Laterza, 2008).

133 See still Nino Calvini, *La rivoluzione del 1753 a Sanremo*, 2 vols. (Bordighera: Istituto internazionale di studi liguri, 1953), particularly vol. I, 13, 125–129; Sophie Caillieret, *L'affaire de San Remo, un episode méconnu des relations diplomatiques entre la France et la cour de Vienne (1753–1772)*, Mémoire de maîtrise (Université

d'Angers, Angers, 1999); Vittorio Tigrino, *Sudditi e confederati: Sanremo, Genova e una storia particolare del Settecento europeo* (Alessandria: Edizioni dell'Orso, 2009), 334–360. On Genoa's territorial state in international context, see recently the essays collected in *Libertà e dominio. Il sistema politico genovese: le relazioni esterne e il controllo del territorio,* ed. Matthias Schnettger and Carlo Taviani (Rome: Viella, 2011). On Genoa in the period see generally Matthias Schnettger, *'Principe Sovrano' oder 'Civitas Imperialis'? Die Republik Genua und das Alte Reich in der Frühen Neuzeit (1556–1797)* (Mainz: Verlag Philipp von Zabern, 2006), on the San Remo affair particularly 363–412.

134 See, on these issues, still Venturi, *Settecento riformatore,* vol. V, book 1, 3–222. On the importance of the Enlightenment influence on the Corsican revolt in the context of Venturi's lifelong Anti-Fascism, connecting his youthful writings on Paolo for *Giustizia e libertà,* see Giuseppe Ricuperati, *Un laboratorio cosmopolitico: Illuminismo e storia a Torino nel Novecento* (Naples-Rome: Edizioni scientifiche italiane, 2011), 160. On contemporary Genoese worries linking the revolts of Sanremo and Corsica, see Tigrino, *Sudditi e confederati,* 339.

135 Doge, Governatori e Procuratori della Repubblica di Genova to Girolamo De Ferrari [???], 23 June 1764, ASG, *Archivio Segreto, 2600, Vienna Anni 1763–1765, Mazzo* 83, 1r; 'Progetto di Convenzione colla Repubblica di Genova per gli Stati di Terraferma,' attached to Gastaldi to the Doge and others, 9 May 1764, 1v; and, for the roads, Gastaldi to the Doge and others, 13 June 1764 both in ASG, *Archivio Segreto 2505, Torino Anni 1764–1765, Mazzo 18.*

136 Coded missive from Gastaldi to Doge and others, 21 March 1764, deciphered by an anonymous Genoese functionary, ASG, *Archivio Segreto 2505, Torino Anni 1764–1765, Mazzo 18.*

137 See among others the report in Girolamo Gastaldi to the Doge and others, [29?] February 1764, ASG, *Archivio Segreto, 2505, Torino Anni 1764–1765,* Mazzo 18, 2v; Doge and others to Girolamo De Ferrari [???], [9?] March 1767, ASG, *Archivio Segreto, 2600, Mazzo 83, Vienna 1766–1767, Lettere del Governo di Genova al M. Deffornari,* 1r, 2r–2v. See also the lengthy letter of 18 June 1766.

138 Coded missive from Gastaldi to the Doge and others, 20 June 1764, ASG, *Archivio Segreto 2505, Torino Anni 1764–1765, Mazzo 18.*

139 AST, *Milano, Lettere diverse, 1751 in 1765, Mazzo 12, #1, Lettere dei Conti Cristiani, e di Firmian...,* volume entitled *1754 Milano, 1754... 1765,* Viry to Firmian, 18 May 1765, 86v–93v, particularly 91v–92r.

140 Calvini, *La rivoluzione del 1753 a Sanremo,* vol. II, p. 151.

141 Coded missive from Gastaldi to the Doge and others, 13 August 1764, ASG, *Archivio Segreto 2505, Torino Anni 1764–1765, Mazzo 18,* 2r.

142 AST, *Materie Politiche, Negotiazioni con Genova, Mazzo 9, 1753 al 1798, n. 5,* manuscript entitled 'Ristretto delle intelligenze coerenti alla trattativa intrapresa nel 1764,' 2 Settembre 1772, 1v–4r, as well as Kaunitz to Firmian, 23 June 1766, in ASM, *AG 28, Arresto e consegna di rei, convenzioni... (Genova), 1581–1799.*

143 J. M. Munn-Rankin, "Diplomacy in Western Asia in the Early Second Millennium B.C.," *Iraq* 18/1 (1956), 68–110, at 93.

144 James J. Kinneally III, "The Political Offence Exception: Is the United States–United Kingdom Supplementary Extradition Treaty the Beginning of the End?," *American University Journal of International Law and Policy,* 2/1 (1987), 203–227, at 206. See, for the deeper history of this institution, Christine Van Den Wyngaert, *Political Offence Exception to Extradition: The Delicate Problem of Balancing the Rights of the Individual and the International Public Order* (Deventer: Kluwer, 1980).

145 See, among endless others, *Convenzione per l'arresto dei Banditi, e Malviventi frà lo Stato Pontificio per una parte, e gli Stati della Lombardia Austriaca dipendente da S.M.R.I per l'altra,* [Milan?]: N.P., [1755?].

146 Zanini, "Soldati corsi e famegli," 146, 153.

147 Beccaria, *On Crimes and Punishments*, 10–12. See also Frederick Rosen, "Utilitarianism and the Reform of the Criminal Law," in *The Cambridge History of Eighteenth-Century Political Thought*, ed. Mark Goldie and Robert Wokler (Cambridge: Cambridge University Press, 2006), 547–572, at 552.
148 Beccaria, *On Crimes and Punishments*, 10.
149 Ibid., 11. See on the inevitability of crime in Beccaria's moral universe, Harcourt, *The Illusion of Free Markets*, 64–65.
150 Beccaria, *On Crimes and Punishments*, 52.
151 Ibid., 46–7, and 55. For a typical case of this form of punishment, see for example Enzo Ciconte, *Banditi e briganti: Rivolta continua dal Cinquecento all'Ottocento* (Soveria Mannelli: Rubbettino, 2011), 55–56. Beccaria's influential resistance to the practice is made emblematic even by legal historians in the tradition of Annamaria Monti, "Illegitimate Appropriation or Just Punishment? The Confiscation of Property in *Ancien Régime* Criminal Law and Doctrine," in *Property Rights and Their Violations: Expropriations and Confiscations, 16th–20th Centuries / La propriété violée: Expropriations et confiscations, XVIe–XXe siècles*, ed. Luigi Lorenzetti, Michela Barbot and Luca Mocarelli (Bern: Peter Lang, 2012), 15–35, particularly at 15.
152 Cesare Beccaria, "Estratto del quinto tomo dei 'Mélanges' di D'Alembert," in *ENDOCB*, vol. II, 311–346, p. 341, originally published in *Estratto della Letteratura europea*, 1767, II, 142–159, IV, 83–97; 1768, I, 113–126, extracting from and commenting on Jean Le Rond d'Alembert, *Mélanges de literature, d'histoire et de philosophie* (Amsterdam: Zacharie Châtelain et Fils, 1767 [but 1766]).
153 Beccaria, *On Crimes and Punishments*, 50.
154 Ibid., 25.
155 Cesare Beccaria, "Piano delle lezioni di pubblica economia che si danno nello spazio di due anni dal professore di questa scienza," in *ENDOCB*, vol. III, 67–77, pp. 74–75. On railways and nationbuilding in nineteenth-century Italy, see Albert Schram, *Railways and the Formation of the Italian State in the Nineteenth Century* (Cambridge: Cambridge University Press, 1997), and 152 for their economic and security consequences.
156 Cesare Beccaria, "Elementi di economia pubblica," in *ENDOCB*, vol. III, 97–591, pp. 170–171.
157 Cesare Beccaria, "Materiali preparatori e stesure rifiutate," in *ENDOCB*, vol. III, 593–599, p. 595.
158 Verri, "Meditazioni," 466.
159 Verri, "Meditazioni," 506.
160 On the multiplying power of roads, see Verri, "Meditazioni," 506.
161 Verri, "Pensieri del conte Pietro Verri sullo stato politico," 413–414.
162 See the vast conceptual arc from Jean-Jacques Rousseau, "The Social Contract," 74 to David Stasavage, *States of Credit: Size, Power, and the Development of European Polities* (Princeton: Princeton University Press, 2011), 158
163 See, for example, Christopher J. Fuhrman, *Policing the Roman Empire: Soldiers, Administration, and Public Order* (Oxford: Oxford University Press, 2012), 155–156; Henry Kamen, "Public Authority and Popular Crime: Banditry in Valencia, 1660–1714," *Journal of European Economic History* 3 (1974), 654–687; Kim A. Wagner, *Thuggee: Banditry and the British in Early Nineteenth-Century India* (Houndmills: Palgrave Macmillan, 2007), 5 and *passim*; Margareet Van Till, *Banditry in West Java 1869–1942*, transl. David McKay & Beverley Jackson (Singapore: National University of Singapore Press, 2011), 107, 189–191, and *passim*; Anton Blok, *The Mafia of a Sicilian Village 1860–1960: A Study of Violent Peasant Entrepreneurs* (New York: Harper and Row, 1974), for useful perspectives on which see Filippo Sabetti, *Village Politics and the Mafia in Sicily* (Montreal: McGill-Queen's University Press, 2002). For a world-historical perspective on such 'military entrepreneurship' emphasizing

the role of land distribution, see Gallant, "Brigandage, Piracy, Capitalism, and State-Formation," 30 and *passim*.

164 For a selection of essays fruitfully charting the virtues and limitations of this perspective in the variegated case of Latin America, see Richard W. Slatta, ed., *Bandidos: The Varieties of Latin American Banditry* (New York: Greenwood Press, 1987).

165 Eg. Elizabeth Pisani, *Indonesia Etc.: Exploring the Improbable Nation* (New York: Norton, 2014), 68.

166 Quoted in Parmy Olson, *We are Anonymous: Inside the Hacker World of LulzSec, Anonymous and the Global Cyber Insurgency* (London: William Heinemann, 2013), 424. For a similar statement of criminality and spatial alienation online, see Julian Assange, *The Unauthorized Autobiography* (Edinburgh: Canongate Books, 2011), 76 (for the appropriately complex authorship of which see Andrew O'Hagan, "Ghosting," *London Review of Books*, 6 March 2014, 5–26) and, for an explanation based on pure spatial anxieties, Kevin Mitnick with William L. Simon, *Ghost in the Wires: My Adventures as the World's Most Wanted Hacker* (New York: Back Bay Books, 2011), 3.

167 John Yoo, *The Wall Street Journal*, Op-Ed, 7 June 2012, "Obama, Drones, and Thomas Aquinas;" and quoted in Jane Mayer, *The Dark Side: The Inside Story of How the War on Terror Turned into a War on American Ideals* (New York: Doubleday, 2008), 153. On the 'torture memos,' see David Cole, ed., *The Torture Memos: Rationalizing the Unthinkable* (New York: New Press, 2009).

168 Durand and Vergne, *The Pirate Organization*, 13–14, and again 56: 'Somali bandits are not pirates'.

169 For a salutary reminder that Somali pirates encapsulate piracy as real rather than 'self-referential', see Rennie, *Treasure Neverland*, 270.

170 *City of God* 4.4.

171 Giuseppe Gorani, *Storia di Milano (1700–1796)*, ed. Alcesti Tarchetti with a foreword by Carlo Capra (Bari-Rome: Cariplo-Laterza, 1989), 231.

172 The literature on human rights is massive, but see, for the context of eighteenth-century Italy, Vincenzo Ferrone, *The Politics of Enlightenment: Constitutionalism, Republicanism, and the Rights of Man in Gaetano Filangieri*, transl. Sophus A. Reinert (London: Anthem, 2012). Needless to say, eighteenth-century Italy played an important role in the often neglected pre-history of Samuel Moyn, *The Last Utopia: Human Rights in History* (Cambridge, MA: Harvard University Press, 2010).

Part VI

Economic reason of state and its survival in modern economic discourse

14 The long shadow of Cameralism

The Atlantic order and its discontents

Francesco Boldizzoni

There is a view according to which globalisation is a phenomenon both spontaneous and irresistible. For this line of thought, it represents an order that is created by market forces and stems from universal principles such as the human propensity to exchange, the division of labour and comparative advantage. But there is also an alternative view according to which social order is constructed; it is a product of history and reflects power relations.

The origins of this latter view can be traced back to seventeenth- and eighteenth-century Cameralism. The term Cameralism describes a set of doctrines more specific then those of mercantilism and, at the same time, a more interesting intellectual category. Mercantilist attitudes were shared by nearly all countries in a phase or another of their modern histories. They have proved to be the only effective approach to development. Britain, Continental Europe, the US, Latin American and Asian countries: all have developed, or attempted to develop, through state intervention in the form of investment and/or protectionism. What was once a paradoxical thesis that only brave iconoclasts such as Paul Bairoch dared to maintain, is today rather conventional wisdom, *pace* the enlightened preachers of the 'enlightened economy'.[1]

Cameralism, on the other hand, is the intellectual product of a very specific context. It has to do with the geopolitical situation and with the form of the state typical of Central European countries, a vast region extending from Scandinavia to Northern Italy with Germany at its centre. Geopolitically, these countries are defined as landlocked polities and economies. Their penchant for absolutism has also been stressed by scholars who have investigated the politics of Cameralism.[2] Such features, however, are still too vague. After all, France too had its form of absolutism which found in Colbertism – and dirigisme more generally – its economic counterpart.[3]

But while Colbertism was essentially economic technology aimed at pursuing national power, Cameralism represents a totalising category embracing all the spheres of political action; even 'a technology for governing man and nature'.[4] It is a discourse about the *Polizeistaat*, or the ideal of well-ordered states actively promoting societal flourishing.[5] This concept, and its troubled relationship with the *Rechtsstaat* (following the encounter with western ideas brought by the French Revolution), remained central to German thought in its search for a non-liberal way to modernity. As Albion Small writes, 'to the cameralists the central problem of science was the problem of the state', and the latter is assumed at the same time as the main unit of analysis in social research and the veritable object of social policy.[6] This feature also persisted until World War II and distinguishes German discourse from Anglo-Saxon and other varieties of western thought. It is within this general framework that a conception of economics as statecraft, as opposed to positive science, took shape.

The legacy of Cameralism in the modern world is mostly indirect. If a line of filiation can be adumbrated from *Kameralwissenschaften* to later continental scholarship up to the mid-twentieth century, less obvious is how these ideas spread to the Global South and East. Even paradoxical is the fact that Cameralist motives have been revived, often unconsciously, by actors, such as the anti-globalisation movement, normally associated with other intellectual reference points. This might not surprise those who subscribe to J. M. Keynes's dictum that we are all the slaves of some defunct thinker. More interestingly, it suggests that the dynamics of contestation and resistance that could be observed two centuries ago in a certain part of the world are still at work elsewhere; they emerge whenever political and economic sovereignty is threatened by a global order.

Closed commercial states

The point of departure for this survey is Johann Gottlieb Fichte. On the surface his ties to Cameralism might appear to be weak. He was heir to Kant and Rousseau – both of whom wrote in the tradition of the social contract – and enthusiastic about the prospects opened up by the French Revolution. But he is also credited for founding German nationalism.[7] His *Der geschlossene Handelsstaat* (1800) was dedicated to the Prussian finance minister Carl August von Struensee. It made the case for closing off the German lands, caught between the rivalry of Britain and France, to international trade. No territorial expansion was contemplated beyond 'natural borders'.[8]

Fichte put forward a model for a planned economy, socialist in a pre-Marxian sense; a proposal that, although highly abstract and admittedly utopian, spoke directly to the presentist concerns of Prussian decision-makers. The state, according to Fichte, has an emancipative function; it fulfils human potential and promotes welfare. The respect for individual freedom must be combined with the need to ensure social justice. Rights do not exist in an absolute sense. Ownership is defined not as an exclusive right over things but rather as an exclusive right to perform certain actions on things. It draws its legitimation from a mutual agreement whereby individuals are excluded from each other's sphere of action. Society is divided into three classes (the producers of primary goods, the artisans and the merchants). The state regulates their size and proportions, and sets prices for the goods according to their intrinsic (i.e. objective) utility as determined by physical need. Income is distributed in proportion to the labour supplied by the workers. The schema clearly entails a reversal of the market logic and the triumph of regulation over economic anarchy.

However, this order, and the principle of justice it embodies, could be made vulnerable by any economic relationships evading the rule of law. This is why the economy must be closed. Gold and silver must be withdrawn from circulation and replaced with a territorial currency. It is the very nature of the state as 'a closed realm of laws and individuals' to require its commercial closure: 'Every living human being is either a citizen of the state, or he is not. Likewise, every product of human activity either belongs within the compass of its commerce or it does not. There is no third possibility'.[9] Only a national government can exercise jurisdiction over international trade, 'just as it is alone the task of the government to conclude war or peace or alliances'. At the same time economic competition between states is harmful because it causes war. Autarchy, then, is also a means to achieve perpetual peace.[10]

After the humiliation suffered by Prussia in the Battle of Jena of 1806, a distaste for Napoleonic imperialism added to Fichte's already intense anti-English hatred. In the *Addresses to the German Nation* he reminded his countrymen how 'alien to the Germans is the freedom of the seas so often preached these days', hinting at its deceptive character:

> Let us finally realize that all those swindling theories of world trade and manufacturing for the world might well suit the foreigner, and are among those weapons with which the foreigner has always fought us; but they have no use for the Germans and that, after inner unity, internal self-sufficiency and commercial independence are the second means for their salvation and, through this, for the salvation of Europe.[11]

The 'closed commercial state' utopia remained, of course, just words on paper. G. W. F. Hegel pointed out on several occasions that Fichte's concept of a 'rational state' was actually a mechanistic construction that depended on coercion for its functioning. It could hardly take root in the heartland of Europe. By contrast, as he maintained in the *Elements of the Philosophy of Right* (1820), the basis for the transition from nation (*Volk*) to state (*Staat*) had to be an ethical one.[12] However eccentric Fichte's proposal might appear, it nonetheless documents an important step in the historical process leading from ancien régime to modernity.

Economics national and cosmopolitical

The economic world in which Fichte and Hegel lived had still much in common with the one analysed by the theorists of the eighteenth-century *Fürstenstaat*; a state where different productive sectors coexisted but which largely drew its revenues from agriculture, as Simon Peter Gasser described it in his *Einleitung* (1729).[13] This world came to an end with the British industrial revolution and the most emblematic interpreter of this phase was Friedrich List. Hegel had, of course, recognised the sources of conflict inherent in the new 'civil society' created by capitalism. But capital-intensive industrialisation posed problems on a larger scale.

The debate is open as to what extent the roots of List's thought lie in German Cameralism. Keith Tribe has argued, with good reason, that some of the most significant ideas of this author took shape during his American sojourn. From the arguments of the northern industrialists, favourable to protectionism, he would draw his aversion to British free trade.[14] This notwithstanding, it is difficult to overlook the fact that List had spent many years in public service in the State of Württemberg, culminating in his short-lived appointment as professor of administration in the newly established faculty of *Staatswirtschaft* at Tübingen. List's career before his exile is in all respects that of a *conseiller du prince*.

The years spent in the United States made him aware of a problem, one which Germany too would soon have to face: how can a developing economy survive in an international context characterised by the dominance of a player who wants to keep the rest of the world (not just her colonies) in a state of inferiority and subservience? The synthesis between these two moments – training and experience – was made in the 1830s when, after his return to Germany, List set to work on the essays that make up his *National System of Political Economy* (1841).

The tenet of classical economics that List meant to overthrow – although he curiously never mentions it directly – is the doctrine of comparative advantage associated with David Ricardo and Robert Torrens.[15] This theory holds that free trade between two or more countries, if there is specialisation, is mutually advantageous. The condition is that each country should specialise in producing certain goods, namely those that it can produce at a lower opportunity cost than other countries. 'It is this principle', Ricardo wrote, 'which determines that wine shall be made in France and Portugal, that corn shall be grown in America and Poland, and that hardware and other goods shall be manufactured in England'.[16]

There are two problems with this theory and they are intertwined. If only one country specialises in goods incorporating greater quantities of capital, there occurs what the French-speaking authors call *échange inégal*: a situation where international wealth disparities widen rather than narrowing.[17] The second problem is that the economy described by Ricardo is static, and the starting conditions are assumed as immutable. In other words there is no understanding of economic development, a process that, once set into motion, changes not just the rules of the game but the game itself. Why should a country be doomed to produce forever low-value-added goods?

This second aspect is at the core of List's thought. He exposed the opportunistic motives behind the shift from mercantilism to free trade on the part of the British. At a time when Britain became the first industrial power, it needed to beat Napoleon and restore the old European monarchies in order to be able to impose a new commercial order. 'Now for the first time the English were heard to condemn protection and to eulogise Adam Smith's doctrine of free trade, a doctrine which heretofore those practical islanders considered as suited only to an ideal state of Utopian perfection'.[18] The 'cosmopolitical economics' theorised by Smith and his followers – depicted by List as a pseudoscience whose function was to legitimise British imperialism – posited the existence of universal laws in this domain. It removed the category of 'nation' from economic discourse, which meant doing away with any form of mediation between 'the individual' and a humanity subject to the law of the strongest. In contrast to these developments, List claimed a central role for the nation and, at the same time, reasserted the nature of economics as *Polizeiwissenschaft*, following in the footsteps of his predecessors.[19]

If the Cameralists were not foreign to the idea that manufacturing matters, List was the first German-speaking author to realise that for a modern state there could be no future without industrialisation. Had he lived until the end of the nineteenth century, which marked the peak of the German industrial revolution, he would have seen how the effects of his prescriptions went beyond the expectations. The *Zollverein* he had fought for led to the political unification of the country. But the young German economy grew to the point of directly threatening the interests of Britain and the United States. The Wilhelmine Reich could then aspire to the role of twentieth-century superpower.

Doux commerce and war

Through the Hegelian Lorenz von Stein and the Older Historical School, the legacy of Cameralism was picked up by Gustav Schmoller and his contemporaries. At the time of Schmoller, the separation of economic thought from political-legal thought was already complete, but the same service-minded attitude, and the same reforming spirit, prevailed among intellectual elites. The welfare of the state was pursued by focussing on the analysis of social phenomena in their historical concreteness. The government, in the person of the *Reichskanzler*, was a key interlocutor for these academics, just as the rulers of the pre-unification states had been for the Cameralists.

In the years of sustained economic growth following the German take-off, the efforts of economic thinkers were directed to maintaining social peace. By rejecting liberal individualism, the *Verein für Socialpolitik* entrusted to the state and its 'intermediate bodies' the task of mediating between particular interests, drawing on the Steinian model of the 'monarchy of social reform'.[20] However, those years were also a prelude to the showdown between the national and the cosmopolitical conceptions of international order. The conflict would soon move from the arena of trade to that of war. And since British influence had extended well beyond the borders of Europe, changing the geopolitical map of Asia and Africa, the two wars that nearly destroyed the old continent in the first half of the twentieth century became world wars.

Thus Werner Sombart, in his *Streitschrift* from 1915, *Händler und Helden*, proclaimed that 'Germany is the last dam against the muddy flood of commercialism that has either already overwhelmed all other nations or is about to do so unhindered'.[21] He stressed that Germany, unlike Britain, had no colonial ambitions but only aimed 'to grow within organic limits'. Its mission was that of consolidating its heroic spirit, a spirit that could not be exported as the British used to export commodities. Indeed, he observed, 'the great "talent for colonisation" attributed to the English is nothing but an expression of their spiritual poverty' or 'shopkeeper mentality' (*Krämergeist*).[22]

The criticism levelled against Atlantic values – subsumed by the triad of individualism, utilitarianism and hedonism – and their corrupting potential for Europe became increasingly bitter in the post-Versailles period. These motives pervaded German intellectual circles and can be found in such diverse works as Oswald Spengler's popular best seller *The Decline of the West* and Otto Brunner's subtle, scholarly attempt at debunking the liberal contract theory of the state.[23] The cliché of *doux commerce*, which had been around since the Enlightenment, was obviously a frequent target for those invoking a new reason of state.[24] This is the background against which Sombart's *Deutscher Sozialismus* (1934), with its denunciation of the international financial system and its call for action, should be read. Just five years later, however, when Hitler invaded Poland, came the disillusionment: 'It's the end of Germany!' he told his son Nicolaus, disgusted with the regime's foolishness and tired of living.[25]

Similar feelings of disenchantment were shared by Carl Schmitt (once the Third Reich's crown jurist) who, in the midst of the war, wrote a short history of the world, *Land und Meer*.[26] At the origin of the modern international order was the separation between land and sea, with England progressively detaching her own fates from those of the European continent and embarking on the conquest of the seas. Sir Walter Raleigh famously maintained that 'whosoever commands the sea commands the trade; whosoever commands the trade of the world commands ... the world itself'. In the nineteenth century, at the zenith of British sea power, this maxim became 'All world trade is free trade'. Just as for List, British political economy and its 'absolute and eternal truths' were seen by Schmitt as instrumental to the legitimation of imperialism, which also required a new international law. In this way, Britain (the 'island') and the US (the 'larger island') prepared for a new era of crusades.

In the aftermath of World War II, the understandable guilt complex about the nation's past affecting German culture and the globalisation of academia under Anglo-American hegemony put an end to the statecraft school of economics with its blend of political economy (*Nationalökonomie*) and public finance (*Finanzwissenschaft*). Political science ceased to be a 'science of the state' and legal positivism dismissed the *jus publicum europaeum*. For many decades German historiography was ashamed of being associated with the *Volk* and the *Volkstum* and turned to the 'social' and the 'political'. This dissolution of the old system of knowledge represented the real death of Cameralism (and the beginning of its afterlife).

Outposts of resistance: an epilogue

The post-war demise of colonial empires did not immediately give way to the reproduction of the old dependency ties in neo-colonial guise. During the post-colonial period many countries in the Global South and East cultivated hopes for a better future. Some of them found in Marxism the tools for lifting themselves out of 'subalternity'. But many other intellectual influences drove the agenda of the non-aligned Third World.[27] As the world peripheries realised that their former colonisers had been 'kicking away the ladder' leading to prosperity, there was a veritable List revival.[28] Thus, as late as 1988, Roman Szporluk could say that 'the Third World today is Listian in its outlook and ... even Marxism has become "Listianized"'.[29]

In India protectionism and Keynesianism were combined and shaped the post-war developmental state. In 1951 Prime Minister Jawaharlal Nehru launched the first of a long series of five-year plans. The origins of Indian nationalism, however, can be traced back to the late nineteenth century when the German Historical School had been a major source of inspiration for intellectuals and early leaders of the Indian National Congress including Mahadev Govind Ranade and Romesh Chunder Dutt. According to Dutt:

> While British Political Economists professed the principles of free trade from the latter end of the eighteenth century, the British Nation declined to adopt them till they had crushed the Manufacturing Power of India .... [I]n India the Manufacturing Power of the people was stamped out by protection against her industries, and then free trade was forced on her so as to prevent a revival.[30]

The last quarter of the nineteenth century also saw the reception of List in Japan (his magnum opus being translated in 1889). It was not just a case of migration of ideas from one context to another. In fact, similar concepts had been developed by Maeda Masana, a senior official in the Meiji administration, and Takahashi Korekiyo, a statesman who eventually served as the first Minister of Commerce and Industry in 1925. List's ideas found fertile ground because Japan had had for at least two centuries its own Cameralist tradition, that of *kokueki* (national interest) writers. As Mark Mezler writes in his fascinating study:

> *Kokueki* ideas were developed and disseminated by traveling administrative and economic policy advisers, who loosely approximated the cameralist 'consultant administrators' of eighteenth-century Germany. In this comparative view, *kokueki* could be translated as the eighteenth-century Latin-German term '*policey*' (Germanized as '*polizei*'), which is what the cameralist advisors called their own statecraft practice.[31]

In 1875 Takahashi observed that:

> while war itself was becoming rare, now 'the enemy uses manufacturing machinery instead of cannon'. The 'so-called civilized countries', above all Britain, employed this 'civilized and enlightened form of war' to widen their territories, gain resources, and build permanent overseas bases.[32]

In order to prevent the country from suffering the same fate of deindustrialisation already experienced by Portugal, Turkey and India, formerly commercial powers, Takahashi advocated a system of protective tariffs. Withdrawing from the free trade treaty that Japan had been forced to sign in the 1850s was the only way to survive in this uneven fight. Takahashi's views were in tune with those held in the 1880s by the critics of westernisation who were reacting against the liberal ideas introduced by an earlier generation of intellectuals led by Yukichi Fukuzawa. It was in this milieu that the teaching of German political economy replaced that of British political economy at the University of Tokyo. But this new system based on import barriers, centralised industrial planning and coordinated capitalism only found full application in the 1930s and 1940s. It would lead to the high-speed growth of the post-war period.

In Argentina, Chile and Brazil, the German approach to trade and industrial policy was the subject of careful consideration since the turn of the century. The debate on international trade acquired new piquancy during the Great Depression. Following the Spanish translation of the *National System of Political Economy* in Mexico City in 1942, a renewed interest in the application of Listian recipes spread throughout Latin American countries. In the post-war period, the economists associated with the United Nations Economic Commission for Latin America (ECLA), most notably Raúl Prebisch and Celso Furtado, borrowed from List (along with Romanian economist Mihail Manoilescu) the tenets of 'structuralist' developmentalism, which was to be the dominant Latin American approach to policy-making until the 1970s.[33] In an oft-cited text from 1949, which reads like the ECLA manifesto, Prebisch questioned the international division of labour between exporters of raw material and producers of high-value-added goods. Free trade, he argued, does not ensure that all countries can equally reap the fruits of technological progress. These fruits are seldom transferred from the core to the periphery. The slower pace of technological progress in the sector of primary products compared to the industrial sector results in a progressive deterioration of the terms of trade. Peripheral countries should pursue their own strategy of industrial growth based on import substitution.[34] The dependency theory developed by Fernando Cardoso and Enzo Faletto in the 1960s reasserted the role of the state in emancipating such countries from economic, political and cultural subordination. The state was also called on to regulate the internal power and class relations maintaining inequality, which were reinforced by the dynamics of dependence.[35]

In the 1980s the foundations were laid of the Washington Consensus, under the auspices of the IMF, the World Bank and other organisations serving the interests of the US Treasury. After installing (in the late 1970s and early 1980s) military dictatorships in Latin America and elsewhere, the United States imposed structural adjustment programmes – namely free trade, privatisation, financial deregulation and austerity – on the developing regions. In the same years, the term 'globalisation' appeared, with increasing frequency, in newspapers and other media.[36] It was a (relatively) new word used to describe an old process, one that had been around, with its ups and downs, since the eighteenth century. Why, then, was a neologism needed now? The creation of the Washington Consensus coincided with the collapse of the Soviet Bloc. With no rivals left to fight, unlimited possibilities of conquest through *doux commerce* were opening up before the North Atlantic metropole. The message had to be presented in a positive, reassuring way.

Resistance from within the system grew gradually in the following decades, from Seattle to Genoa, from New York to Athens. When Joseph Stiglitz lamented the 'hypocrisy' driving 'the globalization agenda' and blamed the United States and its allies for 'push[ing] poor countries to eliminate trade barriers' (or for taking advantage of the loosening of capital markets control in the developing world) he used Listian arguments; and so did Naomi Klein when she targeted the 'trickle-down economics' applied on a global scale.[37] By a strange accident of history, at the dawn of the twenty-first century the conservative Carl Schmitt was acclaimed by the global left, and his legal theory invoked to contest preventive wars against 'rogue states' and 'outposts of tyranny'.[38] The Cameralists may no longer be with us but their ideas are alive and will stay around as long as the modern international order lasts.

Notes

1 Paul Bairoch, *Economics and World History: Myths and Paradoxes* (Chicago: University of Chicago Press, 1995); Philipp R. Rössner, "Heckscher Reloaded? Mercantilism, the State, and Europe's Transition to Industrialization, 1600–1900," *Historical Journal* 58.2 (2015), 663–83.

2 Pierangelo Schiera, *Dall'arte di governo alle scienze dello stato: il cameralismo e l'assolutismo tedesco* (Milan: Giuffrè, 1968).

3 See Philippe Minard, *La fortune du colbertisme. Etat et industrie dans la France des Lumières* (Paris: Fayard, 1998).

4 Sophus Reinert, *Translating Empire: Emulation and the Origins of Political Economy* (Cambridge MA: Harvard University Press, 2011), 234.

5 On the continuity of German thought in this respect see Keith Tribe, *Strategies of Economic Order: German Economic Discourse, 1750–1950* (Cambridge: Cambridge University Press, 2007).

6 Albion W. Small, *The Cameralists: The Pioneers of German Social Polity* (Chicago: University of Chicago Press, 1909), viii.

7 E.g. Heinrich August Winkler, *Germany: The Long Road West*, vol. I (Oxford: Oxford University Press, 2006), 52.

8 Johann Gottlieb Fichte, *The Closed Commercial State*, transl. Anthony Curtis Adler (Albany, NY: SUNY Press, 2012), 156, 171.

9 Ibid.,108.

10 Isaac Nakhimovsky, *The Closed Commercial State: Perpetual Peace and Commercial Society from Rousseau to Fichte* (Princeton: Princeton University Press, 2011).

11 Johann Gottlieb Fichte, *Addresses to the German Nation* (Indianapolis, IN: Hackett, 2013 [1808]), 162–63.

12 G. W. F. Hegel, *Grundlinien der Philosophie des Rechts* (Frankfurt am Main: Suhrkamp, 1986 [1820].

13 Simon Peter Gasser, *Einleitung zu den ökonomischen, politischen und Cameralwissenschaften* (Halle, In Verlegung des Wäysenhauses, 1729).

14 Tribe, *Strategies of Economic Order*, 44ff.

15 On List's omission cf. Andrea Maneschi, *Comparative Advantage in International Trade: A Historical Perspective* (Cheltenham, Elgar, 1998), 92. However, one should not forget that the book departs from academic conventions in many ways.

16 David Ricardo, *On the Principles of Political Economy and Taxation* (Cambridge: Cambridge University Press, 1951 [1817–21]), 134.

17 There are several versions of the theory of unequal exchange, not only in the Marxist literature. The concept is perhaps most commonly associated with Arghiri Emmanuel, *L'échange inégal: essai sur les antagonismes dans les rapports internationaux* (Paris: Maspero, 1969).

18 Friedrich List, *The National System of Political Economy*, trans. Sampson S. Lloyd, London, Longmans, 1909 [1841], p. 60.

19 The preface to the original edition (*Das Nationale System des politischen Ökonomie*, Stuttgart, Cotta, 1841) contains a very explicit defence of this tradition along with sarcastic comments on Jean Baptiste Say and other 'Pariser Genies' who misunderstood it.

20 Schiera, *Dall'arte di governo alle scienze dello stato*, 120.

21 Werner Sombart, *Händler und Helden. Patriotische Besinnungen* (Munich, Duncker & Humblot, 1915), 145.

22 Ibid., 143–44.

23 Oswald Spengler, *Der Untergang des Abendlandes: Umrisse einer Morphologie der Weltgeschichte* (Munich, Beck, 1923 [1918–1922]); Otto Brunner, *Land und Herrschaft. Grundfragen der territorialen Verfassungsgeschichte Südostdeutschlands im Mittelalter* (Baden bei Wien: Rohrer, 1939).

24 On *doux commerce* see A. O. Hirschman, *The Passions and the Interests: Political Arguments for Capitalism before Its Triumph* (Princeton: Princeton University Press, 1977).

25 Werner Sombart, *Deutscher Sozialismus* (Berlin, Buchholz und Weisswange, 1934); Nicolaus Sombart, *Jugend in Berlin, 1933–1943. Ein Bericht* (Frankfurt am Main: Fischer, 1991), ch. 1.

26 Carl Schmitt, *Land und Meer. Eine weltgeschichtliche Betrachtung* (Leipzig: Reclam, 1942).

27 Francesco Boldizzoni and Pat Hudson, "Culture, Power and Contestation: Multiple Roads from the Past to the Future," in *Routledge Handbook of Global Economic History* (London: Routledge, 2016), 431–49, at 439–40.

28 Ha-Joon Chang, *Kicking Away the Ladder: Development Strategy in Historical Perspective* (London, Anthem, 2003).

29 Roman Szporluk, *Communism and Nationalism: Karl Marx versus Friedrich List* (Oxford: Oxford University Press, 1988), 237.

30 Quoted in Prasannan Parthasarathi, "The History of Indian Economic History," in *Routledge Handbook of Global Economic History*, 281–92, at 283.

31 Mark Metzler, "The Cosmopolitanism of National Economics: Friedrich List in a Japanese Mirror," in *Global History: Interactions between the Universal and the Local,* ed. A. G. Hopkins (Basingstoke, Palgrave Macmillan, 2006), 98–130, at 108.

32 Ibid., p. 110.

33 Mauro Boianovsky, "List and the Economic Fate of Tropical Countries," *History of Political Economy* 45.4 (2013), 647–91.

34 Raúl Prebisch, "El desarrollo económico de la América Latina y algunos de sus principales problemas," *El trimestre económico* 16.3 (1949), 347–431.

35 Fernando H. Cardoso and Enzo Faletto, *Dependencia y desarrollo en América Latina* (Mexico City, Siglo Veintiuno, 1969). On the evolution of the intellectual debate within the ECLA, see *Cincuenta años de pensamiento en la CEPAL: textos seleccionados*, ed. Ricardo Bielsthowsky, 2 vols. (Santiago, Fondo de Cultura Económica/CEPAL, 1998).

36 For example, Theodore Levitt, "The Globalization of Markets," *Harvard Business Review*, May–June 1983.

37 Joseph Stiglitz, *Globalization and Its Discontents* (London, Penguin, 2002), 6–7. Naomi Klein, *Fences and Windows: Dispatches from the Front Line of the Globalization Debate* (London, Flamingo, 2002).
38 Cf. Benno Teschke, "Decisions and Indecisions: Political and Intellectual Receptions of Carl Schmitt," *New Left Review* 67 (2011), 61–95.

Index

For Product Safety Concerns and Information please contact our EU
representative GPSR@taylorandfrancis.com Taylor & Francis Verlag GmbH,
Kaufingerstraße 24, 80331 München, Germany

Printed and bound by CPI Group (UK) Ltd, Croydon, CR0 4YY
08/05/2025
01864351-0003